Rocky Lives!

MORE SPORTS TITLES FROM POTOMAC BOOKS

Boxing's Most Wanted™: The Top 10 Book of Champs, Chumps, and Punch-Drunk Palookas, David L. Hudson, Jr., and Mike Fitzgerald, Jr.

Indy: The Race and Ritual of the Indianapolis 500, Second Edition, Terry Reed

You Can Quote Me on That: Greatest Tennis Quips, Insights, and Zingers, Paul Fein

Forging Genius: The Making of Casey Stengel, Steven Goldman

The Super Bowl's Most Wanted™: The Top 10 Book of Big-Game Heroes, Pigskin Zeroes, and Championship Oddities, Walter Harvey

Big Play: Barra on Football, Allen Barra

Wrigley Field: The Unauthorized Biography, Stuart Shea

Pro Basketball Forecast: 2004–05 Edition, John Hollinger

Pro Football Forecast: 2004 Edition, Sean Lahman and Todd Greanier

ROCKY LIVES!

HEAVYWEIGHT BOXING UPSETS OF THE 1990S

DAVID E. FINGER

Potomac Books, Inc.
Washington, D.C.

Library of Congress Cataloging-in-Publication Data

Library of Congress Cataloging-in-Publication Data

Finger, David.
  Rocky lives! : heavyweight boxing upsets of the 1990s / David Finger.
  —1st ed.
    p. cm.
  Includes bibliographical references and index.
  ISBN 1-57488-905-2 (alk. paper)
  1. Boxing—United States—History.   2. Boxing matches—United
States—History.   3. Boxers (Sports)—United States—Biography.   I. Title.
GV1125.F52 2005
  796.83′0973—dc22   2004027238

Printed in Canada on acid-free paper that meets the
American National Standards Institute Z39-48 Standard.

Potomac Books, Inc.
22841 Quicksilver Drive
Dulles, Virginia 20166

First Edition

10   9   8   7   6   5   4   3   2   1

To my parents,
who never bet against this underdog.

CONTENTS

CHAPTER SEVEN: 1996

CHAPTER EIGHT: 1997

CHAPTER NINE: 1998

CHAPTER TEN: 1999

x CONTENTS

PHOTOGRAPHS

ACKNOWLEDGMENTS

Special thanks to David Hudson, who helped make sure this book didn't drop the ball. I would also like to thank the many people who helped me while I researched this book, including Danny Pluckett, Lonis Tuna, Dana Smith, Greg McClelland, Pat Dwyer, Bela Szilagyi, Pat Merrick, John McDermott, Joe Kiniski, Henrik Risum, John Davis, Scott "Flattop" Pope, Ron Scalf, Neil Hunter, *The State Paper* (Columbus, SC), Ron Peterson, Troy Harrington, Simon Nam, Paul Soucy, Greg Juckett, Pat Orr, Ray Bailey, Tom Hogan, and many more. And I would like to thank the many fighters who were kind enough to allow me to interview them, for some about the greatest fights of their career, and for others the lowest points of their careers. Each was classy and respectful, and it is truly a shame that more athletes couldn't be more like boxers.

Introduction

Boxing by no means has a monopoly on the upset. The upset is something that transcends sports as a whole. It is what made Super Bowl III so memorable. It is what made the "Miracle on Ice" a miracle, it is what makes every graduate of a tiny school in Hawaii smile whenever they see a college basketball game on Christmas Eve.

But in boxing, upsets often tell a story that could never be duplicated anywhere else, a story of one man's courage, one man's belief in his own ability. There is probably no place lonelier in the world than in the ring when you are an underdog, and the upset often becomes a reflection of the boxer himself and a reflection of his struggle—against his opponent, against his critics, against the adversity of his life, against himself.

As professional sports changed in the 1990s, so did the upset. Professional sports transformed from being a national diversion and pastime into a national corporation of sorts, a merchandising empire, where skill often took a back seat to marketability. But skill was still a necessary element of the equation, even if it became secondary in many ways. Nike's attempt to pass off Harold Miner as a new, "baby" Jordan failed about ten games into his rookie season, and Brian Bosworth's persona didn't keep him in the NFL any longer than his poor performance could justify. But in boxing in the 1990s, skill soon would become a mere optional attachment, something the lack of which would by no means derail a marketable fighter. Boxing provided a ripe environment for misrepresentation. We knew Harold Miner was no Michael Jordan from week one. We never got the opportunity to find out Gerry Cooney was no Rocky Marciano until he had already fooled nearly everyone into earning one of the biggest paydays in boxing history.

Gerry Cooney's 1982 fight against then heavyweight champion Larry Holmes would prove to be significant—we knew it as soon as the fight was signed and shamelessly promoted as a black vs. white fight. Its impact was felt all over boxing, but it would continue to influence boxing for years to come. Suddenly businessmen all over the world realized something. There was money to be made in a white heavyweight, and the fighter didn't have to take a particularly hazardous road to reach that payday. With that realization an explosion of white heavyweights emerged, each less skilled than the one who preceded him, and each trying to earn the undeserved payday. Few insiders paid much attention to the phenomenon; after all Gerry Cooney was at least a legitimate contender when he got his title fight, and a good fighter to boot. What he was not was a great fighter who deserved such a large payday against such an established champion as Larry Holmes. But when Peter Mc-Neeley earned nearly a million dollars (more than most champions made in their entire career) everyone realized that boxing was a different sport than it was just fifteen years prior. Suddenly managers and promoters were working hard to keep untalented fighters undefeated, a recipe than would often produce countless upsets over the decade, most in boxing's money division: the heavyweight division.

But an even bigger event took place in 1991 that also would change the face of boxing forever. It would prove to be one of the most uplifting and memorable moments in sports history, but would lead to a tragic trend in boxing that would discredit the sport. A middle-aged overweight preacher from Texas, nearly two decades removed from his last title fight, gave the undisputed heavyweight champion one of the toughest fights of his career to that point, losing a close decision. George Foreman had walked into that fight to one of the largest paydays in boxing history, and walked out of it with the guarantee of even bigger paydays. All over the world former champions and contenders were suddenly given the motivation to do what George had done. But Foreman was the exception. Each comeback thereafter ended without a belt, and all, except that of Larry Holmes, ended without a million-dollar payday. Still, the fighters kept fighting, hoping to find lightning in the bottle, just as George had. No matter how many times one lost, there was still that hope, that unrealistic hope, that kept fighters fighting on. When Rocky Marciano knocked out Joe Louis, there was no question that Joe had to retire. But in the 1990s, a former champion could lose and lose again, until it became a nearly meaningless statistic to have a former champion's scalp on your resume. Boxing had become the arena of the upset, and the heavyweight division was this arena's Super Bowl.

CHAPTER ONE

1990

"They came here to see Godzilla."

Larry Merchant on the Japanese fight fans attending the
Mike Tyson–James "Buster" Douglas fight

February 11, 1990—Tokyo, Japan
Mike Tyson (37–0, 33 KOs) vs. James "Buster" Douglas
    (29–4–1, 19 KOs)
Favorite: Tyson
Result: Douglas scored a tenth-round knockout.

It was supposedly the easiest title defense "Iron" Mike had taken since
he won the title in 1986. After clearing out the division of almost all
recognizable heavyweights from the 1980s, Tyson was ready to start
taking on the "new" generation of up-and-coming heavyweights such as
Gary Mason, Francesco Damiani, and, most notably, former undisputed
cruiserweight champion Evander Holyfield. However, after his first-
round TKO over Carl "The Truth" Williams, it appeared as if Don King
would try to squeeze in another overseas payday for Tyson against a
lightly regarded heavyweight. Initially, the talk centered on Jose
"Nino" Ribalta, a fighter that he had already fought. But despite Ribalta's winning eight straight bouts and hanging in with Tyson three years
prior, few were interested in seeing Tyson-Ribalta II. In the earlier
fight, Ribalta was battered mercilessly from the opening bell before getting stopped in the tenth round. At best, Ribalta could be expected to
duplicate his previous performance, but more likely Tyson would score
a quicker knockout.

1

After realizing that James "Buster" Douglas might be a more marketable opponent, Team Tyson decided to lean towards the Columbus, Ohio, native. Although Douglas was highly ranked by all three sanctioning bodies (second in the International Boxing Federation, third in the World Boxing Conference, and fourth in the World Boxing Association), it was more of a reflection of how Tyson had already cleaned out the heavyweight division than Douglas's ability. But though he was slightly more marketable than Ribalta, Douglas was hardly a recognizable opponent (despite his ranking and his frequent fights on the undercard of Mike Tyson's fights). Douglas was a journeyman who had already lost his first title fight against Tony Tucker, in which Douglas seemed to quit after giving Tucker early trouble. As a result there were many questions about Buster's "heart." He had been knocked out by David Bey and Mike "The Giant" White as well as losing to Jesse Ferguson in a fight he had been expected to win. Although he seemed to rebound from his loss to Tony Tucker quite nicely (with impressive wins over Oliver McCall and prospect Mike Williams), even at his best, it was hard to see how he could possibly compete with the devastating Tyson. If Tyson's power didn't rob Douglas of his heart, his somewhat suspect chin would surely fail him. Most of Vegas, anticipating a potential big loss on Tyson bets, refused to set odds on the fight; the few casinos that did placed Douglas's odds at 42–1.

By the time the HBO-televised fight began, it appeared that even the Japanese fight fans weren't buying into what seemed to be a mismatch. Although they had been eager to witness Tyson's destruction of Tony Tubbs two years earlier, the Korakuen Stadium in Tokyo saw nearly 20,000 empty seats by the time Tyson and Douglas entered the ring. Even HBO commentators Larry Merchant and Jim Lampley seemed resigned to the fact that Douglas's chances were slim to none—hardly the tactic to keep viewers glued to their TV screens for the fight. Prior to the fight, Lampley referred to the upcoming fight as another "apparent mismatch for Mike Tyson in defense of his heavyweight crown," and he then went as to say "in the important game of expectation, this fight is over before it begins or soon thereafter." Lampley then prepared fight fans for what was the commonly held best-case scenario by acknowledging that Douglas could still give the fans a few rounds, but gave no indication that the fighter had even the slightest chance of winning.

Douglas didn't have just Tyson to overcome. It seemed to many outsiders that Douglas's world was unraveling around him. His mother, Lulu, had just died, and the mother of his eleven-year-old son fell seriously ill. That along with a separation from his wife, as well as a bout with the flu in the days prior to the fight, seemed to seal Douglas's fate. For a fighter who in the past showed little in the form of toughness, it seemed that the avalanche of tragedy that was befalling him would prove too great a distraction. Most felt that he simply couldn't regain focus in time for the fight.

With all that was happening to Douglas, it was easy to diminish the negative impact that the distractions in Mike Tyson's life would play on his performance. Besides, he had, after all, overcome them before. In fact, his most significant professional win, a first-round knockout over Michael Spinks, came at a time when his life was in complete turmoil. Even though the months leading up to the Douglas fight were filled with a fair amount of Mike Tyson–style mayhem, it almost appeared mild compared to what preceded his earlier fights. His firing of trainer Kevin Rooney, which initially seemed to be the thread from which his dynasty could be unraveled, proved to be a mere blip on the radar screen when Tyson successfully knocked out Frank Bruno and Carl "The Truth" Williams in impressive fashion. Even his knockdown at the hands of Greg Page during sparring was quickly dismissed as a ploy to garner some hype for what was quickly looking to be an unmarketable fight (or perhaps to hype a future Tyson-Page fight). The only distraction that raised eyebrows leading up to the Douglas fight was his scheduled fight with undefeated Evander Holyfield planned for four months after his fight with Douglas, clear indication that he didn't think Douglas would be any trouble.

As it turned out, both fighters reacted quite differently than expected to the prefight distractions. Douglas not only overcame the tragedies that were befalling him, but he in fact used them as motivation for his upcoming fight. He trained with a renewed vigor and weighed in at an impressive 231½ pounds, the best shape he entered a fight in some time. Tyson, on the other hand, reportedly trained without much fire, and it seemed to many observers that he was in fact looking past Douglas to Holyfield.

Nonetheless, Tyson's prefight behavior was forgotten by fight time, as he seemed his usual menacing self. He refused to take part in a belt-awarding ceremony prior to the fight and seemed eager to start mixing it up with Buster. But as soon as the bell rang, it was clear that Mike was not his usual self in the ring. Instead of the onrushing freight train that would thrust into (and through) opponents with relentless pressure and powerful hooks in the first round, "Iron" Mike fought a fairly docile round. He predominantly exchanged jabs with Buster—an exercise in futility for the shorter Tyson—and the two times he did try to bulldog into Buster he found himself matched punch for punch by a surprisingly quick-footed Douglas.

Although most observers felt Douglas had won the first round clearly—Larry Merchant went so far as to say it was the best round Douglas had ever fought—many assumed that Mike would pick up the pace in the second, and Douglas's brief flirtation with success against the invincible "Iron" Mike would come to an end. But it started to sink in about a minute into the second round that Mike was ineffective not by choice but because Buster was fighting well. A left jab followed by a right hook snapped back Tyson's head. Then, when Douglas landed a beautiful right hand that landed flush, it seemed that Douglas had a winning strategy for which Tyson might not have an answer. The left jabs and right hand leads began to pepper Tyson, and Douglas showed signs of setting the tempo of the fight by punching first. Still, Tyson's chin seemed to be able to withstand Douglas's best punches, and ring-siders wondered if Douglas had the power to really hurt Tyson, despite his success in the ring to that point. But with the damage inflicted on Tyson by the end of the second round, the doubts of Douglas's power were quickly put to rest.

A neutral observer would have recognized by the second or third round that Tyson was in trouble and that Douglas was on his way to a knockout victory unless something drastic changed. But Tyson's power was a great equalizer in any fight, and though Douglas clearly had control of the fight, it seemed only a matter of time before Tyson landed a left hook that would salvage the win. But the left hook was not coming. Douglas's jab and movement were completely neutralizing Tyson's offense.

It was then that the firing of Kevin Rooney appeared to play a role in Mike Tyson's career after all. Tyson failed to use much head movement in the fight, even when Douglas repeatedly snapped his head back with the left jab. (In fact it seemed Tyson was a fighter without a game plan.) His trainers Jay Bright and Aaron Snowell recognized his failings in the ring; Snowell actually told Tyson after the fourth that he had to "move that head." But it wasn't the advice, head movement (or lack of), or even the lack of combination punches from Tyson that convinced much of the world that Tyson made a mistake when he fired Rooney. It was the missing Enswell. When Jim Lampley pointed out towards the end of the fifth round that Mike Tyson's left eye was closing from excessive swelling, everyone assumed that Tyson's corner would use an Enswell iron to try to bring the swelling down. After all, the Enswell iron was one of the most basic tools in a boxing trainer's bag of tricks. It would be unheard of if a trainer failed to have one—tantamount to a trainer forgetting a water bottle or a stool. But when Tyson sat on his stool, his trainers placed what appeared to be a water balloon on the swelling. It became apparent that they were unprepared for the fight, and even though they were unjustly accused of being completely unqualified as trainers after the fight, one thing was certain. Kevin Rooney would have had an Enswell.

Douglas continued his dominance well through the seventh round, fueling the growing belief that an upset was in fact in the making. And although Tyson seemed a bit more active for much of the eighth, it was hardly effective in turning the tide of the fight, and, with a minute left in the round, Douglas began to move Tyson back with solid shots to the head. When a right uppercut put Tyson against the ropes with less than twenty seconds left in the round, it appeared that the end was near for Tyson. Douglas quickly unloaded on the champion, who it appeared was actually trying to hold on. But with a mere three seconds left in the round, Tyson finally caught Douglas with a picture-perfect right upper-cut that dropped Douglas. Douglas, in apparent disgust with his care-lessness, pounded the canvas with his glove as referee Octavio Meyran began to count over him. (Keen observers noticed that Meyran's count was a full three seconds behind that of the ringside timekeeper.) When Douglas looked up at Meyran at the count of five, it was apparent that he was clearheaded. Douglas, in an apparent attempt to maximize his recovery time, rose at the count of nine. Meyran let him continue, and Tyson was unable to capitalize on his punch's result as the round ended.

The question suddenly became how hurt James Douglas was, as the fighters came out for the ninth round. Tyson, realizing that he was behind, came out winging punches in an attempt to finish off a woozy Douglas. But it quickly became clear that it was Tyson, not Douglas, who had to worry about getting knocked out. Douglas started where he left off prior to the knockdown; he threw hard jabs and overhand rights, and occasionally sneaked in uppercuts of his own. When Douglas landed a beautiful combination forty seconds into the round that had Tyson backpedaling into the ropes, it effectively quelled any notion that Tyson had taken control. Douglas then staggered Tyson with a combination a little over a minute later, causing viewers to brace themselves for the unthinkable: Buster Douglas knocking out Mike Tyson. Tyson appeared helpless as Douglas teed off on him, and when Tyson fell backward into the ropes, there was no question that Mike was in serious trouble. But then Douglas appeared to run out of gas, and it seemed that Mike Tyson had dodged a bullet when he survived the round.

But the gunslinger in James Douglas was reloading for the tenth round, and Mike Tyson soon seemed to be in a no-win situation. He had been badly hurt in the ninth, and seemingly needed a knockout to win the fight. But he was running out of time. At the start of the tenth, Douglas continued his methodical dissection of Tyson with the jab. To "Iron" Mike's credit, he continued to move forward, hoping to land the solid punch that could turn the fight around. But, by a minute into the round, he failed to respond to (or even block) five lazy Douglas jabs, seemingly frozen by the rather unspectacular shots. Douglas quickly jumped on his advantage, firing a powerful right uppercut that snapped Tyson's head back. Douglas, realizing that Tyson was on the way down, followed it up with a left hook, straight right, and an overhand left to ensure he stayed there.

To the shock of the entire sports world, Mike Tyson was flat on his back. As he tried to get up, HBO viewers could look into Mike's eyes, which showed that he was not going to continue. Confused, he wasted four seconds fumbling around trying to find his mouthpiece and, when he did, put it back into his mouth backwards. Although he began his rise at seven seconds, he failed to beat the count of Octavio Meyran, and the fight ended at 1:23 of the tenth round.

Larry Merchant recognized the magnitude of Douglas's shocking win over "Iron" Mike when he proclaimed only seconds after the fight that it was the "greatest upset in boxing history." Few could argue with him.

More than just being a shocking upset, it was a shining moment for a sport that was constantly mired in controversy. Boxing had given the world a fairy tale that even the movies couldn't duplicate. For all of the tragedy that followed "Buster" Douglas into the ring, he was able to win against all odds. Viewers around the world embraced the greatest feel-good story of sports since "The Miracle on Ice" (when Team USA defeated the Soviet Union in hockey in the 1980 Winter Olympics). James "Buster" Douglas suddenly was a superstar, and a likeable one at that. Boxing had a real-life Rocky Balboa.

But in a move that could only come from the sport of boxing, the joy quickly subsided when promoter Don King attempted to rob Douglas of his victory. Initially, the only real controversy in the fight seemed to be the judge's scorecards. Although one judge had it appropriately scored 88–82 after nine rounds, two other judges had completely ridiculous scores of 87–86 Tyson, and 86–86. But then King appeared the following day with a docile-looking Meyran at his side, claiming that in fact Mike Tyson, and not James Douglas, won the fight by knockout because Meyran failed to pick up the timekeeper's count and instead initiated his own count. Although there was no question that Meyran did in fact miss the count and that Douglas was down for approximately thirteen seconds, it was also equally clear that Douglas could have risen sooner and had remained on the canvas until the count of nine to maximize his time to recover. Nonetheless, the WBA and WBC stated that Douglas would not be immediately recognized as champion until "further review," indicating that they might actually strip him of their titles. With that decision, the sport of boxing, which seemed to have been raised instantly from the depths of illegitimacy into mainstream sports, found itself suddenly thrust back into the sewer. The fans and media went into a justified uproar, and though the WBA and WBC relented three days later, the damage was done.

The upset shocked the boxing world and forever changed both fighters. For Tyson, it initially appeared to soften his jagged personality. Although he refused to congratulate Douglas after the fight, he began to soften his image over time. It appeared that he, and not Don King, chose to pull the plug on the protest, admitting that he wanted to win his title back in the ring and not from behind a table. When he signed to fight Henry Tillman, the press was shocked to find a more hospitable and lighthearted Mike Tyson, one who openly joked with them and was quick with a smile. In fact, when he proceeded to knock out Tillman in the first round, he actually rushed to Tillman's aid immediately after the fight in an attempt to help his defeated foe. But the George Foreman–like image change was short-lived. His childish rivalry with HBO commentator Larry Merchant damaged his reputation, as did his abrupt departure from HBO to Showtime over that rivalry. When he called fellow heavyweight Donovan "Razor" Ruddock a "transvestite" and promised to make him his "girlfriend," there was no question that the old Mike Tyson was back. Unfortunately, the Mike Tyson of old was on a downward spiral towards self-destruction, and by the time he was convicted of raping a beauty queen contestant in 1991, there was little doubt that Tyson was out of control.

For Douglas, the swan song was as short as it was sweet. Immediately after his victory, he began cashing in on his newly found fame. He teamed up with Hulk Hogan to knock out Randy "Macho Man" Savage on a World Wrestling Federation wrestling card days after his title-winning fight. But a bitter court battle with Don King ended up costing the newly crown champion four million dollars of his upcoming twenty-four-million-dollar payday against Evander Holyfield. Then came rumors of poor training habits and a rapidly expanding waistline. When boxing insiders heard that Douglas ordered a plate of food from room service while sitting in a sauna to shed some weight, it seemed clear that his heart was no longer in the sport. Still, many assumed that the gladiator who slew the mighty dragon in Mike Tyson would be able to defeat the smaller Holyfield. Even when Douglas weighed in at a whopping 246 pounds, many still expected a competitive fight. But Holyfield proved too much for the under-trained, unwilling Douglas. When Holyfield countered a wide uppercut with a counter right that dropped Douglas to the canvas, Douglas seemed clear-headed, rubbing his nose to check for blood. But as the count reached ten, Douglas remained on his back, never attempting to get up. It was widely seen as one of the most disgraceful performances of a heavyweight champion in history, and he effectively ended any chance of a second Tyson fight, as few who witnessed Douglas's shameful performance wanted to see him in the ring again. Although Douglas made a comeback in 1996, it was not particularly successful. A first-round knockout loss to Lou Savarese was the only significant fight he had. Nonetheless a second Tyson fight seemed possible as late as 1999, but Douglas again eliminated himself from a potentially big payday when his weight ballooned so much that the fight no longer appeared marketable.

May 19, 1990—Las Vegas, Nevada
Greg Page (31–8, 24 KOs) vs. Mark Wills (10–9–1, 8 KOs)
Favorite: Page
Result: Wills won by way of sixth-round knockout.

Seldom in boxing is a fighter made the underdog after knocking out an opponent in decisive fashion, but when Mark Wills was picked as an opponent for former heavyweight champion Greg Page (who held the WBA title from 1984–1985), a fighter he destroyed in nine rounds four years prior, most experts picked Page to avenge the loss. Most boxing insiders felt that Wills just caught an under-trained, ill-prepared Page, and they assumed Page wouldn't underestimate him a second time. Also Wills failed to capitalize on his big win. He followed it with a twelve-round decision loss to Larry Alexander later that year, and then proceeded to get knocked out by Dee Collier and Tim Witherspoon in his next two fights. Going into the rematch with Greg Page, he was also coming off a decision loss to undefeated Briton Gary Mason. It looked to most boxing fans that Wills was clearly an "opponent" and that his win over Page was an aberration.

Besides, Page was positioning himself as a very marketable fighter. After dropping Mike Tyson in sparring prior to Tyson's fight with James "Buster" Douglas, Page found his damaged credibility instantly restored. To many boxing fans, it looked very likely that Don King was grooming him as a future Mike Tyson opponent. But it would take more than just a knockdown in sparring with Mike Tyson to make believers of the vast majority of boxing fans, and Page realized that. So he did the one thing that many boxing fans had been waiting for him to do for years: he got into shape.

For most boxing fans, Greg Page was the classic out-of-shape heavyweight that defined the 1980s. He often entered the ring overweight, with a paunchy belly, and relied on his natural talent to get him by. Although he did briefly hold the WBA heavyweight title, most boxing fans felt that Page never lived up to his potential—he was groomed by some early on as the second coming of Muhammad Ali—and many felt that the main reason he never accomplished more was because of his poor training. Against Gerrie Coetzee, the fighter he beat for the WBA title, he weighed in at a fleshy 236 pounds, and when he lost the title to Tony Tubbs eight months later he weighed in at 239. (Most boxing insiders felt that his ideal weight was in the low 220s.) For many boxing fans, it was distasteful that he could actually take a title fight so lightly, and when he proceeded to lose two of his next three fights (including the knockout loss to Wills) many fans saw it as a case of "instant karma."

But for much of 1989 Page had dropped down to the low 220s in weight, and when he weighed in against Mark Wills, he was an impressive 218 pounds. For many boxing fans, the common sentiment was that they were finally going to see Greg Page at his best, and most felt that Wills would not "luck out" against a Greg Page in such good shape. But unfortunately for Greg Page, although he rebounded from the Mark Wills fight quite well in the ring, he never was able to overcome the psychological damage done from his only knockout loss. Mark Wills was in fact one of those fighters who just had the "style" that would always give Page trouble, a straight-ahead brawler who relied on the overhand right over his opponent's jab. Also, as ringsiders quickly noticed, Page's weight loss still didn't remove his soft belly, and some wondered if he had properly worked the weight off, or if it was a result of a short-term crash diet.

Still, Page looked sharp early, staggering Mark with a flashy three-punch combination in the first round. But it soon became clear that Page was not as "in shape" as his weight would have ringsiders believe. He showed signs of fatigue after the first round and spent much of the second round throwing one punch at a time and then holding on to catch his breath. The tide began to turn dramatically for Wills in the third round. Within the first minute, Wills reached the chin of Greg Page, landing a hard overhand right. Page's knees buckled, and it became clear that the former champion was out on his feet. Wills came out swinging for the fences against Page, but the experience level of the former champion enabled him to survive the round. By the start of the fourth, it looked like Page had recovered. However, he still had no defense for the overhand right of Mark Wills, and Wills recognized that, throwing it as his primary punch for the next two rounds. The end came for Greg Page in the sixth round. After getting tagged again with the right hand, Mark Wills jumped on Page while the former champion was on the ropes. In the onslaught Page lost his mouthpiece, prompting referee Carlos Padillia to call a break in the action to let him recover it. However, as soon as Padillia resumed the action, Mark Wills immediately attacked, firing another hard overhand right. It was a picture-perfect shot, one that many ringsiders felt was one of the most devastating they had seen in some time. Page was caught blinking and dropped to the canvas like a ton of bricks after the shot landed squarely on his chin. Although he did beat the count, the fight was wisely waved off. With it, Mark Wills became the only man to knock out Greg Page twice.

For Wills, the win didn't open the doors of the top ten, but it did reaffirm that he was one of the toughest in the game and one of the more dangerous journeymen in the division. But just as his first knockout over Page failed to revitalize his career, neither did his second. Avoided like the plague, he remained sidelined for nearly two years before landing his next fight against James "Bonecrusher" Smith (losing in a decision). The loss to Smith, however, reintroduced him to the journeyman ranks, and he had little trouble landing fights after that. Although he won his next three fights against fair opposition—Garing Lane, Jerry Jones, and Vince Jones—a loss in 1993 to Michael Bent brought his winning streak to an end. He finished his career in 1997 with seven straight losses, four of them by knockout.

For Page, the loss again seemed to discredit him, and end any possibility of a fight with Mike Tyson. But the veteran still had a few tricks up his sleeve, and he would prove to be a very resilient heavyweight for much of the decade. After winning three meaningless fights, it appeared as if he were being thrown to the lions in 1992 against "Razor" Ruddock. But for the better part of seven rounds he gave Ruddock all that he could handle before finally succumbing to a hard barrage of punches in the eighth. He then went on to a decision over James "Bonecrusher" Smith in ten rounds and, with it, found himself again close to a big money fight. But a loss to Francesco Damiani later that year ended all talk of another payday for the former champion.

June 12, 1990—Fort Bragg, North Carolina
Pinklon Thomas (30–3–1, 24 KOs) vs. Mike "The Bounty"
    Hunter (14–2–2 5, KOs)
Favorite: Thomas
Result: Hunter won a lopsided ten-round decision.

By the middle of 1990, it was becoming increasingly clear that the
George Foreman comeback was about to land the former heavyweight
champion a multimillion dollar payday, and for many former champions
and contenders George Foreman's "second" career provided a blueprint
on how to stage a successful comeback. Gone were the days of one tune-
up fight and then a big fight with some young up-and-coming fighter or
a top-ten opponent. Comebacks like those were risky, and though they
were beneficial in that they often were mercifully short, they seldom
paid (unless of course the aging fighter pulled out the upset). Instead,
the new "George Foreman" comeback was one in which a former champion fought monthly on cable TV against unranked (and often un-
skilled) opponents. These journeymen often allowed the former
champion to win (and win impressively). Unfortunately, it was a long-
term investment of time for many former champions. It could be years
before the questions about their skills were answered, and Foreman-
like paydays were reserved for those few with unforgettable "Big
George"-like personas. By the decade's end these comebacks proved to
be less successful, and often more damaging, than the "traditional"
comebacks, but in 1990 it was still a relatively new formula that promised success for many fighters whose best days were clearly behind
them. One such fighter was the former WBC heavyweight champion
Pinklon Thomas.

Initially groomed as one of the "future stars" of the sport, Pinklon
emerged when then IBF king Larry Holmes appeared near the end of
his Hall-of-Fame career. He won the WBC belt in 1984 in impressive
fashion from Tim Witherspoon and appeared to many boxing writers as
the heir apparent in the heavyweight division, a view held until he lost
to Trevor Berbick in March 1986. Thomas was never able to completely
recover from the loss to Berbick, losing back-to-back fights with Mike
Tyson and Evander Holyfield to finish out the 1980s. The loss to Holyfield was particularly devastating, as Holyfield battered Thomas merci-

lessly for the better part of eight rounds. In that fight Thomas looked the part of a "shot" fighter, clearly unable to get his once-dominant left jab working and seemingly without any legs at all. Thomas, whose troubles with drugs prior to his loss to Holyfield were well documented, slipped into a depression that saw him return to many of his old bad habits. Still, a comeback was not completely out of the question. Although Evander Holyfield had yet to win the heavyweight champion against James Douglas, he was still regarded as one of the best fighters in the heavyweight division.

Thomas began his Foreman-like comeback with a less than impressive win over Curtis Isaac in May 1990, and within three weeks he appeared on *USA Tuesday Night Fights* on the undercard of the Anthony Hembrick vs. Booker T. Word light heavyweight fight. Following the Foreman formula, Thomas took on a seemingly overmatched Mike "The Bounty" Hunter. Hunter was the classic 1980s opponent for a heavyweight contender: a ranked cruiserweight looking for one quick payday before jumping back down in weight to try and land a title shot. Considering the overall weakness of the cruiserweight division in the 1980s, these fighters tended to be contenders in name only. They were almost all failed light heavyweights or heavyweights (such as J.B. Williamson) with an occasional aging former champion (like Dwight Qawi) looking to win an extra title thrown in for good measure. Although S.T. Gordon, a blown up cruiserweight, was able to upset Trevor Berbick by decision in 1983, by and large the cruiserweights tended to fold with relative ease against the heavyweights.

But by the end of the 1980s things were beginning to change in what was widely perceived as boxing's weakest division. Legitimate prospects, rather than rejected heavyweights and light heavyweights, began to emerge. For a division so devoid of "young" talent, the introduction of these fighters, such as Bert Cooper, Evander Holyfield, Henry Tillman, and to a lesser degree Mike Hunter, was a welcome addition. Boxing writers even appeared initially generous to the heavyweight ambitions of these fighters. Bert Cooper was quickly embraced when he knocked out Olympian Willie Dewitt at heavyweight, and Evander Holyfield was elevated to the status of most legitimate opponent for Mike Tyson after he unified the cruiserweight titles and effectively cleaned out the division. But Hunter, despite his cockiness and incredible self-promotion, was unable to garner the same sort of support. In part it was because of his apparent lack of power, with only five knockouts in eighteen fights at cruiserweight. Although he entered the fight with Thomas on the heels of his biggest victory of his career (a twelve-round decision over Dwight Qawi), he seemed to be an ideal opponent for Thomas, who (despite questions that lingered about what skills he retained) still possessed an excellent chin.

But early signs began to surface indicating that an upset could be in the works. When Pinklon Thomas's name began to surface as a potential opponent for the undefeated Riddick Bowe, many boxing insiders wondered if Team Thomas might have been conceding that Pinklon would never put it together again. Also, the brash Hunter (who once called out Mike Tyson after his knockout over Tyrell Biggs) seemed unusually cocky, even for himself. He agreed to fight heavyweight prospect James Thunder only one month after his scheduled fight with Thomas, despite the fact that Thomas was clearly the toughest fighter he had faced to date. Although both fighters had no love lost, it seemed that the more upset Hunter made Thomas, the less chance he would have to "sneak up" on the former champion.

It took less than ten seconds in the first round to show that age had snuck up on Pinklon Thomas. After taking down Thomas, WWF style, in the opening seconds, Hunter jumped all over his bigger opponent. When Hunter landed a big left less then ten seconds later, Pinklon Thomas's legs abandoned him. He buckled back into the ropes and covered up. Although Thomas seemed to begin to have his jab pumping later in the round, it was clear that his legs were still unsteady, and by the round's end Hunter began to taunt the former champion.

In the second round Thomas began to abandon his only weapon, his jab. Although the jab was not particularly effective against the unorthodox Hunter, without it he became nothing more than a plodding boxer. The thirty-two-year-old Thomas was left to walk in with Foreman-like speed, hoping to land a jab or a right hand. His lack of speed began to come into play when he dropped his hands down to his waist, a bad habit he carried from his days as a champion. However, while he was able to get away with it when he was younger, against Hunter he paid a steep price for it.

It became the pattern for the fight as Thomas failed to recover or mount an effective offense. When Hunter trapped Thomas in a corner nearly a minute into the third round, it was clear to even the most ardent Thomas supporters that he was nowhere near the fighter he had been five years prior. Continuing his taunting ways, Hunter began holding his arms up in the air in an attempt to show even more disrespect for the former champion. Even when faced with an opponent in such a position, Thomas couldn't land a blow. In fact, it became so one-sided that after just the fourth round Thomas's corner began telling him that he needed a knockout to win. Thomas never altered his strategy, perhaps unable to pull the trigger. His punch output continued to decline, and after getting stunned in the eighth round, he virtually shut down completely. It was clear going into the tenth and final round that he needed to do something big. But even when Hunter took the round off, Thomas could not find his target. It was so bad that USA network commentator Al Albert told viewers that there was "no signs of life from Pinklon Thomas." In the end the scorecards were academic, as Hunter won a lopsided decision—one judge scoring the fight a shutout while the other two gave Thomas one round each.

For Mike Hunter the win should have propelled him into the "big time." Although he chose not to return to the cruiserweight division, criticism of his decision to remain a heavyweight was muted when Hunter continued to win impressively against James Thunder (KO 4) and Ossie Ocasio (W 10). But Hunter's success quickly stagnated when inactivity plagued his career. After his successful year in 1990, Hunter remained inactive throughout 1991, and although he resurfaced in 1992, a loss to Francois Botha by way of eight-round decision seemed to be the end of the line for him. But Hunter rebounded impressively with a big win over Tyrell Biggs for the USBA heavyweight title in another upset (page 77).

For Pinklon Thomas, the loss confirmed what Evander Holyfield had already proven, that Thomas was washed up. He followed the Hunter loss with a TKO loss to Riddick Bowe. Although he did extend Bowe into the ninth round, he took a frightful beating, and many wondered why the fight was not stopped sooner. Thomas, who was now showing signs of neurological damage, then took on young Tommy Morrison. Although he was an underdog against Morrison, questions remained about the blonde bomber, and many wondered if Thomas could pull off the upset. But after getting battered in the first round, Pinklon Thomas quit on his stool. For the one-time WBC champion, it was the end of the line, although he did launch an unsuccessful comeback a few years later. Robbed by drugs and the age of his skills, he was a fighter with only his championship chin and heart. But against Tommy Morrison he was robbed of even those by the powerful left hooks of "The Duke."

November 14, 1990—Madison, Wisconsin
Yuri Vaulin (9–0, 6 KOs) vs. John "Hogg Man" Sargent
  (7–0, 5 KOs)
Favorite: Vaulin
Result: Sargent won after Vaulin quit in the eighth round due
  to a hand injury.

When Mikhail Gorbachev introduced "perestroika" and "glasnost" to the Soviet Union in the late 1980s, many throughout the world were optimistic at the changes being embraced by the Communist super-power. Suddenly, Soviet citizens were given the opportunities and free-doms long denied them, and many in fact clamored for more. But buried in the excitement of the Soviet reformation was the release from state bondage of what many felt was the single greatest athletic force in the world: the Soviet "amateurs." Unable to turn professional due to the strict restrictions of the Soviet state, many of the Olympic athletes that fought for the Soviet Union were seen as amateurs in name only. They were seasoned men competing against boys, often with well over a dozen years experience in their chosen field. But besides the edge in experi-ence, they also "benefited" from a Communist state determined to prove its superiority to the capitalist West in every endeavor. The Soviet hockey team became a thing of legend, in part due to the limited choice offered the players—one story told of the Red Army virtually kidnap-ping a promising young hockey player from his home—but also due to the talent of the players and the investment in time and money by the state. By the 1980s the Soviets had molded some of the best sports teams on the face of the earth, from the Olympic hockey teams that won seven Olympic gold medals from 1956–1988 to their Olympic basketball team that upset the United States for Olympic gold in 1972.

Although somewhat overshadowed by their Communist ally Cuba, which followed the Soviet model in creating the best Olympic boxing program on earth, the Soviet boxing team was still a widely feared group. Capturing a total of fourteen gold medals in boxing, the Soviets were second only to the Cuban and the Americans in Olympic success, and several fighters (such as light middleweight Boris Lagutin, who won the gold in 1964 and 1968) were seen as the best amateur boxers in the world. Needless to say, when several Soviet boxers relocated to the United States to launch professional careers in the ring, boxing fans around the world were transfixed. How good were these Soviets fighters? What would they accomplish as professionals? Boxing fans had little to go on other than the brief (but highly successful) boxing career of Hungarian László Papp in the 1950s. Papp, who won three Olympic gold medals as an amateur, came within one fight of a world title before the Communist government of his country pulled his reins back. As a result, many were optimistic about the future of the Soviet imports, and some boxing insiders felt that trainer Tommy Gallagher and promoter Lou Falcigno literally found gold in their stable of Soviet boxers. Although lacking in any Olympic medals, these Soviet boxers were younger than many other Soviet boxers, but no less talented in the eyes of many boxing insiders.

Although many boxing insiders were impressed with the early skills of Alex and Sergei Artemiev (both were lightweights), the attention was primarily focused on a heavyweight named Yuri Vaulin. Vaulin was a matchmaker's dream: he had no qualms about wearing red trunks in the ring and looked and acted like the villainous Ivan Drago (from the movie *Rocky IV*). But he seemed to be much more than a cheap gimmick. He was one of the most talented and fluid boxers that had emerged in years, and amateur boxing insiders were in awe of his quick jab and incredible footwork. If that alone didn't make him a slippery fighter, there was also one other thing: he was a southpaw. Trainer Tommy Gallagher admitted in an interview on *USA Tuesday Night Fights* that he felt Vaulin was the best prospect of the bunch, an opinion shared by many fans. Although somewhat scrawny for a heavyweight—he usually weighed around 210 pounds—he stood 6'4" and appeared to have plenty of time to bulk up in the coming years. With a World Cup championship as well as a European championship in 1987 (both at 178 pounds), Vaulin already had a glossy and impressive resume, and with over three hundred amateur fights many felt that he had enough experience to become a heavyweight contender in just a year or two. But his experience in many ways became as a hindrance. In his first professional fight against a last-minute substitute named Don Coats, he showed a curious lack of "killer instinct," fighting passively behind a cautious right jab. After winning a lopsided four-round decision, many began to wonder if he perhaps was too well schooled in the amateur style of boxing to adapt to the professional ranks. What became clear after his first fight was that Vaulin didn't need to work on his technical skills but his overall toughness. However, Vaulin rebounded quite well, winning his next eight fights—six by way of knockout and four of those in the first round—against fair, if not spectacular, opposition. After winning a decision over William Morris in October 1990, boxing insiders again began to show interest in the Soviet prospect. But unknown to insiders and fans alike was something that would plague many of the first Soviet athletes who turned professional in all sports. After moving to the United States, Vaulin's desire and dedication began to wane. Admitting that he wanted to become both a champion and a millionaire, it would soon become abundantly clear that he was more interested in enjoying the benefits of capitalism. For Vaulin, he already won a championship by escaping the Soviet Union, and he had little left to motivate him. That factor, coupled with his lack of toughness, would prove his downfall.

In November 1990 Vaulin traveled to Madison, Wisconsin, to take on a fellow undefeated fighter, a little known regional fighter named John Sargent. Although the fight was a matchup of two undefeated heavyweights, it failed to generate much excitement nationally. Sargent appeared to be a "soft touch"; he was somewhat obese and was perceived as a slow, plodding, feather-fisted clubfighter who had yet to be exposed. After all, he fought from the state of Minnesota, a state not known for producing any serious boxing talent. Also, he was a Native American, from the White Earth Indian reservation in Minnesota. Never before had there been a Native American heavyweight champion, or even a serious contender, and Sargent appeared an unlikely exception. But Sargent was a deceptively solid fighter despite his limitation in speed and size. Although he weighed in at a fleshy 244 pounds on his 5'10" frame, he was a ferocious body puncher, something that would come into play. Vaulin weighed in at a career low of 203 pounds.

Although Sargent was from neighboring Minnesota, Wisconsin was clearly Sargent country. Vaulin had never before been in such hostile territory. As both fighters entered the ring the chants of "U-S-A! U-S-A! Let's go U-S-A!" emerged from the pro-Sargent crowd, who played along with Vaulin's red trunks by entering the ring in Rocky-Balboa-style U.S. flag trunks. Vaulin retained his calm demeanor though and quickly silenced the crowd when the bell rang that started the fight. Although both fighters opened the first round cautiously, Vaulin, the more polished boxer, quickly took control with his quick right jab and footwork. Sargent appeared completely unable to close the gap; his lack of speed always left him one step behind Vaulin. Vaulin continued his dominance in the second round, sticking, moving, and peppering Sargent with countless jabs. Frustrated, John Sargent tried to employ a jab of his own, to little avail. Halfway through the round Sargent appeared finally to reach the lanky Latvian, briefly pinning Vaulin on the ropes, but Vaulin easily escaped trouble when he sidestepped Sargent while firing jabs (all the while making the undefeated Native American look foolish). When Vaulin was finally forced into a serious exchange in the last thirty seconds of the second round, he more than held his own. For ringsiders, it appeared that Sargent's one chance at a victory, a slugfest, would equally suit Vaulin. Despite his success in the exchanges, Vaulin retuned to his slick boxing in the third, and Sargent began to show signs of desperation, winging wild right hands. When one missed its target by nearly a foot halfway through the round, Vaulin answered with a quick (and effective) upstairs combination.

Sargent finally began to close the gap in the fourth, firing a hard right hand to Vaulin's body followed by a hard right to the head that had Vaulin holding on in the opening minute. The listless crowd suddenly erupted, but Vaulin quickly returned to fighting behind the jab and resumed his dominance. Still, it was soon clear that Sargent was indeed closing the gap with his constant pressure, and when he again rattled Vaulin in the final minutes of the round with two hard body shots followed by a hard left jab that sent Vaulin back, many ringsiders felt that the tide was turning. Although Sargent still seemed to lose the fourth, it was a close, competitive round, and Vaulin's legs showed signs of wilting. Sargent aggressively stalked Vaulin in the fifth, and while Vaulin continued to box well, Sargent's pressure continued to wear him out. But Sargent's conditioning was also tested by the continued pressure, and the Native American began to fade in the second half of the round, allowing Vaulin to cement another close round. Although Sargent rallied in the final seconds of the round, pinning Vaulin on the ropes, it was not enough to steal the round, and with only three rounds left in the fight it looked as if Sargent might run out of time before Vaulin ran out of gas.

Appearing to have gained his second wind, Vaulin regained some bounce in his legs at the start of the sixth round, dancing around a forward-moving John Sargent. Although John Sargent did land a short right hand inside moments later, it failed to serious rattle Vaulin. But in the final minute of the round, Sargent would finally turn the tide, catching Vaulin with a right hand as the Latvian was moving back. Vaulin emerged clearly rattled as well as seriously troubled by the pressure. Suddenly, Vaulin appeared fatigued by the end of the round and began to hold, which proved to be a momentous mistake. Sargent, an inside fighter who liked to attack the body, was suddenly in his ideal range, and he capitalized on it by further attacking the body of Vaulin. Cries of "C'mon John! He's tired, get him!" began to emerge from the crowd at the start of the seventh—something that Sargent recognized even without the advice of ringsiders. Vaulin started the round bouncing and moving, but he fooled nobody, least of all Sargent. The big Native American stalked Vaulin relentlessly, and found his chin with a hard right that pushed him to the ropes. Vaulin again held on, but Sargent pressured relentlessly even as Vaulin clinched. Sargent again rattled Vaulin with a hard overhand right at the bell, cementing his most dominant round of the fight.

Going into the final round, however, many felt that Sargent's recovery was too little, too late. Vaulin appeared to have won the first five rounds decisively, and barring a knockout, few felt that Sargent could pull out the win. Although he had Vaulin holding and rattled him on several occasions, he had yet to knock Vaulin down or seriously hurt him. Many ringsiders viewed the eighth round as the most important in the career of John Sargent, a clear test of his resolve, and they anticipated a whirlwind attack. But it was not the desire and resolve of

Sargent that would decide the fight, but the lack of desire and resolve of Vaulin. Badly winded, Vaulin continued to hold as Sargent moved forward, but thirty seconds into the round Vaulin began to shake his right hand as if it was bothering him. A potentially devastating injury had it occurred in the opening round, most felt Vaulin could simply hold on for the last round and still win. But Vaulin's lack of toughness and lack of heart had finally pushed past its limits. He called out to the referee, asking that the doctor be called to examine the injury. As the doctor examined his wrist, it was clear to all that the decision was now up to Yuri: if he wanted to go on, he would be permitted to. If he didn't, the fight would be stopped. Vaulin meekly told the doctor that he was not interested in continuing, and the fight was waved off, with a little over two minutes left before the final bell would have given Yuri Vaulin a decision victory.

Although many boxing insiders in Minnesota saw the Sargent win as proof that he was in fact a legitimate heavyweight prospect, credit would be slow in coming. Sargent still had to prove that he was the best heavyweight in Minnesota, as an undefeated heavyweight named Jimmy Lee Smith also was based in that state. But when Sargent won a lopsided decision over Smith in his very next fight, national boxing insiders began to take Sargent a bit more seriously. Although Sargent struggled in his next fight in January 1991—his first ESPN televised fight (winning a six-round decision over Ross Puritty)—he followed it with six more wins before the year's end and suddenly was being mentioned as a possible opponent for both Riddick Bowe and George Foreman. Sargent was in line to earn a six-figure payday, but on the threshold of finally breaking into the big leagues, Sargent lost his desire and dedication. A brief visit to his home at the White Earth Indian Reservation became an eighteen-month layoff in which his conditioning completely deteriorated and his battles with alcoholism resurfaced. By the time he returned to the ring in August 1993 he was a forgotten man, and any hope of revitalizing his career quickly disappeared when he lost his comeback fight to unknown Carl McGrew (page 104).

For Yuri Vaulin, the fight exposed his lack of toughness, and for American boxing fans (in which grit was the most important trait of any fighter), it removed him from the classification of prospects. Many insiders began to openly question the hand injury when he returned to the ring against Jesse Boston less than two months later. For Team Vaulin, it was clear that he needed a big win to reestablish himself as a fighter worth keeping an eye on, and to put to rest any questions about his grit. If he was lacking in heart, it was better to know it quickly, before too much time was wasted on a fighter with no future. So in April 1991, Yuri Vaulin was thrown in against one of the hottest prospects in the sport on one of the biggest fight cards of the decade. In the chief supporting attraction to Evander Holyfield's heavyweight title defense against George Foreman, Yuri Vaulin was matched with a popular boxer who played opposite Sylvester Stallone in *Rocky V*, one Tommy "The Duke" Morrison. It was a fight that was still easily marketable despite the blemish on Vaulin's record, a virtual *Rocky IV* vs. *Rocky V*. Even casual boxing fans took an interest in the fight even though most felt confident that Morrison would easily dismantle Vaulin. But for the better part of four rounds Vaulin shined, outboxing Morrison and almost dropping him in the third round. But his lack of intensity would again be exposed, this time in front of the biggest boxing audience in the world. Less than twenty seconds after getting tagged with a Morrison left hook to the chin, Vaulin curiously bent over in pain due to an alleged body shot—one that video replay could not find. Although allowed to continue, he quickly turned his back and quit after Morrison landed a body shot. For the second time, Vaulin handed a victory away due to a suspect injury that most boxers would have been able to tough out. Any questions about the legitimacy of the injury were quickly answered when his trainer Tommy Gallagher yelled at him to "stop the bullshit and get up" while the ringside physician examined his ribs. Everything that he did correctly that night was erased by how he gave up the fight, and Gallagher dumped him shortly after the fight. Although he would eventually return to Gallagher, his career as a heavyweight was over, and Vaulin returned to the ring as a cruiserweight, a move that many fans felt could repair his career if he could emerge as a cruiserweight contender. He initially impressed them, winning his first fight at cruiserweight in impressive fashion over contender Siza Makhathini by way of third-round knockout. He followed that win with another impressive win over the first man to beat Al Cole, Leon Taylor, for a minor title. But in a fight for the vacant USBA in cruiserweight title in December 1992, Vaulin was stopped by a young prospect named Arthur Williams, a fighter who would go on to win the IBF cruiserweight title several years later. It was his last fight as a boxer, but nearly five years later Vaulin reemerged in the most unlikely place—as a contestant in Ultimate Fighting Championship 14. Vaulin took on Joe Moreira, losing by unanimous decision in a performance that showed surprising grit from a fighter who showed so little of it as a boxer.

CHAPTER TWO

1991

"Right now he looks all the part of a beaten fighter"

Barry Tompkins on Bruce Seldon, moments before Seldon
was stopped by Oliver McCall

April 18, 1991—Atlantic City, New Jersey
Bruce Seldon (18–0, 15 KOs) vs. Oliver McCall (15–4, 9 KOs)
Favorite: Seldon
Result: McCall won via ninth-round TKO.

Although the heavyweight division never had a shortage of young, undefeated heavyweights throughout its history, there usually was only one
or two who would eventually emerge as legitimate standouts. The rest
would fade into oblivion almost as quickly as they emerged. Nineteen
ninety-one was no exception to this phenomenon. While fighters like
Jerry Goff, Cleveland Woods, and Derek Williams fell off the radar
screen, five promising heavyweights seemed to emerge from the rest of
the pack, impressing fans and experts alike. Olympians Riddick Bowe,
Ray Mercer, and Lennox Lewis were pounding away at the usual collection of former champs, former contenders, and journeymen in impressive fashion, and most expected them to all become contenders. Bowe
was openly being groomed as the heir apparent to Mike Tyson. But two
other fighters began to emerge as well: hard-punching Tommy Morrison
and the quick-fisted Bruce Seldon. Although Seldon was generally
ranked a bit lower than the other four, his quick, hard jab was one of
the best many boxing insiders had seen since Larry Holmes. Although
Seldon was not a traditional boxer in the Holmes/Muhammad Ali
mold—he was a relatively smaller heavyweight compared to Bowe and

Lewis—he was a fairly aggressive boxer with a good punch. For many insiders, "The Atlantic City Express" was not only a very well rounded fighter, but he also had an engaging personality (a trait that made him popular with the boxing writers as well). However, of the aforementioned fighters, Seldon's opposition was by far the weakest, and he showed some signs of struggling with fighters he was expected to beat. Only three months earlier he was dropped in the opening seconds of his fight with Jose Ribalta. Although it appeared to be some sort of comic stunt when an apparently unconscious Seldon suddenly jumped to his feet unfazed, Seldon later admitted that it was not a hoax and that Ribalta had in fact hurt him. He also showed signs of struggling against former contender David Bey as well, struggling for ten rounds with the chunky brawler. But the most significant criticism of Seldon was of his alleged dislike of training, even earning the disparaging nickname "Seldon in the gym" by some boxing writers.

At the time of his bout with Seldon, few expected Oliver McCall to put up much of a fight. With four losses in nineteen fights, as well as two losses (to James Douglas and Orlin Norris) in his last three, most assumed that McCall was "just another journeyman." They thought that McCall would give the young up-and-comer Seldon some rounds of work and a chance to show off his vaunted jab on national TV, but little else. It seemed a safe bet. Although McCall's losses to Douglas and Norris were nothing to be ashamed of considering Douglas went on to knock out Mike Tyson in his very next fight, and the fight with Norris was a split decision that could have gone either way, losses to Joey Christjohn and cruiserweight Mike "The Bounty" Hunter were harder to justify.

The only question seemed to be if Seldon could become the first man to actually knock out the "Atomic Bull." In what proved to be the most significant (and overlooked) statistic in McCall's resume, few gave his chin much credit. Although most regarded McCall as tough, little did the boxing world (and Seldon) realize that the beard of Oliver McCall was quite possibly the best in boxing. Had Seldon realized that, he might have been in better condition to go ten rounds, or at the very least, he would have better paced himself for a ten-round fight.

When the fight began, it appeared as if Seldon would use the jab to dictate the pace. For most of the first round Seldon used his bread-and-butter punch to pepper McCall, who appeared to be throwing far too few punches to seriously trouble Seldon. However, a McCall jab seemed to shake up Seldon at the end of the first, and it appeared as if the fight would hardly be a whitewash. Nonetheless, Seldon picked up where he left off in the second, pumping the jab. But when he found himself slugging with the "Atomic Bull" just over thirty seconds into the round Seldon began to flirt with disaster, even though he won the exchanges. Although Seldon wisely jumped on McCall when it was apparent that Oliver was having trouble with his right eye, he never completely returned to the smooth boxing that would have given McCall the most trouble. Seldon spent most of the second round chasing down McCall and, by round's end, was not winning the exchanges like he had earlier.

The third round continued to see Seldon stand in front of McCall throwing hard punches, but it seemed that McCall was in fact wearing him down in the process. A right hand stunned Seldon halfway through the round, and when McCall snuck in another right hand that caught Seldon with a little under a minute left, it became abundantly clear that Seldon was fighting the wrong fight. Although Seldon would periodically return to the jab throughout the fourth, he never really had it working, and fatigue was slowly setting in. But rather than rest behind the jab, he seemed intent on slugging it out with McCall whenever he felt winded, a strategy that only wore him out even more. In the fifth, Seldon initiated an early brawl—something which McCall gladly obliged— and even had McCall stunned in the last minute of the round with a right hand. But the chin of Oliver McCall continued to hold up. Even though Seldon attempted to start the sixth with a jab he quickly returned to his flat-footed ways after getting badly rattled early on by a hard McCall right. Although it led to an interesting brawl, with Seldon landing a right of his own that stunned McCall halfway through the round, there soon was little doubt that both fighters were badly worn out from the previous round. Seldon still kept marching forward against McCall during the seventh and eighth, but it also started to become apparent to some that Seldon in throwing wide hooks that missed McCall completely, was way too wild at that point, and was wearing out even more. When he again instigated another brawl with McCall at 2:30 of the eighth round—an exchange he won decisively—he effectively emptied his tank of the last drops of fuel that he had.

For most of the ninth Seldon tried to keep away from McCall, who had yet to realize how badly fatigued his opponent was. But as it became apparent that Seldon was not throwing punches, ringsiders wondered if McCall would pressure Seldon in attempt to decisively win the last two rounds. Although most observers had the fight quite close—ESPN commentator Barry Tompkins going so far as to say at the beginning of the round that it was "one of those fights that could still be had by either man"—they also realized that the Seldon was the "name" opponent, fighting in his hometown. Finally halfway through the round the last fumes that had been keeping the "Atlantic City Express" going ran out. When Seldon was pushed back into the ropes, McCall proceeded to drop the weary Seldon with an unimpressive left uppercut that didn't land cleanly. Seldon quickly rose, but found himself back on the canvas when a weak overhand right of McCall's that landed on his arm dropped him again. It suddenly became apparent that Seldon was a beaten man. With nearly a minute left in the round, he needed to avoid one more knockdown to avoid being TKO'ed courtesy of the three-knockdown rule. McCall also realized the situation and immediately jumped all over Seldon, trapping him in the corner. Although Seldon did punch back initially, it was clear that the corner was the only thing keeping him up, and when another left uppercut (followed by a right hook) dropped Seldon a third time, referee Tony Perez ended the contest at 2:36 of the round.

In hindsight, this fight saw the birth of a new heavyweight contender in Oliver McCall, a man who would go on to win a world title and became a fixture in the top ten for much of the 1990s. But at the time it seemed only to be a journeyman who got lucky. When McCall struggled against Jesse Ferguson in winning a decision in his next fight, it seemed that the win over Seldon was just a fluke. In fact, when he stepped in the ring against Tony Tucker in 1992, most felt that the faded former champion would destroy McCall. But McCall gave Tucker all that he could handle to lose in a highly questionable decision that became the basis for his entrance into the top ten (thanks also to his connection to Don King). Although many boxing insiders felt that McCall was unworthy of a top-ten ranking, he did silence some of his critics when he stopped Francesco Damiani the following year.

Seldon, on the other hand, seemed to be a discredited heavyweight and found himself quickly dropped from the list of heavyweight up-and-comers. Although three other fighters in the "big five" struggled in fights about the same time as Seldon's loss—Mercer struggled with Francesco Damiani, Bowe won an unpopular decision over Tony Tubbs, and Tommy Morrison had problems with Yuri Vaulin—all still remained undefeated, and in the heavyweight division that was what mattered most. Seldon tried to rebound by taking on Riddick Bowe in his next fight, with the assumption that with a defeat of the highly touted Bowe he would jump right back into the picture. But it proved to be a terrible miscalculation; Bowe knocked out Seldon in the first round, almost ending his career. By the time he lost a decision to Tony Tubbs the following year, most expected Seldon to fade into journeyman status or retire from the ring. No one could have predicted what was to come. Although the idea of a Bruce Seldon title shot seemed a long shot, he found out shortly after signing on with Don King that having connections was half the battle in boxing. He skyrocketed up the rankings, despite fighting no one of note (except for Greg Page) and soon found himself the number two-ranked WBA contender. Then-champion George Foreman refused to fight Tony Tucker (who was the number one contender at the time), and Seldon found himself in a fight with Tucker for the vacant title. Although Tucker was a slight favorite going into the fight, Seldon proved to be a resilient and tough opponent and stopped the former IBF champ in the seventh round. The title reign was short-lived however. In only his second defense he took on Mike Tyson and found himself on the losing end of a very questionable first-round knockout. (It seemed he was dropped by a phantom punch.) That was Seldon's last fight as a professional until 2004, when Seldon launched a lackluster comeback.

November 4, 1991—Inglewood, California
James "Bonecrusher" Smith (30–8–1, 24 KOs) vs. Levi Billups
(15–5, 9 KOs)
Favorite: Smith
Result: Billups won a ten-round unanimous decision.

It almost seemed too good to be true for the fighter known as "Bonecrusher." George Foreman had punched his way into the history books when he extended Evander Holyfield the twelve-round distance only seven months prior, and with that Smith's George Foreman–like comeback looked like it might just pan out. Smith found himself closing in on the WBC's "top ten," with a number thirteen ranking and had already pulled the trick in the WBA (the sanctioning body which recognized him as heavyweight champ back in 1986–1987) where he was ranked number eight. Few felt that these rankings were unwarranted. *KO Magazine* had him ranked number twelve in their "KO Ratings" for the Heavyweight division,[1] and many experts and fans were openly discussing a possible title fight in the near future. Even sports authorities that normally shunned boxing started to give Smith some coverage: his first round knockout over lightly regarded Poncho Carter made the rounds on national sports reports throughout the country.

The "Bonecrusher" comeback already had a major boost because Smith was becoming a favorite of almost all of the major cable networks, and with Foreman's "promotion" to exclusive fights on HBO, "Bonecrusher" was called upon to fill the void. Michigan's *Fight Night at the Palace of Auburn Hills* televised his first-round knockout over Jeff Sims, and *USA Tuesday Night Fights* regularly televised "Bonecrusher" fights in their main events (including his knockouts over Everett "Bigfoot" Martin, Kimmuel Odum, and Marshall Tillman).

Smith wisely took advantage of his good fortune as well. He remained active, fighting six times in 1991 before his November showdown with Billups, and had gone 11–0 with ten knockouts since he last tasted defeat at the hands of Donovan "Razor" Ruddock in 1989. Although most of his opponents were similar (and in many instances identical) to those fought by George Foreman, he would occasionally take on a recognizable opponent like journeyman Martin (who had extended George Foreman the distance), or the former WBA champion Mike Weaver. When he did fight "non-entities" like Terry Armstrong he tended to look quite dominant.

However, in all the hoopla over the reinvented James Smith, many fans forgot the James Smith who was so thoroughly discredited as little as three years ago. Widely regarded as one of the worst heavyweight champions of all times, few who witnessed his title defense against Mike Tyson wanted to see Smith in a big fight again. Also, Smith had suffered losses too in the years prior to his comeback—to fighters like Jose Ri-

---

[1] "KO Ratings," *KO Magazine* (January 1992): 60.

balta, Marvis Frazier, and Adilson Rodrigues, a fighter that George Foreman knocked out in the second round.

"Bonecrusher" was looking to continue his diversification of cable appearances with a fight on *Prime Networks Fight Night at the Great Western Forum*. But his opponent, former United States Football League linebacker Levi Billups, seemed hardly the fighter to expose the ex-champion. Even those who disregarded the "Bonecrusher" comeback did not consider Levi Billups much of a threat, and almost everyone felt that the fight would be over quickly. Although Billups had briefly held the California State heavyweight championship (1988–1989), he had been TKO'ed in three rounds by young heavyweight up-and-comer Michael Moorer just four months prior and most anticipated that the fight with Smith would be a repeat. "Bonecrusher" stepped into the ring in what appeared to be the best condition he had been in some time, a lean 250 pounds, further diminishing the possibility of a Billups victory. In fact, few could envision a scenario where Billups could pull off the upset. Although Smith tended to have trouble with boxers such as Tony Tubbs, Billups didn't appear capable of duplicating the smooth boxing of a Tubbs. He was a puncher, and though great punchers (such as Tyson and Ruddock) tended to also give Smith problems, few regarded Billups as a "great" puncher. He seemed to be a strong (but limited) brawler who would get knocked out in a slugfest with the bigger, stronger Smith.

In the opening round, however, Billups showed the world the strategy that would carry him to victory. While "Bonecrusher" tried to establish the jab, Billups bulldogged into his bigger opponent with left hooks and winging overhand rights. Although Billups seldom used the jab to get in, he effectively robbed Smith of his ability to mount an effective offense. Smith was limited to an ineffective left jab, which Billups was able to avoid with ease. Still, despite Billups effectiveness, most expected Smith to come alive and start throwing the combinations. Even though Smith was sluggish in the early rounds, everyone assumed that once he warmed up, the fight would change pace. But when Billups staggered "Bonecrusher" in the fourth, it looked as if Billups's power was in fact the reason for Smith's unwillingness to mix it up. A Smith uppercut seemed to stagger Levi in the fifth, but Billups survived and turned the table on Smith. With Smith reeling by round's end, it finally began to sink in for even the most ardent Smith fan that this was not going to be his night. In fact, it seemed that whenever "Bonecrusher" seemed to turn things around and tag Levi, Billups would quickly regain control by staggering the thirty-eight-year-old former champ.

But as the old boxing adage goes, you can never count a puncher out, and Smith was a puncher. Although Smith seemed to be a clearly beaten fighter going into the ninth round, Levi had yet to pay for the reckless-ness of his punches. He had thrown wild, looping hooks and overhand rights throughout the fight without suffering any serious punishment. But his luck finally ran out when, after getting clocked halfway through the ninth with a picture-perfect overhand right, he tried to counter with one of his own. Smith recognized how damaged Billups was and matched the shot with another right that dropped Billups in his corner. Billups looked to be in serious trouble when he rose at the count of five sporting a cut over his left eye. Even though "Bonecrusher" was re-nowned for his finishing skills, Billups survived the Smith onslaught and, with one round left in the fight, realized that he just needed to sur-vive to win. He decided to use the jab in earnest in the tenth round, which proved to be quite effective as a clearly spent "Bonecrusher" was simply unable to mount an offense. The decision was a mere formality— although one judge had it fairly close at 96–94, the other two had it at a more realistic 98–91—with Billups winning the well-earned decision.

For Billups, it was the biggest win of his career and introduced him to the heavyweight division, if not as a contender, then as a one of the more reputable journeymen in the division. That reputation was recon-firmed when, three months later, he extended young up-and-comer Len-nox Lewis the ten-round distance without hitting the canvas. In fact, until his first-round knockout loss to Corrie Sanders in 1993, Billups almost emerged as a borderline contender. He returned to the Great Western Forum to knock out Joel Humm in the first round and followed that win with a good decision over journeyman Nate Fitch.

Smith, on the other hand, saw his career completely unravel after the loss to Billups. Although he defeated Mark Wills via a ten-round deci-sion in early 1992, a loss to Greg Page later that year (in which he was dropped in the opening round) followed by an ugly decision loss to Mi-chael Moorer ended any possibility of restoring the damage that Levi Billups had done to his career. Ultimately, the loss to Levi Billups was one of his most devastating losses. The night of November 4, 1991, was the last time that James Smith was a ranked contender. He never came close to restoring that position in the years after that fight, and when interviewed over ten years later, Smith admitted that the Billups fight was one of his "toughest" losses.

November 12, 1991—Jacksonville, Florida
Terry Davis (26–2–2, 20 KOs) vs. Nathaniel Fitch (5–1, 3 KOs)
Favorite: Davis
Result: Fitch won via first-round TKO.

For heavyweight Nathaniel Fitch, it had become apparent that his career would fail to amount to much. Despite an impressive amateur resume, Fitch failed to impress as a professional, losing to Fred Whittaker in his first fight. Although he came back to win his next five fights against less-than-stellar opposition, it seemed that his management team recognized that he would never be more than a heavyweight opponent when they matched him, in only his seventh fight, against the more experienced Terry Davis. It was seen as another "gimmie" fight for a Terry Davis who had twenty-six wins in his career. Still, Davis was, despite his record, seen as a club fighter by most boxing experts. He appeared to be the typical white heavyweight with a padded record against soft opposition. Although he did have a pair of wins over Lionel Butler, they were wins over the "old" Butler (the Lionel Butler who lost ten of his first twenty fights), not the Butler who turned his career around to become a solid heavyweight contender. Also, a loss to Lionel Washington and a draw with Harry Terrell seemed to indicate that Davis owed his record more to great matchmaking than actual ring skill. Any doubt to that assessment was laid to rest when, on the undercard of the George Foreman–Evander Holyfield fight, he was destroyed in two rounds by the only world-class opponent he had faced, Michael Moorer.

Still, it didn't seem entirely out of the question that Davis could resurface in a big money fight. White heavyweights were always in demand, and despite his setback against Moorer, Davis still had an impressive record. George Foreman had already selected a complete unknown named Jimmy Ellis to fight in his first comeback, and most experts regarded Davis to be just as good (or, more accurately, not quite as bad) as Ellis. Ellis, like Davis, was white, and there was the possibility that if Davis could further pad his record, he could land a fight like that. Also, with his fight with Fitch thrown in on the undercard of Larry Holmes vs. Jamie Howe, it was a strong sign that he was possibly being groomed as a potential future opponent for the former champion.

It was with that in mind that Nate Fitch entered the ring, a safe enough pick for a fighter like Davis whom could ill afford to lose but lacked the skill to guarantee a victory against a competent heavyweight. With thirty fights under his belt, Davis had the big edge in experience, and that alone was viewed as enough to tilt the odds in his favor. Despite his padded record, the opponents he fought were better, and little was known of Fitch other than he was considered a flop as a pro. That assessment, however, proved woefully limited. Fitch was indeed a fighter with considerably less professional experience, but his amateur credentials more than made up for as soft a record as Terry Davis's. Also, with so little known about him, he was able to enter the fight as a complete question mark, a valuable commodity considering how evenly matched the fight turned out to be after the intangibles were taken into account.

When the fight began, most expected a slugfest. Davis was, after all, a straight-ahead brawler with some power. Also, although Moorer stopped him in the second round when they had fought, he did seem to have a decent enough chin. His defense had been porous, but he had been able to hold up against the power of Moorer a bit before succumbing to the clean power shots of the hard-punching southpaw. Although little was known of Fitch, there was little question that he was not the puncher that Michael Moorer was, and the assumption was that a slugfest was in Davis's best interest. Davis apparently thought so as well as he came out and met an onrushing Fitch in the center of the ring. Both fighters threw hard hooks at each other, with Davis targeting the midsection and Fitch going high. But it was Fitch who did damage, landing a picture-perfect left hook behind a wild right hand that backed Davis into the ropes less than ten seconds into the fight. Although Davis seemed only mildly stunned, Fitch saw an opening and pounced. He recklessly threw shots in an attempt to take out his hurt opponent and landed another left hook on the chin. Davis tried to cover up, but when a third left hook (followed by a straight right hand) landed, he crumbled to the canvas face-first, prompting an immediate stoppage from the referee. In less than twenty-three seconds, Fitch upset the favored Terry Davis and secured the quickest knockout of his professional career.

It seemed initially that Fitch had rejuvenated his career with that win, but he was quickly handed back-to-back losses to Jerry Jones and Everett Mayo in his next two fights. It effectively destroyed the momentum that he had with the Davis win, and by the time he faced Lou Savarese and Jeremy Williams in 1993, he was officially a heavyweight journeyman, a role he held for the rest of his career.

Davis, however, rebounded somewhat, knocking out former Olympic gold medallist Henry Tillman the following year on *USA's Tuesday Night Fights*. For Davis that would be his biggest win. It gave him the NBA heavyweight title—even though the NBA is not one of the more highly regarded sanctioning bodies, it's still a nice acquisition for a hard luck fighter like Davis—and also restored a small bit of credibility lost after the Fitch fight. But rather than use that win to land another big televised fight, he seemed content to fight in the minors. He made a defense of his meaningless title in Beijing, China, against former world-contender David Bey and then sat on the sidelines for over a year before resurfacing against undefeated contender Andrew Golota. Golota starched Davis in the opening round. In the end, although he never was able to make it the world heavyweight picture, the loss to Fitch didn't hurt his ongoing success as a regional heavyweight fighter of some note.

CHAPTER THREE

1992

"Larry! Larry! Larry!"

Crowd during the later rounds of the
Larry Holmes–Ray Mercer fight

February 7, 1992—Atlantic City, New Jersey
Ray Mercer (18–0, 13 KOs) vs. Larry Holmes (53–3, 38 KOs)
Favorite: Mercer
Result: Holmes won a twelve-round unanimous decision.

By early 1991 Ray Mercer appeared to have finally caught up with fellow 1988 Olympian Riddick Bowe in the important game of public perception. Although he had captured an Olympic gold medal, his early career was marred with life-and-death struggles with very ordinary fighters like Ossie Ocasio and Bert Cooper, and by 1991 it was clear that he was not the "top prospect" in the division. Although he did score a knockout over undefeated WBO heavyweight champion Francesco Damiani in 1991, it was hardly an awe-inspiring performance. Damiani clearly outboxed Mercer before an uppercut that broke his nose prompted him to quit in the ninth. When Mercer backed out of a fight with Riddick Bowe later that year, it was enough to relegate him to the end of the line of up-and-coming heavyweights. But in October 1991 Mercer finally silenced the critics with the most destructive performance in a heavyweight fight since Gerry Cooney knocked out Ken Norton ten years before. With his brutal fifth-round knockout of Tommy "The Duke" Morrison, Mercer jumped to the front of the pack in the heavyweight division, and it looked like he would be next in line for a fight with Evander Holyfield. But a fight with Holyfield was at least a full year away from happening, so in the meantime a payday seemed in order. The opponent needed to be marketable, but safe. Therefore the mandatory WBO number one contender, Michael Moorer, was out. Although he was marketable, he was too dangerous for a fighter on the verge of a title fight. Besides, there was more money to be earned with a bigger name fighter who, on paper, seemed to be the perfect foil—namely the forty-two-year-old former heavyweight champion Larry Holmes.

Nobody questioned that Holmes was a one of the greatest heavyweights of all time, holding the title for over seven years and defending it twenty times. But at forty-two, he appeared years past his prime. Many insiders saw signs of trouble as early as 1985 when he lost for the first time to Michael Spinks. Against Spinks he appeared unable to "pull the trigger" against a younger, quicker foe. After another loss to Spinks he called it quits for the first time, but in 1988 he made an ill-advised comeback against Mike Tyson. After getting humiliated in four rounds against "Iron" Mike (the only time he was ever knocked out as a professional), Holmes again retired, and most assumed it was for the last time. But when George Foreman's comeback landed him a title fight with Evander Holyfield and a multimillion dollar payday, Holmes was motivated to lace up the gloves again. For most boxing insiders, the comeback was a disaster waiting to happen. Although he was actually younger than Foreman, Holmes had had wars against fighters like Ken Norton, Mike Weaver, Gerry Cooney, Tim Witherspoon, James "Bonecrusher" Smith, and Carl "The Truth" Williams.

But perhaps more importantly, Foreman was able to make a successful comeback on the basis of his power. Like many older fighters his speed and reflexes had suffered over the years, but for Foreman, his power, along with a newly discovered relaxed fighting style, were alone enough to compensate. However, for Holmes, speed and reflexes were his strength in his prime, not his power. Larry depended on a quick left jab, he would be unable to bomb his way through the opposition like Foreman. The critics were brutal in their opinion of Larry's comeback, and early on it appeared as if they were justified in their skepticism. Holmes looked ordinary against journeymen Eddie Gonzalez and Art Card (going the ten-round distance with both of them), and many felt that had he been in with a higher grade of opponent he would have lost. Perhaps realizing that a Foreman-like comeback—where Larry would fight twenty or so clubfighters without fighting a top of the line heavy-weight contender before landing a title fight—was not going to land him a fight for the world title, Holmes decided to take a quantum leap in competition in his comeback by agreeing to fight Mercer. Although the WBO withdrew recognition of Ray Mercer as champion for his refusal to fight Michael Moorer, the fight did remain a twelve-round fight, and few questioned that the Mercer's stock was unaffected by the WBO's move.

Although the fight landed on pay-per-view, it seemed a mismatch to many. Few gave Holmes any chance, and the odds of 4–1 for Mercer seemed actually generous to the former champion. Even though Mercer weighed in at a career high 228¾, and Larry Holmes appeared in excellent shape at 233 pounds, it didn't change the prevailing wisdom that the former champion was washed up. Also, although he tried to repackage himself as a loveable old grandfather like Foreman did, the act just wasn't flying, and he failed to win over many new converts in Atlantic City (a city that staunchly stood behind the local boy in Mercer). In fact, boos could be heard as he entered the ring and during his introduction. He was undoubtedly a fighter in hostile territory.

Early in the first, it appeared as if the critics were right. Ray Mercer fired a hard left jab that clearly troubled the older fighter. Larry tried to fire back, popping Mercer with a hard right behind his own left jab a minute into the round, but when a Mercer left jab had Holmes reeling with a little under a minute in the round, it appeared clear that Holmes would not be able to cope with the power of Mercer. Fans began to cringe, anticipating a "Merciless" knockout over a once-great fighter. But Holmes shocked everyone, including Mercer, by quickly firing back and in fact had Mercer covering up in the final minute.

From the second round, Holmes was in control. As Mercer stalked, Holmes boxed and pumped the jab. But Holmes also used almost every veteran trick in the book such as holding out his left hand to throw off Mercer's offense. He also would occasionally give his legs a rest by fighting from the ropes or the corner (a trick that few fighters not named Ali had the skill to pull off) and would often grab the top rope with his right hand as he punched with the left for extra leverage. Larry fired a hard right hand that landed on the chin at 2:00 of the second round, and at the bell, there was little question which fighter controlled

Larry Holmes looking dapper as ever. *Scott Romer*

the round. Holmes recognized the weakness in Mercer's defense and was using every veteran trick to expose it, landing a shocking seventy-six percent of his punches in the second round.

By the third Larry began taunting the younger man by dropping his hands to his sides. He also discovered that he was most effective in the corner after Mercer trapped Holmes there. Larry fired right hand after right hand and, whenever Mercer punched, the former champion tied him up to derail his offense. At the halfway point of the round Holmes fired six straight right hands that caught Mercer upstairs. It didn't stop Mercer's ever-forward march, but it did show everyone how ineffective it was. Although Mercer exploded in the final thirty seconds, it was not enough to turn the tide, and Holmes blocked most of the shots before resuming his dissection of Mercer. In fact, Larry's domination became so clear that he began talking to ringsiders and the TVKO cameraman. It was classic Ali, but for the first time in his career, Holmes was able to do it on his own and not be accused of being a copycat. By the fifth round the pro-Mercer crowd began chanting "Larry! Larry! Larry!" in a clear sign that he was winning over the crowd. In the sixth round he turned to the cameraman, telling the viewers to "watch this!" With that Mercer jumped on the former champion with an ineffective combination, which prompted Holmes to tell the camera, "I'm not Tommy Morrison!"

Holmes continued to box well and even began to incorporate the uppercut into his offense in the seventh. But Holmes slowed down in the eighth round. Although Larry still fought well out of the corner and off the ropes, Mercer showed the first signs of reaching the former champion, and some ringsiders were wondering if the forty-two-year-old Holmes was beginning to tire. But Larry bounced back in the ninth, resuming his dominance. At the bell to start the round, Larry fired a hard right to the head of Mercer and never looked back. By the end of the round it appeared clear that Larry had his second wind, and the upset looked more likely than ever. Boxing well over the last three rounds, Larry cemented a clear and lopsided decision. The scores were 117–112, 117–111, and 115–113 for Holmes, giving him the biggest win of his career since his knockout over Gerry Cooney in 1982.

In many ways, it was one of the most rewarding wins of Holmes's career. With it he was able to win over many new fans and emerge from the shadow of Muhammad Ali. Also, he finally established himself as something of a "fan favorite" rather than the bitter, sour fighter with a tongue that stung as much as his jab. Boxing fans also were eager to see what now looked like one of the more intriguing fights of the heavyweight division: Larry Holmes vs. George Foreman. It was a fight that fans wanted to see (even though many claimed that they didn't want to watch it) and it seemed like a natural. But that fight never materialized. Larry Holmes was in fact rewarded for his win with a title fight against Evander Holyfield. Although fans reluctantly admitted that Holmes earned the fight, few were eager to see another forty-year-old fighting for a world title. When Holmes gave "The Real Deal" all that he could handle in losing a twelve-round decision, the same critics who praised Foreman for extending the former champion were now saying that it was Holyfield's weaknesses rather than anything Holmes did that caused the fight to be so competitive. Larry continued fighting after the loss to Holyfield, and after winning seven straight fights against weak opposition he received a second title fight, this time against one of the most beatable champions in recent memory: Oliver McCall. But Holmes ended up on the losing end of a close decision, a clear sign to his many fans that his time was up. If he couldn't beat Oliver McCall then he simply was never going to win a world title. But Larry kept fighting on, losing to Brian Nielsen in 1997 before capturing the "Legends of Boxing" heavyweight title in 1999 against James "Bonecrusher" Smith. By the end of his career, he was out of the heavyweight picture, but still taking on occasional fights for decent paydays, like his fight against Butterbean in 2002.

For Mercer, the fight with Holmes initially appeared to expose him as a limited fighter who would never overcome his flaws to become a world-class heavyweight. He bounced back from the loss with a grueling TKO over Mike Dixon eight months later, and scored a follow up knockout over Wimpy Halstead in December 1992. But nearly a year to the day after his fight with Holmes, Ray Mercer again lost in shocking upset, this time to a journeyman named Jesse Ferguson (page 84).

March 6, 1992—Callicoon, New York
Paul Roma (Pro Debut) vs. Jerry Arentzen (1–2–1, 0 KOs)
Favorite: Roma
Result: Arentzen won via fourth-round TKO.

Buried on the undercard of the ESPN televised Kevin Pompey–Stephan Johnson was a relatively insignificant four-round heavyweight fight, a fight that had few boxing fans particularly excited. But the fight did generate more interest than it probably deserved, as it turned out that the fight had an unusual crossover appeal with fans of professional wrestling. Debuting Paul Roma was a former star of the World Wrestling Federation (WWF) and was looking to continue his success in the ring in a second sport (if pro wrestling could be considered a sport). He was well known as part of a tag team (with Jim Powers) called "The Young Stallions," who proved to be a recognizable, if not spectacular, duo in the WWF in the mid to late 80s. (Their greatest moment in the WWF came when they defeated the legendary "Hart Foundation," a tag team that included future WWF world champion Bret "The Hitman" Hart.) However, Roma's career with the WWF seemed to fizzle. Although he had a handful of minor rivalries early in the decade, he failed to generate a successful career as a single's wrestler and, as a result, wasn't particularly missed when he left to pursue a career in boxing.

Roma hardly set boxing ablaze with his decision. Boxing already had several high profile celebrities who were discrediting the sport and embarrassing themselves in pursuing ill-advised boxing careers. Actor Mickey Rourke and former NFL star Mark Gastineau were both in the middle of what amounted to circus shows, and many boxing insiders shuddered at the thought of another "wannabe" donning the gloves.

However, Roma took his career seriously. To maximize his chances of being a successful boxer, he hired former Mike Tyson trainer Kevin Rooney and proceeded to drop forty pounds of added bulk to weigh in at a trim 210. Unlike Gastineau, who continued to train like a football player (with an emphasis on lifting weights), it seemed as if Roma was training like a boxer, a promising sign. With Arentzen, he had a safe opponent for his debut. Arentzen was a blown-up cruiserweight (although he weighed in at 208½, his previous fight two months prior was at 187 pounds), with a knockout loss in his pro debut and little in the form of boxing skills or punching power. A correct assessment, Arentzen's lack of talent made Roma's defeat all the more humiliating.

Roma proved completely ineffective at mounting an offense, a defense, or much of anything else, although one boxing writer noted that he did have some skills at "grabbing."[1] Arentzen thoroughly dominated Roma, dropping him in the first and third rounds. Not only did Roma fail to win a single round, he had not won even an exchange going into the fourth, and final, round. With Roma needing a knockout to win, cornerman Kevin Rooney threw in the towel when Roma continued to get pummeled for the first minute of the fourth, awarding the TKO victory to Arentzen at 1:10 of the round.

For most observers, it was a clear indication that Roma had no business being in the ring. Arentzen was so lightly regarded that it was hard to imagine how any fighter who lost to him could possibly rebound. However, Roma did continue his career for two more months, scoring two knockout victories before calling it a career in boxing and returning to pro wrestling. His second stint in pro wrestling proved to be considerably more successful, winning the WCW tag team title and becoming part of the most recognizable partnership in modern wrestling history, the legendary "Four Horsemen"—a wrestling alliance that included hall of fame wrestlers Ric Flair and Arn Anderson, with whom he won the tag team title. Although that alliance was short lived, he remained a fixture in WCW, going on to win the tag team titles two more times (with Paul Orndorff) in 1994. By early 1995 he had become what amounted to a star in wrestling, with a trading card made up in the WCW/CARDZ series. It was unquestionably enough to keep him in the sport at which he truly excelled, and he never stepped into the boxing ring again.

Arentzen failed to win many converts from his performance that night, and he never matched that victory with another. It was Arentzen's only career knockout, and the last win he would have in the boxing ring. He would go on to get knocked out in the opening round against Peter McNeeley the following month and then went winless for the rest of the decade, with knockout losses to the likes of Jeremy Williams, Michael Bentt, and James Stanton. By the end of the decade his record stood at a dismal 2–11–1, 1 KO.

March 22, 1992—Atlantic City, New Jersey
Carl "The Truth" Williams (25–4, 19 KOs) vs. Jerry Jones (8–4,
    6 KOs)
Favorite: Williams
Result: Jones won a unanimous ten-round decision.

---

[1] Jack Obermayer, "Results Around the World," *Boxing Illustrated* 34 (August 1992): 59.

For perennial heavyweight contender Carl "The Truth" Williams, it already appeared that his career was coming to a close. Although he had established himself as a recognizable and respected heavyweight contender in the 1980s (with a solid, albeit losing, effort against then IBF champion Larry Holmes), a controversial first-round knockout at the hands of then undisputed heavyweight king Mike Tyson seemed to end any possibility of another shot at the title. Though some questioned the stoppage, there was little doubt that "The Truth's" fragile chin would most likely fail him again if he stepped back into the ring with "Iron" Mike. A somewhat sluggish knockout over Melton Bowen kept him in the top ten, but a follow-up loss to Tim Witherspoon, in a decision that most observers felt should have gone to Williams, seemed to indicate that he would not be given any favors from the judges if he should step into the ring with another contender.

Still, Williams was a popular fighter and one that ESPN enjoyed featuring in the early 1990s. His fights were usually competitive, and his less-than-stellar chin tended to make almost any fight interesting. He also benefited from his nickname, one of the most original (and catchy) in boxing history. Despite the fact that he never won a world title, he was more recognizable than many fighters who did (such as Witherspoon) thanks in part to a parody of him done on the television show *In Living Color*. But by 1992 it appeared that his career was stuck in neutral. He was fighting infrequently against limited opposition, and though he was known for his impressive conditioning and physique in the 1980s—against Mike Tyson he weighed in at 218—he started to resemble many of the pudgy, overweight contenders from that era. In his previous fight against Marshall Tillman, "The Truth" weighed in at a very Greg-Page-like 235, and for Jones, Carl actually added an extra pound to that. His first fight after his controversial loss to Tim Witherspoon was an ugly ten-round decision over the very ordinary Kimmuel Odum, a decision that was later ruled no-contest. Though Williams quickly rebounded with a second-round knockout over the usually durable Marshall Tillman, his defense seemed shaky in that fight as well. Many observers even felt that that Tillman was taking control before being caught by a Williams overhand right.

Still, Williams was in heavyweight limbo. Many young up-and-comers still regarded Williams as too risky an opponent, but Williams himself was not impressive enough to move up the rankings (he was ranked number ten by the IBF, and number fifteen by the WBC). It appeared that he was doing the same thing Tim Witherspoon was doing: fighting every few months for pocket change on cable television networks. It was certainly not the strategy to land another title fight, but it was enough to keep from falling off the radar screen completely.

For southpaw Jerry Jones, it was a huge jump in class, and few regarded the relatively unknown Jones to fare much better than Tillman did two months earlier. Jones was most recognizable for extending a young Ray Mercer the distance in an eight-round fight, as well as a TKO loss to another prospect in Bruce Seldon. Still, some insiders felt that Jerry was nonetheless a competent, if less than spectacular, heavyweight. He knocked out future WBO heavyweight champion Michael Bentt in one round and scored an impressive decision over amateur standout Nathaniel Fitch only six weeks prior to his bout with Williams. But even those who thought well of Jones felt that he was going to be out of his league against Williams. Competing with young, raw heavyweights seemed woefully inadequate in preparing the inconsistent Jones for a fight with the seasoned veteran. With only twelve professional fights, few anticipated much of a contest. Most felt that lack of experience alone would prove to be Jones's undoing.

Jones may have been the only one to believe he could upset "The Truth," but it appeared that he didn't realize it for much of the first round. Williams came out strong with a left jab, pushing Jones around the ring and stunning him in the first minute. Jones's offense seemed wild; he resorted to wide right hooks in an apparent attempt to compensate for his inability to get inside "The Truth's" jab. With a full 1:30 left in the opening round, Jones was felled by a less-than-impressive left hook–right uppercut combination as he lunged in with what seemed like an amateurish offense. It seemed to many ringsiders that "The Truth" was about to pull a somewhat rare feat (for him) in scoring a first-round knockout. Williams had already decided that Jones was ready to go, as he marched into the wobbly Jones in an attempt to end the fight quickly. It was at that point that "The Truth" discovered the truth about Jerry Jones's lunging right hooks. They may have looked sloppy, but they were backed up with power. In what looked like a Hail Mary, Jones landed a wide right that landed square on Williams's chin. Williams dropped to the canvas like a man shot, and though he quickly rose at the count of four and indicated to his corner that he was not hurt, it was clear that Williams was in serious trouble.

In a flash it appeared that Jones, rather than Williams, was on the verge of scoring a first-round knockout. With nearly a minute left in the round Jones came out strong, attempting to finish off Williams. "The Truth" still had the experience of a cagey veteran, however, and he pooled all of it in a desperate attempt to survive. It appeared to work, as Williams survived the round. However, any question as to how much damage Jones inflicted was quickly answered when "The Truth" stumbled into the wrong corner.

At the start of the second round, many were curious as to how Williams was affected by the knockdown. He appeared to be doing well early on, pumping the left jab with authority. But he seemed gun-shy, backing away from Jones's looping shots rather than countering them as he had done before the knockdown. It quickly became apparent why when Williams was rocked again in the second and dropped a second time in the third. By that point it looked like the fight would not make it to the scorecards, because Williams appeared completely unable to cope with the Jerry Jones's right hand. Even though Williams was repeatedly stunned throughout the first five rounds, Jones was unable to finish off the gutsy veteran. However, Williams was not able to regain control of the fight. Although it appeared that he had later closed the gap, Jones so decisively won the early rounds that few could see how Williams could get the decision. In the end, Williams was able to make it close—two judges had it 96–94, while the third had it 96–93—but still ended up on the losing end.

For Williams, the loss to Jerry Jones effectively ended his career as a contender. He quickly dropped out of the top ten in the IBF rankings, and slipped down to number twenty-three in the WBC. Although he defeated former cruiserweight champion Ossie Ocasio and Jimmy Lee Smith before the end of the year, not even the most ardent supporters of "The Truth" could see him getting back into the top ten after such a decisive loss. Williams, to his credit, rediscovered the dedication to his career that had been lacking, weighing in the mid 220s from that point on. He even lined up a fight with Tommy "The Duke" Morrison, who was looking to rebuild his career after a devastating loss to Ray Mercer. But when Williams found himself on the losing end against Tommy

Morrison, he slid out of even the most liberal classification of contender, and became a "name opponent."

For Jones, the fight with Williams catapulted his career into the big leagues. He found himself ranked number twelve by the IBF despite not hitting double digits for wins. Unfortunately for Jones, though he was no longer an "opponent," he was unable to shake the mentality of one. When asked who the opponent was for his next fight, he was quoted as saying "I am."[2] In fact, he was, as he quickly found himself lined up to fight Donovan "Razor" Ruddock only two months after his career defining victory (at a time when most boxing insiders regarded "Razor" one of the top heavyweights in boxing at the time). Though the Ruddock fight fell through, he remained inactive until stepping into the ring with Alex Garcia for a minor title nine months later. Although he gave Garcia all that he could handle in losing a close decision, it effectively ended Jones's brief stint in the world rankings.

May 11, 1992—Inglewood, California
David Dixon (11–1, 10 KOs) vs. Lionel Butler (11–10–1, 7 KOs)
Favorite: Dixon
Result: Butler won when Dixon was disqualified in the fourth round.

Although the Great Western Forum was home to some of the best boxing in the United States in the early 1990s, much of this was in the lighter weight classes. While fighters like Victor Rabanales became regulars and even won world championships, there had yet to be a major heavyweight to emerge from the Forum. However, fans in Southern California were becoming increasingly impressed with a hard punching heavyweight prospect named Dave Dixon, a fighter who seemed to have just what was needed to punch his way into the heavyweight division's top ten. Although there were still many unanswered questions about him, many stemming from a decision loss to Tui Toia in his seventh pro fight, he had shaken much of the negative stigma of that loss by winning his next five fights by knockout. But it was his previous win (a first-round knockout over journeyman Mike Acey) that caused his first ripple

---

[2] Eric Bottijer, "East Coast Line," *Flash* 93 (April 30, 1992): 8.

in the heavyweight division. Acey was a classic opponent, better known for his knockout losses than his wins, but the ease upon which Dixon blitzed Acey impressed many. Many boxing insiders openly wondered how he would fare against a higher caliber of opponent, and it appeared to many Southern California boxing fans that he was indeed taking a natural, if not huge, step up in class with Lionel Butler.

Butler was another noteworthy California-based heavyweight with solid power that accounted for his five straight knockout victories. But his early career was noteworthy in that he lost four of his first five fights. Although losses to Phil Jackson and Riddick Bowe in his first two fights proved that management was the major factor for his dismal start, it appeared too little too late for Lionel when he hooked up with Dan and Joe Goossen. Nonetheless, his signing with the Goossen brothers revitalized his career to a certain extent, leading to his streak of five straight knockout victories. But for the cynics, it was hardly enough to convince them that he was a new Lionel Butler. He was still a fighter barely over the five hundred mark, and some cynical boxing writers felt that Goossen had turned a bottom-of-the barrel heavyweight (the type that fighters in their first five fights would feast upon) into a higher-grade opponent (the type that fighters in their twentieth fight would feast upon). A loss to Dixon was seen as his inauguration into the less-than-lucrative world of heavyweight journeyman status.

But it took Lionel Butler less than a minute to prove that he was no Mike Acey, despite the fact that both fighters had nearly identical records. He showed no fear of his bigger foe as he crowded Dixon on the inside and threw bombs on even terms. He also shocked fans with his defense, for despite his crowding and ever-forward motion, he seemed quite capable of slipping Dixon's punches.

Perhaps realizing his natural advantage in reach (he had a full eleven inches of reach on Butler), Dixon began to use his jab in the early part of the second round and was moderately successful in keeping Butler at bay. But when a lunging Butler overhand right stunned Dixon a minute into the round, it became clear that Lionel was just as dangerous from the outside as he was from the inside.

Realizing that Butler was about to pull off the upset, or perhaps caving in to frustration, Dixon began to employ a strategy that would completely turn the fight around. Whereas the first two rounds were close (and entertaining), involving power and will, the last two rounds involved a ridiculous number of low blows from Dixon. After getting stunned by a left hook twenty seconds into the round, Dixon responded with a low blow that caused Butler to buckle over in pain. After being given a short break Butler came back angry, crowding Dixon. But seconds later Dixon fired a second low blow, a move that cost him a point. It seemed a clear sign that he needed to stop throwing south of the border, but seconds later Dixon did it again. When it was not called, Dixon tried to push his luck again with a fourth low blow. It was seen by referee Robert Byrd and resulted in Dixon losing his second point of the round. With two points deducted in one round, it became clear that Dixon was very close to being disqualified, but nonetheless he again went low at the bell.

Perhaps because he was watching another fight, or even not realizing the precarious spot his fighter was in, Dixon's cornerman Andrew Trusdale gave his fighter terrible advice as the fourth round began, telling him to "work the body, and then we'll get him to the head later." Less than thirty seconds into the fourth Dixon again went low, and with it the patience of Robert Byrd hit its limit. Byrd promptly (and appropriately) called the fight off, awarding Butler the disqualification victory at 0:33 of the round.

For Dixon, a fighter who entered the fight as the hottest heavyweight prospect in Southern California, the loss initially seemed devastating. Almost everything that a fighter could do wrong he had. He came into the fight overweight (at 254 pounds), seemed to quit behind the low blows (which he later attributed to his attempt to throw the uppercut to the stomach), and showed an inability to deal with the pressure of a fighter not regarded as world class. But Dixon quickly rebounded with a win over Larry Davis two months later. When he followed that win with a first-round knockout at the Forum over Mike White he reestablished himself as a minor prospect. (He was aided in Butler's rise to the top ten as a legitimate contender in the years to come.) However he never took the second step up in competition, and although he fought to a technical draw with Larry Donald in 1995, it was hardly enough to convince the critics that he was ready for the big leagues. A first-round knockout loss to Tony Tucker shortly thereafter ended his status as a prospect, and in a bizarre case of déjà vu, Dixon would go on to lose the final fight of his career in 2000 (to Lance Whitaker) when he was disqualified for low blows.

For Butler, credit was slow in coming. Despite the win he was still not regarded as a fighter with any sort of future at all, and many experts seemed sure that the unlikely streak would come to an end when he signed to fight Tony Tubbs in his next fight. But again Butler pulled off the upset, starching Tubbs in the first round (page 64).

June 9, 1992—San Francisco, California
Mark Gastineau (9–0, 9 KOs) vs. Tim "Doc" Anderson
** (25–15–1, 13 KOs)**
Favorite: Gastineau
Result: Anderson won a five-round unanimous decision.

After a high profile career as a defensive lineman in the NFL with the New York Jets (in which he set an NFL record for sacks in a season), along with an equally high profile relationship with actress Brigette Nielsen, there was little doubt that people knew who Mark Gastineau was. But when he announced at the ripe age of thirty-six that he was beginning a career in professional boxing, few anticipated a successful career for the former AFC defensive player of the year. For one thing, he lacked any amateur background, never having so much as stepped into the boxing ring. Considering most boxers first laced on the gloves before they hit puberty, there was little question that Gastineau was at least two decades behind. Most expected Mark to fail, and fail miserably, if he were ever to step into the ring with a legitimate contender, but most also assumed that he would at least win his early fights. More likely than not he would be thrown in with complete tomato cans early, allowing him to pad his record. But controversy erupted as soon as he turned pro. When Gastineau knocked out a former professional wrestler named Derrick Dukes in less than twenty seconds with a very questionable shot to the shoulder, the boxing world began to realize that the fix was almost certainly in—a claim also made by Dukes, who said he was paid to take a dive. It appeared that promoter Rick "Elvis" Parker would take no chances in padding the record of Gastineau, and he had no qualms about dragging the entire sport of boxing into the sewer to land Gastineau a big money fight. Then rumors began to circulate that

Parker was fixing even more fights, not only those of Gastineau but also of some of his other fighters. It was enough to prove to many boxing insiders that Gastineau's boxing career was just a circus act, and many closed the book on him. Although he hardly had much support from the boxing world before, he was now seen as a literal cancer to the sport, and even movie star Mickey Rourke was given more respect for his attempts at boxing than Gastineau.

But there was still one person who was very interested in Mark Gastineau's career and was very interested in the money a fight with him could generate. George Foreman began to throw out some signals to Parker that if Gastineau could pad his record to 12–0, he might fight him. Although nobody thought Gastineau could possibly beat Foreman, and few thought he would survive past the opening round, everyone admitted that the fight was a sellable fight (even if it were for all the wrong reasons). All Parker needed to do now was to keep Mark winning while slowly increasing his national exposure. First came a one-round blowout over a limited clubfighter named Lon Liebergen on the undercard of the little seen Ray Mancini vs. Greg Haugen pay-per-view card in April 1992. Although he did win in the opening round, many ringsiders were actually surprised at how bad he looked in the process. He had a terrible defense, an atrocious jab, and it appeared that the only thing he did well in the ring was the sack dance after the fight was over. Still, when it was announced that he would fight Tim "Doc" Anderson on *USA's Tuesday Night Fights* most felt that he would win. Anderson was widely seen as the bottom of the barrel when it came to journeymen (despite his somewhat glossy record for a fighter of his caliber). Although he had defeated former heavyweight contender Jimmy Young in 1988, most felt that it was more a reflection of how far Young had slipped rather than how good Anderson was. Besides, in the four years since he beat Young he had gone on to lose fights to such limited opponents like Tim Morrison, Art Terry, Danny Wofford, and, in a first-round knockout loss, Larry Holmes. But the most telling fight appeared to be a ten-round draw with a forty-one-year-old doctor who had just taken up boxing as a hobby, Dr. Harold "Hackie" Reitman. Reitman had just as little experience as Gastineau and considerably less size (he weighed around two hundred pounds for most of his fights), and most boxing experts felt that as bad as Gastineau was, he had to be better than Reitman—after all, he was a professional athlete. Considering Reitman dropped Anderson twice, many felt that the size and power of Gastineau would shine through against his smaller opponent. Besides, the conventional wisdom with many boxing insiders was that Parker wouldn't have made the fight if he didn't already make "arrangements" for a Gastineau win.

As Tim "Doc" Anderson would later claim, Parker attempted to do just that by promising Anderson a future cut of a potential $500,000 payday for a Foreman fight. But Anderson refused, intending to give it his all. It still was not enough to scare Team Gastineau into dropping out, but it did created a real concern that Mark could conceivably embarrass himself, even if he were to win, and possibly remove himself from consideration for a Foreman fight. As it would turn out, Mark did more than embarrass himself: he put up possibly the single worst performance by any professional boxer ever in the history of televised boxing. Gastineau started cautiously in the opening round, occasionally flicking out his comical jab as his equally cautious opponent circled around the ring. It soon became apparent that Gastineau, a man accustomed to playing in front of packed football stadiums in the NFL, had a severe case of stage fright. He moved slowly, and it was clear to everybody watching that Gastineau was extremely tense. With each jab he threw he appeared to flinch in fear of the counter punch that could come in response, and he seemed to freeze and close his eyes in fear whenever Anderson even looked like he was about to throw a punch. By round's end he was visibly fatigued, and many at ringside were already laughing at his performance. Sadly for Mark, it would actually be his best round. Heeding his corner's advice to "move" his hands, Gastineau jumped all over Anderson at the bell to start the second and quickly pinned "Doc" in the corner while firing a hard combination. But he looked utterly ridiculous in the process and failed to rattle Anderson at all. Realizing that Gastineau could not hurt him, "Doc" began to open up his own offense, throwing wide, but effective, overhand rights. Initially Gastineau tried to slug back, but he quickly spent what little gas he had left, and when Anderson smiled and waved him back in, it became clear to all that Mark simply couldn't hurt "Doc." It was the last hurrah of Mark Gastineau's offense, as he began to backpedal and hold as Anderson attacked. In the final twenty seconds of the round Anderson fired a quick combination upstairs, and in the final five seconds of the round a hard right hand spun Gastineau around and into the ropes. It was the first time he had been really hit in the boxing ring, and he completely fell apart as a result. Gastineau virtually ran to the ropes, turned his head and closed his eyes out of fear and anticipation for the follow-up punch he was sure would land. It was a clear example of a fighter not knowing what to do when he was hit, something that is common in the novice class in amateur boxing, but not in the professional ranks. Saved by the bell, Gastineau returned to his corner, a confused and completely exposed fighter.

Anderson jumped on Gastineau early, recognizing the complete inability of his opponent to deal with a real boxer. Mark continued to flinch and close his eyes whenever Anderson threw anything. With his confidence surging, Anderson began to bounce and move around the ring. With just over a minute left in the round, a quick combination upstairs again drove Gastineau into the ropes, and once there, a hard left hook caused him to again turn his head away from, and his back to, Anderson. It was enough for referee Marty Sammon to step in and call it a knockdown, even though technically Gastineau didn't hit the deck. Gastineau, whose fatigue was evident as early as the first round, now appeared totally spent as his hands were down to his waist with his chin up (and his mouth open). The fourth round turned into another dominant one for Anderson, as he had Gastineau backpedaling from the bell on. Gastineau's mouthpiece now began to stick out, a clear sign of how tired he was. Although Anderson initially worked behind his footwork and jab to start the round, he began to press his attack again in the final minute. Clearly not wanting to engage Anderson, Gastineau held on whenever "Doc" came in close. But with a little under thirty seconds in the round, a left hand to the belt prompted Gastineau to turn to the referee looking for help. It would not come, but rather an Anderson left hook would, dropping Gastineau flat on his back and seemingly finishing him for the night. Gastineau, however, did get up at the count of eight, and although he stumbled around the ring, he was "saved" by the bell.

It was clear that Gastineau had eliminated himself from any big money fight with Foreman, but he still had one more round to try and salvage the win. Although prompted by his trainer to "get on him," Gastineau simply didn't have the energy to do anything, and when Anderson spent the better part of the fifth and final round moving away, Gastineau obliged him. By round's end it was clear that the deceptive undefeated record of Mark Gastineau was gone, and that the charade of his boxing career was now exposed. All three judges had it a complete shutout (Marshall Walker and Elmer Costa scored the fight 50–43 while Rudy Ortega scored it 50–42) for Tim "Doc" Anderson, giving him the biggest win of his career.

For boxing fans, Gastineau's fall was a small bit of comic relief. Many fans had a hard time watching the fight without laughing, and Anderson appeared to be a nice guy and a likeable underdog. Even Gastineau's post-fight interview was comically funny, blaming his loss not on conditioning or lack of skill, but rather his girlfriend, who kept him up all night arguing with him. Citing his determination to rebound from the loss, Gastineau declared that he was "going to probably get a new girlfriend," a claim that became a virtual punch line in the boxing world. But the comedy quickly turned into a tragedy, and before long nobody would be laughing. Determined to erase the stigma of his loss to Anderson, Gastineau rebounded with three meaningless wins to finish off the year before stepping into the ring with Anderson again in December 1992. Although the fight was not televised, most assumed that Anderson would repeat his earlier performance and beat Gastineau again. But Gastineau appeared to have improved his conditioning and stopped Anderson in the sixth round of a fight in which Anderson appeared to completely run out of gas. But then came the chilling claim from Anderson, who was sure that Parker slipped him an LSD mickey during the fight. He claimed that he began feeling sick in the third round, and shortly after the fight he was rushed to the hospital. Anderson never recovered, suffering from dizziness, as well as having problems with his kidneys and liver from that point on. He never fought again, and his anger at Parker never subsided.

In October 1993 *Sports Illustrated* featured an article entitled "the fix was in" on Parker and his antics. It was about as unflattering a story as one could find, and although one boxer mentioned in the story (Randall "Tex" Cobb) sued *Sports Illustrated* over the article, Parker was notably not included in the lawsuit. A *60 Minutes* feature followed, in which Parker was again attacked for his role in fixing fights, a piece that did more damage to the sport of boxing than perhaps anything in the last ten years. Boxing insiders were disgusted with Parker, and he soon became a pariah in the sport. Although boxing had many problems, it had kicked the problem of fixed fights that defined the sport in the 1950s—that was, until Parker jumped into the sport. Many openly sympathized with Anderson, the common assumption being that poisoning "Doc" was not beneath Parker. Anderson's anger, however, would soon explode in a most unforeseen and tragic way. In May 1995 Anderson called Parker over to his hotel room in Lake Buena Vista, Florida, to try and work out their differences. He then pulled out a .38-caliber handgun and shot Parker eight times (reloading once), killing him. When the police arrived, Anderson was waiting for them and was quickly arrested. He was later convicted of murder and sentenced to life in prison.

For Gastineau, his association with Parker soon became a major detriment, and when reports emerged that he may have been in on the "fixed" fights, many boxing fans began to openly scorn the former NFL star. Gastineau, an unpopular athlete even before the controversy, suddenly found himself the most hated boxer in the sport. He did reemerge in November 1996 in a most unusual fight, against another former NFL star, Alonzo Highsmith. Although Highsmith was not seen as a legitimate prospect, he was a fighter who took his new career seriously. The professionalism of Highsmith shined as he destroyed Gastineau in two rounds, a fight that ended up bringing the career of Gastineau to an end (although he was briefly considered a potential opponent for Butterbean). Even his personal life took a tragic turn when in February 1998 he was charged with assaulting a woman. Seven months later he again was in legal trouble, arrested for slapping and choking another female. Suddenly his ridiculous comments about blaming his girlfriend for his loss to Anderson seemed considerably more disturbing. By the end of the decade there was nothing amusing about the Gastineau-Anderson fight. It was all too disturbing.

July 30, 1992—Stanhope, New Jersey
Mark Carrier (27–1–1, 22 KOs) vs. Jimmy Lee Smith (9–2, 5 KOs)
Favorite: Carrier
Result: Smith won by way of seventh-round TKO.

For twenty-one-year-old Mark Carrier it looked as if his career was finally taking off. After turning pro at the tender age of fifteen he finally was getting some attention outside of his home state of Tennessee, as he took on his second straight fight on network television. He had impressed many boxing insiders with his second-round destruction of the usually durable Ken Lakusta in Atlantic City and was subsequently invited back by ESPN to fight on the undercard of Al Cole's challenge of IBF cruiserweight champion James Warring four months later. Although the quality of opposition on his resume didn't exactly shine, he still was a white heavyweight with a good left hook and a surefire moneymaker if he could keep winning on network TV. After passing his first test with flying colors, many assumed that he would shine a second time, especially considering his opponent, the unknown Jimmy Lee Smith.

Smith was a classic second-tier regional fighter who seemed destined to become an opponent. After winning eight of his first nine fights (with his only loss from an undefeated John Sargent), Smith was thrown in with the lions, taking on former champion Tim Witherspoon. Smith's inexperience, coupled with the right hand of "Terrible" Tim, did him in as he froze up in his first big test and was knocked out in the first round. For a legitimate prospect, the rebuilding process would have taken years, but within five months he was back on network TV in the fight with Carrier in which he saw himself the prohibitive underdog. Although it appeared a mismatch on paper, it would prove to be anything but in reality. Although Carrier had twenty-nine fights to Smith's eleven, the quality of opposition was heavily in Smith's favor. Also, Carrier was a young fighter who clearly was not fond of roadwork, and it was apparent that unless his conditioning improved, he would be unable to overcome adversity in a grueling fight. Although he weighed in at 221¼, it seemed that at least twenty pounds of that weight was located around his belly. Smith, on the other hand, appeared to be in excellent condition at 226½, and to many undiscerning ringsiders, Smith looked like the favorite.

It didn't take long for Smith to start fighting like the favorite. Although both fighters came out swinging, Smith quickly stepped back and began pumping the jab. Although it was not landing, the jab was enough to make the difference in a close round in which both fighters were missing more than they were hitting. It appeared obvious, when he was unable land it, that Carrier's sharpness was off—a sure sign of poor conditioning. Although Smith landed only five punches of twenty-two thrown, Mark Carrier didn't fare much better, landing only eight shots of thirty-two thrown. It may not have been the war of attrition that Team Carrier feared, but it was clear that swinging and missing twenty-four punches per round would wear him out quickly.

The second round started in similar fashion with Carrier loading up with wild left hooks and looping right hands while Smith fired back with jabs that hit everything but Mark Carrier. The first serious sign of trouble came halfway through the round when a hard left hook landed on Carrier's chin, briefly stunning him. Things continued much the same way for the next two rounds, with Carrier throwing, missing, and failing to use the jab, while Jimmy Lee Smith continued to box and counterpunch. As each round slowed down, it became clear that Smith was slowly taking control of the fight. In the fifth round Smith began to bounce around, showing off his conditioning, while Carrier huffed and puffed with his mouth wide open. A Smith counter right that landed halfway through the round shook up Carrier, and although he fired back, it was not enough to gain Smith's respect.

Carrier came out swinging at the bell to start the sixth round, and initially it appeared as if he might have gotten a second wind. A mere ten seconds later, Carrier slowed back down while Smith returned to his aggressive boxing that had Carrier totally befuddled. Mark did land one hard left hook at 1:40 of the round, but when Jimmy Lee fired back instantaneously, it became clear that Carrier simply didn't have anything with which to answer back. It was the last hurrah for Mark Carrier. He started the seventh round pumping a slow, tired hook without much luck. A left hook from Jimmy Smith actually staggered Carrier and sent him back into the ropes. Then Smith unloaded with several hard shots (including a right hand to the body and face) that robbed Carrier of what little gas he had left in the tank. At that point Smith discovered the missing weapon in his arsenal to finish the fight: the uppercut. A hard right uppercut snapped Carrier's head back, and although he remained standing he was clearly spent. He emerged with a cut over his left eye, adding another problem to the list. Smith continued to tee off, snapping Carrier's head back with another uppercut in the final twenty seconds of the round. At the bell ending the round, Carrier slowly walked back to his corner. Insiders were now wondering what the young prospect would do as he faced the toughest test of his career. How would he handle adversity? As it turned out, Carrier would reveal what he was made of when he cried out to his trainer, Dennis Hardesty, "I can't do this! I can't make it!" Although his corner tried to convince him to fight on, they were unable to change his mind, and with that referee Tony Orlando waved the fight off.

With the win, it seemed that Smith actually had the possibility to become a prospect again. After all, he had lost only two times early in his career, and with the high-profile win over Carrier he had the basics to build a successful run. But Smith was a fighter without a great manager, and four months later he found himself fighting former contender Carl "The Truth" Williams on ESPN. Smith did land a handful a hard shots in the first two rounds, but was taken out in the third, ending any hope of him becoming a contender. He would fight only one more time, winning against Rocky Sekorski in 1993.

For Carrier, the loss discredited him and robbed him of the momentum of his previous twenty-seven wins. He floundered as a heavyweight after the loss to Smith, and although he would resurface with a decent win over former cruiserweight contender Michael Greer in 1995, it was the last noteworthy fight for the chunky bomber; he disappeared from the heavyweight picture later that year. Before long Mark would reemerge as a race car owner with his brother, Andy, in the NHRA drag racing circuit.

July 21, 1992—Auburn Hills, Michigan
Tim Witherspoon (37–3, 24 KOs) vs. Everett "Bigfoot" Martin
    (17–14–1, 8 KOs)
Favorite: Witherspoon
Result: Martin won a ten-round split decision.

In July 1992 the top four heavyweights in the world were slated to fight each other in a mini-tournament to establish boxing's true heavyweight superstar. This made the number five ranking in the world a most attractive position. It was widely assumed that whoever was the fifth ranked fighter at the end of the tournament would jump to the number one ranking, and thus a title fight. This put Tim Witherspoon as close to heavyweight gold in over five years, as his number five ranking in the

WBC (along with his number six ranking in the WBA and IBF) put him in a place he had not been since losing his WBA title to James "Bonecrusher" Smith in December of 1986. With a pending lawsuit against Don King, and a King-controlled heavyweight division for much of the late 1980s, Witherspoon found himself on the outside looking in, and knowing that the deck was so heavily stacked against him, he failed to fight with the fire that would excite fans. Now it appeared that his persistence was about to pay off. With twelve straight wins since his last loss, Witherspoon finally was in a position where he could get his title fight, and Don King was nowhere near the top of the heavyweight division.

The big things that he needed were to fight regularly and come to each fight in shape, and maybe throw in a defense or two of his valuable USBA heavyweight title. But Tim Witherspoon was a fighter with a reputation, and it was looking more and more like this reputation was justified. The first knock on Tim was he never trained properly and often came into fights grossly overweight. This was complicated by his somewhat fleshy body, which often appeared softer than his conditioning actually was. Nonetheless, his ideal fighting weight was always in the mid 220s, and he was regularly weighing in at 235 or more. (Against Jim Smith in February that year, he weighed in at a whopping 247.) The second knock on Tim was his tendency to be distracted by outside forces, affecting his performance in the ring. Many boxing fans felt that it was Witherspoon's legal problems with Don King that led to his humbling defeat at the hands of James "Bonecrusher" Smith in one round in 1986. (He decisioned Smith easily over one year prior.) His record was filled with fights in which he appeared flat due to his lack of mental preparation, and many boxing insiders felt that Tim lacked the mental discipline to ever mount a serious run. But these same critics also admitted that *if* Tim were mentally sound, physically fit, and given the opportunity, he could beat just about any heavyweight in the world—a theory that caused fighters like Michael Moorer to avoid him like the plague.

Recognizing Tim's enviable position, promoter Dennis Rappaport decided to try and increase the fight activity of the thirty-four-year-old former champion. (Tim had three fights in 1990 and two in 1991.) In February Witherspoon knocked out Jimmy Lee Smith in the opening

round and followed it up with a boring decision win over James Pritchard the following month. Although Tim took a four-month break after
the Pritchard fight, he already had his next opponent (Tony Willis) lined
up for August, and there was even talk of another fight before the end
of 1992. But in that brief four-month hiatus, Witherspoon became disillusioned with Rappaport, and once again found himself mentally unready for a fight. Rappaport had undertaken a vicious, verbal-attack
campaign in an attempt to land Michael Moorer as an opponent for
Witherspoon. (In Rappaport's defense, that is by no means an uncommon practice by promoters and is seldom frowned upon by fighters or
boxing insiders.) But Witherspoon would later claim that he became
concerned over what he felt were Rappaport's verbal attacks on the city
of Detroit, where his fight with Martin would be taking place—Auburn
Hills was about twenty five miles north of Detroit. It also revealed that
the Witherspoon camp was not taking Martin at all seriously as an opponent, something that could prove costly in the long run for "Terrible"
Tim.

Even though the evidence was pointing to a lackluster performance
by Witherspoon, few anticipated an upset. Martin, after all, was a
fighter who was three years removed from his last victory (over Bert
Cooper) and in the middle of a nine-fight losing streak. Even the fight
program at the Palace of Auburn Hills wrote that "Bigfoot" had a "fat
chance" of pulling of the upset—not a great way of getting the ringside
fans excited about the upcoming fight. But in those nine losing fights,
"Bigfoot" had earned the reputation as the possible best journeyman
heavyweight in the world. He went ten full rounds with George Foreman in 1989 and, in fact, was the first fighter to extend "Big" George
the distance since the former champ had come out of retirement. He
even rocked Foreman in the final round. He then became only the third
fighter to extend hard-punching, undefeated Brit Gary Mason the ten-
round distance in 1990. Perhaps his most noteworthy performance was
his previous visit to Auburn Hills against Michael Moorer in March
1992. Against the hard punching Moorer, Martin held his own for the
full ten rounds and even dropped the undefeated Kronk southpaw for
the first time in his career. When he entered the ring with Witherspoon,
many felt that Martin was almost certainly going to extend Witherspoon the distance, and it was up to Witherspoon to prove them wrong.

A Witherspoon KO looked even less likely when Witherspoon weighed in at a fleshy 239³/₄. Although Martin appeared soft himself, weighing in at 232, it was an improvement for him as he had been weighing in the upper 240s for much of 1990 and 1991.

The fight would prove to be an ugly affair, with a great deal of wrestling and holding, and little action. The pattern of the fight was set in the opening round as Witherspoon fired a slow overhand right that missed the target, and "Bigfoot" moved in to smother Tim. Seconds later a pause was called as the tape on Witherspoon's glove came loose. By the end of the round it became apparent that the sluggish Witherspoon was not going to give fans an exciting night, and early boos began to fill the Palace at the bell. The pattern continued in the second, and an uninterested Witherspoon continued to treat the fight like a sparring session, flicking a weak, lazy jab and failing to utilize his feared overhand right. Martin continued to outwork Witherspoon, but most of his activity was on the inside, where he smothered Witherspoon's punches as well as his own. Martin's attack seemed ineffective, and most assumed that once Witherspoon started throwing the left jab with some fire and keeping Martin on the outside, he would begin to take control. But after more of the same in the third round it began to appear that Witherspoon was simply not going to fight with any intensity that night. Martin did sneak in a solid uppercut in the opening minute of the fourth round, but it was hardly enough to impress Witherspoon or the fans in attendance. Few disagreed with *USA Tuesday Night Fights* commentator Sean O'Grady, who said at the opening of the fifth round that "Tim's not looking very impressive in those first four rounds."

In the fifth round, however, it looked as if Witherspoon was given a golden opportunity when Martin began to ease away from his holding and wrestling tactics on the inside and began to fight more on the outside. For many ringsiders it looked as if Witherspoon would now be able to establish the jab and, more importantly, fire the right hand. But the clearly winded Witherspoon was unable or unwilling to take advantage. He continued to paw with his slow, lazy jab and gave Martin little reason to fear the right. It was enough to finally convince "Bigfoot" that Witherspoon was ripe for the taking, as Martin jumped on "Spoon" in the sixth round, pushing Witherspoon into the ropes. Nearly two minutes into the round Witherspoon walked into a hard right hand that snapped his head back. Although Tim shrugged the punch off, it was enough to turn the tide in a rather uneventful round. Witherspoon continued to show signs of fatigue in the seventh, breathing heavily and holding his left hand at his waist, and never getting his second wind, as he continued to drag for the rest of the fight. Although Witherspoon opened the tenth round strong, throwing hard shots to the head of Martin, "Bigfoot" gladly stood his ground, and it wasn't long before both fighters returned to the dragging pace. By the end of the round Tim was backpedaling, apparently convinced that he had the fight wrapped up.

In fact, many felt that was not an unreasonable assumption. Although most fans booed Witherspoon, it was more due to his lack of activity and his inability to impress than anything Martin had done. Sean O'Grady assumed Witherspoon had emerged victorious as well, telling viewers that "I think Witherspoon comfortably kept control of this fight and I think he won." Besides, fighters like Martin seldom got the nod in close fights, and there was little to indicate that this would be the exception. But judges John Chaulk and Eugene Acey voted for Martin by scores of 96–95 and 97–93—they overruled judge Herman McKalpain Jr. who voted for Witherspoon by a score of 96–94—giving "Bigfoot" the biggest win of his professional career.

Financially, the win over Witherspoon proved to be very beneficial to the career of "Bigfoot" Martin. However, it didn't change the status of Martin as a journeyman or get him any closer to the top ten. Two months later he lost a ten-round decision to another former heavyweight champion, Tony Tucker, and would go on to lose his next three fights to Larry Holmes, Herbie Hide, and Tony Tubbs. However he would continue to impress, lasting the distance with all three. (In fact Hide was 22–0 with 22 knockouts when Martin extended him the distance.) Over the next seven years Martin would go on to lose over twenty fights (almost all by decision) while winning only two. But in the process Martin saw the world (fighting in such exotic locations as Hawaii, The Netherlands, Uzbekistan, and Denmark), fought for a third rate world title (the WBF), and continued to be the fighter who would test the endurance of many a young prospect such as Wladimir Klitschko, to whom he extended the distance in 1998.

For Witherspoon, the loss proved devastating. His potential world title fight was gone, as was his fight with Michael Moorer. Again Witherspoon found himself on the outside looking in, as he was both discredited and too dangerous. He did go through with his fight with Tony Willis the following month but again failed to impress, winning a ten-round decision. Witherspoon then disappeared for nearly two years, but his subsequent, second, comeback proved surprisingly successful. With his lawsuit against Don King behind him, Witherspoon won seven straight wins over respectable opposition before losing a highly questionable ten-round decision to Ray Mercer in 1996. Initially the loss to Mercer sent his career into freefall—after winning his next fight against Levi Billups Witherspoon went on to loose five straight—and when he was held to an ugly twelve-round draw with Mike Sedillo (a former light heavyweight journeyman with a 33–24–2 record), almost everyone assumed that the career of Witherspoon was over. But the classic hot-and-cold fighter proved to have a few overhand rights up his sleeve, and after winning eight of his next nine fights, found himself again close to the top ten and another title fight in 2002 before losing to Lou Savarese.

August 18, 1992—Pensacola, Florida
Tony Tubbs (31–3, 19 KOs) vs. Lionel Butler (12–10–1, 7 KOs)
Favorite: Tubbs
Result: Butler won by way of first-round knockout.

When former WBA heavyweight champion Tony Tubbs announced that he had kicked drugs, was a born again Christian, and was planning on fighting more regularly than before, most boxing insiders rolled their eyes and politely nodded. Tubbs wasn't the first fighter who claimed he would begin fighting more frequently—Tim Witherspoon was making a living fighting on *USA Tuesday Night Fights* every five months against journeyman opponents. Though boxing fans wanted to believe that Tubbs's notorious problems with drug addiction were in fact behind him, it was a line heard many times before from many other fighters (and in fact Tubbs himself). But the thirty-four-year-old former champion had one thing going for him: he could still fight. Only eighteen months previously, he gave up and coming heavyweight Riddick Bowe all that he could handle before losing a highly controversial ten-round decision. It was living proof that Tubbs still was a fighter not to be underestimated in the heavyweight division. In fact, Tubbs had even defeated another heavyweight hopeful back in 1989 (Orlin Norris) but saw his victory changed to a "no-decision" when he failed a post-fight drug test—voiding what was his first significant victory since his loss to Mike Tyson. Even his somewhat fleshy appearance and his less than impressive weight of 241 didn't seem to be a strike against the former champion. He was well know for coming into the ring overweight, and it was not particularly high for him: he weighed 243 pounds for his fight with Bowe. But based on his loss to Bowe, Tubbs saw his ranking remain unaffected—he was ranked number sixteen in the WBC—and it seemed that a quick and easy win over Lionel Butler would be the first step to entering the top ten.

Butler seemed a safe enough opponent for the slick moving Tubbs. He was big and strong, but somewhat slow and easy to hit. Also, he was on a six-fight winning streak that included a shocking upset over Forum heavyweight hopeful Dave Dixon (page 48) that ensured that he could be a marketable opponent. Lionel had one major factor working in his favor: at 226 pounds he was a bona fide heavyweight. Six months earlier Tubbs had labored to a somewhat sloppy seventh-round technical knockout over cruiserweight contender Leon Taylor. (Although Taylor seemed to be a fairly competent opponent going in, Tubbs manhandled his smaller man for much of the fight. It became so tedious that ringsiders began to criticize Tubbs inability to knock out a fighter seen as too small to compete.) Tubbs, stung by the criticism, disappeared for six months before resurfacing against the larger Butler on the undercard of the Roy Jones vs. Glen Thomas fight, and he was eager not to allow his critics any opportunity to criticize his performance.

Unfortunately, it was Tubbs's desire to take on a seemingly overmatched foe that led to his demise. Determined to overwhelm Butler early and score a rare knockout, Tubbs abandoned his early boxing to lean into Butler and trade bombs. It was a strategy that favored Butler, although at first it hardly appeared to be the case. Fighting a classic "phone booth" war, Tubbs leaned into his shorter, stockier opponent firing quick hooks to the body. Two minutes into the round Tubbs fired a hard chopping overhand right that briefly staggered Butler, and seeing his opponent in trouble Tubbs proceeded to jump on Butler, although he was unable to land anything significant. However, with less than ten seconds left in the round, Butler was able to break through and pushed Tubbs into the ropes. Seizing the opportunity Butler fired a picture-perfect left hook that landed on the chin of the former champion. Determined not to let Butler steal the momentum in the final seconds of the round, Tubbs tried to fire back but made the fatal mistake of dropping his hands in the process. A right hand to the chin by Butler landed on the former champion, dropping him instantly with seconds left in the round. Without the option of being saved by the bell, Tubbs had no chance as he was counted out at 3:00 of the first round.

Suddenly, there was a new heavyweight contender in Lionel Butler. With a solid win over the former champion Tony Tubbs, Butler became a regular on the USA Network, and he continued his winning ways all the way into the top ten. With dominant knockouts over normally durable journeymen like Eric Curry and Jerry Jones, as well a solid knockout victory over James "Bonecrusher" Smith, Butler became a virtual Freddie Pendelton (a fighter who overcame early troubles to become a contender) of the heavyweight division. But rumors began to surface of Butler's drinking and drug problems, as well as reportedly erratic behavior. By the time he finally reached the pinnacle of his success—a WBC elimination bout against Lennox Lewis for the highly coveted number one ranking in the WBC—Butler was a psychological and physical wreck. He weighed in a whopping 261 pounds. Lewis dominated Butler and scored a rather lopsided fifth-round knockout, ending Butler's run as a contender. Ugly losses to Michael Grant and Chris Byrd followed, and by the end of the decade Butler was no longer considered anything other than a "name" opponent.

For Tony Tubbs, the loss to Butler seemed to mark the end of his career. For many fans it was hard to see how Tubbs, who never was particularly active at any point of his career, could possibly motivate himself to make a serious run after such a devastating loss. Those suspicions seemed to be confirmed when it was announced that he was going to fight Bruce Seldon just two months after the Butler debacle. It appeared to many that, rather than take the necessary steps to regain his confidence against limited foes, Tony was simply cashing in on his name. But to the surprise of many, Tubbs went on to outbox his younger foe, winning a ten-round decision. It was a win that not only restored the damaged credibility of the former champion but also reestablished him as a legitimate heavyweight contender.

October 30, 1992—Aurora, Colorado
Jerry Quarry (53–8–4, 33 KOs) vs. Ron Cranmer (3–4–1, 2 KOs)
Favorite: Quarry
Result: Cranmer won a six-round unanimous decision.

Although the 1990s had countless ill-advised comebacks—from Alexis Arguello to Earnie Shavers—none were as foolish, and tragic, as the comeback of 1970s slugger Jerry Quarry. A popular Irishman who initially turned pro in 1965 at the tender age of eighteen, within two years Quarry had established himself as one of the better prospects in the sport (no small task considering the era) when he held former heavyweight champion Floyd Patterson to a draw. By 1968 he was fighting for the world title (against Jimmy Ellis) and, at the start of the 1970s, was already regarded as the best white heavyweight since Rocky Marciano. In fact, most boxing fans felt that he would have been world champion in any other era. But in the late '60s and early '70s, he had the unenviable task of fighting in the same era as Joe Frazier, Muhammad Ali, and George Foreman. Although he never defeated the likes of Frazier (he was stopped in seven rounds by Frazier in 1969 and five rounds by the Philadelphian in 1974) or Ali (stopped in three in 1970 and seven in 1972), he had fought on more than even terms with most of the other noted fighters from that era. He held impressive victories over Earnie Shavers (KO1 in 1973), Ron Lyle (a decision win in 1973), Floyd Patterson (W12 in 1967), and Buster Mathis (W12 in 1969) and was widely regarded as the fifth or sixth best heavyweight from the 1970s (behind Ali, Frazier, Ken Norton, and Foreman).

But Quarry was in many ways the quintessential Irish fighter. He often abandoned his better judgment to engage in crowd-pleasing slugfests with his opponents even though most observers felt that his underappreciated boxing skills were better suited to carry him through. In fact, after a knockout loss to Ken Norton in 1975, most boxing writers hoped that he would wisely quit. After a sixty-two-fight career that involved too many wars for the health of the witty Irishman, it was widely assumed that he was putting his well-being into danger if he were to continue his career. Initially Quarry resisted the calls for retirement. After all, it was tough for any fighter as good as Jerry to quit without a world title. But after an ugly win over Lorenzo Zanon in 1977, Jerry finally retired. Although he did engage in a brief, two-fight return in 1983, Jerry had little in the way of motivation for a comeback. (After all, for much of the 1980s Larry Holmes and Mike Tyson completely dominated the heavyweight division and their domination over the division in both their respective reigns was more than enough of a reality check for Quarry.) Besides, the deteriorating condition of Muhammad Ali was a stark reminder of what could go wrong when a good fighter fought too often. But by the end of the 1980s, the career of George Foreman had numerous former legends (including Quarry) salivating at the potential payday a comeback could garner.

Quarry, who had earned an impressive $2.1 million in the ring (but who was nearly out of money in the 1980s), realized what a match-up with George Foreman could make, and he decided for another comeback in 1992. But there were several major obstacles standing in Jerry's way. First was the embarrassment of a previous comeback that was derailed when he was injured in a fistfight with the promoter of his comeback fight several days before the fight. Many boxing insiders felt, not unreasonably, that Jerry must have slipped if he was taken out of commission by a mere promoter. Second, and considerably more ominous, was the early signs of pugilistic dementia that Jerry had been showing since 1982. Although Jerry denied the effects of the disease—he was able to name each of his professional opponents, the date of the fight, and the result—there was little doubt in boxing circles that Quarry was "damaged goods." That, along with a reported alcohol and cocaine problem earlier in his life, made him a boxing commissioner's poster boy for mandatory retirement. There was little doubt that the Nevada Athletic Commission was not going to let Quarry fight in their state, guaranteeing that he would never fight Foreman. In fact, Quarry was unfit to pass the medical requirements of any state's boxing commission. Faced with this insurmountable obstacle, it seemed apparent to most that the Jerry Quarry comeback was going to go the same place as the Jim Palmer and Mark Spitz comebacks: absolutely nowhere. But Jerry was not going to let anything stand in his way and so in 1992 signed to fight Ron Cranmer in Aurora, Colorado, one of the few states that (at the time) did not have a boxing commission to prevent the fight from happening. The very fact that Jerry Quarry had to fight under such conditions told most boxing fans all they needed to know about Jerry Quarry's viability as a heavyweight contender, but with the slim possibility of a Foreman fight in the horizon, Jerry went ahead.

By fight time it was looking more and more like the fight was a total farce. At forty-seven years old, Quarry hardly looked to be the physical specimen that fans remembered from his prime. He looked soft around the middle (despite weighing in at a fairly light 205 pounds) and, for many close to him, was acting like a middle-aged man going through a midlife crisis. Even his most ardent supporters began to realize the futility of his comeback. Nonetheless, the fight at least offered an opportunity for his fans to see him in the ring again, and a quick $1,050 payday. After all, Ron Cranmer seemed a safe opponent, and Jerry, it was assumed, still possessed enough skills to win against a limited and inexperienced journeyman like Cranmer.

Cranmer had fought almost exclusively at cruiserweight, and against extremely weak opposition, he was only able to muster a 3–4–1 record. He was also coming off a first-round knockout loss to an unknown fighter named Eric Brown. It was assumed that if there were any snap left behind the once-vaunted left hook of Quarry, he would knock out the smaller Cranmer. Quarry even appeared somewhat solid in training leading up to the night of the fight, and as he entered the ring to a warm reception from the few hundred fans in attendance that night, many hoped for a brief return to boxing's glory years of the 1970s. In fact, for ten seconds boxing fans were in fact returned to 1970 when a solid left hook was fired perilously close to Cranmer's chin at the bell. But it became the lone highlight for Quarry as Cranmer recovered to pressure Quarry into the ropes, throwing looping shots at the older man's chin and body. Although Jerry tried to box and move, his smaller opponent was determined to keep him on the ropes and continued his forward march. Quarry was still in the fight although Cranmer was clearly getting the better of the exchanges, until a bizarre call by the referee at the halfway point of the round pushed Quarry even further in the hole when he deducted a point for a low blow (despite never warning him prior). It seemed to many a questionable call at best but really had little impact on the actual fight itself, as Cranmer continued to pound away at Jerry for the duration of the round. With less than twenty seconds in the round, Cranmer landed a solid right cross that snapped Quarry's head back, cementing his dominance of the round. The second round continued where the first round left off, with Quarry backed into the ropes by an onrushing Cranmer. However, Jerry began to find his range a bit more in the second, landing off the ropes with a handful of counter shots. After landing a trio of hard left hooks, it seemed to many in attendance that Jerry had begun to turn the tide, but again the referee made a poor call when he deemed another shot had strayed low and again deducted a point. With the one point deduction in the second, Quarry found himself on the losing end of a very close round, and when Cranmer again stole the round with a solid right hand to the chin in the last twenty seconds, it was abundantly clear that he was in a very deep hole going into the third.

By the third round, fatigue had robbed Quarry of what little skills he had left, and the fight was completely dominated by Ron Cranmer. Cranmer trapped Quarry on the ropes and unloaded numerous hard shots to the head of a clearly spent Jerry Quarry, whose only answer seemed to be the clinch. Cranmer, realizing what little Jerry had left, jumped on his opponent at the fourth-round bell and, despite the chants of "Jerry! Jerry!" from the crowd, found little in the form of resistance from the Irishman. A wide right cross staggered Jerry later in the round, and after eating more punishment in the fifth, there was absolutely no question in anyone's mind going into the final round that he needed a knockout to win the fight. It was not to be for Jerry, who was unable to turn the tide of the fight in the sixth. Although Ron did end up losing a point for an elbow that round, he used an uppercut in the final ten seconds to stagger Quarry, punctuating his dominance over the one-time great heavyweight.

Initially the fight seemed merely an embarrassing loss for the former contender, and some even wondered if it alone would convince Jerry to retire for good. But within twenty-four hours the damage done to the popular Irishman would prove that not only was the career of Jerry over, but that an even greater battle was ahead. With two teeth knocked out, there was clear evidence that Jerry had indeed taken a "beating." The following day he had no recollection of the fight the previous night, and the symptoms of dementia began to accelerate. The fight had triggered a rapid deterioration of his damaged brain, which after being examined by a doctor had been compared to a "grapefruit that has been dropped dozens of times."[3] In fact, the examining physician in 1997 compared Quarry's brain deterioration to that of an 80-year-old man, and the head of research for the Jerry Quarry Foundation in 1997 stated "the center part of the brain should be divided; you should see a line. With Jerry . . . the middle of the brain is not there anymore; it's not separated, as it should be."[4] With his condition worsening by the day, the one-time millionaire was forced to survive on Social Security checks and required constant care from family members. When he was inducted into the World Boxing Hall of Fame in 1995, he was unable to sign autographs for fans due to his condition and, within two years, was in a confused, child-like state. His motor skills and brain function began to deteriorate so badly that his brain was unable to recognize hunger.[5] On December 28, 1998, Quarry was hospitalized with pneumonia and suffered a cardiac arrest while in the hospital. He died on January 3, 1999, one of the most depressing endings to one of the most exciting careers in boxing.

October 31, 1992—London, England
Donovan "Razor" Ruddock (27–3–1, 20 KOs) vs. Lennox Lewis
    (21–0, 18 KOs)
Favorite: Ruddock
Result: Lewis won via second-round TKO.

With the incarceration of "Iron" Mike Tyson earlier in the year, it seemed that boxing was left with a huge void. The prospect of a Tyson-less heavyweight division seemed grim, and many fans were left to wonder who would fill the void in his absence. Although Evander Holyfield was the undisputed champion, he was rapidly losing respect with less than stellar performances against Bert Cooper and Larry Holmes. These fights left many boxing fans with the impression that Holyfield was a weak champion and would most likely have lost if he had fought

---

[3] Dr. Peter Russell, quoted in *People* magazine, 1995. Quoted by Thomas Gerbasi, "Jerry Quarry," *The Cyber Boxing Zone Journal*, September 1998, http://www.cyberboxingzone.com/boxing/box9-98.htm#Jerry. (Accessed January 2002.)

[4] Linda Rogers, quoted in *Newsday*, n.d. Quoted by Gerbasi, "Jerry Quarry."

[5] Gerbasi, "Jerry Quarry."

Tyson. However, he was "the man who beat the man" (namely James Douglas), which put him in a small circle of fighters who were regarded as the elite. With Tyson temporarily out of the picture, boxing fans began tossing around three names around as the most likely successor to "Iron" Mike, the fighter who would be champ when Tyson was released and be part of a superfight sometime after 1995. First was, of course, Holyfield. Second was undefeated puncher Riddick Bowe. And third was the man who gave Tyson all he could handle for over eighteen rounds of warfare: Donovan "Razor" Ruddock.

Ruddock owed his high standing with boxing fans to his two losses to Tyson (by controversial seventh-round TKO and unanimous decision). It was more of a testament to the "Tyson myth" than Ruddock's actual accomplishments as a fighter, or even his performance against Tyson. After years of knockouts, it seemed amazing when a fighter was able to last the distance with Tyson without running (like James Tillis) or clinching (like James "Bonecrusher" Smith) for the entire fight. Ruddock stood toe-to-toe with Tyson, bombing away against the power-punching former champion. But he failed to win more than three rounds combined and was dropped four times in those two fights. Nonetheless, Ruddock was one of the top fighters in the game in 1992, with some experts (including legendary trainer and broadcaster Gil Clancy) calling Ruddock the best heavyweight in the division. It also seemed that he had taken a major step in repairing the only major weakness he seemed to have by hiring former two-time heavyweight champion Floyd Patterson as his trainer. Although he was seen as a technically flawed fighter, the addition of Patterson to Ruddock's camp was seen as a big plus. As a fighter, Patterson made his career boxing and moving, and the commonly held belief was that all Ruddock needed was a solid jab to make him a complete fighter. Although he struggled with Greg Page in his first comeback fight, a follow-up win over undefeated Phil Jackson had redeemed him.

Lennox Lewis, however, was not totally ignored. He was regarded by many as the fourth best heavyweight in the world—behind Ruddock, Holyfield, and Bowe. He even had some experts lumping him in with those three fighters into a "big four" classification. But Lennox had one big strike that seemed to destroy his credibility with American boxing experts: he was British.

Although he won a gold medal in the 1988 Olympics for Canada, Lennox decided to base his career out of the United Kingdom, which seemed a fatal blow. Britain hadn't had a world champion in the twentieth century. The drought wasn't for lack of trying either: Britain had numerous high profile fighters in the heavyweight division, and a few of them were even pretty good. But they always fell a little short in the big fight, even though some gave decent performances against great champions (like Henry Cooper). Henry Cooper, Joe Bugner, and Frank Bruno were the most recent to fail, and though all three were legends in Britain, none ever won world titles. It had gotten so bad for British boxing that their heavyweights were given the disparaging nickname "horizontal heavyweights." Baseball had the Chicago Cubs, football had the Detroit Lions, and boxing had Great Britain.

Combined with the "British" factor working against Lennox Lewis was the American obsession with Riddick Bowe. Boxing writers were fascinated with the loud, personable Bowe. He was a big man with the wit of an Ali and the punch of a Tyson, and his repeated performances on national TV made him the obvious choice for boxing experts looking for their next superstar. In the hype that surrounded Bowe's career prior to the fight, Lewis saw his career virtually ignored. His opposition was roundly criticized, despite being as good as Riddick Bowe's. In fact, after Riddick Bowe struggled to stop former Olympian Tyrell Biggs in eight rounds on network television, *KO Magazine* put him on their cover under the heading: "Is he destined to be heavyweight champion?"[6] This despite the fact that Lennox had just scored a knockout over top ranked Gary Mason, who not only had knocked out Tyrell Biggs but also possessed an impressive record of 35–0 with 32 KOs. When Lewis knocked out Biggs a few months later in more impressive fashion than Bowe, the win was dismissed; the assumption was that Bowe had already beat out whatever Tyrell Biggs had left. By the time he fought Ruddock, most American boxing writers regarded Lewis as woefully inexperienced and unprepared to fight such a seasoned fighter as Ruddock. Even the fight's location in Britain didn't figure to hurt Razor's chances much. If it hadn't helped Frank Bruno against Tim Witherspoon (one of the most beatable champions in recent memory) then it certainly wouldn't help Lennox.

---

[6] On the cover of *KO Magazine*, July 1991.

Although Lennox was the underdog, he was still regarded as a live underdog. Most, in fact, were surprised that either fighter agreed to the fight. With Ruddock ranked number one in the WBC and Lewis ranked number two, it seemed that all either fighter had to do was wait a few months for a title fight. The winner was guaranteed a shot at the winner of the upcoming Evander Holyfield vs. Riddick Bowe championship fight, and many experts assumed that the winner would be regarded as a slight favorite over the Holyfield-Bowe winner.

When the fight started it became immediately clear that Ruddock had indeed refined his style under Patterson's tutelage. He bounced around the ring, using footwork and a decent jab to try and set up his legendary "smash" (a combination left hook/uppercut that knocked out former champs Michael Dokes and James "Bonecrusher" Smith). Lewis seemed a bit tentative, hiding behind his jab and backpedaling away from "Razor" whenever he got too close. It seemed as if the boxing world was about to witness a chess, rather than a boxing, match, when the Ruddock of old began to emerge. Within a minute Ruddock was loading up and winging left hands from the outside, abandoning his jab and footwork. At the same time, Lewis was coming alive, throwing in a few hard shots as well. Although the knock on Ruddock had been that he was predictable, no fighter had yet capitalized on that weakness until the last ten seconds of the first round when Ruddock leaned forward trying to reach in with a left hand. Timing the move perfectly, Lewis came over the top with a picture-perfect right hand that robbed Ruddock of his legs and dropped him to the canvas like a bag of rocks. Ruddock arose on shaky legs and was clearly more hurt than he had been at any point in his career (even against Tyson), but he was saved from further punishment as the bell rang. Recovered by the start of the second, he came out strong, moving and trying to reestablish the jab. That charade was quickly ended when a Lewis left hook staggered him again. After falling back into the corner, Ruddock was again felled by a Lennox Lewis barrage of punches. Rising again on unsteady legs, Ruddock had over two minutes left in the round and tried to resort to survival tactics to clear his head. But he was unable to cover up enough against the onrushing Brit, and a Lennox Lewis left hand caught Ruddock on the chin as he tried to hold on, dropping him for the third time in the fight. Although referee Joe Cortez began to count, he quickly surmised Ruddock was too damaged to continue and waved the fight off, awarding Lennox the biggest win in British heavyweight history (or at least since Bob Fitzsimmons had won the belt nearly 100 years prior).

Lewis immediately became the hottest fighter in the heavyweight division, with a title fight was not only guaranteed but very winnable for him: Holyfield seemed weak, and he had already stopped Riddick Bowe in the Olympics for the gold medal. But his title shot was never to come. After defeating Holyfield for the undisputed heavyweight title, Bowe taunted Lewis in the ring and promised to punish the Brit in similar fashion. He then proceeded to avoid Lennox at all cost, even going so far as to dump his WBC title belt in a trash can to avoid being forced by the organization to fight Lewis. Lewis was awarded the belt, which carried with it the stain of being picked out of the trash. His first title defense against Tony Tucker went poorly, with Lewis struggling at times against the former IBF champion. Although he did score two knockdowns against the steel-chinned Tucker, he was rocked on one occasion and failed to score a stoppage. His second fight went even worse; fellow Briton Frank Bruno battered Lewis for the better part of six rounds before fatigue (and a Lennox Lewis left hook) did him in halfway through the seventh round. When Bowe lost in his rematch with Evander Holyfield, Lewis was elevated briefly to the mythical status as best heavyweight in the world. However, he quickly lost that distinction after an upset by Oliver McCall in 1994 (page 160).

For Ruddock, his career was effectively over after the loss to Lewis. Although he was still a recognizable heavyweight, he allowed inactivity to rob him of valuable time and exposure. Nearly fifteen months after the loss, in his first comeback fight he struggled with light-punching Anthony Wade before winning a ten-round decision. He then took another sixteen months off before resurfacing again in 1994 against Tommy "The Duke" Morrison. Although he performed well, knocking Morrison down in the first, he lost by way of sixth-round TKO. Ruddock then took another three years off before beginning a comeback that included five straight wins by the end of the decade. However, when he struggled with blown-up light heavyweight Egerton Marcus in 2001 in a bid to win the Canadian heavyweight title, it became clear to even the most diehard supporters of Ruddock that he would never be the same fighter he was as when he fought Mike Tyson.

CHAPTER FOUR

1993

"That's your cut man! . . . I'll give it to you tomorrow!"

Ray Mercer during his fight with Jesse Ferguson
(as heard by viewers watching the fight tape)

January 17, 1993—Las Vegas, Nevada
Tyrell Biggs (25–5, 17 KOs) vs. Mike "The Bounty" Hunter
(19–3–2, 8 KOs)
Favorite: Biggs
Result: Hunter won a twelve-round unanimous decision.

It wasn't because the thirty-two-year-old Biggs was regarded as a great heavyweight that made him the prohibitive favorite going into this twelve-round battle for the vacant USBA heavyweight title. Many boxing experts regarded Biggs as the Andre Ware of boxing: the "can't miss" prospect who missed. His career started on the wrong foot when he was booed mercilessly while winning a six-round decision over Mike Evans in his pro debut, and he never really got back on track after that. He did have a few highlight moments, such as his decisions victories over James "Quick" Tillis and Jeff Sims. But by and large his career was regarded as a colossal disappointment.

Biggs had won an Olympic gold medal in 1984 and was being groomed as the best heavyweight boxer since Muhammad Ali, but his pro career saw him fighting in the shadows of Mike Tyson. When the two finally met in the ring in 1987, Tyson brutalized Biggs in scoring a seventh-round TKO. Biggs won only one round before Tyson completely dissected Biggs with punishing body shots, and in fact later claimed that he carried Biggs for several rounds to extend the punishment. Biggs followed the loss to Tyson with knockout losses to Francesco Damiani (a fighter he had defeated in the Olympics) and hard-punching Englishman Gary Mason. Although Biggs briefly revived his career after the Mason fight, back-to-back knockout losses to Riddick Bowe and Lennox Lewis seemed to end any notion of becoming anything but a "name opponent." Although many boxing writers began calling for his retirement Biggs wanted to give it one more serious run. After five meaningless wins against soft opposition, he signed to fight Michael Dokes on a *USA Tuesday Night Fights* televised contest. But when Dokes heard his name being mentioned as a possible opponent for Riddick Bowe in a WBA-IBF championship fight, he bowed out, leaving last-minute sub Marion Wilson to fill the void. It seemed Biggs was given a gift, an easy win on network television. But Biggs struggled badly against Wilson and even found himself dropped in the third round before winning a close ten-round decision. It was hardly the kind of performance that excited fans or would line up big fights in the future. Nonetheless, when he was matched against Tony Tubbs for the vacant USBA title, it appeared that at the very least one dead end comeback would end on January 17. Tubbs was favored to win as he was coming off two impressive ten-round decisions over Bruce Seldon and Jesse Ferguson. But most experts felt that Biggs had at least a decent chance to pull off the upset: Tubbs had been knocked out in the first round by Lionel Butler five months earlier, and his problems with drugs were well documented.

As it turned out, Tony Tubbs's problem with drugs did play a major factor in the fight; it axed it. When Tubbs failed a drug test the day before, he was told by Nevada athletic commissioner Mark Ratner that he would not be permitted to fight, and ESPN scrambled to find a last-minute substitute. Enter Mike "The Bounty" Hunter.

Hunter was one of the most underrated fighters in boxing in the early nineties. He had defeated the likes of Dwight Qawi in 1990 and followed it up with impressive wins over Pinklon Thomas (page 12), James Thunder, and Ossie Ocasio. (He also had a win over Oliver McCall in 1988.) But he was a fighter who fought infrequently and had lost an eight-round majority decision to the then-unknown Frans Botha four months earlier. At the time, it seemed a devastating loss. Although most ringsiders felt Hunter should have been given the nod, Botha was still seen as an unspectacular cruiserweight prospect with little punching power. (Botha would prove these critics wrong when he won the IBF heavyweight title and later nearly upset Mike Tyson.) It seemed to be a sign that the thirty-three-year-old Hunter was slipping, for him to have even allowed the fight with Botha to be close. Even with that loss, most observers would have made him a live underdog against Biggs, but with less than one day to prepare, nobody gave Hunter any chance of winning. He didn't have the power to knock out Biggs, and how could he go twelve rounds having not trained for the fight? The question seemed to be not if Biggs would win, but if he would struggle like he did against Marion Wilson.

When the fight began, ringsiders were expecting Biggs to use his jab to keep the smaller Hunter at bay or his advantage in size and power to wear down the unprepared Hunter. But the awkward Hunter proved elusive to hit, and Biggs found himself the recipient of bizarre punches from unorthodox angles. When an overhand right stung Biggs in the first minute, it was clear that this was not going to be an easy night for Biggs. However, Biggs was a known slow starter, and it seemed only a matter of time before Hunter ran out of gas. But Hunter continued his awkward offense and, by the second round, began taunting the bigger man. He bloodied Biggs's nose, and though Biggs returned to his corner with a smile, there was no question that he needed to turn things around.

As the fight continued, a confused Biggs was unable to land his vaunted jab with much effectiveness, and Hunter proved to be in surprisingly good condition, never relenting from the pressure. In fact, through the middle rounds it seemed that Biggs (rather than Hunter) was fading. Hunter continued his showboating and taunting, and continued to land wild (and wide) punches from angles that he had no business landing. (The uppercut from across the ring was one of his more effective punches.) By the fifth round, Biggs began to look as if he were weeping—a fairly common occurrence whenever he began to take a beating—a sure sign for everyone watching that Biggs was losing. It was clear that he simply didn't have a game plan (or an answer) for dealing with the awkward Hunter.

Although the pace began to slow somewhat in the later rounds, most felt it was up to Biggs to up the ante and pressure Hunter. However, he continued to allow Hunter to set the pace; whenever Hunter failed to win a round convincingly, he would steal it with flurries at the bell. By the tenth round the failure of Biggs, who now was also sporting a badly cut lip, to land any power shots, seemed to indicate that Biggs would not repeat his stunning come-from-behind knockout over David Bey back in 1987. In fact, he seemed to be fighting as a beaten fighter, and the hope of Hunter running out of gas was proven futile when Hunter actually upped his punch output in the ninth and tenth rounds. When referee Richard Steele took a point away from Tyrell Biggs in the final round, it proved to be moot. Hunter was so far ahead on the scorecards that the point did little more than pad his sizeable lead. By fight's end Mike "The Bounty" Hunter was given a lopsided unanimous decision by one score of 118–109 and two of 117–110.

The loss effectively ended any hope Biggs might have had for returning to the top ten, even though he would fight on for several more years. Later that year he entered the People's Choice Superfights tournament, but found himself beat by—ironically enough—Tony Tubbs. A second shot for the USBA title followed, against Buster Mathis Jr., and though Biggs actually put up a decent fight, he found himself on the losing end via twelve-round decision. But when Ray Anis (12–1, 8 KOs) knocked him out in the third round in his very next fight, Biggs was effectively done as a contender for even the lightly regarded USBA title. It seemed that Biggs was no longer even a viable test for young up and coming heavyweights. He made an ill-advised comeback after a short layoff, and a second-round knockout loss to Larry Donald put him back into retirement.

Hunter, on the other hand, used the win over Biggs to explode into the heavyweight division. Although he never landed a title fight, he did score impressive wins over the likes of Alex Zolkin, Cecil Coffee, and the undefeated Buster Mathis Jr. (although the decision was later changed to a "no-decision" when Hunter failed a drug test after the fight). That drug test effectively ended any possibility of landing a title shot, as well as his career as a contender. Although he fought Alex Zolkin again, he ended up on the losing end of a split decision and followed that up with a controversial loss to undefeated Cuban heavyweight Aurelio Perez (8–0, 7 KOs). A win over Will Hinton followed, but by the time he lost a split decision in October 1995 to journeyman Marion Wilson (page 192), he became what Tyrell Biggs thought he was on January 17, 1993—just another opponent.

January 29, 1993—Columbia, South Carolina
Pinklon Thomas (43–6–1, 34 KOs) vs. Lawrence "Poncho"
**   Carter 21–5, 17 KOs)**
Favorite: Thomas
Result: Carter won by way of seventh-round TKO.

For any boxing fan that witnessed Pinklon Thomas's losses to Evander Holyfield, Mike Hunter (page 12), Riddick Bowe, or Tommy Morrison, the question was not whether Pinklon was washed up, but rather how could anyone let him continue to fight. His legs were clearly gone, he was unable to slip or duck any of the shots coming his way and, most telling, his once vaunted jab was completely ineffective against those fighters. He was also showing early signs of neurological damage. Boxing writers cringed at his slurred speech and curiously worded statements. In a telephone conference before his fight with Tommy Morrison he was quoted as saying, "You'll be *bombfounded* by my performance," and then added, "People say my head is messed up, but my EGG was good."[1] After quitting while on his stool between the first and second round against Tommy Morrison, most boxing insiders were glad to hear that Thomas had finally called it a career, and it appeared that he found an ideal profession training young fighters. But it took less than a year for the call of the ring to beckon Thomas back, and in May 1992, Pinklon Thomas launched his ill-advised comeback with a third-round knockout over Herman Jackson. For most insiders, it was clear that the road led nowhere near a world title, but most reluctantly agreed that Thomas could conceivably snatch one last big payday (although even that seemed highly unlikely considering how badly he lost to Bowe, Holyfield, and Morrison). Recognizing the George Foreman recipe for a successful comeback, Pinklon fought, and fought often. Although he racked up twelve wins over the next six months, the opposition was hardly awe-inspiring. In November 1992, Pinklon took the next step in his comeback, fighting former amateur standout Craig Payne for the

---

[1] "The Tattler," *KO Magazine,* July 1991, 62.

vacant IBO heavyweight title. The IBO was not exactly one of the more highly regarded sanctioning bodies, but it was still a belt, and Craig Payne was still a major step up in class from the fighters he had been feasting upon for much of the year. Although Pinklon was expected to beat Payne, it was not seen as a walk in the park, and many predicted a difficult fight for the former champion. But even those critics were shocked to see Payne give Thomas a life-and-death war over twelve rounds before dropping in a disputed decision. Even Thomas's most ardent supporters were left wondering how much longer the comeback could continue and assumed that a rest was in order for the aging champion considering the punishment he had taken from Payne. But Pinklon would have none of that, for he now saw a clear path to a title fight. He immediately signed to fight for the vacant WBF heavyweight championship, which was to take place a little over two months after the Payne bout against former light heavyweight prospect Lawrence "Poncho" Carter. If he were able to collect enough of the third-tier belts, he could turn himself into an attractive opponent for a big name fighter and possibly even a champion. Besides, most observers regarded Carter as a softer touch than Payne.

Lawrence "Poncho" Carter initially turned heads at light heavyweight fights when he won fifteen straight (thirteen by knockout) to start off his career. But an upset loss to "Bigfoot" Martin appeared to end his run up the rankings, and his conditioning soon began suffer as he moved to heavyweight. At that weight he appeared to be the ideal opponent: glossy record, somewhat recognizable name, and almost no chance at pulling off the win. For those reasons former champions James "Bonecrusher" Smith and Tony Tubbs wisely picked him as an opponent, and both stopped him. By 1993, his record was beginning to fall apart. When Carter was knocked out by Oliver McCall, many felt that his selection as an opponent for Thomas was an attempt to cash in on him one last time—before he racked up too many losses to "sell" him as an opponent.

For Pinklon Thomas in decline, "Poncho" was a fighter easy to underestimate, and he openly tossed the names of contenders "Razor" Ruddock and George Foreman around. But when Carter weighed in at a somewhat fleshy 232 pounds, the questions soon turned to Lawrence, and many ringsiders wondered how seriously he could be considering the opportunity he was presented. Lawrence held his own as the fight progressed. Although Pinklon still had some pop left in his jab and got the better of many of the early exchanges, it was clear that one thing he didn't have an answer for was "Poncho's" left hand. Carter reached in with sweeping left hooks that seemed never to fail to find their mark, and after three rounds many ringsiders were wondering how much longer Pinklon would be able to brush them aside. Still, the fight remained on even terms over the next three rounds, with Pinklon jabbing and out-hustling Carter while Carter fired strong left hooks. But the accumulated damage of fifty professional fights—thirteen of them in the previous seven months—along with the damage done by his well-documented problems with drugs, finally caught up with Pinklon in the seventh round. After tagging Pinklon with a sweeping left hook, Carter noticed that the defensive capabilities of Pinklon Thomas had fallen apart completely. (It almost appeared as if he was unable to raise his arms.) Carter marched in, firing with both hands and prompting the referee to call for a standing eight count. Although Pinklon claimed he was all right, it took Lawrence Carter only a few seconds to prove that was not the case. After resuming the fight, the referee quickly waved it off when Carter caught Thomas with a devastating combination. Although Thomas never hit the canvas, there was little controversy in the stoppage. When he returned to his corner, Pinklon Thomas was unable to bend his legs to sit on his stool, and it was clear that Pinklon was in bad shape when a cornerman was overheard saying, "my fighter is badly concussed."[2] Suddenly the worst fears of boxing fans seemed close to being realized when Thomas was removed from the ring on a stretcher, covered in blankets. He was rushed to Baptist Medical Center, but for Pinklon, luck was in his corner in the hospital, if not in the ring. He was released the following day and quickly announced his retirement. This time it stuck, and he never returned to the ring.

For the winner and new WBF champion, the victory didn't turn him into a world champion overnight (even if he was classified as one by the WBF). But what it did do for Carter was land him a fight against Phil Jackson on *USA's Tuesday Night Fights*. Although he was the under-

---

[2] Jim McLaurin, "After Carter Fight Thomas Decides to Hang Up Gloves," *The State Paper* (Columbia, SC), Feb. 1, 1993, 3.

dog, many were curious to see the fighter who so decisively ended the career of the former champion Pinklon Thomas. If they were expecting to see lighting strike twice, they were left wanting: Jackson destroyed Carter in three rounds. Another knockout loss for Carter followed later that year, this time against Lionel Butler, which effectively ended his brief flirtation with potential contention.

February 6, 1993—New York City, New York
"Merciless" Ray Mercer (20–1, 15 KOs) vs. Jesse Ferguson
   (18–9, 13 KOs)
Favorite: Mercer
Result: Ferguson won a ten-round unanimous decision.

When Ray Mercer was picked to fight on the undercard of Riddick Bowe's heavyweight title defense against Michael Dokes at Madison Square Garden, it was by no means an accident. The heated rivalry between Mercer and Bowe was arguably the most volatile in the heavyweight division at the time (second perhaps to only the Bowe–Lennox Lewis rivalry), and a Bowe-Mercer championship fight seemed only natural. For Mercer, the heavyweight gold medallist at the 1988 Seoul Olympics, the reasons were obvious. Discredited since his loss to Larry Holmes (page 37), Mercer realized that a win over Riddick Bowe would give him two belts and the respect of the boxing world as the "man who beat the man who beat the man." He could easily erase the ugly memory of Larry Holmes taunting and peppering him at will with the left jab, and also secure the largest paycheck of his career. Besides, there was also the matter regarding a proposed fight several year prior, one from which Mercer pulled out when he injured his ankle. Using the incident to question Mercer's courage, a claim against which Mercer was powerless to defend, Riddick Bowe and his management had ridiculed Mercer and his manager.

However, Riddick Bowe also had plenty of motivation going into a potential Mercer fight. He genuinely disliked Mercer ever since their days as Olympic roommates and had wanted to lure the steel-chinned Mercer into a fight for some time. Fans and boxing writers were openly excited about the match, and though Riddick Bowe was still the prohibitive favorite, everyone agreed that Mercer would be a major step up from Michael Dokes.

All Ray had to do was win in impressive fashion against a soft touch on the undercard to help hype the potential future title fight. Enter Jesse Ferguson. To say that few gave Ferguson a chance of winning would have been an understatement. Although he would later go on to earn a reputation as one of the most dangerous journeymen in the heavyweight division, in 1993 he was not yet held in such high regard. His knockout loss to Mike Tyson in 1986 had become something of boxing "tall tale" due to Tyson's claim to have tried to drive Ferguson's nose bone into his brain, and with knockout losses to Carl "The Truth" Williams and Bruce Seldon on his resume as well, it was hard to see that he had the durability to last more than a few rounds with Mercer, even on his best night. Although Ferguson had extended Tony Tubbs and Michael Dokes the distance the previous year, neither had been considered a power puncher like Ray, and the very fact that he lost to them seemed to indicate that he was not going to put up much of a test for the younger Ray Mercer. But Ferguson's record was somewhat deceptive. After winning his first thirteen fights (including a decision over James "Buster" Douglas) his management threw him in with the lions in matching him up with Carl "The Truth" Williams in 1985. He fought bravely and even dropped Williams twice, but his inexperience eventually led to his demise as Williams went on to score the tenth-round knockout.

A year later he fought with Mike Tyson, and from there it was the fast road to journeyman status, losing to James "Bonecrusher" Smith, Anders Eklund, and Orlin Norris before the end of the decade. By 1988 it appeared as if his career were over, but two years later he made a comeback and lost to Oliver McCall by way of a boring ten-round decision. Although Ferguson failed to win many fights in his comeback (he was 2–4 in the 1990s going into the Mercer fight), he was showing some signs of improvement—something he was denied in his first career when he was thrown in as an opponent rather than developed into a prospect. Unfortunately his improvement was coming in the gym, but not in the ring. Developing a reputation as an excellent sparring partner, Ferguson had yet to put it together in an actual fight. Against Seldon, Tubbs, and Dokes he foolishly let each opponent dictate the pace of the fight and never pushed their weaknesses enough to seriously threaten them. And it appeared that Mercer's only major weakness was an inability to deal with slick jabbing boxers, which Ferguson was not.

The only question going into the fight was whether Ferguson would KO the Bowe-Mercer fight by making Ray look bad enough to make the fight unmarketable—something that seemed a remote possibility when Ray weighed in at a fleshy 238¾. Ferguson accomplished that feat within three rounds, and over the next seven would accomplish the more unlikely feat of winning the decision. Mercer initially started out with the left jab, a weapon he was trying to develop. But it was clear early on that the Mercer jab was not going to be much of a factor in the fight, and that the relentless body attack of Jesse Ferguson would be. When Ferguson landed a straight right to the chin of Ray Mercer in the opening minute of the round most felt that, despite Mercer's granite chin, Ferguson's power was in fact able to rattle the bigger man. Mercer's inability to avoid Ferguson's punches was so noticeable that at round's end HBO commentator Jim Lampley said, "Even against a relatively slow fisted puncher like Ferguson, Mercer remains an open target." The body attack mounted by Jesse Ferguson continued through the second round as Ray Mercer foolishly let himself slip into a pattern of holding Ferguson's head (rather than his arms) while the underdog pounded away at Mercer's body. By the end of the second many ringsiders were openly wondering if Mercer's conditioning would fail him if he continued to take body shots for ten rounds. In fact, HBO commentator George Foreman noted at round's end that "Ray Mercer is allowing himself to be hit in the body a little too much . . . those body punches are doing more damage to Ray Mercer than the head shots."

It was clear in the third round that Mercer was wilting as his jab became even more ineffective—fatigue caused him to paw with it. Although the fight itself continued in the same pattern as the first two rounds, with Ferguson pounding away at Mercer, the single most important aspect of the fight first surfaced in the third when Jesse Ferguson began to "trash talk" his opponent with stinging verbal barbs—"you ain't got nothing!"—that could be heard even on the HBO telecast. At the beginning few ringsiders paid much attention to the verbal exchange as Jesse continued to pound away at Ray over the next several rounds, implementing his own jab that peppered Ray's face in the fourth and staggering him with a right in the last thirty seconds of the round. The fifth round saw Jesse's relentless pressure forcing Mercer to back away from his stalking opponent, and the sixth ended up being one of the most dominant for Ferguson; he hurt Ray on the ropes halfway through the round and stunned him with a left hook in the closing seconds.

The "talking" factor resurfaced in the seventh when Ray Mercer responded to a Jesse Ferguson pounding by talking to him. The talking continued through the round and became so prevalent that all three HBO commentators began discussing it, and even began joking that Ray Mercer was "trying to make a deal" with the underdog Ferguson—and that a dive, or setup, might be in the works. However, it seemed that any notion of Jesse Ferguson taking a dive ended when, after seemingly bizarre behavior in his corner between rounds, he came out in the eighth like a pit bull. It was now abundantly clear that Jesse was intent on fighting and winning, while Mercer seemed more interested in talking, leaving many wondering what he was doing. In the ninth round the "setup" theory was given some disturbing legitimacy when Mercer was overheard by the HBO camera, saying, "I ain't never lied to you before!" But few anticipated the matter would be looked at again when Ferguson continued to pound away at Mercer and won the tenth (and final) round. Although one judge (Steve Weisfeld) gave Mercer one round (which seemed appropriate) the other two judges had the fight a bit closer than it actually was, giving the nod to Ferguson by scores of 96–94 and 97–94. It was enough to remove Ray Mercer from serious consideration for a title fight, and many felt that the career of Mercer was dealt a fatal blow.

Although many boxing fans immediately began focusing their attention on the main event, New York boxing commissioner Randy Gordon began investigating the "bribe" accusations as soon as Mercer and Ferguson left the ring. Within days the tarnished career of Ray Mercer was dealt an apparent knockout when rumors of a $100,000 bribe offer to Ferguson emerged. A reporter, Rosemarie Ross of the *North Jersey Herald & News*, broke the story when an unidentified member of the Mercer camp confirmed the accusation. Within days Ray Mercer was indicted and charged with Sports Bribery by the Manhattan District Attorney's office. Initially Ferguson denied the allegations, claiming that Mercer had not made any offers during the fight. But faced with the

While in control here versus Jesse Ferguson, Ray Mercer (right) would later allegedly resort to a mid-fight bribe to stave off an eventual defeat. *Ray Bailey*

threat of perjury, Ferguson recanted on the stand and claimed that Mercer had in fact offered him $100,000 to "go down." However, the impact of Ferguson's testimony was not enough to convict Ray. When the HBO tapes failed to provide any clear-cut evidence (although he was heard to say such things as "I'll give it to you" and "I swear on my mother, man")[3] and referee Wayne Kelly stated that he heard no bribery offer, the jury was left with a classic "his word against my word" case, and after a little more than five hours of deliberation, the jury concluded that there was not enough evidence, and was enough "reasonable doubt," to find Ray Mercer not guilty.

Despite winning the biggest fight of his career in a New York courtroom, it appeared that the boxing career of Ray Mercer was all but dead.

---

[3] Robert Cassidy, "Not Guilty! Ray Mercer Finally Wins a Big One," *Ring Magazine,* August 1994, 61.

He lost twice to fighters he was suppose to beat, in Larry Holmes and Jesse Ferguson, and suddenly his tougher-than-expected wins over the likes of Bert Cooper and Ossie Ocasio were used as proof that Ray had never been that good. Shortly before the trial Mercer won a hard-fought decision over Mark Wills and afterwards made legal history when he became the first defendant to legally beat up his accuser during a pay-per-view fight with Ferguson entitled "Final Verdict." However, his win over Ferguson in the rematch was hardly decisive—Mercer won a close split decision—and seemed to confirm the critics who felt he was overrated. When Ray was held to a controversial draw with club fighter Marion Wilson (in a fight that most observers felt Wilson won decisively) in July 1994, it seemed the final step into journeyman status for the once promising Olympian. But Mercer was far from finished. After losing to Evander Holyfield in a ten-round war, he resurrected his career by losing a controversial decision to Lennox Lewis and then rebounding with a ten-round decision win over Tim Witherspoon to cement a place in the top ten.

For Ferguson the "bribe" allegations initially seemed the only bit of fame he was going to bring from the fight and that he would return to fighting as a journeyman opponent for the up-and-comers in the sport. When it appeared that he was going to fight Herbie Hide, many felt that it was an indication that bigger things did not await him. But in a shocker, he was selected instead as Riddick Bowe's second opponent for the defense of his heavyweight championship. Many insiders were openly hostile of Ferguson as an opponent for Bowe in a title fight—he had lost to two fighters that Bowe knocked out in the first round: Bruce Seldon and Michael Dokes—but Jesse recognized the opportunity that was presented to him and came into the Bowe fight in the best shape of his career. Unfortunately for him, it was not enough to compensate for the huge advantages in size, strength, and skill that Bowe possessed. Although the loss was a huge disappointment to Ferguson, who attributed his poor performance to the classic sports "choke," it was not the end of his career as a contender. A big win on ESPN over Rocky Pepeli followed before his split-decision loss to Mercer in a rematch, a fight that earned him an impressive $150,000.

February 27, 1993—Beijing, China
"Smokin" Bert Cooper (29–9, 25 KOs) vs. Mike Weaver
    (35–16–1, 26 KOs)
Favorite: Cooper
Result: Weaver won a ten-round unanimous decision.

For those who saw the fight live, no heavyweight fight in the 1990s gen-
erated more excitement and anticipation than the Bert Cooper–Mike
Weaver fight for the vacant NBA heavyweight title. It would go down as
one of the most historic and widely seen fights in the history of the
sport. This despite the fact that most boxing insiders regarded it as
fairly weak, with a somewhat limited contender and a badly faded forty-
year-old former champion. But for the millions of boxing fans in the
People's Republic of China, it was their first taste of the sport that had
been banned by the Communist party for decades. As part of a fight card
titled "Brawl at the Wall," the Cooper-Weaver fight was one of three
fights that would be part of the first boxing broadcast in China's history.

Perhaps due to the relative naivety of the Chinese fans, it also appeared to many of the viewers as something it was not: a legitimate fight
between two contenders for a vacant heavyweight title. Unaware of
what runaway capitalism had done in creating a profitable business in
sanctioning organizations, few Chinese fans questioned the validity of
the NBA (which ranked alongside the WBF in the United States as the
least credible of the sanctioning organizations). After all, you had a
hard-punching contender against a seasoned former champion. What
more could you ask? But for fans in the United States, it looked like
mismatch, and few fans outside of China showed interest in the fight. It
was just a case of Bert Cooper cashing in on a foreign trip while padding
his record against a recognizable former champion.

For many boxing insiders, no fighter had a more erratic and unpre-
dictable career than "Smokin" Bert Cooper, but by 1993 it appeared as
if he finally had put it all together to become a legitimate contender.
After turning pro in 1984 as a cruiserweight, Cooper quickly established
himself as one of the more attractive prospects in the division when he
racked up ten straight wins (nine by knockout). But in fight number
eleven (in 1986) it appeared as if he would fail to deliver. Unknown Reggie Gross knocked him out in eight rounds in a fight during which ques-

tions surfaced about his heart and conditioning. However, Cooper quickly bounced back with a huge upset over Olympic gold medal winner Henry Tillman two months later. Cooper captured a twelve-round decision and the NABF cruiserweight title and, in the process, reestablished himself as a prospect worth keeping an eye on. Therefore, it initially appeared as if Cooper was making a major mistake when he decided to abandon the cruiserweight division to chase the bigger money fights in the heavyweight division. But after a huge upset over undefeated prospect Willie DeWitt in 1987, in which he starched the Canadian Olympian in two rounds, Cooper appeared to have proven the critics wrong. Suddenly he was one of the most talked about heavyweight prospects in the sport, and many were comparing him to both Mike Tyson and his own trainer, Joe Frazier. But the roller coaster career of Bert Cooper was hardly done, and in his next fight he was battered for eight rounds by Carl "The Truth" Williams before quitting on his stool. The loss to Williams prompted him to return to the cruiserweight division, but the move failed to reignite the fire in his heart, and he failed to establish himself as a contender, losing decisions to Everett "Bigfoot" Martin in 1988 and Nate Miller in 1989.

The freefall that Cooper's career was taking was not without reason. His training regime had deteriorated, and he was preparing for fights by indulging in cocaine and sex. With his drug usage out of control by the end of 1989, his career was all but dead. After quitting on his stool against George Foreman after two rounds in his first fight back in the heavyweight division, even his strongest supporter (trainer Joe Frazier) walked out on him. For most boxing fans it appeared as if he hit rock bottom, and he was still digging.

But Cooper decided to whip himself into shape for a last shot at redemption. After stopping Orlin Norris in 1990 in a fight for the NABF heavyweight title, Cooper engaged in one of the most exciting heavyweight fights of the decade, brawling on even terms with Ray Mercer before dropping a close decision. Although Cooper's career took another dip when Riddick Bowe stopped him in two rounds, he returned to his winning ways by stopping his next three opponents. Cooper then pulled off an upset of sorts when he stopped heavyweight prospect Joe Hipp in five rounds, a win that put him in position for the biggest fight of his career: a title fight against Evander Holyfield in 1991. As a six-day substitute, Cooper had little time to properly train for the fight, but nonetheless almost pulled off the second biggest upset of the decade when he rocked Holyfield in the third round, scoring the first knockdown over the steel-chinned champion ever. The match revitalized his career, and after stopping Cecil Coffee, Bert found himself in his second heavyweight title fight, this time against Michael Moorer for the vacant WBO belt. Again Cooper stunned the world with a better-than-expected performance. After dropping Moorer in he first and third, Cooper was stopped in the fifth round in what one of the best heavyweight fights of the decade. With his solid showing against Moorer, Cooper's stock actually rose in losing, and his ranking and status remained high. It looked as if the twenty-seven-year-old Cooper finally had put it together, and it was hard to see how the somewhat soft-chinned Weaver would be able to stand up against Cooper at the top of his game. After all, most insiders felt that Weaver was completely shot after getting blitzed by James "Bonecrusher" Smith in one round in 1986. In the seven years since that loss, he fought only twelve times, losing four times—to Donovan "Razor" Ruddock, James "Bonecrusher" Smith (again), Lennox Lewis and even the lightly regarded Johnny DuPlooy. In fact, going into the Cooper fight, Weaver had only one win in almost three years.

For the former champion Mike Weaver, Cooper was a very beatable opponent. The blueprint on how to beat him had already been written nine times, and Weaver understood what he needed to do. Although his career was defined by his face-first style that produced such classic wars as Weaver–Larry Holmes and Weaver–Gerrie Coetzee, he also recognized that mixing it up in a slugfest with Cooper might prove unwise. So he worked on an aspect of his game that had always been somewhat underrated: his boxing skills. Weaver honed his jab and prepared for a defensive match focusing on his footwork to get him out of trouble. For Team Weaver, if the early reports on Cooper's poor conditioning proved true, it might just be the strategy that could wear down the hard-punching contender.

As expected, Cooper started the fight swinging wildly, trying to catch the forty-year-old with one of his trademark right hands. If ring rust would play any part in the fight, Cooper was determined to expose it quickly. But reports on Cooper's poor conditioning would in fact prove correct when Cooper quickly fizzled after a mere ten seconds. It was the opportunity for which Weaver was looking, and he began to box and move, trying to keep Cooper away. For many of the American fans watching, it initially looked like an exercise in futility. You can't teach an old dog new tricks, and Weaver was about as old as they got. But within a minute those same fans were stunned to discover Weaver's jab actually keeping Cooper at bay and, more importantly, tentative. When Cooper tried to close the gap, Mike Weaver held on well and used every veteran trick in the book to keep his lead. Although the Weaver jab at times was a pawing flick for much of the second round, it still worked. Cooper did find the range with a hard overhand right halfway through the round, but it was hardly enough to turn the tide in what was appearing to become a very dominant Weaver fight.

Perhaps realizing that he let the slow-starting Weaver off the hook in the first round, Cooper came out in the third swinging for the fences. However, for the normally fast-starting Cooper it was too little too late as Weaver soon had his jab working again. Cooper still continued his forward march, swinging and missing wildly. But employing another veteran trick, Weaver stole the round with a solid attack in the final ten seconds. The fluid boxing performance of Weaver continued in the fourth as Cooper began to show signs of slowing down. Cooper began to show a more serious problem as well; he was beginning to appear uninspired. But, with a little over a minute in the round, Cooper seemed to turn the tide of the fight when he staggered Weaver with a hard right hand. His follow-up attack had Weaver staggering into the ropes, and many ringsiders felt that Weaver was one punch away from calling it a night, but Cooper's lack of conditioning robbed him of a golden opportunity as he failed to attack. Weaver quickly held on and threw in a few hard body shots of his own for good measure, and the opportunity was quickly gone for Bert Cooper. Still, the power of Bert Cooper was beginning to shine, and for many ringsiders it was clear that Weaver had to be careful. Weaver came out boxing and outworking his younger opponent again in the fifth, but once again Cooper found a home for his right hand. Although the first one that landed at 1:20 of the round did little real damage, it was followed up by another forty seconds later, this time stunning Weaver again. Again Weaver stumbled into the ropes, and again Cooper attacked. But just as he had in the previous round, Bert

Cooper quickly wore himself out and by the end of the round was willingly allowing Mike Weaver to wrestle with him.

Going into the sixth, the momentum was clearly in Bert Cooper's corner, and it was looking as if Weaver would be hard pressed to last the distance. The power of Cooper was taking its toll on Weaver, and his jab was becoming less effective as the round's went on. Weaver began to mix it up more with Cooper in the sixth, reaching Cooper with a long right hand of his own in the opening seconds of the round. Cooper tried to fire back with a left hook but fell short with the counterpunch. However, despite Weaver's early success, the slugfest was clearly a fight that Cooper was better suited to compete in, and as the round continued Cooper began to stalk the former champion. Although he didn't punch well when he did close the gap, it appeared as if Weaver was not willing to capitalize on Cooper's inactivity, choosing instead to run. A Cooper left hook staggered Weaver again towards the end of the round, but once again Cooper failed to follow through, letting his wounded foe off the hook. By the seventh round, Cooper was pumping his own jab as he stalked the fleet-footed Weaver. But his lack of activity on the inside was a sign of trouble. His poor conditioning was not suited to handle such a physical fight, and by the round's end it was clear that he had let Weaver back into the fight.

Although Cooper still appeared in control for much of the eighth round, with his stalking of a timid Weaver, the tide would quickly turn back in Mike Weaver's favor. Weaver began to find a home for his jab again, and in the final ten seconds of the round a hard combination upstairs staggered Bert Cooper for the first time in the fight. Determined to test the somewhat suspect heart of Bert Cooper, Weaver jumped all over him at the bell to start the ninth round. Although he quickly backed off, it was clear that he was now in control as he began to stand and mix it up with Cooper. Suddenly the smirk that Cooper carried for much of the fight was gone, replaced with a look of frustration and fatigue. A Weaver left hook landed upstairs one minute into the round, and from that point on it was Weaver who pressured Cooper and tried to engage his opponent into a slugfest. Cooper, who had been waiting for this for the previous eight rounds, was simply too tired to keep up.

Going into the final round many ringsiders felt that the fight was still up in the air and that whoever won the tenth round could very well win the fight. Weaver initially returned to his bicycle, boxing and jabbing as he had so effectively in the first three rounds. After landing a hard right hand Weaver held on as Bert Cooper tried to respond. Cooper then tried to jab his way inside but failed to land a single jab. Suddenly Weaver was looking like the second coming of Ali as he danced and moved, making Cooper look foolish with his wild attacks. When Weaver landed a hard left hook in the final minute of the fight it looked like the icing on the cake, but Cooper quickly responded with a left hook of is own, one that briefly stunned Weaver. But the success was short lived. Mike Weaver quickly recovered and actually had Cooper stunned as the bell ended the fight.

With Weaver's solid performance in the final two rounds, he was able to cement a surprisingly lopsided decision (by scores of 97–93, 98–93, and a more realistic 96–94), this despite the fact that many ringsiders felt the fight could have gone either way. Initially it appeared to be just the fight to put him back in the picture for a big money fight in the heavyweight division. A title fight was a long shot, but a fight against George Foreman seemed a very real possibility. Weaver recognized what he needed to do to land that fight, promising after the Cooper fight to "fight someone else in the top ten" and to "stay busy." But Weaver failed to listen to his own advice, and for the next fifteen months sat on the sidelines. When he returned to the ring in June 1994, it was against the farthest fighter from a contender, one Ladislao Mijangos. He then returned to China, the one place where he was still one of the biggest stars in the sport, for a quick and easy defense of his NBA title against lightly regarded Bill Corrigan in September 1994, before disappearing for another nine months. By the time he defeated George O'Mara in June 1995, the momentum from his big win over Cooper was gone and so was any possibility of landing a big money fight. After fighting once in 1996, Weaver disappeared for over two years before making an ill-advised comeback in 1998. A knockout loss to Melvin Foster followed, which again prompted him to call it a career. But an old foe convinced him to step into the ring again when Larry Holmes needed an opponent to defend his "Legends of Boxing" heavyweight title in November 2000. Holmes stopped Weaver in six lopsided rounds.

For Bert Cooper, the loss effectively ended his brief fling as a heavyweight contender. He returned to the United States to take on Derek

Williams a month later, and although he won a lopsided decision, many ringsiders felt that was more due to Williams's unwillingness to mix it up than anything Cooper did. After getting starched in his very next fight by South African prospect Corrie Sanders (who stopped Cooper in three rounds), Cooper's career began another freefall—one from which even the resilient "Smokin'" Bert would be unable to recover. Cooper would go on to lose six of his next nine fights before scoring his next meaningful win, a first-round knockout over undefeated Richie Melito (page 248).

May 8, 1993—Lake Tahoe, Nevada
Danell Nicholson (10–0, 8 KOs) vs. Jeremy Williams (8–0, 6 KOs)
Favorite: Nicholson
Result: Williams won by way of second-round TKO.

With a high profile manager in Bill Cayton, a world-renowned trainer in Kevin Rooney, and more television exposure than any other undefeated prospect in the heavyweight division, it appeared to most casual fans of boxing that Williams was the bigger name when he stepped into the ring with fellow undefeated prospect Danell Nicholson. And in fact he was. But in what had to be regarded as a bizarre twist of fate, those factors helped to make him the underdog against the yet-to-be televised former Olympian Danell Nicholson. Williams had already had his share of trouble against opponents who were far from world class, and though that was not particularly uncommon for countless young prospects on their way up, Jeremy's struggles were seen by countless fans on cable TV. Against a feather-fisted, obese heavyweight named Robert Smith, Williams had struggled to win a six-round split decision. He followed that win with the toughest fight of his young career, coming up from the canvas to win a close decision against Marion Wilson. Getting dropped wasn't that uncommon for many young fighters, but whereas nobody saw undefeated prospect Kirk Johnson hit the deck against Ty Evans, every serious boxing fan in the country saw Williams when he was felled. It was enough to dim the Williams star, prompting many insiders to say that Williams was simply too small to compete with the bigger heavyweights. After all, he gained a whopping forty pounds since his

Olympic trials loss to Montell Griffin (although he carried his weight very well, and looked quite fit in the ring).

But Cayton was seen as a man who managed his fighters cautiously (stemming from his management of heavyweight contender Tommy Morrison), and most assumed that he would move his fighter along slowly, leaving the questions of Williams's durability unanswered. But when it was announced that Williams would fight Nicholson in only his ninth fight, jaws around the boxing community dropped. It seemed an unusually risky gamble for Cayton to take, and many insiders were openly questioning if Cayton was simply throwing his twenty-year-old prospect in with the wolves. It was enough to prompt ABC analysis Alex Wallau to comment that "a lot of people, I think the majority of people I talked to, expect Danell Nicholson to beat Jeremy Williams," this despite the fact that Danell had yet to fight on television, and had yet to fight a fighter with a winning record.

What boxing fans remembered vividly about Nicholson was his near upset in the Barcelona Olympics against Cuban powerhouse Felix Savon. Savon was widely regarded as the best amateur heavyweight to emerge since Teofilo Stevenson, and he usually reserved his best performances for his battles with American fighters. But after two rounds, Savon saw himself trailing on the scorecards against the unheralded Nicholson. Although Savon went on to win the third round big, giving him a close decision victory, it was widely regarded as the best Olympic performance of an American heavyweight against a Cuban in years.

Williams, who was a notoriously fast starter, came out at the bell bombing. Although his punches failed to land, they did expose something in Nicholson that would play a major role in the fight: stage fright. Going from no TV exposure to an ABC network fight was too much for a fighter who would soon become renowned for his choking in the "big game." Nicholson was clearly gun shy, as he fired only one jab at a time before timidly running away from potential counterpunches. Nicholson's failure to put his punches together ensured that Williams would not be discouraged in jumping in with wild power shots to the head.

However, Nicholson seemed to begin to shake some of his stage fright early in the second. Although Williams landed a big left hook ten seconds into the round it was matched with a right-hand counter by Danell. Nicholson then began to stand and trade with the hard-punching Williams, not a smart strategy, but a major improvement from his strategy in the opening round. Although Williams was getting the better of the exchanges, it was still relatively close. With just under a minute left in the second, it appeared that Danell finally had found his "game." A counter right hand buckled the knees of Jeremy Williams, and for a brief second it looked as if the bigger Danell Nicholson was about to test the soft chin of Jeremy Williams. But the advantage lasted only a few seconds. Nicholson, perhaps due to arrogance or inexperience, dropped his hands as he came in to fire another right hand. Williams fired a right hand counter of his own, which landed a split second before Nicholson's reached Jeremy's chin. Suddenly "Doc" Nicholson found himself sitting on the canvas, and although he was up at the count of three, there was little question that the momentum was back in Jeremy's corner. Still, it didn't appear that Nicholson was seriously hurt, and with forty seconds left in the second, it appeared that he would survive the round. But Williams was an exceptional finisher, and he proved it against Nicholson. After trapping Nicholson on the ropes, he fired a right uppercut that nearly decapitated "Doc," followed by a left hook and right cross that dropped Nicholson a second time. The referee waved the fight off at 2:55 of the round, with a clearly dazed Nicholson still on his hands and knees.

For both Nicholson and Williams, the fight would set a pattern that would define their careers. Williams would remain an explosive, but very vulnerable, heavyweight contender. With the win he jumped to the front of the class of 1992 for heavyweight prospects, but a war with Frankie Swindell followed—another fight in which he was forced to rise from the canvas—prompting many experts to again make him the slight underdog when he faced another Olympian, Larry Donald, in March 1994. Against Donald he was not to be as successful, losing a lopsided twelve-round decision.

For Nicholson, he initially took the ideal steps to repair the damage from his loss to Williams. Taking on increasing competition, occasionally on cable TV, he looked impressive against grade C heavyweights. Hiring Manny Steward also helped immensely. But when he faced Andrew Golota on HBO in 1996, he again came up short in the big fight, losing by way of an eight-round TKO. He followed that loss with another, by decision, to Kirk Johnson. The Johnson loss seemed to end his career, but five years and fifteen wins later, he was two fights away from a title fight when he entered a four-way tournament for the IBF number one ranking (and mandatory fight with Lennox Lewis). Although he boxed well against David Tua early on, he was stopped in the sixth round, ending his last serious run as a contender.

June 8, 1993—Las Vegas, Nevada
Alex Garcia (32–1, 26 KOs) vs. Mike Dixon (12–8, 11 KOs)
Favorite: Garcia
Result: Dixon scored a second-round TKO.

For Alex Garcia, a title fight was already his for the asking. But it was a big money payday that kept him fighting limited opponents like Dixon, rather than Lennox Lewis or Riddick Bowe. In fact, he had already been offered a title fight against Riddick Bowe but priced himself out of it. Initially, it seemed that time was on his side. He was, after all, a Mexican American, and boxing had yet to see its first Latino heavyweight champion. Garcia also had a large fan following inside his home state of California and was a regular on *USA Tuesday Night Fights*. But his hope for a big money payday did not gain ground leading up to his showdown with Dixon. Though he had exploded early in his career with devastating knockouts over Jerry Goff, Mike "The Giant" White, and former cruiserweight champion Bernard Benton, he struggled in three of his last four fights. Against Jerry Jones he was extended the distance in winning a close decision, against Mike Williams he was given trouble by the movement of Williams before scoring the fifth-round knockout, and against Eric Curry he was pushed to the brink of defeat before scoring a stunning knockout in the twelfth, and final, round.

Garcia's desire for a big money payday was further complicated by the simple fact that, despite his number three ranking by the WBC, he had yet to face a single top-ten-ranked heavyweight. Some critics pointed to his struggles against Curry, Jones, and Williams to openly question if he deserved a title shot at all, let alone to be paid handsomely for it. The assumption was that against Bowe or Lewis, he would lose, and probably lose badly.

But against Dixon, most assumed that he would probably perform well. Dixon had shown some signs of being a decent heavyweight in extending Bruce Seldon the distance, as well as in his slugfest with Ray Mercer (a fight he lost in the seventh round). But coming off the heels of a second-round knockout at the hands of Oliver McCall five months earlier, most felt that he was now officially a "professional opponent." Jones, Williams, and Curry were fighters who were inactive, but they all had somewhat glossy records. Jones was coming off a win over Carl "The Truth" Williams, Mike Williams was a highly touted prospect in the late 80s who was attempting to make a comeback, and Curry brought in a record of 21–1. Dixon was active, but with seven losses in his last nine fights, he was considered a step down for Garcia, an easy win after a string of tougher than expected fights. Besides, it seemed a perfect opportunity to add two other belts (the WBC Continental Americas and the WBA Fedalatin title) to his resume.

The fight began rather unspectacularly. Garcia seemed content to try and establish the jab. He won the opening round with greater activity and a handful of decent right hands. Dixon, who was noted for slugging with bigger men, seemed gun shy. He also tried to pump the left jab and even tried to rough up Garcia towards the end of the round. But the flurry failed to rattle Garcia much, and Garcia never lost his composure in reestablishing the jab. The second saw more of the same, with Garcia actually pinning Dixon to the ropes early on for a few seconds. Though Dixon would occasionally throw hard hooks to the body or decent overhand rights, they seemed to lack much zip, and it appeared Dixon just didn't have the firepower in his arsenal to really hurt Garcia, whose jab was keeping Mike at bay. But with about thirty seconds left in the fight, Dixon landed an unspectacular left hook right behind Garcia's ear that completely discombobulated and deposited him on the seat of his pants. Although the shot hardly looked devastating, it did successfully shake up Alex's equilibrium. He rose on shaky legs, and suddenly the second round became a race against the clock for Alex Garcia, as he tried to survive long enough to make it to the conclusion. Dixon, however, saw his golden opportunity, and pounced on the woozy Garcia, trapping him in the corner and landing left hooks and overhand rights in an attempt to finish off the stunned fighter. When an overhand right snapped Alex's head back, referee Joe Cortez wisely jumped in and stopped the fight with seventeen seconds left in the round.

For Dixon, he found himself in possession of two championship belts—Garcia's NABF title was not on the line—as well as a resurrected career; he had thrust himself into the heavyweight picture. However, only two months later, he stepped into the ring with heavyweight up-and-comer Phil Jackson. Jackson seemed to be a wise choice for Dixon; he was a ranked fighter coming off a televised victory over Poncho Carter, who also was a former cruiserweight contender (so he would not possess a major advantage in size over Dixon). Though Jackson had an impressive record of 28–1, with 26 KOs, he also had already been defeated by Donovan "Razor" Ruddock via a fourth-round knockout, and it seemed that a Dixon victory was certainly not out of the question. For all intents and purposes, it appeared Dixon's best chance of striking gold a second time was through Phil Jackson. But it was not to be, as Jackson dominated him in scoring a fifth-round TKO. That loss returned Dixon to "opponent" status, and he followed up that loss with losses against Buster Mathis Jr., Herbie Hide, and Brian Nielsen.

The thirty-one-year-old Garcia saw his payday (and his title shot) disappear, never to resurface. Ranked in the top ten by all three sanctioning bodies, he was dropped from all after the loss, his only remaining ranking being a dismal number twenty-four by the WBC. The loss undoubtedly was a letdown for Garcia, but also appeared that his skills as a fighter deteriorated as well as a result of the loss. He followed up the loss to Dixon with an unimpressive twelve-round draw with former cruiserweight champion James Warring (in a decision that many ringsiders felt should have gone to Warring), and then was knocked out in the second round by Garing Lane. He attempted to rebound with a pair of fights over Everton Davis and George O'Mara, but struggled to win ugly decisions in both. A decisive loss to Joe Hipp in 1994 robbed him of the last bit of credibility in the ring that he possessed—his NABF title. Still, he did manage to avenge the loss to Dixon, although not in the impressive fashion that he would have hoped for. On May 24, 1994, on the undercard of Tommy Morrison's fight with Sherman Griffin, Alex Garcia won a ten-round decision over the man who ended his reign as a heavyweight contender. But the fight didn't salvage Alex's sagging career. He struggled with Dixon, and his failure to secure a knockout proved to many that Alex Garcia was no longer a viable heavyweight. Nonetheless, Garcia continued to fight after that, and even lined up a fight for the USBA title with Buster Mathis Jr. in 1995, a fight he lost via twelve-round decision. He never came close to regaining his stature as a contender, and his two short-lived comeback attempts, in 1997 and 1999, were completely ignored by the boxing world.

August 16, 1993—Boise, Idaho
Tony Tubbs (35–4, 19 KOs) vs. Jimmy Ellis (19–3–1, 18 KOs)
Favorite: Tubbs
Result: Ellis won by way of first-round knockout.

When Tony Tubbs found himself on the losing end of a first-round knockout loss to Lionel Butler in 1992 (page 64), most insiders assumed that it was the end of the line for the former champion. But Tubbs was a fighter unwilling to allow the Butler loss to rob him of his career, and by August 1993 it looked like Tony was on pace to win the comeback-of-the-year award. He followed the loss to Butler with a solid decision over Bruce Seldon, a win that revitalized his career, and Tubbs decided to capitalize on his win rather than sit on it (as had been his habit in the past). Over the next ten months he strung together three straight decision victories. All of the wins were on television (televised on *USA Tuesday Night Fights*) against strong opposition, and Tubbs found himself in possession of the number nine ranking in the WBC as a result of his impressive streak. Even the fans were talking. A rematch with Riddick Bowe suddenly seemed a real possibility, and a few were even discussing the remote possibility that Tony might even beat Bowe if they were to fight again. (He lost a controversial decision to Bowe when the two fought in 1991.) The key for Tubbs was to remain active against solid opposition. But four months after his victory over Melton Bowen in Auburn Hills, Michigan, Tubbs decided to take a quick and easy payday against the lightly regarded Jimmy Ellis. After fighting televised fights in each of last seven fights, the Ellis fight would be a non-televised, little-seen fight against a widely discredited opponent.

Ellis was best remembered for his 1991 fight against George Foreman, in which he was dominated before getting stopped in the third round. It was arguably the biggest mismatch ever televised on HBO, and the sight of George literally playing with his overmatched foe did little in helping his career after the fight. Although Ellis had a glossy record of 16–1–1, there were few in the boxing world that felt that Ellis would ever be anything more than a journeyman. When Ellis went on to get knocked out by Tony Willis in his next fight, it seemed that assessment was brutally accurate. Although Jimmy went on to string together three wins after the loss to Willis, a later loss to the lightly regarded clubfighter Joe Brewer seemed to end any hope that he might have had of erasing the stigma of the Foreman loss. By the time he signed to fight Tony Tubbs, Jimmy Ellis was regarded as quite possibly the worst 19–3–1 fighter in the world, and some experts even wondered if Tubbs would score the rare knockout over Ellis.

There was one chance that could give Jimmy the win. It was a long shot, but if everything went perfectly, he could upset the former world champion. Tubbs had already shown a tendency of getting caught early (against Mike Tyson and Lionel Butler) and the fast-starting Ellis realized that his best chance of winning was to jump on Tubbs immediately and test his chin. Although most experts felt that Jimmy's power was grossly exaggerated by his record, they nonetheless admitted that, if nothing else, style-wise he was a brawler.

Ellis also had another factor working in his favor. He was fighting in front of his local fans. In Idaho, Ellis was still regarded as a potential prospect, and he was determined not to let his fans down. As it turned out, he didn't. At the bell Ellis ran out to meet Tubbs in the center of the ring. He quickly fired a right cross to the body (which was blocked) followed by a left hook to the face (which was not). Tubbs crashed to the canvas a mere three seconds into the fight and was clearly out of it as the referee began counting. In fact, a Tubbs corner man entered the ring to attend to his fallen fighter (for the record, eleven seconds into the fight), but the referee oddly ignored him (and Ellis hugging his corner man in the opposite corner) to continue counting. The official end came at twenty-one seconds—after the referee reached ten in a very long count.

For Ellis, the winner in the biggest upset in Idaho boxing history, the victory did erase some of the sting of the Foreman fight but hardly enough to change the prevailing opinion of him as an overrated journeyman. A follow-up win in his next fight (against Ladislao Mijangos) seemed the second step in changing that prevailing opinion of him, but the Mijangos fight turned into a debacle for Ellis, as he in turn was the victim of a first-round upset at the hands of a lightly regarded opponent.

For Tubbs, the win destroyed his run as a contender, and he was forced back to the proverbial drawing board. However, he was able to repair some, if not all the damage inflicted by the loss to Ellis when he went on to win four fights in one night to capture the "People's Championship." He followed that win with televised wins over "Bigfoot" Martin and William Morris, but was never able to overcome the stigma of the Ellis loss. He was not taken seriously as a contender even after the wins. Then end came in 1994, when Tony lost a close, controversial decision to James Thunder for the IBO heavyweight championship. The loss to Thunder finished his final run as a contender, and he went on to lose to Alex Zolkin and Brain Nielsen in 1995.

August 19, 1993—Sedalia, Missouri
John "Hogg Man" Sargent (17–0, 12 KOs) vs. Carl McGrew
   (3–7, 0 KOs)
Favorite: Sargent
Result: McGrew won a questionable six-round decision.

After winning seventeen straight fights, John "Hogg Man" Sargent appeared on the verge of breaking into the world rankings and landing a big money fight. Although widely unknown by most boxing fans, he was in fact winning over a handful of boxing insiders, and these experts felt that he was the best Native American heavyweight in the world (surpassing Joe Hipp). But a curious thing happened just as he began being mentioned as a potential opponent for George Foreman: he lost his desire. What initially appeared a brief trip back to his home at the White Earth Indian Reservation became an eighteen-month layoff that saw Sargent return to many of his old bad habits. Sargent's problems with alcoholism resurfaced as he began to drink heavily, and by the time he returned to the ring, his conditioning had deteriorated considerably. Although he never possessed a particularly svelte physique, he had worked his weight down from the high 240s to 230 pounds. But by August 1993, he had ballooned up to his highest weight ever, a soft 259 pounds. It was clear that Sargent needed to ease into a return to the ring, which wouldn't be too hard considering he was no longer a potential candidate for any big money fight. A fighter once was on the verge of contention, he was now back to square one. Although he landed his first comeback fight on the undercard of an ESPN televised fight, it was a non-televised affair that few boxing fans would have the opportunity to see. For Team Sargent, it was not necessarily a bad thing for the rusty "Hogg Man." What he didn't need at this point was the exposure but rather an easy opponent who would help him shake off eighteen months of ring rust—someone like Carl McGrew.

McGrew appeared to be the perfect foil, a limited journeyman with little actual boxing skill and almost no power despite his 6'6" frame. What he did have was some durability: only two fighters had stopped him, prospects Edward Escobedo and King Ipitan, and only Ipitan blew him out (stopping him in the first round). It was just what Sargent needed, someone who could give him a few rounds of work without threatening him. Even McGrew's conditioning (which saw him weigh in at a career low 268 pounds, down from over 300) was not enough to worry Sargent.

Sargent was so confident of victory that he didn't press his tall opponent in the opening round, electing instead to feel him out. McGrew worked behind a slapping left jab that was as ineffective as his activity in throwing it. Inside the first minute, McGrew did an Ali-style wiggle then quickly moved him out of harm's way before Sargent punished him for his disrespect. Sargent's rather sluggish start prompted ESPN commentator Barry Tompkins to observe that he (John) was "having a little trouble getting untracked here." Although McGrew's jab lacked much pop and was not particularly attractive, he would unleash a loud grunt each time he threw it, an action that would help mask the ineffectiveness of his punches to the judges. Within the final three minutes, McGrew began to incorporate the right hand into his offense against Sargent, who was just moving forward and eating Carl's punches without throwing any of his own, allowing Carl to steal a crucial round.

Recognizing his mistake in the first, John upped the pressure in the second. After McGrew threw an ineffective flurry in the opening seconds of the round, Sargent waded in and fired a left hook that sent the mouthpiece of McGrew flying into the air. Sargent then did what he did best—attacking the body of "Too Mean" McGrew, shaking Carl up almost at once. However, the ring rust and conditioning began to come into effect for Sargent, who attacked with single shots rather than combinations. Although John effectively used his left hook, it was not enough to drop Carl. When Sargent hit McGrew on the break in the final minute of the round, it allowed McGrew a valuable time out to regroup and put Sargent in the referee's doghouse, something that would also play a role in the decision.

McGrew returned to his strategy of pumping his ineffective left jab in the third round while grunting loudly (attracting the attention of the judges). Sargent began to mix up his attack both upstairs and downstairs with a bit more effectiveness. At 2:07 of the round he briefly froze McGrew with a left hook upstairs, but then made a costly mistake by firing two low blows that prompted referee Ross Strada to intercede. Although it was the first, Strada took a point from Sargent. As soon as the fight resumed, McGrew fired a quick upstairs combination that, although not hurting Sargent, did prompt him to cover up. It was McGrew's best moment of the fight and turned what would have been a 10–9 round for Sargent into a 10–8 round for McGrew. That with the first round gave McGrew a two-point lead on the scorecards and put Sargent in serious trouble despite controlling most of the fight. But the body shots of Sargent began to seriously wear out McGrew in the fourth. After starting the round with his usual noisy combinations in the opening seconds of the round, Sargent fired a hard right hand that shook up Carl and for the first time had him holding on. Sargent, a fighter who tended to rely of the left hook, suddenly realized that there was an opening for it and began to pump it in earnest. Suddenly McGrew's offense completely shut down as he held on and tried to keep Sargent's arms from throwing punches. The once-inactive Sargent was now doing all the work as McGrew held and leaned on his shorter opponent. Although McGrew again tried to flurry at the bell, it was not enough to steal the round. It was such a dominant round that Barry Tompkins commented at the start of the fifth that "he's [McGrew] going to have to find something . . . that has not really been there almost at all." McGrew tried to force his way back into the fight, using the jab again, but Sargent found another effective weapon that worked, the right uppercut. It seemed to seal that fate of McGrew, whose energy level had dropped to almost nothing. With the exception of the first round and the final seconds of the third, Sargent controlled the entire fight. By the end of the round all McGrew was doing was holding, and as he returned to his corner his trainer Bill Benton screamed at him "you want this fight? You got to win this round!" It was enough to motivate the badly winded McGrew to come back fairly well in the sixth, moving and jabbing much like he did in the first. But it still appeared too little too late as Sargent picked it up again in the final minute of the fight. McGrew, to his credit, tried to answer in kind but clearly lost the exchanges, the round, and seemingly the fight.

But in boxing, there is seldom a sure thing. Although most ringsiders felt that Sargent won a lopsided decision, the one-point deduction proved costly as McGrew won a close, questionable six-round decision.

For McGrew, it was the biggest win of his career, and although nobody believed that he would emerge as a prospect, some boxing insiders began to openly wonder if a "new" Marion Wilson was born, a fighter whose chin could provide an excellent test for the younger guns of the division. He was given the perfect opportunity to answer those questions when he was chosen as an opponent for an undefeated puncher one month later. Samson Po'uha was widely being seen as one of the better punching prospects in the heavyweight division, and the conventional wisdom was that if McGrew could take him the distance for the first time he could conceivably forge a career as a "chin," something that could in fact be profitable despite the lack of glory involved. (Everett Martin earned a very comfortable living doing just that.) But Po'uha's power proved too much for McGrew, who was felled in the opening round. Although he would go the distance in his next three fights, he would end up losing all of them. In fact, the win over Sargent would be his last. He went on to lose his last nineteen fights over four years (including eleven by knockout).

For John Sargent, the controversial nature of the loss disgusted and disillusioned him. He abandoned his training regime as well as the sport, again disappearing from the ring—this time for over two years. When he finally returned to the ring he lacked any of the desire that marked his early career: he didn't train and continued to drink excessively. Hoping to restore his desire, his manager Ron Peterson let him fight several overmatched foes in 1995, but with Sargent's weight now pushing three hundred pounds, it was clear that he would not make much noise in the sport unless he lost well over fifty pounds. After winning five meaningless fights over three years, Sargent again abandoned the sport. But in 1999 he was presented a fight that promised to revitalize his career if he could finally put it all together. Chris Byrd, reeling from his knockout loss to Ike Ibeabuchi in his previous fight, needed an opponent for his homecoming fight in Mount Pleasant, Michigan. His team contacted Peterson, who realized that it could be just the thing to motivate Sargent. Petersen felt that if John were in shape, he could surprise a Chris Byrd who he was sure was not taking Sargent seriously. Unfortunately for Peterson, Chris Byrd wasn't the only one who wasn't taking John Sargent seriously; John Sargent himself was also not taking the fight seriously. He failed to show up for training at all and arrived to fight in atrocious shape. After running out of gas in the second round, Sargent quit. By the time he reemerged again in 2003 most boxing insiders in Minnesota considered Sargent the biggest disappointments in the history of Minnesota boxing. Although he found himself in a meaningless title fight (for the IBU heavyweight championship) later that year, a seventeen-second knockout loss to Shannon Briggs in that fight proved to everyone that Sargent missed his one chance at glory, and that he would never get another opportunity like the one he squandered.

September 4, 1993—Las Vegas, Nevada
Tim Puller (10–1, 5 KOs) vs. William Morris (9–10–1, 1 KO)
Favorite: Puller
Result: Morris won an eight-round unanimous decision.

For boxing fans, the emergence of Tim "The Hebrew Hammer" Puller didn't exactly bring back memories of Muhammad Ali or Larry Holmes. Although his power was good, it was hardly awe inspiring, and with a lack of speed, an atrocious defense, and a somewhat suspect chin, the assumption was that he would soon be removed from the list of "prospects." In fact, it appeared as if his career had been derailed before it even got off the ground when cruiserweight opponent Sim Warrior stopped him in the fifth round in his seventh pro fight. But redemption came in the form of Bill Corrigan in his next fight. The fight with Corrigan was featured on the undercard of Joe Hipp vs. Jesse Shelby, an ESPN-televised fight in February 1992. Although neither fighter was regarded as much of a prospect, it was widely seen as an even matchup between limited brawlers. When Puller rallied from near disaster in the second round (in which he was nearly TKO'ed) to knock out Corrigan in the fourth, ESPN was won over. Puller found himself on another ESPN-televised fight against Tim Morrison, brother of Tommy. Puller again shined in front of the camera, blitzing Morrison in the second round. The win over Morrison was followed by another impressive win, a decision victory over Sim Warrior, avenging his only defeat. By mid-1993 it was clear that Puller was moving along rapidly, and the assumption was that he was ready to take on some of the more recognizable "opponents" in the division. But his management also recognized his serious shortcomings, and the question arose as to which fighter could allow Puller to shine, while not exposing his poor defense and, more importantly, his soft chin.

Enter William Morris. Morris was widely regarded as a decent, if not spectacular journeyman. He started his career with six wins in his first seven fights but quickly stumbled after jumping up to the heavyweight division. He had earned some credit for his durability, lasting the distance in all but two of his losses (one being in his pro debut and the other coming in the eighth round to hard punching prospect Phil Jackson). Although he had recently scored his biggest professional win, stopping Paul Lockhart for his only knockout, on *Cedric Kushner's Heavyweight Explosion*, he followed the win with an ugly decision loss to John Andrade two months later. The Andrade fight ensured that he remained at the bottom of the "journeyman" barrel, and he seemed an ideal pick for Puller's appearance on the *Heavyweight Explosion*. He was somewhat recognized, would most likely give an honest effort, and probably go the distance. But with only one knockout, it seemed clear that he couldn't take advantage of Puller's weaknesses.

But even if Morris couldn't capitalize on Puller's soft chin, he had no problem taking advantage of his lack of defense. After winning the opening round with greater activity, Morris soon discovered that Puller was unable to seriously hurt him, nor match him punch for punch. Morris began to up the pressure, and by the end of the second round, Puller was sporting a bloody nose. Although Puller closed the gap in the third round, Morris still emerged from the round as the aggressor, even opening up a small cut on the right cheek of his 6'6" opponent.

Realizing that a brawl was not working in his favor, Puller began to utilize his ten-inch reach advantage in the fourth, pumping the jab and trying to keep Morris at bay. But Puller's defense was just as bad from the outside as it was on the inside, and Morris began to fire (and land) wild shots from halfway across the ring. With less than a minute left in the round, Morris began to overcome the jab of Puller as well, pressuring his way inside with quick combinations to the head. In fact, Morris's control of the fight was so complete that the journeyman began to showboat in the fifth round. He began to drop his hand to his waist as he stood in front of Puller, but Tim was still unable to find the exposed chin of Morris. It was enough to cause "The Hebrew Hammer" to succumb to frustration, as he wildly exploded on Morris to little avail. Morris quickly stopped Puller in his tracks with a big right hand and came back with his own wild combination that actually staggered Puller with less than thirty seconds left in the round, and seconds after a break in the action that occurred when the tape on Puller's glove came loose.

The sixth round saw more of the same as Puller tried desperately to establish the jab while Morris easily worked his way inside with quick combinations upstairs and solid counterpunches. Although there was little question that Puller needed a knockout to win, it was also becoming increasingly apparent that Puller was unable to hit his surprisingly elusive target. After another break in the action at the end of the seventh round, Morris again jumped on Puller to put an exclamation point on another dominant round. Still, the journeyman Morris was no stranger to hometown decisions going against him, and he took no chances in the eighth round. Although Puller came out desperate and strong, Morris did not run from his bigger opponent, instead choosing to stand in front of him. As soon as Puller slowed down, Morris responded with his own right hand power shots, which had yet to miss and were considerably more effective than Puller's. Another overhand right stunned Puller halfway through the round, but Puller showed grit in bouncing back. Nonetheless, he was unable to recover enough to win the round, or the fight. When the bell rang, ending the eighth round, there was little question as to which fighter won the fight, and the fans at ringside were only left to wonder if it were possible for the Vegas judges to rob Morris of such a clear-cut victory. The concern proved unwarranted as the judges had the decision on the mark, with two judges having it a shutout while the third awarded Puller one round.

For Morris, the win over Puller was the first step in a brief run as a prospect-buster. He followed the Puller win with a decision victory over

Carl Williams (not the noteworthy contender, but the journeyman of the same name) and then with another upset, this time over top prospect Ray Anis (page 131). It wasn't until he lost in a ten-round decision to Tony Tubbs on *USA's Tuesday Night Fights* in October 1994 that his streak was brought to an end.

For Puller, the loss proved damaging, but hardly fatal to his career. In fact, he found himself back in the run as a minor league prospect when he stopped rugged journeyman Sherman Griffin the following year. The Griffin win was followed by an ugly ten-round decision win over Mike Dixon on *USA's Tuesday Night Fights* in 1995, a win that set up his first big fight against Chris Byrd. But despite the streak, his deficiencies in the ring still remained, and where William Morris exposed Puller, Chris Byrd totally destroyed him in five rounds. It was a loss that introduced Puller to the status of opponent—a status further confirmed with knockout losses to Tim Witherspoon and Lou Savarese in his next two fights.

October 22, 1993—Boise, Idaho
Jimmy Ellis (20–3–1, 19 KOs) vs. Ladislao Mijangos (22–15, 17 KOs)
Favorite: Ellis
Result: Mijangos won via first-round TKO.

For former NFL football scab Jimmy Ellis, his shocking first-round KO over Tony Tubbs (page 102) failed to translate into a newfound respect within his new profession. Most had assumed that Tubbs, who had a history of getting caught cold early in fights (like against Mike Tyson and Lionel Butler) was simply caught off guard by Ellis, who realized that he had to jump on the former champ lest he be out-boxed and most likely stopped. But Ellis was determined to cash in on his win and remained active, maximizing his chances at getting another big money fight like the one he had against George Foreman. Although it was unlikely that a world ranking was in the books (even with his win over Tubbs), Ellis was certainly a likely candidate for a main event against a Larry Holmes on *USA's Tuesday Night Fights*, or a high profile fight against Tony Tucker on one of Don King's Showtime cards. It seemed likely that he was about to resurface on cable, and the first step in resur-

recting his career was a win in front of his hometown crowd on the undercard of the Prime Networks broadcast of Rafael and Gabe Ruelas
against Manuel Hernandez and Mike Grow, respectively.

Although nobody anticipated Ellis to look particularly dominant, and
few thought he could duplicate his surprise win over Tony Tubbs
against another ranked fighter, Mijangos seemed a safe opponent for
Ellis. Ellis had indeed showed that it didn't take much to defeat him
when he lost to Joe Brewer and Tony Willis, but Mijangos had a reputation in boxing as quite arguably one of the worst heavyweights in the
sport. He looked somewhat silly, and with fifteen losses, there was little
on paper to indicate that assessment was incorrect. But the view of Mijangos as a clown and a completely inept fighter was a bit harsh; it had
come when he fought Tommy Morrison the previous year. In that fight,
ESPN commentator Barry Tompkins seemed to light-heartedly mock
Mijangos throughout the fight (which indecently ended in the first
round) and made a statement after the fight ended that a punching bag
would have put up a better fight. Although it was a fair assessment of
Mijangos's chances against a fighter like Morrison, it created a somewhat unjust reputation of Mijangos as the worst of the worst in the
heavyweight division, something that Mijangos was not. Although he
was a club fighter, the type that fighters like Morrison or George Foreman would knock out with relative ease, he was no worse than fighters
like Kimmuel Odum or Art Card, fighters whom Ellis avoided in his career. Mijangos even briefly held a belt when he won the Mexican heavyweight championship in 1985. Ultimately, outside of the Tubbs fight,
the Foreman fight, and his fight with Tony Willis (which he lost), Ladislao Mijangos was undoubtedly the toughest opponent that Ellis had yet
to face in the ring—a clear indication of the type of opposition Ellis had
thus faced as a boxer.

When the fight began, Ellis attempted to come out strong. He apparently believed in his power, based on his victory over Tubbs. But it
quickly became clear that, despite the Tubbs knockout, Ellis lacked real
knockout power. He failed to rattle Mijangos with any of his shots and
began to show signs of having trouble with Ladislao's return fire. When
several of Ladislao's power shots snuck through, Ellis completely unraveled. He proceeded to get battered by the Mexican and was dropped less
than halfway through the round. When he arose, he was unable to keep

the onrushing Latino off, and became clearly disoriented when he assumed a defenseless posture, prompting the referee to wave the fight off at 2:04 of the first round.

Ellis, who had already been exposed by Foreman, was completely exposed again. However, unlike when he fought Foreman, this time there was no coming back. He tried to rebound with another televised fight against a high profile opponent when he took on undefeated Shannon Briggs the following year, but was again stopped in the opening round. The loss was humiliating and decisive, and effectively ended his career.

Ladislao Mijangos never fought again on cable TV, but the win over Ellis was a redeeming victory. For a club fighter who was regarded as a joke, the win proved that even though he would never compete against the top-ranked fighters in the world, the Mark Gastineaus and Peter McNeeleys might be well served to avoid him. Although he would return to his losing ways after the Ellis fight, few who saw his win over Ellis would have agreed with Barry Tompkins's assessment of him. He would not have been outperformed that night by a punching bag.

October 29, 1993—Tulsa, Oklahoma
Tommy "The Duke" Morrison (38–1, 33 KOs) vs. Michael Bentt
   (10–1, 5 KOs)
Favorite: Morrison
Result: Bentt scored a first-round TKO.

For Tommy "The Duke" Morrison, his decisive twelve-round decision victory over George Foreman gave the power to silence his many critics. Against one of the most devastating punchers of any era, Morrison abandoned the face-first style of his previous thirty-seven fights and actually showed the world a versatile Tommy Morrison, one who could box and move. Critics who felt Morrison's chin could not hold up (citing his knockdowns at the hands of Carl "The Truth" Williams as well as his knockout loss to Ray Mercer) were proven wrong when the devastating punches of "Big" George failed to seriously hurt the supposedly china-chinned Morrison. Also, for a fighter who usually fizzled out after the fourth round, Morrison showed surprising endurance in coasting the full twelve-round distance.

When "The Duke" signed to fight vulnerable-looking Lennox Lewis on March 5, 1994, for a whopping $7.5 million, it hardly seemed a mismatch. Lewis, who struggled mightily against fellow Briton Frank Bruno just twenty-eight days earlier, had become increasingly discredited since his stunning second-round knockout over Donovan "Razor" Ruddock in 1992. Though Morrison had many struggles himself since his loss to Mercer, few questioned his power, and many experts (outside of those who resided in Europe) felt he was a much better fighter than Bruno. In fact, *KO Magazine* went so far as to claim on their cover that the real winner of the Lewis-Bruno fight was in fact Morrison.[4] Las Vegas bettors agreed: the sports world saw the odds for Lewis dip to a mere 2–1.

Morrison wanted to cash in on his newly found status as a boxing superstar, and in a move that scared almost everyone involved in the March 5 super fight, he decided to take on a few "tune-ups." Morrison's first tune-up, a title defense against Mike Williams, seemed to be safe enough. Williams was coming off a KO loss to Alex Garcia and seemed a perfect foil for Morrison: a fighter with a glossy record but zero chance of winning. Also, he had some history with Morrison, playing a minor role opposite "The Duke" in *Rocky V*. But when that fight fell through at the last minute, Williams was replaced by the personable, but hardly world-class, Tim Tomasheck. Tomasheck, who had already lost to Morrison KO victims Dan Murphy, Ric Enis, and Jerry "Wimpy" Halstead, gave Morrison a surprisingly tough fight, but few held it against Morrison. Morrison was already dealing with the distractions of his big money payday as well as the mental letdown of having his original opponent replaced on the day of the fight with a fighter whose style was in sharp contrast to the one for which he had been preparing.

Morrison's next opponent, Michael Bentt, had people worried. He was a five-time amateur national champion, and perhaps the best amateur fighter never to go to the Olympics. Though he struggled early in his career, losing to Jerry Jones via a first-round knockout in his pro debut, he was beginning to show signs of pulling his career together. He was coming off a ten-round decision victory over Mark Wills, a win that catapulted him to the top ten in the WBO rankings. Although nobody

---

[4] On cover of *KO Magazine,* February 1994.

regarded Mark Wills as Morrison's equal, Bentt showed grit in winning the fight with a broken right hand (although questions lingered about if Bentt's hand could have fully healed is such a short amount of time). Also, Morrison's antics outside the ring were legendary, and people wondered if Morrison could keep away from the ladies and parties long enough to take Bentt seriously. Rumors of Tommy's wild ways surfaced after each of his fights, and though they often explained away a poor performance, it had been some time since Tommy entered a fight with nothing to prove to the world. Nonetheless, Morrsion was to be paid about one million dollars, an amazing payday for such a perceived non-competitive fight.

When both fighters entered the ring, Bentt appeared relaxed and confident, chewing gum and showing no signs of fear. This despite the fact that this was his first HBO-televised fight and that he was fighting in Tommy's back yard. Morrison's ring entrance was an event in and of itself—involving fireworks—and some ringsiders openly wondered if the fight would match the entrance in length.

It didn't. When the bell rang, Morrison came out with the apparent strategy of methodically breaking down Bentt. He didn't seem wild, and it seemed only a matter of time before his left hook found a home on Bentt's chin. That strategy lasted all of thirty seconds however, until Tommy landed his first left hook. Although the punch didn't land cleanly, Bentt, who was already on the ropes, fell back. Morrison abandoned caution and began winging punches wildly, despite the fact that Bentt appeared more off balance than hurt by the hook. Bentt wisely covered up during Morrison's offensive explosion as if he was just trying to survive the onslaught, but he soon saw an opening and jumped on it when he countered a Morrison left hook with a left uppercut of his own (which missed) followed by a picture-perfect straight right that landed flush on Tommy's chin. Morrison's knee's buckled badly, and he barely remained upright. When Bentt saw how hurt Tommy was, he exploded with a combination that floored Morrison with over two minutes remaining in the round.

Tommy rose at the count of four with a look of partial disgust and confusion on his face, perhaps realizing that his seven-million-dollar payday against Lennox Lewis was in serious jeopardy. To his credit, Morrison came out like the warrior he was. Rather than try to survive and tie up the onrushing Bentt (something he probably should have done), Morrison came out looking to pick up where he left off. He threw a powerful left hook, hoping to match Bentt's homerun with one of his own. But Bentt would not be denied; the left hook failed to so much as slow down the onrushing Bentt, and a quick combination dropped Morrison a second time a few seconds later.

With a little less than half the first round completed, Morrison needed to avoid another knockdown to avoid the mandatory three-knockdown rule. Again he rose at the referee's count of four, and again he came out winging left hooks. Several Bentt right hands had Morrison backpedaling into the ropes, but Tommy never attempted to initiate a clinch. A left uppercut sealed his fate, when it snapped his head back and deposited him on the canvas for a third, and final, time.

In less than two minutes the heavyweight division was turned upside down. Forgotten in the fight was Morrison's victory over George Foreman and Bentt's loss to Jerry Jones. Forgotten as well was the idea of a Lewis-Morrison super fight. Morrison, it appeared, had been completely exposed and discredited.

For Morrison, it proved to be perhaps his most devastating loss. Although he was knocked out by Ray Mercer a little over two years before, he seemed to be in control against Mercer until his nerves got the best of him and he ran out of steam in the fourth round before getting stopped in the fifth. It was easy to find something positive in that loss, since it seemed that had his endurance held up, he might very well have gone on to beat Mercer. Besides, Ray was a highly regarded contender. Bentt was not. There was no explaining away this loss. There was nothing positive to take from it.

Nonetheless, despite the loss, "The Duke" proved to be a resourceful fighter inside and outside the ring and rebounded. He looked like a mere shell of his former self in scoring knockouts over Tui Toia and Brian Scott. When Sherman Griffin extended him the distance and Ross Puritty dropped him twice in securing a ten-round draw, most assumed that Morrison was finished. But a 1995 knockout over Donovan "Razor" Ruddock resurrected his career and landed him the fight with Lewis, although for a much smaller purse. When Lewis stopped Morrison in the sixth round, it appeared that his career would probably be over again. But then Don King entered the picture, and considering how

Don King controlled the heavyweight division at the time, as well as Mike Tyson, one more big fight seemed in line for the blonde bomber. But then Morrison encountered an opponent that would finally end his career as a boxer: human immunodeficiency virus. Just days before a scheduled fight against Arthur Weathers, Tommy was diagnosed with the deadly virus and forced to retire from the ring. Although he did fight once more overseas (against Marcus Rhode), Tommy's career could simply not overcome the stigma of his infection. Within several years the articulate and likeable Morrison appeared to be on an out-of-control downward spiral. Most of his millions were squandered, and legal troubles began to emerge with alarming frequency. By 2000 he was in prison, and in what many regarded as one of the most disturbing interviews in boxing history, Morrison gave a prison interview in which he appeared incoherent and confused and made disturbing comments regarding his infection, his unprotected sex with his wife, his failed relationships with women and family, and his desire to return to acting. Upon Morrison's release, however, he appeared to finally settle down, engaging in a quiet life with his wife and family and avoiding the public spotlight.

For Michael Bentt the fight initially seemed to give him instant credibility as a legitimate heavyweight contender. However, his brief reign as WBO champion was mired in criticism. George Foreman, who regarded Bentt with contempt prior to the fight, immediately dismissed his victory over Morrison, claiming, "Bentt is less than an average fighter." When unsubstantiated rumors that Morrison entered the ring with a hangover surfaced, it also seemed to diminish Bentt's accomplishment. Also, Morrison's determination to land an immediate rematch, going so far as to offer Bentt a complete role reversal in pay (with Bentt getting the one-million-dollar check while Morrison would receive about ten percent of that) gave many boxing fans the impression that Bentt might just go down in history as Tommy Morrison's personal Leon Spinks. But Bentt believed in himself, and many boxing writers were impressed. When Bentt signed to fight Herbie Hide in his first defense, most insiders made him the favorite. Hide, who had wowed British Boxing fans for over four years in padding his record to 25–0, with 24 KOs, was a relative unknown to American boxing fans. But Hide was a legitimate heavyweight prospect with quick feet, quicker hands, and surprisingly stunning power for such a small man (although Riddick Bowe would later find his soft chin). When Bentt struggled in training camp, many insiders began to question whether he could beat the young Brit. Shortly before the fight, a rumor surfaced that Bentt had been knocked out in sparring by King Ipitan, an event that would require the match's postponement under British boxing rules. That threat didn't materialize, and Bentt found himself ruthlessly overwhelmed by Hide. When Hide finally ended Michel Bentt's reign as WBO champion, he also ended his career as a boxer. Bentt was removed from the ring in a stretcher and never again fought as a professional. Boxing fans did see him in the ring again eight years later when he played Sonny Liston in the Will Smith movie *Ali*.

November 6, 1993—Las Vegas, Nevada
Riddick Bowe (34–0, 29 KOs) vs. Evander Holyfield
　　(29–1, 22 KOs)
Favorite: Bowe
Result: Holyfield won a twelve-round majority decision.

For fight fans, it appeared that boxing had been introduced to her newest heavyweight superstar in Riddick Bowe. Boxing writers had already groomed him as the next superstar as early as 1990, when he knocked out Art Tucker and Pinklon Thomas. With a dominant unanimous decision over Evander Holyfield (for the undisputed heavyweight championship) in November 1992, it seemed that he had lived up to their high expectations. Although Holyfield had become increasingly discredited after less-than-spectacular title defenses over Bert Cooper and Larry Holmes, he was still "the man who beat the man who beat the man." Though it seemed that he would go down in history as a transitional champion—who kept the title warm between championship dynasties—his gritty performance against the bigger, stronger Bowe seemed enough to justify one more championship fight before the inevitable slide into obscurity.

After struggling against Alex Stewart five months prior, it looked to many boxing experts that Holyfield was a spent commodity—that after the beating he took from Riddick Bowe he would never again be a championship-caliber fighter. When fans also began calling for Evander's retirement after the Stewart fight, it seemed to many in the Bowe camp that if there would be a Bowe-Holyfield II, it would have to take place soon. The concern was that Holyfield would further discredit himself or might even be defeated, if he was allowed to take one more tune-up fight. This despite the fact that Holyfield, strategically, fought the smartest fight he had in years against Stewart—a rare occurrence because he didn't fight against Stewart to please the fans per se, but to fight the perfect fight against a relatively docile opponent.

As a result, the announcement of a second fight between Bowe and Holyfield didn't electrify boxing fans. Although fans were enthralled when Evander came back from the brink of a knockout loss in the previous fight to have Bowe holding on for dear life in the tenth, it seemed a tall order for him to repeat the comeback. In boxing, after all, it was a commonly held adage that when a fighter got beat in a fight, he usually lost the rematch more decisively. Besides, it was not Holyfield who was regarded as the best opponent for Riddick Bowe, but rather the WBC champion Lennox Lewis. Lewis was awarded the WBC belt when Bowe refused to make his first title defense against him. In an attempt to discredit Lewis's claim to the title, Riddick and manager Rock Newman staged a brilliantly effective press conference at which Bowe dropped the WBC title belt into a trashcan, telling Lewis in no uncertain terms that if he so wished to claim it, he could do so. It undoubtedly took a great deal of the luster off Lennox Lewis's claim to be a co-champion, but when Bowe made his first defense against a badly faded and undeserving Michael Dokes, it seemed to raise questions about who was the better fighter. But a pair of ugly wins over Tony Tucker and Frank Bruno brought the Lewis pedestal down a few notches, and boxing was left with what amounted to a dilemma. Although Lewis was looking increasingly ordinary, his opposition was fairly solid. Bowe, on the other hand, was looking dominant against highly suspect opponents. (After Dokes, he fought Jesse Ferguson.)

By early 1993 Holyfield had become yesterday's news, but for Riddick Bowe he was an ace in the hole. A second win over Evander would eliminate the criticism that he was fighting weaker opposition than Lennox, and most assumed that Bowe's win would most likely be by knockout this time. It seemed like such a safe bet for Riddick that he would win again that he trained without the passion of his first fight with

Holyfield. In his first fight with Holyfield, Bowe had weighed in at a relatively svelte 235 pounds, but against Dokes and Ferguson he weighed in at a somewhat meatier 243 and 244 respectively. Although Dokes and Ferguson were easy fighters to disregard, Holyfield was one not to be taken lightly. However, Bowe's progressive weight increase continued as he prepared for his second fight with Holyfield. After ballooning up to 285 pounds, he settled at a career-high of 246 pounds. Although he looked fit, it was a clear indication that Bowe was not as well prepared for Evander the second time.

Evander also put on some weight for his rematch with Bowe—he weighed in at 217 pounds—but the added twelve pounds were a welcome sight for boxing fans. In the first fight, he had weighed in at a mere 205 pounds, clearly too little for a modern heavyweight when, against Bowe, he appeared too small to compete. His punches failed to seriously hurt the bigger man, and eventually the size and power difference seemed to wear him down badly in the later rounds. Although most felt that more movement and boxing was the key for Evander—something that he had repeatedly been unable to do, always allowing himself to be dragged into a slugfest—the extra weight seemed to indicate that he would be better able to damage Bowe. Holyfield's acquisition of trainer Emanuel Steward was also looked upon as a plus, although few could predict how much of an advantage it would become. Although Holyfield had two of the most respected trainers in the game in George Benton and Lou Duva, he seemed to grow increasingly distant from them in fights, going so far as to virtually ignore the duo's (sound) advice in his fight with Bert Cooper.

In picking Holyfield, it looked as if Riddick was picking the softest touch among the highly respected heavyweights on the scene, and though his waistline brought the Vegas odds down from 5–1 to 7–2 in his favor, it was not a question of if he would win, but whether he would win via knockout.

When the fight began, it indeed appeared as if Evander Holyfield had learned his lesson from the first fight with Bowe. Although Bowe jumped on him at the opening bell, Evander remained defensive, not allowing himself to get caught up in a slugfest. The fight quickly turned into a chess match of sorts, with both fighters exchanging jabs but little else. Holyfield jumped in with a nice combo at 1:20 of the round, but mainly he was sticking to his game plan of moving side-to-side, using speed and the jab, and avoiding a brawl. The second round saw more of the same, with both fighters relying on the jab—Bowe stalking behind his, while Holyfield continued his attempt to control the fight, adding some movement. But it was becoming increasingly apparent that Evander's jab was not quite quick or long enough to reach its target before Bowe's. Even with the jab Bowe appeared the superior fighter.

After more of the same in the third, Evander made a fateful decision at the bell starting the fourth round by marching into the bigger man, looking to initiate a slugfest. When Bowe quickly moved him back with a right uppercut followed by a left hook, it seemed as if Holyfield was making a serious error, but he began a forward motion that never relented. When Bowe was tagged by a right hand with forty seconds remaining in the round, it became apparent that Evander could indeed hold his own in a street fight with Bowe. Evander then revealed a strategy that would go on to win him the fight. When the timekeeper pounded the ring, indicating that the round had only ten seconds left, Holyfield exploded, throwing hard hooks and backing Bowe up to the ropes at the bell. When Bowe tried to land the last punch after the bell, Evander responded by continuing his onslaught, initiating a brawl that lasted nearly ten seconds after the bell sounded. (Referee Mills Lane and Emanuel Steward broke the two fighters apart.) Bowe, sporting a small cut over his left eye, returned to his corner knowing he was in a fight.

Bowe started the fifth round nervously and fought defensively, allowing Evander to out-jab him and pick away at the cut. Although the round appeared relatively close going into the final minute, once again Holyfield upped the pressure at the round's end, staggering Bowe with a right hand followed by a left hook in the last twenty seconds. Although a clearly hurt Bowe tried to hold on, Evander continued to punish him with hard shots until the bell saved Bowe. The sixth also started slowly, with both fighters moving and throwing occasional jabs, but neither seriously initiating an exchange. However, Evander continued his effective strategy of slowing upping the pressure as each second of the round passed. Bowe tried to imitate Evander by coming on strong at the end of the round, but it was not enough to steal the round back. It looked as if Evander was wearing down the bigger man.

Fans sensed that the seventh round would be memorable when Evander landed a solid right hand on the chin of Riddick Bowe, who responded by firing back with a nice combo that had Evander covering up. It appeared that Bowe was turning things around, and fans came to their feet as the fight developed. Unfortunately, one fan was not on his feet. At 1:10 of the seventh round the fight was interrupted when James Miller (AKA "Fan Man"), of Henderson, Nevada, dropped toward the ring via motorized paraglider. Miller, wearing a red jumpsuit and a white crash helmet, became entangled in the top two ropes when his parachute caught on the overhead lights. He failed to land inside the ring and fell back into the crowd where several fans and members of Riddick Bowe's security team gave him a warm, Brownsville-style welcome that (along with the fall from the ring) rendered him unconscious. In a heartbeat the fight was on hold, and fans were left wondering what could have been going through Fan Man's head. When it appeared that his neck was broken, medical personnel took utmost care in removing him, adding to the delay. Both fighters were forced to sit in their corners for twenty-one minutes in the relatively chilly fifty-three degree night air. When the seventh round resumed it appeared as if Holyfield was in control, although with the delay it was hard to say who actually won the round: the three judges were in disagreement on the scorecard.

The eighth round saw more of the same fighting style, with Bowe failing to press his advantage while Holyfield danced and upped the ante as the round progressed. With less than a minute to go, Evander landed a left-hook-and-straight-right combo that had Bowe holding on. A solid last minute by "The Real Deal" Holyfield ended up winning him the round on all three scorecards.

However, the fight was far from over, and Bowe showed some of the power and grit that helped him defeat Evander the first time around when he rattled the "Real Deal" in the ninth round. Evander was left to back up and clinch his way out of trouble for most of the round. Although Holyfield came back towards the round's end (again), it was still not enough for Evander to capture the round on any of the judges' scorecards.

Evander resumed his brilliant display of boxing superiority over Bowe through the next two rounds, narrowly capturing them both.

Going into the final round, it seemed as if Evander was on top of a razor-thin decision victory, but Bowe came alive to win the final round big, staggering Evander with a right hand halfway through the round. With less than a minute left in the round Evander was holding on for dear life as Bowe tried desperately to keep the title with a knockout. When both fighters continued to fire away at the bell ending the fight, Manny Steward tackled his fighter (Holyfield) to avoid the possibility of a disqualification or injury. Nonetheless, Bowe appeared to win even the exchange after the round, and many ringsiders were openly wondering if it was perhaps enough to squeeze out the victory. As it turned out, it was one of the most dramatic and suspenseful decisions in heavyweight history: almost everyone had the fight within a point or two. The suspense was added to when the judges (for once) seemed to be in agreement. Chuck Giampa scored it an even 114–114, while Patricia Jarman and Jerry Roth had it at a razor-thin 115–114 and 115–113, respectively. Fans were breathless with anticipation until Michael Buffer announced the "once again heavyweight champion of the world . . . Evander 'Real Deal' Holyfield!"

Suddenly the heavyweight division was upside down, and boxing was introduced to a new heavyweight rivalry, one that would be the 1990s' version of Ali-Frazier.

With the victory Holyfield suddenly was the hottest heavyweight in the world—something he had never truly been in his career, always fighting under the shadow of Mike Tyson. Evander suddenly seemed a potential hall-of-famer as well, and his lackluster performances against Cooper, Holmes, and Stewart were forgotten. But the magic carpet ride was short-lived, as he lost a decision to undefeated Michael Moorer five months later.

For Riddick Bowe, it hardly seemed a particularly devastating defeat, and most fans were eagerly anticipating a third matchup with Evander Holyfield. But Riddick Bowe became a victim of boxing politics with uncommonly bad luck when Evander Holyfield lost the title in his next fight to Michael Moorer. Bowe continued to remain active, despite this setback, but in his next fight he was nearly disqualified when he hit Buster Mathis Jr. while the smaller man was on the canvas. (The fight was later ruled no-contest.) Just when it appeared that he finally was about to step into the ring with his Olympic archrival Lennox Lewis, his bad luck (and boxing politics) again stepped in to hurt his career after Oliver McCall upset Lennox the following month. After a victory over Olympian Larry Donald, Riddick won the WBO title from Herbie Hide in 1995 and won the third fight in the Holyfield-Bowe trilogy when he knocked out Evander in the eighth round. But after a brutal pair of fights with Andrew Golota, in which he was badly battered before winning by disqualification when Golota ended up repeatedly hitting Riddick low, Riddick retired. With early signs of brain damage from the second Golota fight—after that fight Bowe slurred his speech badly in the post fight interview and never fully regained his speech abilities— his life proceeded to take repeated tragic turns. His attempt to enlist in the Marine Corps in 1997 ended in embarrassment when he quit eleven days into boot camp. Later that year he applied for a job as a school

Riddick Bowe's (center) career ended with a pair of fights against Andrew Golota, including a DQ win after suffering a low blow. *Pat Orr*

guard (which paid $10.49 an hour) and kidnapped his wife the following year (intending to take her from Charlotte, North Carolina, to his home in Maryland). The kidnapping led to an arrest on federal charges. Bowe faced up to ten years in prison, and although he was initially sentenced to only thirty days, his attempt to deny a key element in his defense (that he suffered from a mental disability incurred from repeated punches to the head in his boxing career) led him to prison for considerably longer. It was clear that Bowe had indeed fallen from grace, a tragic turn of events for a fighter groomed as the next superstar of boxing. In the end, it was he, not Holyfield, who became the transitional champion.

The other player in the fight, "Fan Man," ended up spending the night at the University Medical Center, where it was determined that he had not broken his neck, but rather suffered only from "headache." After being released, only three hours later he was quickly booked into the Clark County jail. Unfortunately, the charge (dangerous flying) was a misdemeanor, and Miller was released after posting a $200 bond. In those pre–September 11 days, it seemed a relatively harmless prank to some (although the risk of bringing the lights down on spectators was all too real), and though many complained that it was setting a dangerous precedent—Bowe manager Rock Newman admitted to *Ring Magazine* that he initially thought it could have been a terrorist assassination attempt on one of the dignitaries sitting ringside[5]—Miller got off relatively lightly. He quickly became a sports legend, being parodied on *The Simpsons* and even pulled a similar stunt in the United Kingdom, where he landed on Buckingham Palace. But an illness grounded him from flying, which led to a bout with depression that he was unable to overcome and prompted him to commit suicide in 2003.

December 3, 1993—Bay St. Louis, Mississippi
The People's Choice World Heavyweight Superfights
    Tournament, semifinal fight:
James "Bonecrusher" Smith (39–11–1, 29 KOs) vs. Dan
    Dancuta (9–1, 6 KOs)
Favorite: Smith
Result: Dancuta won a three-round unanimous decision.

---

[5] Jack Welch, "I was in the Neighborhood, So . . ." *Ring Magazine,* March 1994, 42.

When a pair of little-known kick-boxing promoters named Don Arnott and Trevor Wallden announced a one-night sixteen-fighter toughman-style tournament, many in the sport of boxing rolled their eyes. It appeared to be another classic circus show passed off as professional boxing, not unlike George Foreman's five fights against five opponents in one night or Muhammad Ali's foray into pro wrestling. It wasn't that the concept was considered so bad: many boxing fans considered it a dream to pull Lennox Lewis, Evander Holyfield, and Riddick Bowe into a tournament to determine the best heavyweight in the world. But the problem was that tournament included no ranked heavyweight, just a collection a badly faded former champions and contenders and unknown novices with little public appeal. Even with the one-million-dollar purse going to the eventual winner, fighters like Donovan "Razor" Ruddock and Larry Holmes chose to avoid the tournament, citing money issues. Instead, the tournament included three faded former champions (Michael Dokes, Tony Tubbs, and James "Bonecrusher" Smith), several former contenders of note (Henry Tillman, Tyrell Biggs, Jose Ribalta, Bert Cooper, Francesco Damiani, Johnny DuPlooy), only one fighter who was seen as a legitimate prospect (King Ipitan), one who was seen as a complete sideshow act (Joe Savage), and a few fighters with some international credentials but little else to warrant their admission (Yevgeni Sudakov, Derek Williams, Craig Petersen, and Dan Dancuta). The fighters involved appeared so weak that *KO Magazine* featured an article of the upcoming tournament under the headline "A million bucks to the best of the worst."[6]

Initially, the concept appealed to some casual fans who were able to overcome the lack of quality fighters involved. They were asked to call a 900 number to vote for the final fighter to be admitted and to arrange the fights in the tournament's first round. It was a clever, "hands-on" approach that seemed to guarantee a degree of interest. But financial problems soon began to emerge that nearly destroyed the promotion before it got off the ground. Initially the promotion appeared to rest solely on the back of the least-skilled contestant: Joe Savage. Savage, who claimed to be a bare-knuckle boxer in England with a record of 41–0

---

[6] Robert Cassidy, "The People's Choice Heavyweight Tournament," *KO Magazine,* February 1994, 47.

with 41 KOs, attracted the interest of almost all the media personnel covering the fight. But when he pulled out of the tournament citing a wrist injury, the promotion was left without its only marketable fighter. Joe Savage's flight was quickly followed by another departure, one that would prove even more costly: namely that of an unknown businessman from Singapore who also was the major backer of the tournament. As a result Wallden and Arnott were unable to post the $1.4-million bond. Most boxing insiders assumed the tournament would be canceled for lack of funds, but Casino Magic (the venue that planned to host the tournament) bailed it out with a $600,000 investment. The catch, however, was that the payment plan was slashed. Fighters would only make $10,000 per fight, rather than $20,000, and the bonus for first-round knockouts were also slashed in half, to $10,000. Most notably, the winning jackpot fell from just a little over $1 million to $170,000.

Although the tournament was saved, the exodus of fighters from the tournament was crippling. Only nine of the original fifteen remained, and the six replacement fighters were seen as so weak that the tournament lost what little credibility it had. Career journeyman Marshall Tillman was called in, as was Jason Williams, a fighter with no pro experience. Rocky Ray Phillips came in with his somewhat glossy record of 15–1, and so did two unknowns, Leonsio Bueno from the Dominican Republic and Lester Jackson (a fighter with a 5–1–1 record). One-time-prospect Willie Jackson, who saw his star dim after a first round KO loss to Samson Po'uha, was also called in.

The addition of such limited fighters hurt the promotion, but it helped one particular fighter feel a little less overwhelmed. Romanian champion Dan Dancuta was initially seen by many fans as the weakest of the original fifteen fighters in the tournament: he had only nine fights, one of those a loss to the undefeated Larry Donald by way of a six-round decision. Although he had the respected Jesse Reid as his trainer and pulled together a handful of good wins over the likes of undefeated Ed Escobedo, former contender James Broad, and Matthew Brooks, his lack of experience as a pro negated (in the eyes of many) whatever skills he might have possessed as a prospect. Although the addition of such fighters as Jason Williams and Lester Jackson ensured that he was no longer considered the weakest fighter in the tournament, he was still not given much chance against such experienced opponents as Bert Cooper and Tyrell Biggs. Guest commentator Bert Sugar had Dancuta as a whopping 500–1 underdog to win the entire tournament, and few anticipated that he would get past the first or second round.

But Dancuta proved to be one of several dark horses in the tournament. In fact, almost all of the novice fighters in the tournament proved to be considerably more capable than anticipated, and from the first fight until the end of the night the fans, along with veterans themselves, were shocked at the resiliency of many of the younger fighters. James "Bonecrusher" Smith emerged victorious against Lester Jackson, but he was unable to stop, or even drop, the younger man and even emerged from the fight with a small cut. Jason Williams lost by way of split-decision to veteran Marshall Tillman, Yevgeni Sudakov took Biggs the distance and ended up on the losing end of a very questionable decision, and last-minute entry Shane Sutcliffe defeated Ray Phillips in impressive fashion after three lopsided rounds. In fact, the only "rookies" who ended up getting blown out were two of the fighters expected to fare well, namely Willie Jackson (who was stopped in one round by Tony Tubbs) and undefeated Derrick Roddy (who was voted in by the fans in part due to his glossy 17–0 record and was stopped by Dancuta in the opening round). Still, with the exception of Bert Cooper who lost a decision to Australian Craig Petersen after having to deal with promoter Rick Parker's interloping in an attempt to milk extra cash from Cooper, all the favorites emerged victorious and, despite the troubles they faced, it was looking like they would most likely emerge victorious by the end of the night. But fate would prove different. After his quick blowout over Roddy, Dancuta advanced to the semifinals without having to fight a second fight when his scheduled opponent, Craig Petersen, was forced to drop out due to his inability to fully recover from the knockdown he suffered in his win over Bert Cooper. Although Dancuta would still end up the only "rookie" standing by the end of the second round, he was also the freshest fighter left. Smith won another decision (this time over Tillman), Tubbs went the full three rounds (in a decision win over Jose Ribalta), and Tyrell Biggs was briefly rattled in the opening round before rallying to stop Shane Sutcliffe in the second. While each of the other fighters entering the semifinals had already fought four, five, and six rounds, Dancuta had fought less than one. That along with his youth made him a surprisingly dangerous opponent. But the odds still remained firmly stacked against him. He was an unknown fighter in a tournament with two former world champions and a former Olympic gold medallist. Most assumed that the fairy tale would come to an end for Dancuta in his next fight; he was taking on one of the hardest punching former champions of the 1980s, a fighter with nearly five times as many pro fights as Dancuta.

But the twenty-two-year-old Dancuta recognized Smith's weaknesses in his first two fights and, more telling, recognized the fatigue that Smith felt after six surprisingly tough rounds. Dancuta started the fight throwing bombs and actually stunned Smith with a hard right hand seconds into the fight. Dancuta then swarmed all over his forty-year-old foe, not giving him a moment to respond. Although Dancuta was missing with most of his punches, he set a pace that Smith would be unable to match. Although Smith tried to establish his left jab, it was too slow to derail the onrushing Dancuta, who briefly trapped Smith on the ropes just inside of a minute into the round. By the halfway point of the round Smith was relegated to clinching and holding. Although Dancuta slowed just a bit at the round's end, Smith still was unable to capitalize, and there was little question which fighter had won the round.

Dancuta continued his wild domination in the second round, throwing combinations upstairs that had Smith desperately holding on. The fatigue factor also came into play in the round, as Smith's less-than-sizzling offense deteriorated to virtually nothing. Dancuta also began to implement a very effective left jab that further added to Smith's woes. The only thing that seemed to threaten Dancuta was frequent warnings for a variation of minor infractions. Still, with his opponent only throwing fourteen punches in the round (compared to fifty-five for Dancuta), there was little question for ringsiders that Smith needed to rediscover his bonecrunching power if he were to turn the fight around.

However, it was not to be for the former champion. Smith tried to pump his jab to start the third round, but was back to clinching and backing into the ropes as Dancuta returned to his first-round strategy of wildly swinging away without setting anything up with the jab. It got so bad that commentator Al Bernstein said, "all Bonecrusher is doing is holding, he's doing nothing offensive." With just under one minute left in the fight, Dancuta was able to bully Smith into the ropes with another effective combination upstairs. Smith tried to finish the fight bravely when, with ten seconds left in the fight, he initiated a wild slug-fest. However, Dancuta gladly obliged him and actually won the brief exchange, cementing his domination. All three judges scored the fight a shutout (30–27), advancing the most unlikely underdog into the finals.

With the win, Dancuta finally erased the stigma of his loss to Larry Donald and found himself the fan favorite going into the finals. But his inexperience would prove his undoing in his next fight. After Tony Tubbs easily outpointed Tyrell Biggs to advance, Dancuta found himself in the ring with a fighter more like Donald, a slick boxer with a great jab. He was the exact opposite of Smith and the type with whom Dancuta was not prepared to deal. Tubbs used his experience to outbox Dancuta in capturing a three-round decision, winning the Superfights tournament. Still, the tournament as a whole proved to be greatly beneficial to the career of Dancuta, who emerged as a minor prospect in the division. He went on to win his next seven fights over the next two years before seeing his run as a prospect (and his career) brought to an end when James Thunder knocked him out in the second round.

For the former champion James Smith, the loss failed to impact his career very much. He was already so discredited that his loss to Dancuta only seemed to prove what the experts had been saying for years—that he was no longer even a minor factor in the heavyweight division. A third-round knockout loss to Lionel Butler followed, before he went to Europe to cash in on his name in the European theater, losing to Axel Schultz (in Germany) and Brian Nielsen (in Denmark) in back-to-back fights that capped a four-fight losing streak.

CHAPTER FIVE

1994

"There's something wrong with this guy!"

Trainer Teddy Atlas to Michael Moorer during his
fight with Evander Holyfield

February 5, 1994—Las Vegas, Nevada
Ray Anis (12–0, 8 KOs) vs. William Morris (11–10–1, 1 KO)
Favorite: Anis
Result: Morris won an eight-round unanimous decision.

For undefeated prospect Ray Anis, it was looking more and more like he
was more than just another up-and-comer. With twelve wins under his
belt as well as his New York background and his connection to Cedric
Kushner, many fans were looking at Anis as one the top young prospects
in the division. All he needed was to keep winning in impressive fashion
against fighters of a slowly increasing quality, and within a year or two
it seemed quite plausible that he would break into the world rankings.
By February 1994, it was looking like his first small step up would come
in the form of William Morris.

After scoring an upset over fringe prospect Tim Puller on *Cedric
Kushner's Heavyweight Explosion* on September 4, 1993, (see page 108),
William Morris found his stock jump a few points, but when the smoke
cleared he was still seen as a journeyman—one that a quality heavyweight like Anis would most likely dispatch without too much difficulty.
It would take more than a win over Tim Puller for Morris to erase the
stigma of ten losses in a career that spanned twenty-two fights. When
he labored to pull off an eight-round split decision over Carl (not "The
Truth") Williams less than a month after the Puller win, it seemed to

confirm that the Puller fight was nothing more than an aberration. Besides, even if he came in at his best like he did against Puller, it would most likely be too little to derail the undefeated Anis. After all, Anis was seen as a much better prospect and fighter than Puller was. When all was said and done, it looked like Anis had the perfect fight: a journeyman opponent easily recognizable to both the television audience and the ringside fans, a fighter who could give the undefeated fighter some rounds and perhaps even give him a bit of a test, but in the end a fighter who was regarded as a journeyman with little power.

Early in the opening round the fight seemed to go according to plan. Anis dominated much of the round with his jab. By the end of the round it seemed that Anis was winning while playing it safe, but after he rocked Morris with a hard shot with thirty seconds left in the round, it looked as if Anis was about to jump closer to the front of the class, to Shannon Briggs and other young prospects, with a first-round knockout. Anis unloaded, but saw his opponent saved by the bell. Although Morris came out for the second round fully recovered from the previous round's shellacking, there was little question that Anis pulled out the next three rounds by a slim margin. But Morris upped the pressure and closed the gap each round. By the fifth round the jab, which worked so well in the opening round for Anis, was now unable to keep Morris at bay. Morris's work rate also played a major factor in the tide turning in the fight. Anis, who showed signs of fatigue, was unable to match Morris punch for punch. And without the jab to keep Morris honest, he was forced to fight on the inside. Anis was left to hold and clinch against the onrushing Morris. Still, the round appeared to most ringsiders to be close until Morris reached into his bag of veteran tricks and stole the round with a flurry in the last ten seconds.

Anis tried to return to the jab from the outside in the sixth round, but fatigue reduced the jab to a lazy flick, one which Morris easily slipped past on the way in with wild, but effective, body shots. Anis's punch output, which had been hardly great over the previous two rounds, was virtually non-existent for much of the sixth—an unfortunate fact for him since his jab was still effective the few times he was able to set down, plant his feet, and throw it with some authority. By the start of the seventh it looked as if Anis was getting his second wind. He began to pump the jab again and appeared to understand that he was letting Morris win rounds in a dangerously close fight. But when Morris grazed Anis's chin with a wide overhand right, it seemed to cause the undefeated fighter to change his strategy. Rather than rely solely on the jab, he began to pump the right hand and found it to be a very effective tool (landing three straight to the face of Morris). Going into the eighth round few would deny that the fight was close, but most assumed Anis had it wrapped up. After all, it appeared as if he won the first four rounds as well as the seventh. Although almost every round was close, it was difficult to see the hard luck Morris getting the nod in those rounds. Morris knew he needed to win the eighth, and win it big, and fought accordingly. Although Anis returned to the jab, it was not enough to derail Morris's pressure and good punch output. Although the round appeared to be Anis's by a slim margin, those familiar with Morris's win over Tim Puller would encounter a brief moment of déjà vu, when loose tape on the glove of Ray Anis caused a break in the action with twenty seconds left in the fight. Morris came back from the brief pause to explode on Anis, stealing the round and not stopping until the bell ended the fight—not even allowing Anis a chance to respond.

As the judges' scorecards were collected, most ringsiders assumed that Anis got what he wanted—a good win and some rounds with some scary moments that tested the young fighter. Although the win would not be as impressive as he would have wanted, it was still early enough in his career to be overlooked. But when all three judges voted for Morris by a single point each—79–78 three times—Anis suddenly saw his stock plummet to the ground, while Morris saw his shoot up.

Anis was quickly taken of the list of prospects with world champion potential, despite the fact that the loss was disputable. Even an impressive third-round knockout victory over former contender Tyrell Biggs was unable to repair the damage that the loss to Morris had caused. But in August 1995 Anis had the opportunity to finally put the questions about him to rest. Against James Thunder, a fighter with a early shaky career who had punched his way into contention, Anis was presented a huge opportunity to jump into the top ten against a vulnerable opponent—Thunder was coming off a loss to Franco Wanyama—as well as capture the IBO heavyweight title. Anis had some success early, but he was unable to cope with Thunder's power and was stopped in the seventh round. A loss to Michael Grant followed in 1996, and by the time

John Ruiz starched him in less than thirty seconds a year later there was no longer any talk of Anis ever entering the top ten.

For Morris, the win revitalized his career, and suddenly insiders began to talk about Morris pulling a "Lionel Butler" and possibly establishing himself as a lower-level contender of sorts. Unlike Butler, Morris was notorious for struggling in the lower profile fights, and as he entered his next fight against Jack Basting as a favorite, Morris struggled, just as he did against Carl Williams, before winning a ten-round majority decision. Also, unlike Butler, Morris lacked power, and when he fought Tony Tubbs in 1994, that flaw finally caught up to him. Although he taunted Tubbs and clowned with him, he finally met an opponent who could handle his work rate and whose bag of tricks was considerably deeper than his. After ten rounds most of the fans that tuned in on *USA Tuesday Night Fights* had already changed channels, as the fight deteriorated in arguably the worst fight the network had shown in several years. But in a fairly common occurrence regarding Tony Tubbs fights, the decision was later changed to "no-contest" when Tubbs failed a drug test. The stigma of the Tubbs performance hurt him considerably, even if it would not go on his record. When he fought prospect Danell Nicholson in March 1995, the book on how to beat Morris was already well read. Danell danced and moved and did not let Morris jump in with hard shots from the outside. Still, it looked like another ten-round affair until the referee stopped the fight in the sixth round in what was widely regarded as a very fast stoppage. But there was little controversy in his knockout loss to James Thunder in 1996 or Terrence Lewis in 1997, nor was there any question that his brief run at trying to become a contender was undoubtedly over. In fact, after the Tubbs fight, Williams would go on to lose eleven of his next thirteen fights.

February 18, 1994—Boston, Massachusetts
Peter McNeeley (24–0, 18 KOs) vs. Stanley Wright (8–5, 8 KOs)
Favorite: McNeeley
Result: Wright won via eighth-round TKO.

In the early 1990s, heavyweight boxing saw a small revival in the New England area with the regional success of the popular Paul Poirier, a moderately talented undefeated welterweight from the early 1970s who made an unlikely comeback in 1990 as a heavyweight. Poirier lacked power, but he did posses some skills (although the added weight seemed to be a detriment to him as a boxer). Regardless of his limitations, he was a fighter with a heart of gold and an engaging personality that endeared him to New England fans. Although he won the New England heavyweight title in 1991, he found himself grossly outmatched when he finally stepped up in competition and faced world-class fighters. Alex Stewart, Tony Tucker, and Larry Holmes all defeated him with a degree of ease, and Poirier retired shortly after the Holmes defeat, leaving what appeared to be a substantial void in the heavyweight division in New England.

New England fans were not forced to wait long for their next undefeated heavyweight local star when a seemingly tough, hard-punching Irishman named Peter McNeeley exploded onto the scene. Fans in New England who had become somewhat accustomed to Poirier's distance fights—he had only seven knockouts in over thirty fights—were enthralled with the hard punching McNeeley, who surpassed Poirier as a fighter as early as his fifth fight, when he knocked out Jerry Arentzen on *ESPN*. For many New Englanders, McNeeley was just as engaging a personality as Poirier and seemed to have quite a few strengths that Poirier did not possess. Unlike Poirier, Peter appeared to have a little bit of pop behind his punches. His age was also in his favor: in February 1994 he was still only twenty-five. Peter also had an impressive heavyweight pedigree in his father, Tom, who fought Floyd Patterson for the heavyweight title in 1961.

For some fans of boxing in New England, it seemed that Peter could actually go on to become a legitimate contender, and maybe even challenge for a world championship (although few outside the northeast shared that belief). Although his opposition was atrocious, it still seemed early enough in his career to overlook that fact and focus on the future. The assumption was that Peter would eventually reach the point where he would step into the ring with a contender, but the first step in his career was to consolidate his dominance over New England by winning the recently vacated New England heavyweight title.

McNeeley's opponent, Stanley Wright, seemed a safe enough pick. Although he was in the midst of a six-fight win streak (four first-round knockouts and two second-round knockouts) with a rejuvenated career following his acquisition of legendary trainer Tony Petronelli, his early losses to Tim Igo and Garing Lane by way of knockout seemed to indicate that he would fold under the pressure of a hard puncher like McNeeley. More importantly, Stanley was an easily marketable opponent. At 6'10" he appeared a more imposing figure than his record as a fighter indicated, and with all eight of his wins coming by way of knockout it was easy to sell the fight as a potential slugfest. Also, Wright had briefly played in the Colonial Basketball Association (with the Albany Patroons) and played college hoops for Indiana State, which gave him a tie-in of sorts with Boston legend Larry Bird.

Most figured the fight was just a coronation for Peter McNeeley. He had yet to win a belt of any kind in the ring, and the New England title was the first step in taking his career to the next level. Considering the former champ, Paul Poirier, was a close friend and stablemate of his, it seemed almost a continuation of a sort of dynasty—a poor man's Ted-Williams-to-Carl-Yazstremski transition. Wright was looked upon as a sort of novel side story but wasn't expected to upset the real show.

Early in the fight it appeared that Wright had read the McNeeley script. He found himself unable to use his size to an advantage and saw the smaller man crowd and batter him mercilessly on the inside. When McNeeley broke Wright's nose in the opening round with an uppercut, it seemed only a matter of time before he robbed the big man of his heart and ended the fight. With a broken nose, Wright changed tactics to pure survival mode. For most of the next six rounds, McNeeley crowded the big man, who seemed content just to survive to the end of the fight. McNeeley, who had failed to knock out three of his last four opponents, seemed to be resigned to winning another decision against an opponent few felt should have been able to hang in with him. The only real opportunity for Peter seemed to come when Wright complained to the referee in the third round about a thumb in the eye. McNeeley, however, failed to take advantage of his distracted opponent and soon found himself shoved to the canvas in retaliation.

By the start of the eighth round the fight had set into a pattern, with McNeeley crowding and Wright fighting defensively, weak arm punches the only offense in his arsenal. In fact, two of the three judges ringside had Peter pitching a shutout up to that point (with one judge giving Stanley one round). McNeeley seemed totally in control, a small cut over his left eye the only blemish from Wright's punches. But halfway through the eighth round, the fight switched gears when Wright exploded with a sudden barrage of punches that caught McNeeley unawares. Perhaps it was because Wright's offense was virtually nonexistent for most of the fight, or perhaps because he made a rookie mistake, but McNeeley failed to anticipate the combination and was stunned by Wright's six-punch combo to the head. McNeeley lost his mouthpiece in the exchange and appeared generally dazed, but it seemed that he was not seriously damaged when referee Bob Benoit stepped in to administer a standing eight count. In fact, it almost appeared a gift of sorts, allowing McNeeley valuable time to recover. But it suddenly became apparent that McNeeley was in fact in serious trouble when blood from the now-large cut over his left eye began pouring into his eye during the count. The referee quickly called in the ringside physician, who deemed the cut too serious to allow the fight to continue. In a flash, Stanley Wright was the new champion of New England.

For Wright, the success was short-lived. Although it seemed he established himself as a prospect of sorts, the win streak came to an inglorious end when he lost a decision to Kevin McBride in his next fight. McBride was also undefeated (and like McNeeley a puncher), and the loss to McBride effectively ended Wright's brief flirtation with overcoming his five early losses and becoming a legitimate prospect. Wright then decided to use the ace in his sleeve to help accommodate his comeback, namely the New England heavyweight title that he won in his fight against McNeeley. Although it looked unlikely that he would explode on the national scene, he still was a viable and recognizable regional fighter, and a quick and easy defense of his title could further establish himself in New England (and arguably help sell a rematch with McNeeley).

His opponent was a limited clubfighter named Juan Quintana of Springfield, a recognizable opponent in the New England circuit. Whenever a contender or former champion made a trip to the northeast, Quintana was usually the opponent he would tee off on. Donovan "Razor" Ruddock, Alex Stewart, Richard Mason, Bash Ali, and Shannon Briggs all took trips to New England to fight Quintana. Quintana also made the rounds with the top New England fighters as well, losing to Peter McNeeley and former undefeated New England champion Paul

Poirier by decision. Though Quintana fought often in New England, he had yet to score a major win (in fact he had only six in thirty-eight fights), and it seemed a relatively easy defense for the towering Wright. But Wright underestimated his opponent, dropping a ten-round decision that destroyed the momentum garnered from his win over Mc-Neeley. Although he came back to knock out Quintana in a rematch, 1995 saw him lose by way of second-round knockout to both Henry Akinwande and Michael Grant.

McNeeley, on the other hand, saw his career completely unfazed by the loss. He was back in the ring two months later and began padding his record with easy wins against soft opposition. Although the loss was an ugly blemish on his record, his career was not seriously hurt by it. Boxing fans tended to look differently on losses that were the result of cuts than from actual knockouts. Also, for the fans of New England, the image of an infuriated McNeeley in the ring shortly after the fight was awarded to Wright seemed to indicate that Peter was less a victim of Stanley Wright than he was a victim of bad luck. But McNeeley's real career plans became all too clear by the year's end. Although he went on to knock out J.B. Williamson, his opposition remained unusually soft. Even when McNeeley set a boxing record with a six-second knockout over Frankie Hines, he still failed to up the competition. Then came reports that manager Vinnie Vecchione repeatedly rejected offers to fight the likes of Joe Hipp and Tommy Morrison (for $50,000 and $125,000 respectively). It soon became apparent that Peter was being groomed in the classic "Great White Hope" mold. His management was padding his record deceptively to take advantage of his pigmentation in securing a big money fight. When he was signed as Oliver McCall's first opponent after McCall won the WBC title, it seemed clear that Mc-Neeley was indeed a "White Hope"-style heavyweight. Although the McCall fight fell through, he still landed an amazing $800,000 payday when Mike Tyson, fresh out of prison, chose him as his first opponent in over three years. McNeeley failed to make it out of the first round against Tyson.

April 14, 1994—Bay St. Louis, Mississippi
Quinn Navarre (10–0–1, 7 KOs) vs. Ed Donaldson (7–2, 6 KOs)
Favorite: Navarre
Result: Donaldson won by way of second-round knockout.

For many boxing insiders, it was clear that undefeated prospect Quinn Navarre had something working for him, this despite the fact that he was not regarded as one of the best heavyweight prospects in the division at the time. Although he was certainly a fighter that most boxing insiders felt was worthy of keeping an eye out for in the future, even his most ardent supporters admitted that he was still very much a work in progress. With a limited amateur background that included only six fights, nobody expected to see Quinn skyrocket into the top ten for at least several years. But what Quinn had working for him was exposure and lots of it. He had already fought on ESPN twice, knocking out Tony Phillips in impressive fashion and holding fellow prospect Ahmad Abdin to a four-round draw. With the scheduled rematch with Abdin to be his third fight on ESPN, Navarre found himself in the enviable category of a regular. In fact, Quinn had already picked up more ESPN televised fight time than several more highly regarded prospects like Shannon Briggs and Courage Tshabalala.

When Abdin pulled out of the fight, there was little to threaten Navarre's TV time as he was quickly replaced with hard punching Ed Donaldson. Donaldson was in many ways very similar to Navarre. Standing one inch taller and weighing six pounds heavier, Donaldson had a very similar style to Navarre, one that relied on the jab followed by the right hand. But Donaldson lacked the management or the luck of Navarre early on, thus resulting in his status as a potential prospect destroyed in only his third fight. Donaldson was outpointed in that fight by a comically obese boxer named James Gaines (a fighter who appeared to be the farthest thing from a professional athlete). Gaines would later prove that he was in fact a very skilled and competent heavyweight, but in 1992 he had yet to earn the respect of boxing fans, and Donaldson's loss to him in turn hurt his career. He tried to come back and, in fact, strung together four straight first-round knockouts before he was thrown in with the lions in the form of Kirk Johnson, Canada's heavyweight Olympian in the 1992 Olympics. Donaldson was stopped in the fifth round, and when he was thrown in with Navarre two fights later, it seemed clear to many that his career was as a stepping stone for the young guns of the division. Even though it was regarded as something of a step up for Navarre (many ringsiders admitted that Donaldson's power made him more dangerous than Abdin, even if he was not as well rounded a fighter as the Syrian) most still were looking for Navarre to shine. After all, he had shown steady improvement throughout his eleven pro fights, and there was little to indicate that his development would be stunted this early in his career.

In fact, as the fight started, that was exactly what Navarre did. Although the fight started slowly, with both fighters exchanging jabs in an attempt to feel the other out, it quickly heated up when Donaldson landed a hard right hand on the chin of Navarre less than a minute into the round. Rather than stagger, Navarre seemed to walk through the shot as he answered with a right hand of his own seconds later. Donaldson soon began to take a defensive posture, and when Navarre attacked his body two minutes into the round it was clear to ringsiders that he was in control. Donaldson was left wearing "earmuffs," with his gloves up on the side of his face as Navarre punched, and with thirty seconds left in the round Navarre briefly trapped Donaldson on the ropes.

It was looking like it would be Navarre's best performance yet and that everything was going according to plan. But in boxing things seldom go according to plan, and for Quinn things would turn around for him in a hurry. After coming out in the second more cautious, Quinn failed to adequately respond to the Donaldson jab. He stood like a statue as Ed fired several lazy left jabs. Navarre then leaned in with a wide overhand right that missed the mark. Seconds later Donaldson fired a left jab followed by a straight right hand that landed on the Navarre's chin. This time Quinn was not able to brush the shot off. He dropped to the canvas and remained there in a stiff body position that revealed how much damage that one right hand did. Although he attempted to rise, there was no beating referee Elmo Adolph's count. At 0:42 seconds of the second round Navarre was counted out.

Donaldson tried to use the win to position himself into the heavyweight picture, and initially it appeared like it would work for him. He racked up a pair of knockout victories before stepping into the ring with rapidly declining former contender Alex Garcia. It seemed a smart fight to take for Ed, Garcia was increasingly looking like a completely washed-up commodity, but his name still carried enough prestige that a win over him would benefit the career of a young up-and-comer. Also, Garcia's weakness appeared to be his chin, and Donaldson's power seemed more than adequate to knock out Garcia if he were to land flush.

But it proved to be a miscalculation. Garcia had enough left in his tank for one more solid performance, and though the fight was close and competitive, Donaldson found himself on the losing end of a majority decision. The loss was followed by a brutal second-round knockout loss to James Thunder, a loss that ended any notion Donaldson might have had of ever breaking into the top ten.

For Navarre, the loss to Donaldson dropped him off the list of prospects, and he was never able to regain the status of a fighter worth keeping an eye on again. He racked up seven straight wins after the Donaldson debacle, but fans still remembered him for the way in which he was brutally knocked out with one shot. When he stepped into the ring with Jeremy Williams the following year there was little question which fighter was expected to win (hint: it wasn't Quinn). Again he fought well in the opening round, and again he was stopped in the second round. The loss to Williams was followed by a third loss, this time by way of split decision to his old nemesis Ahmad Abdin over ten rounds. Suddenly Navarre's luck, which had been so good early on, seemed to finally run out. However, when he fought Larry Holmes in 1996 he seemed to finally put it all together. After a career best performance from Navarre it appeared to many ringsiders that he pulled off the upset. But without the undefeated record to help nudge the close rounds in his pocket, Quinn found himself on the losing end of a ten-round decision. The loss to Holmes did prove one thing, had his luck remained as good as it was early in his career, he could have been a contender.

April 22, 1994—Las Vegas, Nevada
Evander Holyfield (30–1, 22 KOs) vs. Michael Moorer
   (34–0, 30 KOs)
Favorite: Holyfield
Result: Moorer won a twelve-round majority decision.

For WBA/IBF heavyweight champion Evander Holyfield, the respect that had so long eluded him was finally his. Unable to escape the shadow of Mike Tyson and impress in any of his previous title fights (his win over Douglas was tainted with allegations that an out of shape Douglas quit), Holyfield finally earned respect with his thrilling twelve-round decision over Riddick Bowe the previous year (page 118). With Tyson incarcerated in Indiana, it appeared that Holyfield had but two obstacles to overcome to ensure himself a place in the Boxing Hall of Fame in Canastota, New York: he needed to unify the title with a win over WBC champion Lennox Lewis and win a rubber match with archrival Bowe. For many boxing fans, everything else was just window dressing, and they were becoming increasingly aware of a unusual trait that would define Evander's career: his tendency for looking flat and unimpressive in fights against seemingly weaker opposition.

It was looking increasingly like Moorer was one of those not in Evander's league. Although he was widely regarded as a top prospect since he moved up from the light-heavyweight division in 1991 (where he was the WBO champion), his stock in the heavyweight division was on a downturn. Initially packaged as a hard-punching destroyer, Moorer seemed at first to be living up to his reputation. He blasted out durable Levi Billups in three rounds and scored impressive knockouts over Terry Davis and Bobby Crabtree. Against a respectable (but fading) heavyweight named Alex Stewart, Moorer again showed fireworks in blasting out his opponent in four rounds. He showed great power and a fighter's heart in rallying from a shaky second round (in which he was badly staggered) to secure the win. But the excitement was short-lived. Moorer began showing signs of conditioning problems, allowing his weight to balloon up to a whopping 231 pounds—a full fifty-six pounds heavier than that at which he was fighting when he was a light heavyweight. Then came the Mike "The Giant" White fight on HBO. Against the tall former prospect White, who had scored a knockout over James "Buster" Douglas early in his career, Moorer was extended the distance for the first time. However, it didn't seem particularly devastating at the time since he was more impressive than co-main event fighter Lennox Lewis, who struggled with Moorer KO victim Levi Billups in winning an ugly ten-round decision. Also, White was felled three times in the fight, and it seemed a miracle that he wasn't knocked out (being saved by the bell in the last round). But the win did ruin one of Michael's more impressive stats, ending his consecutive knockout streak at twenty-six.

Nonetheless, the fight marked the birth of a seemingly new Michael Moorer, a fighter who seldom excited the crowds and often looked all too vulnerable. In his next fight against Everett "Bigfoot" Martin, Moorer was dropped in the third and fought an uninspiring performance in winning a boring ten-round decision. Although his next fight (for the WBO heavyweight title) against Bert Cooper could hardly have been called boring, it again showed Michael to be a vulnerable fighter as Cooper dropped Moorer twice before succumbing to Moorer's power in the fifth. Boring decisions against James "Bonecrusher" Smith and Mike Evans followed, and suddenly fans were left to wonder what happened to the Michael Moorer they thought they knew.

But regardless of which Moorer showed up, it appeared unlikely that he would win against Holyfield. If the reckless brawler came to fight, his suspect chin would surely fail him, and if the safety-first boxer showed up, he would clearly be outhustled by Holyfield. Also, although Moorer was a southpaw and would most likely give Evander some trouble with his stance—Evander hadn't fought a southpaw in nearly eight years—boxing had yet to see its first left-handed champion, and most felt that that alone was hardly enough to upset a champion like Holyfield.

Although Moorer was seen as the lesser of the two fighters in the ring, it seemed boxing experts made him a favorite in one area: the corner. Initially boxing experts chastised him for firing his trainer Emanuel Steward, who had guided his career from day one. His original replacement, Tony Ayala Sr., saw his stint as trainer end badly after a few months when Moorer felt that Ayala took too much interest in his personal life. It first seemed that Moorer was looking for a token trainer in the Jay Bright/Aaron Snowell mold, and boxing writers were highly critical about Moorer's apparent disregard for one of the most important aspects of his career. Moorer, however, was very serious about his career, and he shocked (and impressed) many boxing experts with his selection of former Tyson trainer Teddy Atlas as his new head coach.

Evander Holyfield himself was going through a similar situation, but his move appeared motivated for all the wrong reasons. Holyfield quickly dismissed Emanuel Steward after only one fight, which happened to be his career best, and replaced him with the lightly regarded Don Turner. Although a number of reasons were cited, it was apparent that the move was financial. Holyfield then went on to fire cut man Ace Marotta for financial reasons as well: Turner indicated that Holyfield could save around $25,000 of his multimillion-dollar purse by firing Marotta since he could also work as a cut man. A move that was seen as a dangerous downsize, it looked as if Holyfield was possibly shortchanging himself out of the title if he were to be cut. Although the trainer controversy seemed to hurt Holyfield on paper, it did little to hurt his popularity. He still remained a fan favorite due to his two wars with Bowe, and although his odds in Vegas were hurt by the southpaw factor along with the trainer controversy, he still was a prohibitive 2–1 favorite. Although there were many questions regarding Holyfield—Could he handle a southpaw? Is he looking past Moorer to a fight with Lewis? Would he be cut?—those questions seemed miniscule compared to Moorer's seemingly glaring deficiencies.

Early in the fight, it seemed clear that Holyfield was indeed having trouble with Moorer's stance. The first round started slowly, with both fighters flicking jabs at each other. Although it appeared that Moorer's were landing with a bit more pop behind them, it seemed a foolish long-term strategy for the undefeated challenger.

By the second round, however, the jab was beginning to push an oddly passive Evander Holyfield back. Having more than he could handle from the southpaw right jab of Moorer, Evander found himself on the ropes and on the defensive with less than a minute left in the round. But with the round seemingly lost, Evander suddenly came alive with a picture perfect two-punch combination that dropped Michael Moorer to the canvas. Although Moorer didn't seem seriously hurt, it looked as if Evander finally woke up and would begin to up the pressure and take it to Moorer.

But it was Evander Holyfield who returned to his corner a hurt man; having torn the rotator cuff of his left shoulder in the previous round, Evander came out looking more sluggish in the third than he had in the previous two rounds. His punches lacked any force or snap behind them, and he seemed unable to throw more than one or two punches before running out of gas. Moorer, who was now all too aware of Evander's punching power, returned to the jab and embraced a safety-first approach that would prove to be his fight plan for the duration of the night. It proved exasperating for fans (who expected a slugfest) and trainer Teddy Atlas, who recognized that Moorer was fighting too cautiously.

"I want you to use the jab and I want you to work off it! I don't want you to be satisfied with it!" a clearly annoyed Atlas implored Moorer after the third round. "You go in there and start backing this guy up and start doing what we came to do, otherwise don't come back to this fucking corner!"

Although the emotional plea stirred listeners watching the fight on pay-per-view, it failed to have much effect on Moorer. When the fourth round started with both fighters punching, Moorer quickly retreated behind his jab. Still, the jab alone was proving to be highly effective, as Holyfield was appearing to be suffering from severe fatigue as well as his injured left shoulder. In the fifth, it appeared that Moorer had indeed taken complete control behind his jab, but it was also abundantly clear that he was failing to press his advantage over a champion who appeared totally shot. When TVKO commentator George Foreman said that "Holyfield looks tired," it seemed almost an understatement. With over a minute left in the fifth round, Moorer stunned Holyfield with a solid combo behind his right jab and proceeded to tee off on the champion until the bell ended the round.

With the round clearly Moorer's, fans wondered if things could in fact get worse for the "Real Deal." Then they noticed a large cut over his left eye, and it appeared that things had just gone from bad to worse. Holyfield's decision to fire Ace Marotta was now a major factor of the fight, and fans were left to wonder how, and if, Don Turner could deal with the cut. Although Turner actually did handle the cut quite well—it never became a factor in the fight—it proved to be a serious distraction for the trainer-turned-cutman. He spent the first thirty seconds of the break between the fifth and sixth rounds looking for Vaseline to help with the cut (never actually saying anything to a fighter who clearly needed sound instruction), and when he finally did give Evander some advice, it was simple cheerleading in the form of "the Lord is with you." It became abundantly clear that Holyfield was not getting any serious help from his corner, and his decision to release Steward seemed even more of a mistake than it had been before.

After losing the sixth in similar fashion, Evander came out slugging in the seventh but quickly ran out of gas again and by round's end found himself once again peppered by Moorer's jab. Moorer, however, was still refusing to throw anything behind the jab and continued to earn the ire of his cornerman Teddy Atlas. When he slowed down even more in the eighth round, arguably letting Holyfield steal it, Moorer became a first-hand witness to one of the most inspiring and memorable speeches in heavyweight history. As he returned to his corner he saw Atlas sitting in the stool screaming, "Do you want me to change places with you?!" He then told Moorer, in no uncertain terms, that he was letting the fight slip away, and summed up what everyone (except apparently Moorer) had already figured out when he barked, "There's something wrong with this guy," in reference to Holyfield's apparent breakdown.

Although nobody who witnessed the speech was unmoved (it was straight out of Hollywood), it failed to rally the one person it was suppose to: Michael Moorer. Holyfield, in fact, won the ninth round and seemed poised to regain control of the fight solely off the inactivity of Michael Moorer. Although Atlas was unable to inspire some sort of fire in Moorer, it proved unnecessary, as the jab alone was enough to win the last three rounds for Moorer. Most ringside observers had Moorer comfortably ahead, while most of the fans that watched the fight on television felt Holyfield had indeed won. The Atlas speeches, which seemed aimed toward a fighter who was losing, along with the fact that all four TV commentators felt that Holyfield won, made it appear that Holyfield had in fact scored a victory albeit lackluster. But when the scores were read, it was Moorer who emerged as winner via majority decision.

Although the decision seemed just, a scoring controversy soon developed. Judge Jerry Roth, who scored the fight 115–114 for Moorer, had apparently scored the second round an even 10–10. Moorer had in fact seemed to be winning, but the knockdown should have made it a clear Holyfield round, if not by two points then at least by one. It was one of the most ridiculous scoring blunders in recent memory. It could have been a more serious scoring controversy: had Roth scored it 10–9 or even 10–8 the fight would have been ruled a draw.

The scoring controversy was quickly forgotten when Evander Holyfield was rushed to the hospital to have his injured left shoulder treated. When their patient was pumped full of fluids to treat apparent dehydration, doctors discovered a very disturbing reaction to the fluid intake from Evander's heart. He was quickly rushed to Emory University Hospital where the bad news was confirmed: Evander was diagnosed with a heart ailment—a non-compliant left ventricle. The ailment was not life-threatening, but because of the effect it had on a human body under strenuous conditions, it seemed safe to assume that it effectively ended Evander's career. In hindsight, the reason that Evander looked so bad against Moorer was because, to a certain degree, he was having a heart attack. Evander initially accepted the diagnosis with grace. It, in fact, added to his ever-growing myth as a fighter with an almost inhuman tolerance for pain. The idea of a man having a heart attack while fighting on to lose a razor-thin decision to an undefeated fighter seemed to confirm Evander was the greatest warrior of his time. And even if it wasn't a real heart attack per se, it still made for an inspiring story.

The story took a tragic turn to the ridiculous when two months later Evander Holyfield appeared on faith healer Benny Hinn's show. Hinn was a controversial figure that was considered by many to be a charlatan and a con man of the most unethical kind. However, there were also many who claimed that Hinn was a legitimate faith healer with a track record to prove it. Regardless of what people thought about Hinn before Holyfield appeared on his show, one thing was for certain: Evander believed in him, and proudly proclaimed his heart to have been cured. When he returned to his doctor, it appeared as if he did, in fact, have a miraculously repaired heart, although some claimed he was misdiagnosed back in Emory University Hospital. Most who remembered the tragic comeback of basketball superstar Reggie Lewis hoped that Evander would not step back into the ring. (They remembered how Lewis was told never to play basketball again, his search for doctors who would tell him differently, and his death following his return to the court based on the advice of the doctors, who were clearly in the minority.) The assumption was that Evander was doing the same thing, and the hope was that his comeback would not end like Lewis's. It didn't: in fact, the best Holyfield in the ring was yet to come.

For Moorer, being champion proved to be an uphill battle for respect. His reign was discredited from the start, based of the discovery of Evander's "stiff" heart. Also, he had a tendency to be sullen and detached, a trait that didn't endear him to fans or writers, and his performance against Holyfield made him appear to be clearly a rung behind both Lennox Lewis and Riddick Bowe on the ladder of respect. The bubble finally burst for Moorer when he lost his two championship belts in his first defense against George Foreman.

May 21, 1994—Hammanskraal, South Africa
Corrie Sanders (24–0, 17 KOs) vs. Nate Tubbs (12–1, 11 KOs)
Favorite: Sanders
Result: Tubbs won by way of second-round knockout.

There had never been much question which country ruled the heavy-weight division throughout boxing history—that being the United States—but by the early 1990s it was looking as if "second place" was emerging in a most unlikely area. Although there was never a shortage of British heavyweight contenders, their success (or lack thereof) was becoming the thing of boxing lore, virtually parallel to the World Series success of the Chicago Cubs. As the 1980s came to a close, few countries produced more than one or two heavyweights with moderate success except one: South Africa.

It started with a pair of white punchers who found themselves in a four-fight tournament for the soon to be vacated WBA title (surrend-ered by a retiring Muhammad Ali) in 1979. Although both Gerrie Coet-zee and Kallie Knoetze were on opposite ends of the political spectrum, and Knoetze's success as a boxer was hardly comparable to the success of Coetzee, it was still a most unlikely scenario for a country that had yet to produce a heavyweight champion. Coetzee went on to lose to John Tate in a fight for the vacant WBA title, but he nonetheless remained a solid contender throughout the 1980s. In fact, he went on to accomplish something that no British heavyweight had been able to do in nearly a century when he knocked out WBA champion Michael Dokes in 1983 to win the elusive WBA title on his third try. Although the win was tain-ted—Dokes's problems with drugs had become so overwhelming that rumors of reckless cocaine use in the days leading up to the fight sur-faced throughout boxing circles—and few regarded Coetzee as the "real champion" (that was a title held by the WBC champion Larry Holmes), it was nonetheless a proud moment for South African boxing. Most ex-pected South African heavyweight boxing to fade from the picture as soon as Coetzee retired in much the same way that Swedish heavy-weight boxing did after the retirement of Ingemar Johansson in 1963 (resulting with the banning of the sport in the Scandinavian country).

But South Africa proved to be a minor powerhouse in terms of the production of quality heavyweights, and from the 1980s on there was always at least one noteworthy heavyweight in the division whose roots were based in South Africa. In the late 1980s a Lou Duva–trained prospect named Johnny DuPlooy began to excite the boxing world with his dominant wins over David Bey and James "Quick" Tillis. Although he would go on to be exposed by Mike Weaver and Renaldo Snipes—his lack of old fashion "toughness" proved to be his undoing—he was able to land a title fight against Italian Francesco Damiani for the WBO heavyweight title in 1990. Damiani destroyed DuPlooy, ending his status as a contender, even in the then lightly regarded WBO, but he was quickly replaced by another white heavyweight in Pierre Coetzer, a game brawler with a decent punch and a solid chin. Although few international boxing writers regarded him as a top ranked heavyweight he was able to fight his way into the number one ranking of the WBA (and the number two spot in the IBF's ratings). When Riddick Bowe dispatched Coetzer in 1992 by way of seventh-round TKO, South Africa was quick to shift her attention to Corrie Sanders.

Sanders quickly raised eyebrows in South Africa with his impressive first-round knockout over Johnny DuPlooy in 1991, a win that gave him the South African title. It wasn't just that he knocked out DuPlooy: the dominance of the win (as well as the fact that it came in only his eleventh fight) excited his countrymen. But cynical American boxing wanted more than a lone win over a badly discredited opponent before they jumped on the bandwagon. Although Sanders failed to knock out journeyman Mike Rouse in his next fight, criticism of his performance was quickly muted when he shortly after destroyed Art Card (who was coming off a decision loss to Larry Holmes). It was enough to pique the interest of boxing insiders and fans alike. But as Sanders developed it became increasingly clear that he was the classic "hot and cold" fighter, a man who would follow an impressive knockout with a lackluster decision. Sanders fell into a minor slump of sorts when he won his next four fights by decision (against Anthony Wade, Mike Dixon, Mike Evans, and Johnny Nelson). It was enough to raise serious questions about "how good" he actually was until Sanders again entered a hot streak, blitzing Matthew Brooks in one round and setting off a string of dominant wins against solid opposition that propelled him into the top ten. After knocking out former contender Bert Cooper in three rounds in 1993, Sanders stepped into the ring with the rugged Levi Billups, who was coming off a pair of decision losses to Lennox Lewis and Buster Mathis Jr. Few anticipated a Billups win, but most assumed that the tough former USFL football player would give Sanders the "rounds" and would most likely carry the fight to the distance. But when Sanders took care of Billups in the first round, boxing writers all over the country were completely won over, and many predicted that he was the best heavyweight ever to come out of South Africa. With the heavyweight division lacking serious contenders, Sanders quickly jumped to the front of the pack of potential opponents for the newly crowned WBA-IBF champion, Michael Moorer. Boxing writers wondered what Moorer would do if Sanders found his chin with one of his powerful shots. Although many questions still lingered about Corrie's own untested chin, it appeared that he was planning on playing it safe against weak opposition, ensuring that those questions would have to be answered by Michael Moorer himself. After knocking out Marshall Tillman and Mike Williams, Sanders returned to South Africa for a quick payday (and some local exposure) against the little known Nate Tubbs.

Few fans knew anything about Tubbs outside of his ties to former WBA champion Tony Tubbs (his brother), but what they did know was hardly inspiring. Tubbs had fought a collection of anonymous fighters to pad his record with twelve victories, but there was one loss that stuck out. Against the only known opponent he faced, Eddie Gonzalez, Tubbs was out-hustled and lost an uninspiring ten-round decision. Many boxing writers knew of Gonzalez for all the wrong reasons: Gonzalez was part of one of *USA Tuesday Night Fights* highest-rated shows when he was shut out by Larry Holmes in Larry's first televised comeback fight. The image of the chunky Latino was hard to forget. So was his fight with Holmes, which turned out to be one of the worst fights ever televised. To lose to such a fighter seemed a clear sign that Tubbs was not going anywhere, and when he was chosen as Sanders's opponent, it seemed that he was getting there fast. Besides, Tubbs possessed a familiar flaw, the same one that had plagued the career of his brother Tony for years. He was seldom in good shape for a fight. After turning pro at a fleshy 242 pounds, Nate began to work hard to lose weight, and by his fourth fight he was down to 205 pounds. When he decided to refocus his career on boxing and less on weight loss, a mere twelve days after weighing in for a fight at a career low 185 pounds, Tubbs weighed in at a whopping

245. It was shocking for many insiders to imagine a fighter putting on an incredible sixty pounds in twelve days, but somehow Tubbs pulled it off. After the loss to Gonzales, in which he weighed in at a disappointing 254 pounds, Tubbs initially began to whip himself back into shape, but when he stepped on the scales for the Sanders fight, Nate weighed in at a career-high 262 pounds. It seemed that even Nate didn't give himself much chance to win against Sanders, and few could imagine how an out-of-shape Nate Tubbs could win.

By fight time many were predicting a quick blowout, but the local fighter decided to break from the norm and started the fight actually boxing. Using his superior foot speed and his southpaw jab, Sanders proceeded to do his best Muhammad Ali imitation by outboxing his slower opponent. But the strength of Nate Tubbs was quickly revealed when he pushed his fleet-footed opponent to the canvas in response to a missed left cross. Although Sanders was clearly the quicker of the two, it was also clear that he was not doing much damage with the jab. Still, Sanders cemented the round with a quick combo to Tubbs's face in the last thirty seconds of the round. The second round initially saw more of the same, with Sanders boxing and Tubbs stalking. But with a little over a minute in the round, Corrie Sanders's chin failed on its first test when a straight right of Nate Tubbs found its mark. When Tubbs followed the shot with a right cross, the South African crumbled to the canvas, where he was counted out at 1:36 of the round; he didn't even come close to beating the count.

For Sanders, the loss quickly dropped him out of consideration for a title fight against Moorer and sent him back to the drawing board. Although many boxing fans still regarded him as a good heavyweight prospect, the image of his collapse was hard to forget, and it wasn't until 1997 that he landed his world title shot. Unfortunately it was for the lightly regarded WBU belt. Against Ross Puritty, Sanders labored to a twelve-round decision to capture a belt, but earned little respect in the process. Another "hot streak" (when he scored dominant knockouts over Bobby Czyz and Al Cole) was enough to put him within one fight of a title fight again, this time against Hasim Rahman in 2000. The winner was to be in line for a shot at WBC-IBF champion Lennox Lewis, but again Corrie fell short, getting stopped in the seventh round. Most felt that Sanders was a spent commodity by then, but the South

African's power made him a dangerous fighter to underestimate, regardless of his chin. As a result, when WBO heavyweight champion Wladimir Klitschko picked him as an opponent in 2003, Sanders was able to pull off the biggest upset of the year, starching the highly touted Ukrainian in two rounds to finally win a world title.

For Nate Tubbs, the man who accomplished what a boxing publication called "one of the biggest upsets in South African boxing history,"[1] the win propelled him into the top ten although few boxing writers felt that the win over Sanders alone should have put him there. It seemed that he was on the threshold of emerging from his brother's shadow and becoming a fighter of note in his own right, but trouble began to emerge almost immediately. In his first fight after the win over Sanders, Tubbs struggled to win a ten-round decision over Martin Foster. Following up that win with another sluggish decision victory, this time over West Turner, by the time he appeared on *USA Tuesday Night Fights* against the little know Jorge Valdez, his stock had already dropped a few points since his win in South Africa. But a televised win over Valdez seemed a surefire way to get back into the picture. But after struggling for ten rounds Tubbs found himself on the losing end of a ten-round decision, thus ending his brief flirtation with contention in the heavyweight division.

June 30, 1994—Mesquite, Nevada
Samson Po'uha (12–0, 12 KOs) vs. Craig Payne (11–8–1, 7 KOs)
Favorite: Po'uha
Result: Payne won by way of sixth-round TKO.

When unheralded Tongan Samson Po'uha turned pro in November 1992, there were few boxing fans who were particularly excited. After all, Tonga wasn't exactly a boxing Mecca, and Po'uha seemed to possess a glaring flaw because of his size and conditioning. Weighing in at a whopping 273 pounds, Po'uha reminded many of the classic overweight, undertrained heavyweights that littered the landscape in the 1980s, and few insiders had any interest in an addition to that list. Besides, with the recent class of Olympians kicking off their careers at the same time,

---

[1] *Boxing 94,* November 1994, 48.

it proved to be easy to overlook Po'uha. But it didn't take long for the hard punching Tongan to emerge near the front of the pack with his brutal displays of power. It started with his third fight against undefeated Willie Jackson. Jackson was regarded as one of the more attractive prospects in the division, racking up nine knockouts in nine fights, but Po'uha made quick work of the highly regarded fighter, stopping him in the first round. He then went on to crush top-ten-ranked cruiserweight Jason Waller in the opening round in his tenth fight (October 1993). Along the way he also scored quick knockouts over normally durable journeymen like Eddie Gonzalez (who had lasted the distance with Larry Holmes in 1991) and Carl McGrew (who was coming off a big upset over undefeated John Sargent). But most promising was the new dedication to his conditioning. Po'uha worked hard to shed the pounds, and by the time he fought Waller, he appeared fit having lost thirty pounds since his first fight. Although the Waller win propelled him into the heavyweight picture, the success story began to crumble immediately. Po'uha was invited back by USA *Tuesday Night Fights* to fight Mike Rouse, a seasoned veteran. There was little to indicate that he could give Po'uha much trouble, and most predicted an early KO for Samson. As the fight grew nearer, however, Po'uha encountered a series of personal problems that began to rob him of his dedication, and in one month he gained eight pounds. During the fight he struggled with the bigger Rouse before finally stopping him in the eighth round. Afterward, rumors of drinking and partying began to surface, causing many insiders to once again question Po'uha.

Perhaps recognizing that momentum was slipping away from them, Team Samson signed to fight the slick boxing former champion Tony Tubbs, a dangerous opponent whom many expected would bring out the best in Po'uha. But the fight quickly fell apart, and by the end of 1993 it was clear that Po'uha was backsliding. His weight had jumped from the low 240s to the mid 260s, and his power no longer seemed as destructive as it had earlier. After struggling with David Graves in January 1994—Po'uha scored an ugly seventh round knockout—Team Samson decided it would be wise to keep their fighter active but away from the national spotlight until he got back into shape. All they needed was a fighter who wouldn't seriously challenge Samson, but could still sell tickets. Enter Craig Payne.

Craig Payne was one of the most recognizable amateurs in the sport in the early 1980s. With wins over Tyrell Biggs, Mike Tyson, and Cuban legend Teofilo Stevenson, Craig Payne was widely seen as the second best fighter next to Tyrell Biggs in the super heavyweight division. (In fact, he was ranked number two in the world amateur rankings.) After losing in the Olympic box-offs against Tyrell Biggs, Payne's dedication began to wane. His weight increased, and his training became suspect. Initially a heavily courted commodity when he announced his intentions to turn pro, he quickly earned a reputation as a fighter with little motivation and dedication. After moving to Las Vegas to work with the legendary trainer Eddie Futch, Payne quickly lost favor with Futch when he failed to show up to train, due to his fondness for the Vegas "night life." But more upsetting to Futch was that he was also dragging fellow heavyweight James Broad away from the gym on his trips to the strip. Futch was a trainer with little patience for a fighter who lacked motivation, and he was especially not fond of one who was a disruption to other fighters. Payne was sent back to Michigan, blacklisted by many in the boxing business. Although he did fight once in 1985, he would not fight for another six years, and by then it was clear that there would be no fanfare for the former amateur standout. His weight against K.P. Porter in his first comeback fight was 299 pounds, and few could envision the slick-moving Payne as an amateur having much success at that weight. Payne was a fighter who initially appeared to be working hard at getting back into shape, dropping nearly forty pounds for his next fight. Although he ballooned back up near 300 when he fought Robert Smith in December 1991, the lackluster draw seemed to motivate him to get back in shape and he once again dropped down to 259. Payne went on to win his next two fights by decision, but when he dropped a disputed decision to Tyrone Evans in April 1992, he again lost his motivation. From that point, he regularly weighed at least 300, and although he did come close to capturing the IBO heavyweight title in a fight with former world champion Pinklon Thomas in November 1992, it was becoming increasingly clear that he was not going to pan out as a professional. His record after the Evans loss was an unimpressive 6–7, and for many boxing fans, Payne looked like a "waste of talent." By June 1994 Payne was on the heels of a five-fight losing streak, which included losses to second-tier fighters like Garing Lane, Darren Hayden, and John Bray. There was little to indicate that Payne would pose even the slightest problem for Po'uha, even though he too was out of shape. After all, it was unlikely that his conditioning could possibly be worse than Payne's.

But in many ways Payne's weight was deceptive. Although nobody questioned that Payne was a good fifty-to-seventy-five pounds over his ideal fighting weight, he was a fighter who did have the endurance to go some rounds despite his size. He seldom shown signs of tiring in the later rounds, lasting the distance with everyone he lost to except for Frans Botha and Lionel Butler. (Both stopped him in the seventh.) He went twelve rounds against Pinklon Thomas (and actually had Pinklon on the verge of a knockout in the final two rounds), ten with Garing Lane and Mike Hunter, and eight with John Bray. Although Craig was accustomed to going the distance despite his conditioning, the relatively inexperienced Samson Po'uha was not, and it would prove to be the single most telling fact of the fight. For Samson entered the fight in the worst shape of his professional career. Weighing in at a whopping 298 pounds (thirty-six pounds more than he weighed in at five months prior) Samson actually outweighed Payne by a pound, the only time Craig had ever been outweighed as a pro. It was clear that Po'uha had not trained much for Payne, and when he predicted an early knockout it also became clear that he didn't think that the added weight would be much of a problem. And early on it didn't seem to be. Although Payne tried to establish the jab early in the first against the slowly stalking Samson Po'uha, Po'uha began to find the range with his left hook. When a hard right hand sent Craig Payne reeling into the ropes nearly halfway through the round, it appeared to be the beginning of the end for him. However, Payne proved to be both resilient and slick, quickly bouncing out of the corner. However, it was clear at the bell that Po'uha was finding the range with his right hand.

In the second round Po'uha showed early signs of fatigue as his attack slowed down. Payne began to find some range with his own right hand and actually held his own without the jab. Both fighters showing signs of fatigue, Po'uha began to drop his hands. Although much of the second round was close, Po'uha stole it when a hard straight right behind a body shot stunned Payne in the final thirty seconds, but he was again unable to pin down Payne long enough to put him away. Perhaps realizing that his endurance would not hold up for ten rounds, Po'uha came out in the third throwing bombs, but, never able to land cleanly, with each exchange his hands would drop a little more. Po'uha continued his body attack however, and did have success with it, again stunning Payne with a hard right to the body followed by a chopping right to the chin while Craig was on the ropes. Po'uha then went for the gold, firing hard body shots and throwing caution to the wind against Payne, who was on the ropes. But when the bell sounded ending the third with Craig Payne still standing, it marked the beginning of the end for Po'uha. He wearily walked back to his corner, his poor conditioning robbing him of the ability to carry on much longer. Slowing down in the fourth, he still threw bombs that became more telegraphed and less effective. Po'uha again flurried in the final minute, firing a handful of effective right hands, but again Payne survived the round and again Po'uha returned to his corner on tired legs.

Payne, however, was fighting on cruise control, still with plenty of gas in the tank for the later rounds. When Po'uha came out in the fifth slower than he had been in any other round and with almost no zip behind his punches, Payne finally began to up the pressure himself. Craig landed a solid left hook halfway through the round as Po'uha tried to lean back and began to incorporate his dormant left hand into the fight. Although Po'uha would again stun Payne with a left hook of his own in the closing seconds of the round, it was not enough to deter Payne, and it was the last bit of gas in Samson Po'uha's tank. Po'uha came out in the sixth at a snail's pace with his hands at his waist. Initially he tried to outbox Payne behind the jab but quickly abandoned that in favor of switching to southpaw. It was a clear sign of his fatigue, and Payne recognized it. In the final minute of the round Craig fired an overhand right that missed, followed by a left hook that landed on Po'uha's exposed chin. Po'uha dropped to his back and looked like a beaten man as referee Mitch Halpern started the count. But Po'uha rose at eight and was allowed to continue. It would prove to be unnecessary as Payne exploded on his wounded foe, firing three straight left hooks followed by a right hand that again dropped Po'uha. Although Samson again rose, this time at nine, it was clear that he was finished as he rose. Referee Mitch Halpern waved the fight off at 3:00 of the sixth round.

For Craig Payne it was undoubtedly the biggest win of his career, but the success would be short-lived. In his very next fight he was stopped by Ray Anis (in ten rounds) and followed that loss with a decision loss to Shannon Briggs on ESPN. Although he did extend the hard-punching Briggs the distance, his performance was hardly impressive. His lack of offense sent the viewers running for their remote controls and effectively ensured that he would not get a televised fight for some time. (In fact it would be six years.) Payne went into a downward spiral into opponent status after that, losing his next ten fights against badly faded former contenders and champions, like Iran Barkley and James Tillis, as well as prospects like Fres Oquendo and Dan Dancuta. By the time his career came to an end in 2001, he had failed to win a fight since his upset over Samson Po'uha.

Po'uha also saw his career decline after the Payne fight. Although he blamed the loss on poor conditioning, he still looked grossly overweight when he stepped into the ring with Andrew Golota the following year (at an embarrassing 287 pounds). It was a clear sign to many that he hadn't learn his lesson from the debacle against Craig Payne, and many boxing fans effectively closed the book on him as a future contender. Although Samson did give Golota a scare in the fourth round after coming up off the canvas (and nearly knocking out the undefeated Pole), he eventually succumbed to fatigue and the power of Golota in the fifth round. Although he still fought on, few regarded him as a top prospect anymore, and he began to show serious weaknesses in fights against Frankie Swindell and Patrick Freeman. The end for Po'uha's run came in 1997 when Jesse Ferguson knocked him out in the eighth round. After that loss even his most diehard fans were forced to admit that the Tongan would never become a contender, and he never again resembled one. In his next fight against blown-up light heavyweight David Vedder, Samson ended up on the losing end of a six-round decision, and in 2002 he lost a decision to journeyman Sherman Williams.

August 21, 1994—Reading, Pennsylvania
Craig Tomlinson (10–1, 7 KOs) vs. Doug Davis (7–7, 6 KOs)
Favorite: Tomlinson
Result: Davis won a eight-round unanimous decision.

For boxing fans in western and central Pennsylvania, heavyweight Craig Tomlinson was giving them a good reason to get excited about the future. Although he had limited amateur experience and already suffered a setback as a pro in losing to Levon Warner, he was developing rapidly as a regional heavyweight prospect. He seemed to fare well against the limited opposition that he had faced thus far, and even showed glimmers of star potential in a few of his fights. Against Bruce Johnson, a journeyman who lost to almost every named heavyweight on the planet, Tomlinson emerged victorious in the opening round. Although Johnson was expected to lose, the dominance of Tomlinson's victory had some Pennsylvania fans excited, and Johnson had made it to the second round against Lennox Lewis, Larry Donald, and David Tua. Even when he lost his sixth fight to a winless Levon Warner (who entered the fight 0–2–1), the loss seemed easily excusable when Warner went on to upset undefeated Terrence "KO" Lewis in his next fight. Still, few national boxing experts thought highly of Tomlinson, citing his weak opposition and his heavy dependence on fighting regionally: he had yet to fight in a casino or on cable TV. Outside of his home state he was not a well-known commodity. The promotional duo of Marshall Kauffman and George Moliatu seemed content to milk their successful product regionally, but boxing writers knew that Tomlinson would need to establish a greater national fan base if he were to make a serious run at becoming a contender.

All criticism aside, Craig was still slowly moving up the ladder in regards to the quality of opposition, and Davis seemed the perfect opponent for Tomlinson at that point. Davis was a fellow Pennsylvanian, making the fight easily marketable as an interstate rivalry. Also, he was a small step up from the Bruce Johnsons of the world, hardly a fighter with enough skills to give him serious trouble. Davis was noted as something of a mover, but that was over ten years ago, when he was a welterweight. Since Tomlinson never fought anyone who moved or boxed much, Davis seemed a good opponent to introduce him to a style he had yet to face—old and seemingly out of shape. Even if he were to outbox Craig early on, it appeared a safe bet that he wouldn't have the conditioning to go the full eight rounds at sixty pounds over his ideal fighting weight. Also, Tomlinson was a puncher, and Davis had a suspect chin. Against Jeremy Williams a year earlier he was stopped in the opening round, and he had suffered a second KO loss to Vincenzo Cantatore only two months before. Davis had been stopped in all seven of his losses, including two first-round knockout losses at welterweight.

When the fight began few were surprised to see the bigger Tomlinson bulldog into his smaller opponent, using his size and strength advantage to decisively win the round. It seemed like everything was going according to plan, until Davis came out for the second showing off his skills as a boxer. Suddenly Tomlinson was faced with an opponent who wasn't standing in front of him, waiting for him to unload. Instead Davis used his deceptively quick hands, solid foot movement, and every veteran trick in the book to box circles around his slower opponent. It suddenly became a question of Doug's conditioning, if he could keep up such a pace for very long. It seemed that the tank was beginning to run dry when Davis began to slow down in the fourth. A Tomlinson overhand right found its mark, stunning the suddenly flat-footed Davis, and by round's end Davis appeared badly winded. It appeared that the fight was changing gears, and that with solid pressure Tomlinson could indeed take out his pesky foe. But that assumption proved to be incorrect as Davis came out in the fifth with new life, resuming his dominance over Tomlinson as if the previous round had never happened. Although Tomlinson continued to stalk, he was unable to land anything meaningful and began to show signs of frustration. A wicked Davis right hand towards the end of the round staggered Tomlinson, draining Craig of his remaining resolve. When Davis stunned Tomlinson again in the sixth, it became clear that Tomlinson needed a miracle to pull out the victory, and that Davis was not likely to run out of gas. Tomlinson was unable to land the homerun punch, and Davis continued his dominance, sweeping the final two rounds. Davis received a dominant decision to cap what was the single most significant victory of his career, in any weight division.

However, like so many journeymen who score big upsets, Davis was unable to use the victory to turn his career around. He went on to lose his next fight at cruiserweight to Sergei Kobozev (a fighter who had knocked him out two years prior) and went on a nine-fight losing streak that included losses to Brian Nielsen, Darroll Wilson, and even Craig Tomlinson in a rematch.

For Tomlinson, the loss proved devastating. Gone was the talk of a promising heavyweight from Reading with a great punch. Tomlinson found himself completely discredited as a prospect and was never able to fully recover the momentum that he had developed going into the fight. He went on to lose to Dennis Cain, and although he strung together a handful of wins over the next several years, he would continue to lose just often enough to keep him from being taken seriously as a heavyweight.

September 24, 1994—London, England
Lennox Lewis (25–0, 21 KOs) vs. Oliver McCall (24–5, 17 KOs)
Favorite: Lewis
Result: McCall won via second-round TKO.

A little over a month after his title defense against Oliver McCall, Lennox Lewis was featured on the cover of *Boxing 94* magazine, which proclaimed him the "best heavyweight in the world."[2] It was a sentiment that more and more boxing writers were embracing, if reluctantly. Although Lennox was hardly impressive in his title defenses against Tony Tucker, Frank Bruno, or Phil Jackson, he always found a way to win. And although he looked very ordinary in those fights, he still won, which was more than could be said about Riddick Bowe or Evander Holyfield in 1994 (both fighters lost fights earlier in the year). Even British boxing fans (who were a bit cool to the remarketing of Lennox as a Brit after he fought for Canada in the Olympics) were beginning to embrace him with the same affection that they bestowed upon Frank Bruno. Besides, there was strong evidence that Lennox simply was mentally unprepared whenever he fought lower profile heavyweights. After a high profiled match against Tommy Morrison fell through when Morrison was upset by Michael Bentt, Lennox saw his first potential major payday disappear. The Morrison loss forced Lennox to take a huge pay cut to fight the lightly regarded Phil Jackson, which seemed to justify Lewis's lackluster performance. Many wondered if Lennox was just plain bored whenever he fought the Phil Jacksons and Tony Tuckers of the world. Even his fight with Bruno (the biggest heavyweight championship fight in British history) saw Lewis underestimate his opponent (in one instance he was half asleep during a telephone press conference). After

---

[2] On the cover of *Boxing 94*, November 1994.

all, he was such a prohibitive favorite that few gave Bruno much of a shot to win the fight. It was the novelty of two Brits fighting for the championship that made the bout such a super fight in England.

The still lingering question was how would Lennox look against the upper echelon fighters in the division, fighters like Holyfield or Bowe. Though he had many critics, most boxing writers remembered his shocking upset over Donovan "Razor" Ruddock nearly two years prior, a win that indicated that he could rise to the occasion. The question appeared close to being answered when a mega-fight with former champion Riddick Bowe was tentatively planned for March 1995. Although boxing writers were split as to whom they thought would win that fight, it was clear that Lennox Lewis was in a very enviable position. He was the most marketable champion (Michael Moorer looked even less impressive that Lewis in winning decisions over Mike Evans, James "Bonecrusher" Smith and Evander Holyfield), he was undefeated, and he was fighting Riddick Bowe rather than Joe Hipp or George Foreman (the two fighters that Michael Moorer was considering for his first title defense). If he were to beat Bowe, the questions would be laid to rest about his skill, and his struggles against Bruno and Tucker would almost certainly be forgotten. Yes, by November of 1994 things were really looking up for Lennox Lewis.

Unfortunately for Lennox Lewis and *Boxing 94*, Oliver McCall had other plans for the heavyweight division. Lewis was faced with a dangerous scenario. He would fight McCall while scheduled to fight Bowe. For a hot and cold fighter like Lewis, it was a very dangerous gamble. Although the fight was to be held in Lewis's backyard of London, many felt that Lennox would almost certainly be looking past McCall, and if his track record were any indication, he would not impress as a result.

However, although most boxing writers assumed that Lewis might look bad and might bump the odds in Riddick Bowe's favor, few figured McCall to win. After all, Oliver McCall was considered one of the easiest opponents in the top ten. He had lost a decision to Tony Tucker only two years earlier and, with the exception of Bruce Seldon and Francesco Damiani, didn't have any significant wins. Besides, the prospect of a McCall victory seemed grim to many boxing writers and fans. McCall lost a fight early in his career to Orlin Norris, who in 1994 was the WBA cruiserweight champion. Never before had there been a reigning cruiserweight champion who had a victory over a reigning heavyweight champion, and the prospect of such a scenario seemed certain to discredit the sport. Besides McCall was promoted by Don King, and few boxing writers were really eager for a Don-King-controlled heavyweight division again.

In fact, the Don King connection became both McCall's biggest asset and his biggest liability. Few doubted that McCall owed his number one ranking to his connection to King, and almost nobody believed he deserved to be ranked so high. Many assumed that the lack of integrity in the WBA, WBC, and IBF were best exemplified by the fact that Don-King-controlled fighters (McCall and Tony Tucker) were ranked number one and number two by all three organizations (and a third Don King fighter in Bruce Seldon was ranked number three by the IBF and WBA). In the justified backlash over Don King's attempt to con his way back into the heavyweight picture, Oliver McCall saw his credibility suffer. Although everyone in boxing (outside of those connected to Don King) resented McCall's ranking, almost nobody doubted that he did indeed belong in the top ten. He was a solid heavyweight, with a good chin (even if few gave him much credit for it). Had he been ranked number ten when Lennox Lewis signed to fight him rather than number one, nobody would have claimed that he was unworthy of the title shot. He also improved his chances with the acquisition of legendary trainer Emanuel Steward, who along with co-trainer Greg Page formulated a solid and intelligent fight plan. But because of the "King factor" these factors were overlooked. For many boxing writers, Oliver McCall was simply viewed as the latest Don King obstacle to a unified heavyweight champion.

By the time both fighters entered the ring, it appeared that McCall was on the verge of an emotional breakdown. Observers saw a man seemingly consumed with nervous energy, who paced the ring with excessive intensity. Some writers openly wondered if it was, in fact, fear that was causing the bizarre pre-fight performance of McCall, and even those who didn't question McCall's courage still felt that Oliver was on pace to hype himself right out of the fight. When McCall initially refused to participate in referee Jose Garcia's ring instructions, it did indeed appear that either he was trying to pull a Mike Tyson style psyche job or he was frightened of Lewis.

Lennox, on the other hand, appeared the picture of calm. He seemed unfazed by McCall's antics and showed no signs of excitement in his fourth title defense. Although it added to his mystique as a confident fighter before the fight, it clearly worked against him as the bell rang to start the first. Seconds into the fight commentator Jim Lampley remarked how Lewis was "standing like a statue." Lewis seemed content to paw with a lazy jab, all the while ignoring his footwork completely. Although McCall appeared to be loading up with every punch he threw, Lewis was unable to keep away from them as easily would have been expected, partially due to his poor stance. (He kept his feet too far apart to be effective at punching and moving.) With thirty seconds left in the first round, McCall had the undefeated champion on his bicycle, back-pedaling away from the onrushing McCall.

Although Lewis was clearly the loser of the round, fans in attendance assumed that as the fight progressed McCall would slow down. Many wondered if Lennox was simply weathering the storm and would pick up the pace in the second. Unfortunately for Lennox, he did. Ignoring the strong chin of McCall, and perhaps stung by the constant criticism, Lewis came out bombing in the second round. Determined to end the fight and win impressively, Lewis tagged the smaller "Atomic Bull" with a solid left hook as soon as the bell sounded to start the round. However, his technical deficiencies were glaring as he jumped on McCall. His left hand hovered by his waist, and his legs were still way too far apart to throw punches effectively. After firing a left jab, he dropped his left hand again and walked in with an overhand right. McCall, who had been training intensely for that moment, closed his eyes and fired a short right hand that landed right on Lennox's chin and dropped the champion like a ton of bricks. Lewis was clearly hurt, but he rose at six and indicated his desire to continue. However, in one of the worst stoppages in heavyweight history, referee Jose Lupe Garcia waved the fight off at 0:31 seconds of the second. Lewis was clearly upset by the stoppage, as he raised his arms in the air to indicate his disgust in a sort of "what the hell is he doing?" gesture. He had many who agreed with him, including HBO commentators Gil Clancy, Larry Merchant, and Jim Lampley, who said seconds after the fight "that's got to be one of the strangest stoppages I ever saw!"

However, Lewis was clearly hurt, and was leaning on the referee. (It appeared as if the referee was in fact the only thing keeping him up.) With over 2:30 left in the round, it was unlikely that he would have survived the round against an onrushing McCall (a sentiment with which both Clancy and Merchant agreed). But the questionable stoppage tainted McCall's win, and he made no attempt to rectify the controversy. When HBO viewers heard McCall say in the post-fight interview, "I'm a Showtime fighter! You'll see me again on Showtime!" it became abundantly clear that politics had just taken over the heavyweight division. With the most marketable fighter in an Indiana prison, and a Don King fighter with the WBC belt, it was unlikely that McCall would face Lewis in a rematch. Not when he could defend against lightly regarded fighters like Bruce Seldon and Peter McNeeley until Mike Tyson was released from prison. The fears of boxing fans were confirmed when McCall admitted that he would never defend his title against Riddick Bowe (citing Bowe's disrespect towards the WBC in throwing his belt in the trash). Don King then put the nail in the coffin of the heavyweight division when he confirmed that the possibility of a rematch with Lewis was "slim and none, and slim just left town."[3] With a single right hand, the heavyweight division lost almost all of its luster. Although Don King had actually gained a degree of admiration in putting together such strong boxing cards in the 1990s (most featuring Terry Norris, Julio Cesar Chavez, and Azumah Nelson), King suddenly found himself the most hated man in the sport again when he announced Peter McNeeley as McCall's first title defense.

Although the heavyweight division did indeed proceed to fall apart over the next year when Bruce Seldon and Frans Botha became WBA and IBF champs respectively (both controlled by King), McCall never did end up fighting Tyson as was anticipated. He looked uninspiring winning a close decision over forty-five-year-old Larry Holmes in his first defense and proceeded to lose a twelve-round decision in his next fight to Frank Bruno. As a result, Bruno was rewarded with the Tyson fight (in which he was stopped in the third round). McCall still had the Don King connection though, and when the WBC stripped Tyson of his

---

[3] Bernard Fernandez, "Don King, Uh, Oliver McCall Wins the WBC Heavyweight Title," *KO Magazine*, February 1995, 59.

title for refusing to fight Lennox Lewis, McCall found himself back in another title fight with his old nemesis Lennox Lewis in 1997. However, in what turned out to be one of the most disturbing fights in heavyweight history, Lennox Lewis avenged the loss in London when he scored a fifth-round TKO over the granite-chinned McCall. The win was just as tainted as McCall's victory over Lewis. McCall, who had suffered from problems with drugs prior to the fight, had a complete mental breakdown in the ring. He began to weep and refused to engage Lewis at all. After refusing to return to his corner in between rounds and continuing his disturbing behavior in the fifth, referee Mills Lane waved the fight off.

For Lewis, the rematch with McCall failed to erase the questions and criticisms that had surfaced after the first McCall fight. He seemed a completely discredited fighter after the loss, and even the win in the rematch failed to gain him much respect (most writers wondered why he couldn't knock out a man who was not defending himself at all). But the loss to McCall did provide Lennox with a major boost in one area of his career, and in the long run proved to be one of the best things that ever happened to him. After losing to McCall, Lewis hired the man who trained his opponent, Emanuel Steward. Lewis, who lacked proper training from day one of his pro career, suddenly had the best trainer in the business working with him. Slowly, his technique began to improve, and though he still remained a hot and cold fighter, he began to impress more often than struggle (although he would go on to be knocked out in a huge upset to Hasim Rahman in 2001). By the time he fought Evander Holyfield in 1999, Lennox Lewis had developed into a complete fighter and a well-rounded champion, who would rule the heavyweight division until his retirement in 2004.

October 22, 1994—Washington, D.C.
Leon Spinks (25–15–3, 15 KOs) vs. John Carlo (Pro Debut)
Favorite: Spinks
Result: Carlo won by way of first-round TKO.

By late 1994 boxing insiders were nearly unanimous in their opinion of the ill-advised comeback of Leon Spinks. It didn't just fail miserably: it was on pace to becoming the worst heavyweight comeback in the history of the sport. After upsetting Muhammad Ali in 1978, "Neon" Leon quickly emerged as one of the most recognizable athletes in the world. Not only had he beaten the immortal Ali, but his personality, his driving record, and his teeth made him instantly recognizable to almost everyone. Unfortunately for Spinks, his skills could not compensate for his terrible training and his notoriously wild lifestyle. He quickly returned the title to Ali later that year and rapidly faded from the heavyweight picture from that point. Gerrie Coetzee knocked him out in 1980, and although he recovered from that loss to earn a title fight with Larry Holmes, he failed miserably against Holmes (losing in three). When Spinks announced his intention to drop down to the cruiserweight division in 1982, it appeared to many boxing insiders that the career of Spinks would be revitalized. The cruiserweight division was boxing's newest weight class and lacked any big name fighters. A world title appeared to be a no-brainer for the cruiserweight Spinks. But he failed as a cruiserweight (losing by way of knockout to both Carlos DeLeon and Dwight Qawi), and though he returned to the heavyweight division in 1987 the prevailing wisdom was that Leon was beyond finished. Spinks went on to lose six of his next eight fights after his return to the heavyweight division, and following an embarrassing first-round knockout loss to Tony Morrison, Spinks called it a career.

Bankruptcy had left Spinks without any of the millions he won in the ring, and he found himself taking on a collection of degrading jobs in an attempt to survive after boxing. After a brief stint working as a greeter at Mike Ditka's restaurant in Chicago, Leon's craving to return to the ring was fueled by the (at least financially) successful comeback of George Foreman. For the financially destitute Spinks, the image of Foreman earning millions was more than enough motivation, and with that Leon was back. But it didn't take long for Spinks to show why he was never going to land that big fight. After winning his first fight against Lupe Guerra in November 1991 by way of third-round KO, Spinks struggled against clubfighter Andre Crowder in winning a ten-round split decision three months later. Considering Crowder entered the ring with a horrible record of 6–17–2, 2 KOs, it proved without a doubt that Spinks was only fooling himself in thinking he would land the big money fight. Things didn't get any easier for Leon when he went on to win a tough decision over Rick Myers in his next fight and over

Ken Bentley after that. By the end of 1992 the comeback seemed to have been derailed when K.P. Porter, a step up in class for Spinks but still worlds away from the top ten, won a lopsided ten-round decision. Leon then went on to lose perhaps the single most embarrassing fight for any former heavyweight champion the following year when he was upset by blown-up light heavyweight James Wilder. Wilder entered the fight with a record of 2–33–1. From that point on, there was little question that the comeback was over, but Leon still hung around, hoping to land the big money fight. Spinks was able to capture a small degree of redemption when he held his own against young Shane Sutcliffe in early October 1994 before losing an eight-round decision, a performance that made his fight with John Carlo three weeks later appear to be a case of "record padding" for the former champion. It may not have been enough to convince insiders that he could beat a ranked contender, but it seemed to show that he had enough to beat a fighter like Carlo, a complete unknown making his professional debut.

Although the Spinks comeback was a flop, never before in the history of boxing had a former heavyweight champion lost to a fighter making his pro debut, and Carlo hardly appeared to be a candidate to become the first. He had only two amateur fights in the novice class (winning them both), and at thirty-three years old he seemed too old to have a successful career. Realizing the farce the fight appeared to be, Carlo saw his record changed by the promoter to 14–2 in an attempt to disguise his inexperience. Considering what little was known on Carlo, it appeared to be a safe enough move (although when asked by a reporter he was unable to name any of the fighters he fought). Besides, what were the odds that anyone would remember Carlo after the fight was over?

But at forty-one years old, Spinks lacked the recuperative abilities to fight on such short notice (and considering how bad he looked when he was fresh, he needed all the time he could to recover). Carlo came out jabbing and fighting cautiously, but a left hook landed on the chin of Leon twelve seconds into the fight and dropped the former champion. The punch looked harmless enough, but Spinks rolled around the canvas, barely beating the count. Carlo jumped all over Spinks, prompting the ringside doctor to climb to the ring apron to try and convince the referee to wave the fight off. After pushing Spinks into the ropes Carlo fired three straight left hooks that dropped Spinks again. With the ringside doctor still standing on the ring apron trying to call the fight off, Spinks was given one more chance by the referee. But Carlo fired several more left hooks that finally prompted the referee to wave it off at 1:11 of the opening round.

For the debuting Carlo, it was a perfect way to start a professional career. Suddenly he was in all the boxing record books (or at least the trivia books), and suddenly his made-up record of 14–2 was more of a hindrance than it was beneficial. He continued his career as an undefeated prospect, and went on to rack up ten more wins against relatively weak opposition before taking his second step up in class, this time against a fellow New Yorker, undefeated heavyweight Rich Melito, in 1997. Carlo was stopped in two rounds (in a controversial fight in which some would accuse Carlo of taking a dive), suspending his career for five years before returning to the ring in 2002 for a one-fight comeback. By 2004 it seemed that only his success would be in promoting kickboxing events and trash-talking on an Internet boxing message board.

For Spinks, the calls for his retirement were now overwhelming, but he fought on. After winning a decision over Ray Kipping eight months after the Carlo debacle, Spinks took on a thirty-seven-year-old former cruiserweight journeyman named Fred Houpe, who was coming off a seventeen-year layoff following a knockout loss to S.T. Gordon in 1978. Houpe won a decision, prompting Leon to finally call an end to his failed comeback.

November 5, 1994—Las Vegas, Nevada
Michael Moorer (35–0, 30 KOs) vs. George Foreman
**   (72–4, 67 KOs)**
Favorite: Moorer
Result: Foreman won by way of tenth-round knockout.

With two championship belts, and a big decision win over the most recognizable heavyweight not incarcerated in an Indiana State prison, it appeared a no-brainer that Moorer would emerge as a superstar. He was dark, sullen, hard punching, and he was boxing's first southpaw heavyweight champion. For many fans, he brought back memories of Mike Tyson's early championship reign and some boxing insiders were even comparing his personality to that of former heavyweight champion

Sonny Liston (who knocked out Floyd Patterson in one round in 1962 to win the world title). By the time he stepped into the ring seven months later against George Foreman he was widely seen as one of the most little known champions to emerge since the Berbick-Tubbs-Page era a decade earlier. Unfortunately for Moorer, he lacked the explosive power (or nature) of Mike Tyson. He was almost too sullen, to the point of appearing uninterested. (*KO Magazine* would write that some critics felt that Moorer had the "personality of a fence post.")[4] Also, his near mythical power, which alone could have carried him to superstar status, badly fizzled after moving up from light heavyweight to heavyweight in 1991. After knocking out his first twenty-six opponents, he followed up with four lackluster decisions in eight fights, many against less-than-stellar opposition like Mike "The Giant" White and Everett "Bigfoot" Martin. Even his victory over Evander Holyfield was tainted when Holyfield was diagnosed with a mysterious heart ailment. In fact, the fight was more memorable for Teddy Atlas's performance as a cornerman than anything that Moorer did in the ring.

Recognizing Moorer's lack of drawing power, Team Moorer initially focused on finding a familiar (and popular) face as an opponent. Forty-five-year-old George Foreman was arguably the single most recognizable active pugilist in the world, and with the most successful career in advertising in the history of the sport, there was little question that he had drawing power. But a problem emerged almost immediately. Although Foreman's unlikely comeback had landed him financial security, a new fan base, and even a great deal of respectability—he held his own in losing a tough twelve-round decision to undisputed heavyweight champion Evander Holyfield in 1991—most insiders felt that the comeback had run its course and was rapidly fading. In 1992 Foreman was badly damaged after winning a razor-thin majority decision over Alex Stewart, and the calls for his retirement became deafening throughout the sports world. The image of Foreman's grotesquely swollen and bloody face after the fight sent chills up the spines of many boxing insiders who were all to familiar where extended careers often lead (see Muhammad Ali). Although "Big" George rebounded with an impressive win over Pierre Coetzer in his next fight, a twelve-round decision loss to

---

[4] Nigel Collins, "My Best Shot," *KO Magazine*, November 1994, 5.

Tommy "The Duke" Morrison in June 1993 seemed to bring an end to the career of "Big" George. There appeared nowhere left to go; although Morrison boxed better than he ever had in the past against Foreman, there was little question that a loss to the blonde bomber put Foreman out of the running for a shot at another title. In fact, Foreman himself seemed to recognize that fact, not stepping in the ring at all since the loss to Morrison. But all that changed with Moorer's win over Holyfield, as "Double-M" found himself looking to pad his record with an easy defense. Foreman seemed the perfect fall guy, but there was a second problem. The WBA balked at the prospect of a title fight with a forty-five-year-old that was coming off a seventeen-month layoff and was almost two years removed from his last victory. Refusing to sanction the fight, Moorer was forced to seek a new opponent (and found Joe Hipp) for the first title defense of the title. But outside of the novelty of an all-southpaw heavyweight championship, there was little interest from casual boxing fans in a Moorer-Hipp fight, and even Foreman's most ardent critics reluctantly admitted that they would rather see him in a title fight than Hipp (not to mention Moorer, who would have been forced to take a fairly large pay cut). Perhaps motivated by those sentiments (as well as the financial benefits of a fight with Moorer), Foreman decided to take legal action, suing the WBA. Most assumed the WBA would win—after all, in this instance they actually had a pretty sound argument—but in what would prove prophetic, "Big" George pulled off the upset after a Las Vegas judge ruled in his favor.

Considering what steps he needed to take just to ensure that the fight would transpire Foreman realized that his title fight with Michael Moorer would undoubtedly be the last chance he would ever have to finally exorcise the ghost of Zaire. Despite all that he accomplished, one name haunted his legacy: Muhammad Ali. Although Foreman was over twenty-one years removed from his humbling knockout loss to Ali in Kinshasa, it was a loss that unfortunately defined his career. In one night his brutal knockouts over Ken Norton and Joe Frazier were no longer the things of which legends were made, but rather interesting asterisks that made Ali's win all the more significant. Foreman never completely shook the stigma of his loss to Ali, and even after he came back in 1987 as a loveable and personable "old man," he was never able to smile and joke his way out of the shadow of Ali (although he came

George Foreman put down the sausage to prepare for his title fight against Michael Moorer, weighing in at 250 pounds, a six-year low for "Big" George. *Pat Orr*

close after his fight with Evander Holyfield). Ultimately though, Foreman's burden was of his own doing: his desire to regain the heavyweight championship he lost to Ali became a near obsession, made all the more intense by his popularity and the simple fact that he was still a very competent heavyweight. There was little question that Foreman was a man on a mission when he weighed in at a shockingly svelte 250 pounds (the lowest in over six years). But perhaps more telling was his choice of trunks, squeezing into the old, red boxing trunks that he wore the last time he was a world champion, against Muhammad Ali.

Moorer initially appeared unmotivated and uninterested (a perception that was somewhat complicated by his demeanor), but there was little question that with eight added pounds since his last fight against Holyfield, he was taking Foreman at least a little lightly. It was enough to add to the mad rush on Foreman money in Vegas, dropping the odds to a deceptive 2–1 in Moorer's favor. There was little question that most of that money was due more to sentimental reasons than legitimate ones, and boxing writers and insiders put it heavily in Moorer's favor. In fact, when HBO commentator Larry Merchant admitted after the fight he felt that "it [the odds on the fight] was a gazillion to one that George Foreman could ever win the heavyweight championship again," few disagreed.

Initially both fighters fought exceeding expectations. Moorer came out with a solid right jab, but quickly began hooking and mixing it up well against the forty-five-year-old veteran. But Foreman was holding his own quite well in the opening round, landing a few good counters early. But the speed and persistence of Moorer began to take its toll as Foreman seemed to freeze as Moorer peppered the bigger man with jabs and hooks that began to swell Foreman's left eye almost immediately. Although George did land a solid right hand with forty seconds left in the round, it hardly slowed Moorer, who landed twenty-five of fifty-two punches in the round (against only eleven of fifty-two for Foreman). It suddenly looked as if the age, the ring rust, and the speed of a younger opponent would be too much for Foreman to handle. Foreman fans were given even more reason to worry when, in between the first and second round, Moorer's trainer Teddy Atlas told his young fighter "the hardest part of the fight is over . . . our sparring partners were better."

It seemed a valid point; Foreman's power was the main concern of Team Moorer, and now that he tasted it he could move on and do what he needed to do. Without the power Foreman was looking increasingly ordinary in the ring. After a fairly even second round, Moorer's dominance continued in the third round as Foreman was left to reach with his slow right hand while Moorer peppered the big man relentlessly with his jab. Although Foreman again landed a hard right hand in the closing minute of the round, Moorer fired back almost immediately with his own combination that had Foreman backing up at the bell. At the end of the third round Foreman had thrown an impressive fifty-seven punches, but he landed a somewhat ordinary twenty. Moorer, however, landed a shockingly efficient forty of seventy-two, prompting Atlas to urge Moorer to continue the pressure by telling him "don't allow him to bullshit you to go a slower pace." Although Moorer's ability to outbox Foreman shocked nobody, his ability to take Foreman's best punches began to wear away at one of the most unquestionable myths of boxing, that of the power of Foreman. In fact, by the fourth round all three HBO commentators were openly questioning the once undeniable power of "Big" George. Foreman was still reaching with his slow right hand while eating right-hand jabs all the way.

Although Foreman continued to march forward in the fifth, he also continued to take punches from his more active opponent. In the sixth it appeared as if Foreman was throwing caution to the wind. After tagging Moorer with a right hand within a minute, he began to throw more punches, but he paid a dear price for opening up as a Moorer counter to the face further closed the swelling left eye. It was vintage Michael Moorer, who was not only holding his own with one of the best punchers of all time, but also out jabbing a fighter with one of the hardest (and best) jabs ever. Foreman simply appeared unable to pull the trigger, the classic sign of a fighter past his prime. Although it looked like he would go the full twelve rounds, it appeared as if the legend and aura of George Foreman would emerge from the fight in tatters. Larry Merchant would say in the seventh round, "I think the myth of George's power has been exposed by Michael Moorer so far," and although it was a harsh criticism of "Big" George, it looked more and more as if it had merit. Although Moorer would occasionally seem to allow himself to become distracted and stand still in front of Foreman—even when he did move he didn't listen to Atlas's advice to move to his right away from George's power—these lapses were relatively brief and George was unable to capitalize. With each round a duplicate of the one that preceded it, Moorer was pitching a virtual shutout, and although he could not slow the forward march of "Big" George, he was punishing him dearly for it. Early in the ninth he had Foreman backing up, and with Foreman's badly swollen left eye, a TKO started to look like a real possibility. Moorer pounded Foreman for much of the ninth round, landing thirty-three of his seventy-nine punches thrown in that round, but it was the end of the round that signaled the end for Foreman (although at the time few could have seen it). Moorer's early activity took its toll and Moorer decided to slow down for the last minute of the round. Foreman, however, was still moving forward.

Foreman's activity, which had dropped from over fifty punches a round to around thirty-five, seemed to take another break early in the tenth. Still, Moorer himself seemed to want to take a break as well, easing up in the tenth round. The Moorer jab, a powerful weapon for much of the fight, lost its snap early on as Moorer pawed with it, and the movement that was such an important tool in Moorer's fight plan also vanished. Foreman again upped the pressure, firing chopping right hands to the chin of Michael, but Moorer continued to hold his ground, easily brushing off Foreman's punches. When Moorer began to fire back at 1:10 of the round it appeared as if Foreman had missed his only chance. Seconds later Foreman missed with two wild left hooks, indicating that the momentum was clearly back in Moorer's corner. But thirty seconds later Foreman finally found his missing power when a right hand behind a left hook landed on the chin of Moorer. Although Moorer initially didn't appear badly rattled, he did take a step back as a result. It was enough of a window for Foreman, who followed up with another left-right combo. The right hand landed perfectly on the chin of Moorer and the champion bent over before falling flat on his back. In an instant Foreman shocked the world, completely turning around a fight that was clearly all Moorer's. Referee Joe Cortez reached the count of ten without much threat from Moorer, and by the time ringsiders recovered from their shock, George Foreman was in the corner on his knees offering a prayer of thanks for his victory. At 2:03 of the tenth round, George

Foreman had regained the heavyweight championship for the second time, a full twenty-one years after he first tasted gold.

For boxing, the Foreman victory was undoubtedly the biggest, and most significant, upset (regardless of the odds) since Tyson's loss to James "Buster" Douglas in 1990. Suddenly casual sports fans were abuzz, and the following day boxing was again the most talked about sport in the world. Everyone in the country knew the name of the heavyweight champion, and almost everyone loved him. It was, after all, the ultimate feel-good story and a most needed boost of adrenaline to a sport in disarray. Not only was he the oldest heavyweight champion of all time, he was also arguably the most personable since (who else) Muhammad Ali. Although most boxing insiders hoped that he would retire on top, few thought that was likely. Not with a potential $100 million fight with Mike Tyson on the line. If George Foreman was one thing, he was the consummate businessman and there was still a lot of money to be made. Unfortunately it was the businessman in "Big" George that would badly cripple the sport in the years to come. Initially the WBA, which was hardly excited about the fight, began clamoring for Foreman to fight their number one contender Tony Tucker. For neutral fans, it was a gift. Tony Tucker was widely seen as a shot fighter and one of the softer touches in the top ten. But Foreman was unwilling to deal with any Don King–controlled fighter, which immediately put him at odds with both the IBF and the WBA. Although Tucker was not seen as a particularly dangerous opponent, his connection to Don King made the prospect of a scoring decision in that fight potentially hazardous. Still, most assumed that Foreman would take the defense and get rid of Tony Tucker once and for all; few questioned his desire to fight the softest opposition available until Mike Tyson was released from prison, and Tucker was seen as relatively soft. Besides, it was up to Tucker (and King) to eat crow, not him. Although Tucker was a Showtime fighter and Foreman an HBO fighter, it would have been up to Tucker to "cross the picket line" and take the fight on HBO. But Foreman was not going to take any chances and opted out of the Tucker fight, instead choosing to fight unknown German Axel Schultz. It was a stunningly bad decision as it cost him the WBA title and also alienated many fans. Also, Foreman overlooked the simple fact that Schultz was in fact more dangerous than Tucker. He was a young, up and coming prospect with a draw against undefeated Henry Akinwande (as well as a points loss to the towering British fighter), a sign that his lack of international appeal was not indicative of his skills as a fighter. After struggling with Schultz over twelve rounds in April 1995, it looked as if George's strategy had backfired on him. Schultz appeared to have outhustled and outboxed Foreman, and most assumed that he would emerge with the IBF title. But in one of the worst decisions of the decade, Foreman emerged with a majority decision. It was enough for the IBF to demand an immediate rematch, but Foreman no longer wanted any part of Schultz and refused to fight him again, this despite the fact that the IBF threatened to strip him of his only remaining title. Suddenly Foreman was left with none of the belts that he won against Moorer. However Foreman figured that the champion meant more than the belt, something that Larry Holmes proved when he vacated his WBC belt for the (then) unknown IBF championship (giving instant credibility to the IBF). He quickly shopped around for a lesser-quality sanctioning body (of which there were plenty) looking for a championship and found his fit with the WBU. As WBU champion, he was virtually free to defend against anyone of his choosing (his first, against unknown Crawford Grimsley) but again the plan backfired. The WBU gained little prestige from the addition of Foreman, and his poor choice in opposition further discredited him, despite his linear championship. By 1996 his "safety first" approach backfired in every way possible, and the Tyson fight was but a wish. He would continue to fight, defending his "linear championship"—he dumped the WBU title after realizing how worthless it really was—until losing a highly questionable decision to Shannon Briggs in 1997, a fight that would prove to be his last. Considering Don King emerged with two champions due to Foreman's actions (in Bruce Seldon, the WBA champ, and Frans Botha, the IBF champion), the damage had been done. With three of the weakest, most forgettable champions in the history of the sport sitting on top, the sport again spiraled off the radar screen and remained there until Mike Tyson won the WBC title in 1996. Still, Foreman was finally able to catch and exorcise the "Ghost of Ali" once and for all, in a proud and memorable moment for the sport of boxing.

For Moorer, he suddenly found himself a discredited, paper champion. His flaws, which were evident previously, were now glaring, and it looked as if he had a tough road ahead. Winning a lackluster ten-round decision against a minor prospects of sorts in Melvin Foster six months later, Moorer continued to fight with a lack of intensity that would define the rest of his career. Even when he won the IBF title against Axel Schultz in 1996, he did not excite fans the way many anticipated he would early in his career. (Although his fight with Frans Botha later that year did have fireworks, it was not the dominant performance that fans were expecting.) Moorer would eventually lose the IBF title to an old nemesis, Evander Holyfield in 1997, and by the decade's end it became clear that the "ghost of Zaire" was not exorcized but rather repackaged and handed to Moorer to carry on in the form of the "ghost of Big George." Unlike Foreman, Moorer, however, would never be able to shake his ghost. A thirty-second knockout loss to David Tua in 2002 would only confirm his place in history, as the man who George Foreman knocked out in one of history's most memorable heavyweight fights.

November 15, 1994—Erie, Pennsylvania
Tom "The Bomb" Glesby (14–0–1, 11 KOs) vs. Josh Imadiyi
   (9–1, 8 KOs)
Favorite: Glesby
Result: Imadiyi won by way of second-round TKO.

When Canadian Tom Glesby first announced his intentions of turning pro, few boxing insiders anticipated much from the hard-punching amateur standout. Although he went on to become the best amateur super heavyweight in Canada, his failings against such fighters as Felix Savon (who starched him in one round) were glaring, and for many boxing insiders he seemed a mirror image of fellow Canadian heavyweight Willie DeWitt. DeWitt, a Canadian Olympian, turned pro in 1984 with much fanfare only to flounder as a pro. Like DeWitt, Glesby was big and strong, but he also seemed to lack speed and had a porous defense. Despite the criticism, most insiders followed his career with some interest. Most of his flaws were technical (and therefore correctable), and he was a white heavyweight, something that was always in short supply in the division. Besides, his pro debut began in such fashion that it was hard to completely ignore him. Stepping into the ring against rugged veteran

K.P. Porter, Glesby won by way of devastating first-round knockout. Porter was not a fighter to be mistaken for world class, but in the previous fight he extended former champion Greg Page into the eighth round before getting stopped, and the fight before that, he upset former champion Leon Spinks. Most assumed that the durability of Porter, along with Glesby's inexperience, would ensure a tougher fight for the rookie.

Glesby continued to impress following his fight with Porter. Four months and three fights later he captured the Canadian heavyweight championship with an impressive knockout over Conroy Nelson in the fourth round. Although he went on to fight to a four-round draw with Terry Pitts (who would later emerge as a cruiserweight contender under the name Sajad Abdul Aziz), in his next fight in Lansing, Michigan, many ringsiders felt that it was more of a case of the local fighter in Pitts getting a "gift decision" than a major setback. By 1994 he had a decision victory over former IBF cruiserweight champion Jeff Lampkin, a win that helped him land his first fight on network TV against tough Everton Davis. Although Davis's record seemed less than stellar at 9–2, 7 KOs, he had extended former contender Alex Garcia the ten-round limit in losing a majority decision. Although many attributed that to the rapid decline of Alex Garcia, it did make many wonder how Glesby would perform against a fighter with proven resiliency. Glesby did end up stopping Davis in the ninth round, but the win garnered somewhat mixed reviews. In the fight, few questioned his power, but it was also clear that his balance needed a great deal of work. Also, his defense, which had never been great, was clearly not improving quickly enough. Perhaps recognizing the need to slow things down, Glesby's next two opponents were the forgettable Mauricio Villegas and Bill Corrigan. By November he was ready to return to *USA Tuesday Night Fights* for the second time, this time against Nigerian Josh Imadiyi.

For Team Glesby, Imadiyi seemed a safe enough pick. Although he was an amateur standout, compiling an impressive record of 43–2, 38 KOs, and fighting for his native Nigeria in the Olympics, his professional career was defined by his lone loss to Mike Robinson in his fourth fight. Imadiyi was starched in the opening round by Robinson (whose record going in was 4–12–1), and many saw the loss as a clear sign that Josh's chin was never going to pass the test against a top heavyweight.

But in all the attention given to Josh's chin, Team Glesby underestimated a major weapon in Josh's arsenal: his power. Imadiyi had six first-round knockouts in his ten fights, and with eight knockouts in nine wins, he was a dangerous opponent for any fighter with a shaky defense regardless of his chin.

Perhaps recognizing that he was in with a fast starting opponent, Glesby started cautiously in the first, pumping his jab and moving. But Josh was not to be derailed. A right hand counter over the left jab dropped Glesby into the ropes for a standing eight count thirty-seconds into the round. Immediately the Nigerian jumped all over his dazed opponent, trapping him against the ropes and tagging him with several shots to the chin. Halfway through the round Glesby was able to momentarily frustrate Imadiyi, when he attempted to push his shorter opponent over the top rope in the clinch (an action that earned him some boos from the crowd). But Josh was able to repay Glesby when a left hook sent Glesby into the corner and down (in what should have been ruled a knockdown but wasn't). Imadiyi was all over the Canadian again, and when Glesby turned to argue with the referee with ten seconds left in the round, it was clear that he was unable to cope with the relentless pressure of Imadiyi.

By the start of the second round there was little question that Glesby had yet to fully recover from the beating he took in the first, and it didn't take Imadiyi long to capitalize on that. At the bell Josh came out swinging and backed his wounded foe into the ropes. Although Glesby bravely tried to slug it out with Imadiyi from the ropes, a big right hand from the Nigerian landed flush on his chin to rob Glesby of what clarity he may have still possessed. Glesby fell face first to the canvas, and to most ringsiders it looked like the fight was over. But Glesby was able to get up at the count of five and, in fact, was allowed to continue despite being clearly out on his feet. Imadiyi fired two right hands that dropped Glesby a second time, and although the fight was again allowed to continue, a left hook that nearly decapitated Glesby was enough to prompt the referee to finally wave it off less than a minute into the round.

For Josh Imadiyi, it initially appeared as if he had erased the memory of the Mike Robinson debacle and was now on his way up the ladder towards contender status. Unfortunately for Josh, he never reached the top of the ladder or came close to entering the world rankings. Ironically enough it was not an opponent who would erase the memory of his win over Tom Glesby, it was himself. Josh disappeared after the win over Glesby for four months before resurfacing in the New England circuit against unknown Steve Halstead. He went on to win his next four fights, all against local club fighters in the New England circuit and all far away from the watchful eye of a national audience. With only one fight in 1996, it was not hard for boxing fans to forget the once attractive prospect. A six-round loss to Zuri Lawrence in 1997 ended his run for all intents and purposes, and by the time Frankie Swindell stopped him in four rounds, the win over Tom Glesby was a distant memory.

For "The Bomb," his career never completely recovered after losing to Imadiyi. He went on to win six straight by knockout, but disappeared from the ring in mid-1996. He returned in July 1998, but when he was knocked out the following year by undefeated prospect Robert Davis, it effectively ended all talk of Glesby as a fighter with potential. Suddenly, the talk returned to his similarities to Willie DeWitt, and how similar his loss to Imadiyi was to DeWitt's devastating loss to Bert Cooper.

December 10, 1994—Monterrey, Mexico
King Ipitan (13–0, 8 KOs) vs. Bob Crabtree (49–29–1, 46 KOs)
Favorite: Ipitan
Result: Crabtree won by way of first-round TKO.

Although Nigerian heavyweight King Ipitan was not quite in the same league as Shannon Briggs or Jeremy Williams when it came to attractive heavyweight prospects, he was still regarded as one of the best young heavyweights of the future, and by 1994 his stock was skyrocketing. After turning pro in 1991, Ipitan quickly began to win fans with his combination of speed, size, and power. Few questioned that he was the best heavyweight produced by the African country of Nigeria (until the emergence of David Izonritei in 1993), and many wondered if he would become heavyweight champion—after all he already knocked out one reigning heavyweight belt holder. After starting his career with ten straight wins against the usual cannon fodder, Ipitan took a major jump in class when he entered the People's Choice Heavyweight tournament in December 1993, a World-Cup-style, one-night tournament of thirty-two fighters battling for a one-million-dollar prize. Although there were no top-ranked heavyweights in the tournament, there was also no short-age of experience. Many boxing insiders assumed that he entered to cash in on his record or because his team honestly believed his talent was good enough to compensate for his lack of experience. However, when the prize money was slashed, Ipitan bolted from the tournament. Although he lost out on the exposure that the tournament would have brought, he quickly made a name for himself when he was called in as a sparring partner for then-WBO heavyweight champion, Michael Bentt. Bentt, who won the title by way of a first-round knockout over Tommy Morrison, was in training for a title defense against undefeated Brit Herbie Hide, a fighter with a glossy 25–0 (24 KOs) record. But Bentt was given worlds of trouble in sparring with Ipitan and was in fact knocked out cold by Ipitan shortly before his fight with Hide was to take place. Although the rules in Britain (where the fight took place) called for Bentt to pull out of the fight, he covered the event up and went through with his ill-advised title defense, getting knocked out in seven rounds. After being removed from the ring in a stretcher and seeing his boxing career brought to an end, there was little question that he made a poor decision. Suddenly, Ipitan was given more press than most spar-ring partners receive when the reports surfaced that Bentt may have entered the ring as damaged goods and that Ipitan was the man who did the damage. It was enough to spark serious interest in Ipitan as a prospect—enough to land him a fight on the undercard of one of the biggest fight cards of the year, Julio Cesar Chavez's title defense of his WBC Light Welterweight title against Tony Lopez. His opponent was the popular clubfighter Bobby Crabtree, a hard-hitting (albeit limited) journeyman from Fort Smith, Arkansas, who had knocked out forty-six of the forty-nine opponents that he beat. (Most were against weak, re-gional opponents with little skill other than their ability to pad records.) Crabtree was better known for his twenty-nine defeats, almost all inside the distance. He tended to come out swinging before tiring badly within a round or two, as fighters like Trevor Berbick, Craig Payne, Alex Gar-cia, and Tyrell Biggs discovered. His chin was also suspect, with several losses by way of first-round knockout. For boxing fans, it seemed a safe pick: Crabtree's power was overrated, and although a small step up in competition for Ipitan, he was still seen as a safe pick for the undefeated Nigerian.

The referee checks on King Ipitan and calls for a TKO due to a broken ankle. *Scott Romer*

But for Ipitan, the one thing he failed to take into account was the inexplicable. As Crabtree rushed Ipitan at the bell, Ipitan easily blocked a hard right hand and clinched to offset the attack of Bob Crabtree. After the break, as he backed away from Crabtree to establish his own punching room, he was dropped to the seat of his pants by a short left hook. He rose at the count of seven, but it was clear that his right leg was injured. Complaining about a broken right ankle to the referee, Ipitan saw his undefeated record go up in smoke when the referee waved the fight off less than thirty seconds into the fight.

With the win, Crabtree elevated himself into the biggest fight of his career and added to his nearly mythical status as one of boxing's most beloved journeymen. He saw a major story written about him in *Boxing 95*,[5] and saw an opportunity to fight for a third-tier world title in his

---

[5] Tommy Deas Jr., "Taking Lumps and Pounding Out Don'ts: The Saga of Bobby Crabtree," *Boxing 95*, May 1995, 38–51.

hometown. Although still ignored by the major sanctioning bodies, the WBF rewarded him with an opportunity to avenge a fourth-round knockout loss to Kenny Keene in a bid for their cruiserweight title. Crabtree wasn't expected to win (after all, he already had been knocked out by Keene), but he nonetheless trained with renewed vigor, confident of his chances. He extended Keene the full twelve rounds, and although most ringsiders felt that Keene emerged victorious, many felt Crabtree did much better than was expected. Crabtree was awarded the title after capturing a highly questionable decision that had even his hometown fans somewhat stunned. Although he lost the rubber match with Keene three months later (by way of ninth-round KO) he rebounded again with a knockout over young Rick Rofus, a win that led to his biggest title fight, for the WBC Continental Americas Cruiserweight Title, against Eliecer Castillo. A second-round knockout loss ended Crabtree's brief run towards respectability and returned him firmly to the status of opponent.

For Ipitan, the loss proved to be devastating. Immediately after the fight both corners were talking rematch, but fans knew it would have to wait: he would be sidelined for some time after breaking his ankle. However, he was never able to completely shake off his inactivity. Most fans felt that the loss to Crabtree would be easy to explain away and wouldn't affect his career too badly if he resumed boxing quickly and got his name out again. But from February 1996 to June 1998 he was inactive and, as a result, was quickly forgotten by boxing fans. A loss to Zuri Lawrence in 2000 derailed his comeback, and when Jameel McCline knocked him out in one round in 2001 it ended any hope that he might have had of becoming a contender.

CHAPTER SIX

1995

"They told me he was a bum . . ."

—Earnie Shavers after his fight with Brian Yates

March 17, 1995—Bushkill, Pennsylvania
Jerry Ballard (5–0, 5 KOs) vs. Robert Hawkins (2–0, 0 KOs)
Favorite: Ballard
Result: Hawkins won a four-round unanimous decision.

Usually when two undefeated fighters meet each other in the ring early in their careers, the fight is considered "pick'em": neither fighter is considered a favorite. Sometimes one fighter is a little more impressive statistically, a fact which alone would make him the favorite. Hardly a surefire formula for success in picking the winner, but usually the formula is fool proof. More knockouts + size advantage + well-known promoter/trainer/manager + hometown + better amateur experience = winning fighter. Although it was too soon to gauge either Ballard or Hawkins as potential heavyweight prospects, it seemed that Ballard was the man to keep an eye on that night. The formula pointed clearly to a Ballard victory. Although both fighters were the same age (twenty-five years old), Ballard appeared bigger (although he only outweighed Hawkins by a mere three pounds). He also had an impressive 67–1 record as an amateur, compared to a mere five fights in the amateurs for Hawkins. Although both his pro wins were against undefeated fighters (including a victory over amateur standout Rodney Harris). Hawkins went the distance in both those fights whereas Ballard knocked out all five of his opponents.

For Ballard, it was an opportunity to shine on national television, a valuable boost to any young up-and-coming fighter's career. Although there were many questions still unanswered about both fighters, it was certainly not considered a detriment to them at this stage of their careers. Usually an undefeated fighter has yet to have his chin tested that early on, and both Ballard and Hawkins were no exception—in fact, had they been in a situation where their chins were tested so early, it would have been more of a strike than a plus. But as soon as the opening bell rang, it appeared that that question would soon be answered about both fighters. Ballard and Hawkins came out slugging, winging (and landing) hard looping hooks to the chin against each other. Initially, it appeared as if Ballard was winning the early exchanges. Although his offense relied almost entirely on the left hook, it did seem to do some damage as Hawkins seemed to be covering up. However, by the halfway point of the opening round, Hawkins began to open up, landing overhand rights with enough regularity to have Ballard moving on his bicycle before the round's end. Ballard's new attempt to control the fight from the outside proved futile, as he had yet to master the jab in the gym. It was a classic rookie mistake that proved technically fatal. Without a troublesome jab Hawkins was able to control the tempo of the fight from the outside with lunging hooks and combination to the body.

In the second round the fight continued as it ended in the first, with both fighters exploding at the bell. Hawkins seemed to stun Ballard with a solid right hand early in the round and continued to control the fight with solid pressure. Another hook seemed to shake up Ballard again in the last twenty seconds, and although Hawkins slipped at the bell on a wet spot on the canvas, he captured another close round.

In the third both fighters came out bombing again, and the fight was proving to be an entertaining, if not technically sound fight. Both fighters had some success, but it seemed clear that Ballard won the round with a collection of solid left uppercuts and left hooks. However, it seemed that he was winded by round's end, holding on excessively in the last minute of the round. It proved to be the case, as Ballard was clearly unable to match Hawkins punch-for-punch in the final round. Hawkins, realizing he was the "opponent" in the fight, came out wailing hard shots in an attempt to stamp an exclamation point on what was a solid, but not yet dominant performance. A left hook landed at 1:15 of the round and clearly stunned the tired Ballard, and though it proved to be the last major offensive spurt of the fight, it proved enough to win the round (and the fight) for Hawkins.

Although the fight seemed close enough to give to Ballard, it also seemed unlikely. The first round was close, and the third was his, but the second and fourth were clearly Hawkin's. A draw seemed a likely verdict, but Hawkins was rewarded for his work ethic, as he won the four-round decision by scores of 39–37 from all three judges.

For Hawkins, the win should have propelled him into the "prospect" category. It was an impressive televised fight, in which his chin was tested and passed with flying colors. His work ethic and heart also impressed. Although neither he nor Ballard impressed on the technical side (both failing to use the jab and having trouble with defense), it seemed that there was a basic, solid foundation for a potential contender. Unfortunately, his management continued to plan as if he were a mere opponent. He was matched with Oleg Maskaev in his next fight, losing by way of fourth-round TKO. When he lost his next fight to Gary Bell, it seemed that he was just going to be another prospect whose career was shot by bad management. That was, until he fought Gary Bell a second time and scored a stunning tenth-round knockout (page 267).

For Ballard, the loss proved to be a minor bump on the road to a "world title." He appeared simply as a raw prospect who needed some polishing before he could become an actual contender. Ballard continued his stunning display of power against every fighter he faced not named Robert Hawkins, going on to knock out his next fourteen opponents. He even won a minor world title (the IBO championship) against Corey Sanders. But in his first step up in competition, he struggled with former champion Greg Page in 1998, being held to a less than stellar ten-round draw. A knockout loss to John Ruiz later that year seemed to end his run as a prospect, but in 1999 he made one more run. After scoring impressive knockouts over journeymen Jason Waller and Garing Lane, Ballard appeared to be working his way back into the heavyweight picture. But on August 8, 1999 he was found in a Washington, D.C., alley with multiple stab wounds in his chest. He was rushed to the hospital but later died from his injuries at the age of thirty-two.

July 16, 1995—Detroit, Michigan
James Thunder (26–5, 20 KOs) vs. Franco Wanyama (15–3–2, 6 KOs)
Favorite: Thunder
Result: Wanyama won a ten-round split decision.

For twenty-nine-year-old Samoan heavyweight James Thunder it was finally looking as if his career was beginning to take off. Initially ignored by most American boxing fans, Thunder completely revitalized his sagging career after relocating from Australia and New Zealand to train and fight out of the United States. With proper training and sparring, Thunder transformed himself from the slow, ponderous, clubfighter with above average power and a C-minus chin into one of the most exciting heavyweight contenders in the division. It was a far cry from the fighter who had trouble holding onto the Australian title (splitting two fights with Craig Petersen) as well as getting knocked out by Mike Hunter and Derek Williams. Thunder was everything boxing fans wanted in a contender; he was big, hard hitting, remaining active (fighting every two to three months), and extremely personable. Even some boxing purists were won over by Thunder; he was a fighter from the old school, not allowing early losses to deter him and fighting quality opposition as often as he could.

After winning a ten-round decision over Marion Wilson in 1994, Thunder was given his first big break by landing a *USA Tuesday Night Fights*–televised fight against Eddie Donaldson. For many boxing insiders it was a "pick 'em" fight, but Thunder won over many fans, and USA, when he blitzed Donaldson in two rounds. It was one of his most impressive performances, and one that led to his second big break, a network television appearance against Danell Nicholson for the IBO heavyweight title. Although Nicholson pulled out, Thunder gained some valuable exposure (as well as a minor belt) when he won a lopsided decision over last-minute sub Richard Mason. Although Thunder briefly held the WBF title in 1993 (winning it from Melton Bowen before dropping a decision to blown up cruiserweight Johnny Nelson) the IBO belt carried with it more prestige and better opportunities for the future. The Thunder revival reached its pinnacle in his next fight when he defended his title by winning a controversial twelve-round decision over former champion Tony Tubbs in 1994. Although Tubbs was no longer considered a top contender, he was still proving to be a very resilient opponent who had already derailed the careers of several young prospects like Bruce Seldon and Willie Jackson. The win over Tubbs put Thunder in the big leagues, and Thunder cemented his position by winning his next fight against another former champion, Trevor Berbick, three months later. Like Tubbs, Trevor Berbick was well past his prime, but he was a fighter coming off an impressive win streak (of seven fights) as well as a decision victory over undefeated prospect Melvin Foster. Another big win followed, this time a second-round knockout over Romanian heavyweight prospect Dan Dancuta, and by July 1995 it was looking like James Thunder was on the fast track to a title fight. All he needed to do was keep winning in impressive fashion on television.

Although Thunder was making quite a name for himself on *USA Tuesday Night Fights*, he still remembered the boost his career received from his sole network television appearance against Richard Mason, and in July 1995, less than a month after his previous fight, Thunder was given another opportunity to shine on network TV when Tommy Hearns was forced to pull out of his scheduled fight with Franco Wanyama a few days before. With CBS covering the fight, Thunder decided to fill in for the injured "Hitman" and pick up some valuable exposure. Even though Thunder admitted that he "didn't know nothing about him [Wanyama]" and that he took the fight for the exposure, few questioned his wisdom in taking the fight. After all, what could a light punching cruiserweight journeyman possibly do to derail his rapidly rising career? Even though Thunder had considerably less time to prepare for the fight than Wanyama, he still outweighed him by a good thirty pounds, and Wanyama hadn't been training for James Thunder but rather Tommy Hearns. Also, Wanyama looked to be a soft touch, even by cruiserweight standards. He was coming off a draw with unknown Bulgarian light-heavyweight Kalin Stoyanov, a fighter with an 8–11–1 record.

Initially it appeared as if Wanyama was intimidated by Thunder when he started the fight timidly, running from the stalking Thunder. Halfway through the first round, it looked as if the Thunder would wrap things up early when he trapped Wanyama on the ropes and unloaded with a hard combination upstairs. But Wanyama, a fighter with some defensive skills, easily avoided most of the powershots and by round's end was no closer to being stopped than he had been at the start of the round. It was enough to give Wanyama a much needed confidence boost, and at the start of the second Wanyama fired (and landed) first with a big right hand. Thunder showed signs of slowing down and frustration when he fired a low blow 1:15 in the round that drew a warning from referee Monte Oswald. By round's end Thunder was still swinging for the fences, but Wanyama was clearly getting braver. His courage would prove valid in the third round. After getting stunned with a big right hand early in the round, Wanyama was backed into the ropes where James Thunder tried to finish him off. But Thunder actually came in too close, smothering his own shots and robbing them of any effectiveness. For Wanyama however, Thunder's chin was just in range and a counter right hand (in response to a Thunder left hook that missed) landed right on the chin of James Thunder, dropping the bigger man to the canvas. Thunder quickly rose, but it was clear that James was not getting the kind of exposure he was looking for. He still moved forward, but Wanyama now had a weapon that was proving to be very effective against the hard punching Samoan, and he began to pump his own right hand with reckless abandon, hurting Thunder again with another counter right hand. Although Thunder was given a short break in the final minute of the round after losing his mouthpiece, the round remained Wanyama's to the bell.

The right hand continued to work for Wanyama in the fourth, as several right hand uppercuts caught Thunder flush on the chin. Wanyama began to move side to side more in the fifth and continued to control the action for much of the round. But Thunder, whose offense could only be described as ineffective aggression for much of the fight to that point, began to show some signs of closing the gap by the end of the round. He came back strong in the sixth, pushing Wanyama back with several thudding blows. However, his connect percentage was dismal and by round's end Wanyama was back in control, taking advantage of Thunder's fatigue. A solid combination to the head of James Thunder stole a close round for Wanyama, ending Thunder's brief revival.

Thunder came back in the seventh when referee Monte Oswald made a critical error that in turn changed the result of the fight. As Thunder came out strong at the bell, Wanyama once again landed a hard right hand that briefly froze the top-ranked heavyweight. Wanyama appeared in control but with just over a minute in the round Thunder floored Wanyama with a low blow. Upon seeing Wanyama on the canvas Oswald instinctively began to count, only to catch his error after the count began. After Wanyama rose Oswald gave him the customary five-minute reprise to recover from the low blow, a move that left everyone watching in confusion over whether the punch was a low blow or a legitimate knockdown. However, Oswald quickly tried to repair the damage in between rounds by telling the ringside judges that there was no knockdown but rather a low blow.

For the next two rounds the fight continued the same pattern as Thunder stalked but failed to mount a serious offense while Wanyama boxed and counterpunched behind a hard right hand. Going into the final round it appeared as if Thunder needed a knockout to win, but it would not come. Both fighters started the round throwing bombs, but it was Wanyama who took control, doing a brief Ali shuffle as he danced around Thunder. With just under a minute left in the round Thunder trapped Wanyama on the ropes, but once again was unable to find his chin. As the bell sounded ending the round and the fight, everyone at ringside assumed that Wanyama had won.

In a decision that shocked everyone, including James Thunder himself, the judges totals gave the split decision victory to Thunder (Frank Garza and Dario Chiarini both voted for Thunder by a score of 96–93 and 95–94 while judge Phil LeDouceur voted for Wanyama 95–94). The disbelief on Thunder's face answered any question ringsiders may have had about whether or not Thunder actually though he won the fight, and for most of the viewers on CBS, it looked like another hometown decision going to the bigger named fighter.

As viewers saw Thunder awarded the decision, one of the judges noticed something was wrong. Judge Dario Chiarini, who had not been told of the mix-up in regards to the low blow in the seventh round until after he turned in his scorecard, noticed that the correction had not been made. He felt that Wanyama was winning the seventh but, under the assumption that Thunder scored the knockdown, awarded the round to Thunder by a score of 10–9. Upon learning of the referee's error he changed his score to 10–9 for Wanyama. The score was not corrected, resulting in Thunder getting the nod by one point on his card rather than vice versa. Because Michigan commissioner Dale Grable was not present at the card, he was unable to overturn the decision, and thus it took several weeks to clear up the mishap. But after a review by the Michigan commission, Thunder had his victory turned into a defeat.

Ironically the fight had little impact on either Wanyama's or James Thunder's careers. Wanyama returned to the cruiserweight division de-

termined to cash in on his newfound credibility, but was quickly derailed in his next fight, losing his British Commonwealth cruiserweight
title to undefeated Chris Okoh by way of eighth-round stoppage. A decision loss to Garry Delaney followed in 1996, as well as back-to-back
knockout losses to Dirk Wallyn, ending any hope of ever becoming a contender in the cruiserweight division.

Thunder, however, continued his forward march up the heavyweight
rankings without so much as a bump after the Wanyama loss, stopping
prospects Ray Anis the following month and Melvin Foster two months
after that. In fact by the end of 1996 he was being mentioned as a possible opponent to Lennox Lewis if he were to defeat Oliver McCall for the
WBC heavyweight title. But another upset loss (this time by decision to
John Ruiz, page 243) ended discussion of a possible title fight and sent
Thunder back to the drawing board.

October 6, 1995—Atlantic City, New Jersey
Mike "The Bounty" Hunter (25–5–2, 8 KOs) vs. Marion Wilson
(7–16–3, 2 KOs)
Favorite: Hunter
Result: Wilson won a ten-round split decision.

By October 1995, it was clear that Mike Hunter was not going to get a
title shot. His days as a top-ten heavyweight were over. After upsetting
Tyrell Biggs for the USBA heavyweight championship (page 77) in 1993,
Hunter became a bona fide contender with legitimate title fight aspirations.

He followed up the win over Biggs with impressive decisions over
Alex Zolkin, Cecil Coffee, and Buster Mathis over the next twelve
months. But after failing a post-fight drug test after his victory over
Mathis, Hunter saw his win voided and his title stripped. It was a devastating blow for his career, and one from which he never completely recovered. He initially bounced back with solid wins over Craig Payne and
Keith McMurray, found himself on the outside looking into the top ten,
and was forced to watch as the fighter he beat (Mathis) fought Riddick
Bowe in an HBO-televised fight in 1994. It was a fight (and a payday)
that most likely would have been his had his win over Mathis not been
ruled a "no-contest." Out of options, Hunter was relegated to fighting

Alex Zolkin in a rematch for considerably less money in December 1994—a fight in which he saw himself on the losing end of a split decision. After traveling to Brazil for his next fight, Hunter found himself a loser again, this time by way of a controversial ten-round decision to undefeated Brazilian heavyweight Aurelio Perez.

By 1995 things were looking bleak for the "Bounty" Hunter, but he was determined to make one more run for a title shot, and the thirty-six-year-old Hunter started the year in impressive fashion. After back-to-back loses to Zolkin and Perez, Hunter bounced back with his most impressive wins since his first fight with Alex Zolkin, winning a lopsided decision over tough heavyweight Will Hinton. It was a promising start for Hunter's comeback, and a follow-up win over Marion Wilson on the undercard of Lou Savarese's fight against Olian Alexander seemed good. Although Wilson was not regarded as a world-class heavyweight and tended to be easily out-boxed, he was a fighter who guaranteed an honest effort, with a chin regarded as one of the best in the heavyweight division. Besides, for a thirty-six-year-old fighter in the middle of a widely ignored comeback, televised fights were hard to come by, and when they did surface they needed to be embraced.

Marion Wilson was regarded as a journeyman in almost every sense of the word, but he was a fighter whose record was deceptive. Unlike most fighters with a losing record, Wilson was highly regarded in boxing circles. He had never been knocked out, despite fighting such noted power punchers as Shannon Briggs, James Thunder, and Andrew Golota. Also, he occasionally pulled off the upset (or near upset), holding Ray Mercer to a draw (almost everyone agreed he should have been given the decision) as well as knocking down then undefeated Jeremy Williams. But with only one win in his last fifteen fights, few anticipated anything more than an "honest effort."

Although few boxing writers took Wilson lightly as a fighter, there was one person who did: Mike Hunter. When the fight started it became abundantly clear that Wilson had a well thought-out game plan, whereas Hunter had none. Wilson jabbed his way inside, and then fired off hard body shots to rob the aging Hunter of his legs, a strategy that won him the first three rounds. When Hunter returned to his corner with a small cut after the third, it was clear that this was going to be a tough night for him. By the fourth round it was also clear that Hunter was nearly out of gas; his punches were slow and ponderous. Although Hunter had always had success with his unorthodox style—firing punches from unlikely angles—without the speed of his youth he was not only ineffective, but also appeared amateurish. When a Marion Wilson hook sent Hunter's mouthpiece flying out halfway through the round it was apparent to even the most ardent fans of the "Bounty" Hunter that conditioning was not on his side. Although Hunter tried to use some of his clowning tactics against Wilson towards the end of the fourth, turning his back and running from his opponent, Wilson was unfazed. Unlike fighters like Biggs and Zolkin, Wilson simply ran after his fleet-footed opponent until he finally caught up to him.

Hunter, who was "running on fumes" as early as the fifth, again lost his mouthpiece that round (prompting a warning from referee Eddie Cotton). Exhausted and unable to outbox the ever-forward-moving Wilson, Hunter was relegated to that of a one punch bomber, hoping to land a knockout shot that would turn the tide of the fight. It was an ineffective strategy against such an iron-jawed opponent as Wilson, as Hunter only had eight knockouts in his thirty-two fights. In fact, with the exception of a solid uppercut thrown halfway through the fifth round, there was little working for Mike in the fight.

Although the fight deteriorated by the seventh into an ugly affair, with Wilson throwing illegal rabbit punches while Hunter clinched and threw only one ineffective punch, at a time there still was some drama: Wilson was cut over the right eye in the seventh, and while never a major factor in the fight, it did briefly threaten to rob Wilson of his well-earned victory.

Knowing he needed a knockout (or at least a very dominant round) in the tenth, Mike Hunter came out throwing bombs at the bell to start out the final round. But he lacked the energy to maintain that pace and fell to the canvas in exhaustion after throwing a short right hook to Wilson's body. When a hard right uppercut stunned Hunter in the last ten seconds, Wilson seized that opportunity to trap Mike in his corner to finish the fight. It was enough to capture another round in a surprisingly lopsided fight for Wilson.

One judge saw it differently, voting for Hunter with a score of 97–93. However, he was overruled as the other two judges gave the fight to Wilson by scores of 96–94.

For the dejected Mike Hunter (who incidentally left the ring refusing to shake hands with the victor) it marked a disappointing end to his run as a contender. His credibility tarnished, Hunter traveled to Denmark as a sacrificial lamb for Danish heavyweight Brian Nielsen. After getting stopped in the fourth round he retired, ending one of the most unlikely, and at times bizarre, heavyweight careers of the '90s.

For Wilson, the win did little for his career other than confirm his status as one of the best journeymen in the sport. Wilson lost his next fight—the following month—to Jeff Wooden, and proceeded to lose six of his next seven fights (all by decision). However, the veteran still had a few wins left in his bag of tricks. Against then-undefeated Paea Wolfgramm, a fighter with solid Olympic credentials as well as a 14–0 record, Wilson was able to again score the upset in winning a six-round decision.

November 24, 1995—Wisconsin Dells, Wisconsin
Earnie Shavers (72–13–1, 67 KOs) vs. Brian "B-52" Yates
   (5–16–2, 1 KO)
Favorite: Shavers
Result: Yates won by way of second-round KO.

When George Foreman earned one of the largest paychecks in boxing history for his gritty, albeit losing, effort against Evander Holyfield, the floodgates opened. Suddenly, fighters who were decades removed from their primes were jumping back into the ring, hoping to duplicate the financial success of "Big George." However, Foreman was the exception, and one by one the comebacks came to inglorious ends. The little-known Ron Cranmer defeated Jerry Quarry; Alexis Arguello went on to lose a decision to the lightly regarded Scott Walker; Leon Spinks lost to James Wilder. The list went on and on. The only fighter who encountered similar success was Larry Holmes, by earning a sizeable payday for his fight against Evander Holyfield. By 1995 it appeared as if the cycle of attempted comebacks was coming to an end. Ron Lyle, another 1970s superstar, saw his ill-advised comeback fizzle, and many boxing fans assumed that his attempt would be the final one.

But in 1995 boxing fans were surprised to discover that the fifty-year-old former puncher Earnie Shavers was attempting to make a Foreman-like comeback as well. The surprise for many was not that he was coming back, but that he waited so long. After George Foreman made history in 1991 against Holyfield, some boxing experts began to prepare themselves for a return of Earnie Shavers. After all, Shavers was in many ways a mirror image of Foreman. Like "Big" George, Earnie was a hard puncher in the heavyweight division, and most experts agreed that power was the last thing a fighter loses. Besides, Shavers was only a few years removed from his last fight; he scored a first round knockout over Larry Sims in 1987. The Shavers comeback did not materialize, so boxing writers began to lower their guard. But when George Foreman knocked out Michael Moorer for the heavyweight championship in 1994, the temptation became too much, and Earnie began training for a comeback.

Shavers appeared on sports commentator Jim Rome's ESPN2 talk show *Talk2* to help hype his comeback several weeks before his first fight against Brian Morgan, a quick shot of legitimacy for the boxer. (*Talk2* was a sports show and not just a boxing show. In fact few boxers outside of world champions were ever invited on the show.) Shavers reminisced about his wars with Ali and Holmes, as well as his desire to land a fight with fellow puncher George Foreman (a fight that never materialized). There was little question that the Foreman fight was foremost on Earnie's mind as he talked. He believed (as did many fans in the 1970s) that a fight with Foreman was a natural, and it held an important distinction: the winner would almost definitely be crowned hardest puncher in history. With Foreman on top, with his notorious attempts to select weak opposition (the sport was still reeling over the Foreman–Jimmy Ellis fight), there was certainly a great deal of motivation for Earnie. If he could string together a handful of impressive wins over weak opponents, he might sneak into the top ten. When the IBF stripped Foreman of his heavyweight championship for refusing to grant Axel Schultz a rematch, that scenario became all the more lucrative. No longer did Shavers need to secure a ranking in the IBF, now all he needed was to be ranked by the little-known WBU (the only sanctioning organization to recognize Foreman as its champion).

But age and father time were not privy to Earnie's plans, and nineteen days after his fifty-first birthday, the comeback was nearly derailed by the lightly regarded Brian Morgan, who gave all Earnie could handle in losing a close eight-round decision. Morgan entered the ring with a less than impressive record of 4–20–1 (1 KO) when he fought Shavers, and many boxing insiders felt that the Shavers comeback would be hard pressed to make it as far as a fight with Foreman.

Clearly Shavers needed to win some converts, so for his second comeback fight in Wisconsin a mere two months after the first, he selected a fighter who was seen as something of a step down from Brian Morgan: Brian Yates.

Although Yates had a record almost identical to Morgan's, with only one knockout in twenty-three fights and sixteen losses, the level of competition was clearly nowhere near that of Brian Morgan's. Morgan, who fought (and went the distance with) the likes of former cruiserweight champion Carlos DeLeon, Lou Savarese, Vaughn Bean, and Boris Powell, had earned a reputation as a solid opponent who at least could go some rounds while losing. He was even able to upset former cruiserweight contender James Pritchard earlier in 1995. Yates, however, fought only in the Midwest against the Ric Enises of the boxing world. With a knockout loss to Tim Tomasheck and a decision loss to "Wimpy" Halstead (the only recognizable names on his resume), there was little to indicate that he would score the upset.

Yates did have several things working in his favor as he prepared for the Shavers fight. There was some hidden power in his right hand (he staggered "Wimpy" Halstead with it), and Earnie was battling more than just age. With days to go before the fight, Earnie was hit with the flu. Although he refused to back out of the fight, there was little question that Earnie needed all his speed or endurance considering his advanced age.

Nonetheless, Shavers came out looking fairly solid in the first. Working behind a solid left jab, he quickly established the tempo of the fight, pushing a visibly timid Yates around the ring. Yates initially refused to mix it up with Shavers at all, choosing to keep away from Earnie's legendary power. When Brian began to set down in the latter half of the round, he was clubbed with several hard jabs that pushed him back. Shavers then fired a hard right cross that just missed the mark. By round's end it looked like only a matter of time, and even the ring announcer was jumping on the Shavers bandwagon when he oddly took the microphone in between rounds to tell the crowd ". . . this man

[Shavers] is fifty-one years old! It takes a round or two for a man that age to warm up, but when he warms up look out!''

Perhaps irked at the ring announcer, or perhaps realizing that Shavers lacked the speed to seriously threaten him with anything more that a jab, the twenty-one-year-old Yates started the second round working behind his own jab. Then, less than five seconds into the round, ringside fans saw the first sign of trouble for Earnie Shavers. Shavers tried to fire a combination to the body of Yates, but the shots were so slow and ponderous that Yates was easily able to step away from them. It was Earnie's first attempt at a multi-punch combination in the fight, and the results were hardly inspiring. The Shavers jab also began to unravel in the second, going from being a hard, quick (in relative terms) shot to a slow, pawing motion of his left hand. Brian, determined to counterpunch, covered up from Earnie's shots to the head, waiting for the perfect opening. With less than thirty seconds left in the round the opening presented itself. Shavers fired a hard left hook to the body, but Yates quickly bounced back with a short overhand counter right to Earnie's chin that clearly stunned the former contender. Yates, recognizing his opportunity, followed the punch with two more identical rights, and in a crash the Earnie Shavers comeback hit the canvas for the last time. Shavers struggled to return to his feet but was rescued by the referee. At 2:49 seconds of the second round, Brian "B-52" Yates scored the biggest win of his career.

For Yates, the win should have been the first step to bigger and better things. Even if he were not to become a contender, it seemed likely that he would become a more recognizable opponent, perhaps fight a few prospects on ESPN or *USA Tuesday Night Fights*. However, in boxing success can sometimes be brutally short-lived. Brian lost his next fight to little-known Curt Allen, and suddenly his brief flirtation with journeyman legitimacy was brought to an end. Brian went on to lose his next eight fights before tasting victory again, and by the end of the decade he would go on to lose seventy-five fights (against twelve wins). Although he would have a few more decent performances (extending Oliver McCall eight rounds before getting knocked out), none would compare to the knockout over Shavers.

Although the ring announcer told the crowd to give it up for Earnie, and that "he'll be back," there was little question that his quest for a

Foreman fight was over. He simply was not going to be able to overcome the stigma of the loss to Yates to land the big money shot against the WBU champion. Shavers wisely retired from the ring, his fight with Yates to be the last of his career. However, the loss had little effect on the personable Shavers, who left the ring with his physical and mental well being intact. Years after the Yates fight he even joked about his last night in the ring. "They told me he was a bum," Shavers would say with a smile, "they forgot to tell him."

December 15, 1995—New York City, New York
Butterbean (13–0, 9 KOs) vs. Mitch Rose (1–6–1, 1 KO)
Favorite: Butterbean
Result: Rose won by way of second-round TKO.

When former tough-man champion Eric Esch decided to try his hand at boxing in late 1994, few boxing writers anticipated that he would encounter much success in the ring. Although he had an impressive 67–4 record in toughman competitions, many boxing fans held a degree of distain for the semi-professional, seldom-sanctioned "barroom brawling" styled competitions. It was regarded as a sort of bastardized amalgamation of boxing and professional wrestling, and it was widely frowned upon as a form of "minor leagues" for professional boxing. Although several successful fighters did in fact emerge from the unlikely world of toughman competitions (like former welterweight champion Greg Haugen and former WBO heavyweight champion Tommy Morrison) they tended to be few and far between. Butterbean seemed to be one of the "in betweens." He was extremely obese, weighing over three hundred pounds on his short 5′10″ frame, and he appeared too old to start a successful career—he was twenty-eight when he started. Although he had reported great power, it was widely assumed that great power in the toughman circuit hardly equated great power in pro boxing. When he struggled in his first fight to knock out lowly Doug Norris in the final round of his pro debut, it appeared that the assessment was correct. His alleged "great punch" would not be enough to compensate for his glaring deficiencies as a fighter. After his pro debut he returned to his home state of Michigan, where he won an ugly six-round decision over Ed Barry in the city of Saginaw. With the win it appeared as if

Butterbean would slip into relative obscurity, fighting on the Michigan club circuit before disappearing from the scene without so much as a ripple in the heavyweight picture. But after his first-round knockout over Alvin Ellis on the undercard of the Tommy Hearns vs. Lenny Lapaglia fight at the Joe Louis Arena in Detroit, a peculiar thing began to occur. Esch (later to be known as Butterbean) began to become a cult figure in heavyweight boxing, the "four-round phenom." He became a fighter in high demand, and after the financial (if not pugilistic) success of Peter McNeeley in his boxing career, it was clear that Butterbean was a potential gold mine. Dollar signs began to attract investors and promoters alike, and by 1996 Bob Arum was working closely with Butterbean. Initially it appeared that the most marketable fight that could be made was a showdown with McNeeley, a fight that was sure to generate a good deal of money despite its lack of true significance in the heavyweight picture.

Although there were bigger paydays down the line (some insiders began throwing around the name Mike Tyson) it was widely perceived that even the Butterbean's cult status would not be able to compensate for the obvious discrepancy in skill between the two fighters, and that with the exception of a possible fight with McNeeley, nobody would really "pay" to see a major fight with Butterbean in it. Butterbean was, quite simply, not a good fighter; Although he did show flashes of power, he also showed serious flashes of complete boxing incompetence. He was dropped by lightly regarded Adam Sutton in his ninth fight (he went on to win a four-round decision) and in his eleventh pro fight Butterbean was battered for the better part of four rounds but somehow escaped with a highly questionable decision against Kenny Meyers (a fighter with a 3–6–1, 1 KO record). It was clear that keeping Butterbean undefeated was not going to be an easy task, but against the limited opposition he was fighting it appeared quite possible.

When he fought for the first time in the boxing Mecca of Madison Square Garden in December 1995, the assumption was that this was not the time to "test" Butterbean but rather allow him the opportunity to shine in from of one of the most important boxing audiences in the world. It was decided that his opponent would be the lightly regarded, and step down for Butterbean in terms of opposition, Mitchell Rose. Rose had managed only one victory in eight pro fights, and had been knocked out three times already (including a knockout loss to Darroll Wilson). Rose was regarded as a fighter with a porous defense and a soft chin, the perfect combination to ensure a Butterbean victory. But overlooked in the Rose resume was Rose's extensive amateur background, that in fact made him a much more seasoned fighter (and a much better fighter) than his record indicated. Also, the early book on how to beat Butterbean was already out: it called for a solid jab and lots of lateral movement, something Rose did have some skills at doing.

When the fight began Butterbean attempted to bulldoze his opponent and score the early knockout like he had two weeks earlier against Lou Monaco (whom he had knocked out early in the opening round). Butterbean jumped all over Rose, throwing hard hooks and trying to find Rose's questionable chin. But Rose proved to actually be a somewhat sound fighter defensively, and easily avoided the Butterbean assault. Butterbean quickly slowed his pace in an attempt to pick his shots, but he was suddenly faced with something that nobody expected to encounter: a real boxer. Rose immediately began to utilize his footwork, as well as his left jab, to thoroughly outbox Butterbean, whose offense became almost ridiculously predictable. Butterbean tried the jab followed by the right cross, but it was simply not enough against the slick moving Rose. Rose then began to pump the punch that would prove to be decisive in the fight: the right cross. After peppering Butterbean with five straight jabs two minutes into the round, Rose fired the first of his hard right crosses that found its mark on the face of Butterbean. Although the punch did not deter the ever-forward-moving Butterbean, it showed Rose that his bald-headed opponent was clearly open for the punch. Seconds later another right caught Butterbean, this time clearly wobbling the three-hundred-pounder who stumbled back into the ropes. Although he was "saved by the bell" there was little question that Butterbean was in more of a fight than he anticipated. Imploring his fighter not to "wait" for Rose and to fire first, Butterbean trainer Murray Sutherland tried to get his fighter to alter his unoriginal and ineffective offense. As the bell rang to start the second it seemed as if Butterbean heard the message as he came out winging punches. But he still didn't have an answer for the right hand, and within seconds a Rose right cross had him hurt again. Butterbean stumbled into the corner where Rose immediately jumped all over his groggy foe. When a straight right

snapped Butterbean's head back referee Joseph Santarpia jumped in
and stopped the fight (somewhat prematurely) at 0:48 of the second
round.

Immediately Butterbean complained about the stoppage, clearly
upset by what he perceived as an unjustly quick intervention. But the
damage was already done. Gone was talk of big money fights in the future. One boxing writer commented after the fight that the "circus act"
was finally over. In fact, even the proposed fight with Peter McNeeley
seemed dead as few thought Butterbean would last against the more experienced McNeeley. But oddly enough the fight had little impact on the
popularity of Esch, who still remained the "king of the four rounders"
in the hearts of many fans. Besides, Butterbean had something going
for him: he did in fact have legitimate power and he had a great trainer.

Eric "Butterbean" Esch (right) may have been the "king of the four
rounders" but Mitchell Rose stopped him in the second at MSG for
Butterbean's only loss in six years. *Pat Orr*

Slowly but surely Butterbean began to improve with each fight, working on his "take four to land one" style that got him in so much trouble against Rose. He even tried desperately to land a rematch with Rose, who disappeared shortly after the win (and was finished as a boxer within a year). Although he was unable to land the rematch with Rose, he was able to fight with Peter McNeeley in 1999. In the most impressive performance of his career, Butter destroyed McNeeley in the first round, gaining a small degree of respect in the boxing world. He even won a minor title belt (whose very existence was created to accommodate Butterbean's career), and by the decade's end Butterbean was not only still fighting, but had yet to taste defeat again. Although the competition was limited, there were a handful of recognizable names in his resume (and his win over Monaco increased in significance as Monaco became more and more successful as a heavyweight journeyman). Although no boxing insider ever considered him a real contender, he did go on to rack up over sixty wins (against the lone loss to Rose) in the next six years before losing, in Utah, to a local fighter named Billy Zumbrum. It was proof that if nothing else Butterbean had improved, and no longer was that difficult to keep him undefeated.

CHAPTER SEVEN

1996

"He just caved in."

Jim Lampley on Shannon Briggs's upset
loss to Darroll Wilson

March 15, 1996—Atlantic City, New Jersey
David (Izon) Izonritei (18–0, 16 KOs) vs. Maurice "Mo" Harris
(5–6–2 2, KOs)
Favorite: Izonritei
Result: Harris won an eight-round unanimous decision.

When HBO decided to showcase some of the undefeated fighters in the
sport for an impressive card titled "Night of the Young Heavyweights"
and including David Tua, Shannon Briggs, Courage Tshabalala, and
David Izonritei, it looked like a great opportunity for boxing fans to
gauge the "young guns" of the division in an attempt to determine who
could go on to be the next great heavyweight. Although there was little
question that Briggs was the most exciting fighter on the card, many
were also curious about the hard-punching Nigerian Izonritei. Having
only fought in the United States twice there was little to go on, but what
was known was that he was a talented fighter with Olympic pedigree
and a solid amateur background. Unfortunately he also had a "French
connection" (he fought out of France for much of his career), which in
boxing was about as was about as helpful as a Communist Party mem-
bership card attached to a job application going to Joseph McCarthy.
However, few anticipated anything less than a win for Izonritei on the
night of March 15. His opponent, the little-known Maurice Harris, was
regarded as a blown-up light heavyweight (the Izonritei fight was his

first fight over 200 pounds) with no chin and little power. At 175 pounds he was knocked out by lightly regarded Richard Frazier and Scott Lopeck, and had already been stopped by heavyweight prospect Vaughn Bean two years prior. After the loss to Bean he slipped into a period of inactivity, fighting only once in 1995 (losing to Dale Brown in three rounds). Even if Izonritei turned out to be dud as a heavyweight, most assumed that he would not be exposed that night.

But it took Maurice Harris less than one round to show something that the boxing world had yet to see in him, and something for which David Izonritei was ill-prepared. Immediately pumping a beautiful jab through the early round, Harris controlled the action as the undefeated Nigerian looked confused and unable to overcome the slick boxing of his lanky foe. Harris proceeded to thoroughly outbox Izonritei for much of the round and even briefly stunned his opponent when a hard overhand right clipped David's chin halfway through the round, causing him to pull back and cover up in the corner. Although Izonritei tried to come back with hard shots of his own later in the round, he had absolutely no answer for Harris's slick movement and solid jab. After continuing his dominance in the second, Izonritei was looking increasingly like a man about to be upset. But a jab, with less than ten seconds left in the round, was able to connect on the chin of Harris and shake him up enough to knock the mouthpiece out of his mouth. It was hardly a devastating punch, nor something that had many ringsiders particularly impressed, but it did shake up the underdog just a little bit—something that was confirmed seconds into the third round. With a mere fourteen seconds down Izonritei again connected with a left jab, one that was able to knock down the fleet-footed Harris. Harris appeared too hurt considering the punch that felled him, and when he rose at the count of five many assumed that he would fold under Izonritei's followup attack. Harris had showed little durability in the past (it was more a reflection of his lack of motivation that his physical ability), but he easily brushed off Izonritei's onslaught and began firing back overhand rights of his own that were finding the mark. Although Izonritei won the round, there was little question that the second half of the third was extremely close and that Harris was right back in the fight.

By the fourth round Harris had reverted to what worked so effectively for him in the first two rounds—foot movement and the jab. Izonritei also revealed what would be the pattern for the duration of the fight: he would stalk his opponent but not put together much of an offense in regards to punches. Although instructed not to "wait" for Harris between rounds, the fifth round saw David do just that. After opening the round with some solid pressure, Izonritei's attack quickly fizzled, and by round's end he was back to eating the jab as he followed Harris around the ring. Although Harris himself showed some momentary signs of frustration (in a clinch he grabbed David Izonritei's leg and lifted it up), there was little question which fighter was in control of the fight. Although David came back to win the sixth round by the closest of margins, Harris introduced a second weapon in that round—one that would further confound his opponent. Occasionally throwing lightning quick flurries to the head of David, Harris was able to awe the judges with the relatively soft (but flashy) punches. David's attempts at counterpunching proved to be ineffective against the faster Harris; he was unable to respond effectively to the flurries. However, the "Sugar Ray" style combinations took their toll on the relatively inexperienced Harris, and in the seventh round he showed clear signs of fatigue. Perhaps tired himself, Izonritei was completely unable to take advantage of the situation. Although the movement of Harris had slowed down and the jab had been replaced with the clinch, David still failed to mount an effective offense that seriously pressured Harris, and the golden opportunity for Izonritei disappeared with the bell ending the round. Realizing that he was on the threshold of a major win on the undercard of one of the biggest heavyweight cards of the year, Harris came out and put everything he had into the eighth, and final, round. He combined quick footwork, hard jabs, and flashy combinations to dominate the round and seal the fate of the Nigerian. There was little doubt as to which fighter won the fight; the only question was if Harris would be robbed. The scores were dangerously close on two judges' cards (John Stewart and Melvina Lathan both had it scored 76–75), but Maurice was nonetheless rewarded for his dominant performance with the unanimous decision.

Disgusted at the loss Izonritei quickly congratulated Harris and walked out of the ring and back to his dressing room. Initially most ringsiders assumed that he would continue past his dressing room and head right back to France, never to be seen again. He had been exposed as a "club fighter" with little future in the sport in the United States. That assessment was solidified when Harris went on to lose to Dayton Wheeler (by decision) and Gerald Nobles later that year, but it proved a most incorrect assessment of the career of David Izonritei. After remaining inactive for the next nine months Izonritei reemerged on a major HBO card, this time against the undefeated Samoan David Tua. With devastating first-round knockouts over John Ruiz and Darroll Wilson behind him, most assumed Tua would stop Izonritei early. But the Nigerian slugged it out with the hard-punching Tua for the better part of twelve rounds before finally getting stopped in the final round of the fight. The loss redeemed Izonritei, and when he followed the Tua fight with a big win over Lou Savarese, there was little question that he had overcome the loss to Harris in impressive fashion.

Although it appeared to be lucky break for Harris (he initially returned to his losing ways), it in turn proved to be the first step in the revitalized career of the opponent-turned-contender in Maurice Harris. He started 1997 with a solid win over Sam Hampton and followed it up with another big upset over James Thunder. The Thunder win solidified him as a Lionel Butler–style prospect, a fighter whose early failings in the ring were hardly a reflection of his skills as a fighter.

March 15, 1996—Atlantic City, New Jersey
Shannon Briggs (25–0, 20 KOs) vs. Darroll Wilson
    (15–0–2, 10 KOs)
Favorite: Briggs
Result: Wilson won by way of third-round knockout.

For boxing fans, the night of March 15, 1996, was already a night of upsets before Shannon Briggs and Darroll Wilson even stepped into the ring. Undefeated David (Izonritei) Izon had just lost an eight-round decision to the unknown Maurice Harris, and in the fight in which many experts actually anticipated an upset or at least a competitive fight, (that being the David Tua–John Ruiz fight), the experts were left in awe of one of the most brutal knockouts in recent memory. Boxing fans were shocked at the manner in which the undefeated Samoan destroyed his highly regarded foe in less than twenty seconds, and even the most ardent Tua supporters were left speechless. All that was left was the HBO debut of hard-punching New Yorker Shannon Briggs in a fight that few anticipated would be much of a contest.

Briggs had immediately jumped to the front of the pack of young heavyweights after turning pro, and by 1996 he was widely regarded as the "future" superstar of the division. His popularity was in part due to his background. From the Brownsville district of New York, he came from what was widely regarded as the breeding ground of future heavyweight champions. Brownsville produced champions Mike Tyson and Riddick Bowe in the 1980s and 1990s respectively, and Shannon Briggs was seen by many the logical third in the trilogy that was Brownsville's boxing legacy. By 1997 Brownsville was being compared to the Dominican Republic's reputation for great shortstops in baseball, and Shannon Briggs was already being groomed as her brightest star. Besides the obvious assets in Briggs's favor (he was a big, hard punching heavyweight), he also had personality and tons of it. He was instantly recognizable due to his golden dreadlocks; he played the piano, spoke a touch of French, and was a decent rapper to boot. Also, he was articulate. Not since Muhammad Ali did boxing have as quotable a boxer (excluding those fighters who were quotable for Duran-like comments that tended to be somewhat vicious), and he was quickly emerging as one of the more engaging personalities in all sports. Many thought him to be the next heavyweight champion after the Holyfield-Lewis-Tyson era came to a close, and with a string of destructive knockouts (many in the first round) there was plenty to back up that assertion.

Despite his growing popularity, by 1997 there were a growing number of critics who felt that Briggs was at the front of the class more because of wishful thinking than because of his actual abilities as a boxer. They felt that the boxing writers who were so high on Briggs did so because the *wanted* him to succeed (a Briggs championship would have been greatly beneficial to the sport and would have given the sport a valuable boost with casual fans), but that if they examined the evidence closely, they would recognize his faults. His opposition was by far the worst of any young, undefeated up-and-comer, a fact had many boxing experts (including HBO commentator Larry Merchant) wondering what his management might have known that the public didn't. Although Briggs fought a handful of recognizable opponents, they were better known for the ease upon which they were knocked out than for their ability to push a fighter. And then there were the performances that hardly seemed awe-inspiring. Against Craig Payne, Danny Wofford, Danny Blake, and Ken Bentley he was extended the distance (all against fighters with losing records), and against Mark Young (a fighter with twice as many losses as wins) he struggled before scoring the dramatic knockout in the final round. Even in what was regarded as one of his better performances (against Marion Wilson) he struggled after stunning the steel-jawed Wilson in the first round. But it was the fights that people hadn't seen that had the critics most abuzz. Rumors of life and death wars in the gyms and numerous knockdowns in sparring had many wondering if Briggs was all flash and no substance. Although knockdowns were not all together uncommon in sparring, even among the best fighters, the frequency upon which Briggs was getting hurt in the gym indicated that there were potential serious flaws in the Briggs package.

Even with the critics, Briggs was still regarded as the best prospect in the division by the vast majority of fans and boxing writers. With Darroll Wilson as opponent, there was little to indicate that the magic carpet ride that was the career of Shannon Briggs soon would be grounded. Wilson appeared to many boxing fans to be weak despite his undefeated record, and he had shown little in any of his wins to indicate he was world class. In fact, some went so far to say that he was about as bad a fighter as Briggs could have gotten away with fighting in an HBO main event. (These individuals obviously never sat through the George Foreman–Jimmy Ellis fight.) Although Wilson was coming off a big decision win over another undefeated heavyweight (James Stanton), even Briggs's critics felt that Stanton was nowhere near the fighter Briggs was. Besides, there also were the two glaring blots on his record in the form of two draws. The first draw was early in his career against Levon Warner and the second was with cruiserweight Terry McGroom. Although both McGroom and Warner were good fighters (McGroom was widely regarded as one of the better cruiserweight prospects in the division, and Warner had upset Terrence Lewis and Craig Tomlinson early in his career), most felt that if he were in fact "world class" he would have found a way to win. The draws, along with Wilson's perceived lack of power, burdened him going in against Briggs. He was, for all intents and purposes, an undefeated fighter who was not widely regarded as a prospect. Besides, Briggs was younger by five years (twenty-four to twenty-nine), bigger (a full twelve pounds and four inches taller) and seemingly stronger (with twice as many knockouts). Wilson didn't match up, even on the tale of the tape.

As soon as the bell rang it looked like Briggs would add another early knockout to his growing highlight reel. Charging at Wilson, Briggs threw caution to the wind in throwing hard left hooks and chopping right hands. Seconds into the fight, Briggs hurt Wilson with the left hook. Although Darroll punched back (tagging Shannon Briggs with a right hand) there was little question Briggs was in command when another left hook badly wobbled Wilson. Although most ringsiders assumed Wilson would try and clinch his way out of trouble, he shocked everyone (including Briggs) by electing to punch his way out of trouble. Initially Briggs seemed to welcome the slugfest—it appeared to be suicide for the smaller Wilson—but Wilson actually began to win the exchanges, forcing Briggs to take a step back and work behind his jab. He had the physical tools to outbox Wilson, with a two inch reach advantage, but Briggs never fully utilized his jab early in his career and found it to be ineffective against Wilson, who began to pepper Briggs with his own jab.

By the second round Shannon Briggs began to show signs of concern on his face, as Wilson found Briggs's ever so stationary head to be an inviting target. Briggs was relegated to stalking, following Wilson around but offering absolutely no diversity in his attack. During the few exchanges when Briggs did reach Wilson with a shot of his own, he tended to step back and admire his work, another serious flaw that was emerging in Shannon's offense. Although Wilson tagged Briggs repeatedly with shots to the head, Briggs was able to steal the round when a left jab briefly stunned Wilson, knocking him back into the ropes. Wilson was able to recover and landed a straight right to the head to punctuate that fact, but Briggs got the round. By that point, there was little question in the eyes of most ringsiders that Shannon was slowly unraveling. That fact was not lost on his trainer Teddy Atlas, who screamed at his young fighter to "pull yourself together . . . and act like a goddamn pro!"

But even with the harsh assessment of his performance by Atlas, Briggs failed to rectify his mistakes. Although he came out strong in the

Darroll Wilson (right) focuses in on Shannon Briggs during his upset victory. *Pat Orr*

third round, landing a straight right hand in the first minute, he resorted to fighting the smaller man's fight. Pounding away on the insider, Briggs gave Wilson an easy-to-reach, stationary target, and Wilson took advantage of his gift. He landed a right hand followed by a pair of left hooks, another right cross, and a final left hook all on Shannon Briggs's chin. Shannon backed away from his opponent, emerging with a cut over his right eye. It was the final straw for Shannon, who was sinking in quicksand. Unable to handle the increasing pressure of the fight, Briggs folded when Darroll landed a wide overhand right followed by a left hook. He collapsed face first to the canvas in a heap and gave no indication that he was going to rise when referee Tony Orlando waved it off at the count of six, 2:17 seconds into the third round. "He just caved in," remarked HBO commentator Jim Lampley on Briggs's total meltdown in the ring.

For Wilson, the win propelled him into the class of undefeated prospects along with David Tua. But his ascension was short-lived. He struggled against limited Rick Sullivan in his very next fight (winning an ugly decision) and was quickly knocked out of the major leagues when he was destroyed by David Tua inside of a round in September of that year. It seemed as if he would fade from the picture completely, but Wilson again rebounded with another shocking upset against another highly regarded (but untested) prospect in Courage Tshabalala (page 255).

For Briggs, he was never completely able to recover from the loss. Suddenly his bandwagon was not so crowded (outside of his management team, there was hardly anyone on it), and many fans regarded him as a something of a fraud. Even his likeable personality took a hit when he claimed that the loss was as a result of an asthma attack, an accusation that Teddy Atlas (now his former trainer) denied—he claimed that he was never informed of any such difficulties during or after the fight by Briggs. But in a bizarre way, his sudden lack of credibility landed him the biggest fight of his career. The highly cautious George Foreman chose him as an opponent in November 1997. Foreman felt that Briggs was a perfect foil—a recognizable fighter with little chance of winning. And after twelve rounds of boxing it appeared as if his assessment was correct, as Briggs seemed gun-shy and tentative, running from "Big George" for much of the fight. It was, to many, another example of his lack of toughness. But Briggs stunned Foreman by winning the decision—one that was regarded as highly questionable at best by most boxing fans—and found himself the new "linear champion of the world." (Foreman didn't have a belt, but was still the "man who beat the man who beat the man.") That title was able to land him a fight with WBC champion Lennox Lewis the following year. Few anticipated much of a contest, but Briggs put to rest the criticism of his grit in an entertaining brawl with the hard-punching Englishman. After rocking Lewis in the first round, Briggs hung in (despite taking a frightful beating) before finally succumbing in the fifth. Although critics still pointed to his chin and his lack of defense, the fight silenced those who felt that he was not "tough" enough to hang with any of the bigger named heavyweights.

May 13, 1996—Kansas City, Missouri
Greg Suttington (12–0, 11 KOs) vs. James Pritchard
  (29–14–2, 24 KOs)
Favorite: Suttington
Result: Pritchard scored a fourth-round TKO.

For much of the 1990s, the common assumption was that, with the exception of the classic club fighter/journeyman, there were only three types of heavyweights that came from the Midwest (which in boxing, included Ohio, Missouri, Oklahoma, Wisconsin, and several other states not regarded as midwestern). Fighter A tended to be a balding, chubby white guy who had somewhere around fifty to seventy-five wins against opposition with which your typical Butterbean opponent would pad his record. Fighter A would usually fight other midwestern fighters similar to him in record once in a great while, and might even have faced a few top-ten heavyweights. However, his claim to fame ultimately would be a knockout loss to Tommy "The Duke" Morrison. Jerry "Wimpy" Halstead, Tim Tomashek, and Dan Murphy all fell into the category of a Fighter A. Fighter B was a fighter with a grossly protected undefeated record that tended to overemphasize his power (i.e., he scored knockouts in all or nearly all of his fights). After padding his record to around 15–0, he would usually take a quantum leap in competition and get knocked out by Tommy "The Duke" Morrison. Marcus Rhode, Brian Scott, and Derrick Roddy all qualified as Fighter B–type fighters. Fighter C was Tommy Morrison.

But by 1995, it looked like there would possibly be a legitimate heavyweight prospect, a Fighter D if you will, emerging from the state of Missouri: Greg Suttington. Few national boxing writers paid much attention to Suttington early in his career (he seemed just another Fighter B type of heavyweight), until he established himself as a popular regional prospect in Kansas City with his brutal knockouts. In only his seventh pro fight Suttington caused his first ripple in the boxing world when he destroyed Jerry "Wimpy" Halstead in the second round. Although nobody regarded Halstead as a world-class heavyweight, he was still viewed as solid opponent for the top fighters in the world, too seasoned for such a raw fighter like Suttington. Halstead tended to lose only to the best fighters in the world (like Morrison, Ray Mercer, and

Herbie Hide), and Suttington was not seen as a world-class fighter. Though "Wimpy" was widely viewed as past his prime, he was nonetheless still able to give respectable performances. (He nearly pulled off a major upset over Alex Stewart two years prior.) Besides, how could a fighter with only six fights possible compete with a fighter with over ninety-three? But when Suttington handed "Wimpy" the most decisive defeat of his career, it seemed that Greg was a fighter to watch out for in the future.

Although the win over Halstead seemed to indicate that Suttington could in fact be a world-class prospect, he returned to fighting "second rate" opponents like John Jackson and Brian Morgan. It wasn't until nearly a year after his win over Halstead that the twenty-nine-year-old Suttington took on his second recognizable opponent in thirty-five-year-old James Pritchard.

Pritchard was a well-known commodity in the heavyweight division, unfortunately for all the wrong reasons. After starting his career off as a heavyweight prospect, Pritchard was upset by former heavyweight champion Mike Weaver in 1987. After losing to Michael Dokes, Johnny DuPlooy, and Pierre Coetzer over the next two years, Pritchard tried to salvage his disappointing career by dropping down to cruiserweight. Although he was able to land a title shot for the vacant IBF belt (against James Warring), he quickly ended any notion of a successful career when he set a world record by getting knocked out in a mere twenty-four seconds (becoming the fastest KO in a world title fight). With the loss to Warring ending any hope of fulfilling the early promise of his career, Pritchard proceeded to move back up to heavyweight and became a journeyman opponent. Unfortunately for him, he was a failure at that as well. His knockout loss to Warring caused him to be gun shy and fearful against the bigger heavyweight punchers, and his initial heavyweight fight against Tim Witherspoon was one of the worst fights ever televised on *USA Tuesday Night Fights*. Pritchard ran and clinched through ten rounds of boredom before losing the decision. After trying to pull the same stunt against Michael Moorer (who was able to pin down the timid Pritchard in the third round long enough to knock him out), it appeared that Pritchard was finished even as a journeyman. No network was eager to televise another fight with Pritchard, and few fans wanted to see him in the ring again after his disgraceful performances.

However, his soft chin and recognizable name kept him employed against regional fighters in non-televised fights. Although he was regarded as a forgotten man by the time he signed to fight Suttington, he did remain active enough to lose nine of his previous eleven fights.

Initially it appeared to be a smart fight for Suttington to take. Pritchard had gone the distance with fighters like Witherspoon and Zeljko Mavrovic based on his survival skills (i.e., running and clinching), and it appeared to be an ideal fight for the power-punching Suttington to develop his skills as a puncher. Suttington could learn how to fight against an opponent looking only to survive. Besides, if he failed to score the knockout it wouldn't have been held against him, and if he did it could further enhance his reputation. But when Suttington entered the ring at a whopping 240 pounds (nearly twenty pounds heavier than he was against Halstead), it became apparent that the strategy could very easily backfire. Suttington, besides looking physically out of shape, also appeared mentally unready. (One boxing writer commented that Suttington appeared "uninterested" as he entered the ring.)[1] If he were unable to score an early knockout, he could find his conditioning might betray him if Prichard were to up the pressure in the later rounds.

As it turned out, those initial worries were right on the mark. Realizing that he didn't have the stamina to go the full ten rounds, Suttington tried to test Pritchard's chin early. After staggering Pritchard on several occasions in the first two rounds, Suttington began to show signs of fatigue in the third. Pritchard recognized his opportunity and began to pressure his rapidly fading opponent. After a tough third round, many ringsiders wondered how much gas the clearly winded Suttington had in the tank, and how much longer he could continue in his current condition. Those questions were quickly answered when Pritchard began to tee off on Suttington for much of the fourth. Unable to defend himself, Suttington was rescued at 2:14 of the round when the referee (Ross Strada) jumped in and ended the fight.

Although it was a big win for James Pritchard, it failed to do much for his career other than give him a second life in Europe (where he lost to Brian Nielsen and Wladimir Klitschko). A return to Missouri the following year followed though, where he lost a ten-round decision to Topeka born heavyweight prospect Damon Reed.

---

[1] Bob Carson, *International Boxing Digest* 38 (August 1996): 42.

For Suttington, the loss quickly ended talk about him becoming a legitimate contender, and initially it appeared to end his career. Although he fought five months after the Pritchard loss (scoring a knockout over Robert Jackson) he disappeared for nearly three years after that. By the time he resurfaced in 1999, he was a forgotten fighter, even in Missouri. After losing to prospect Boris Powell in his second comeback fight, Suttington seemed finished. However, redemption seemed to call in the name of Ty Fields. Although Fields had an impressive record of 14–0 with 14 first-round KOs, he was seen as a joke to many boxing writers. It was the perfect opportunity for Suttington to resurrect his career, scoring a win over an overhyped opponent. But Fields proved to be more resilient than his critics assumed, knocking out Suttington in the second round. After that loss, there was no coming back for Greg. No boxing fan would take him seriously after losing to Fields. He was clearly a Fighter B.

July 13, 1996—Denver, Colorado
"Hurricane" Peter McNeeley (40–2, 34 KOs) vs. Lou Monaco
   (3–3–2, 1 KO)
Favorite: McNeeley
Result: Monaco won via fifth-round TKO.

"Hurricane" Peter McNeeley had accomplished exactly what manager Vinnie Vecchione had set out for him as a professional boxer. He landed a huge payday against former champion "Iron" Mike Tyson, but in less than one round McNeeley was completely discredited as a fighter and earned the scorn of boxing insiders for receiving such a large payday despite never having taken any of the hard knocks that came with being a fighter. He never fought a ranked, or even respectable, opponent and yet landed an $800,000 payday. He even seemed to relish in his newly found fame, doing a self-mocking Pizza Hut commercial that made fun of his soft chin. In the world of boxing, Peter McNeeley was despised by many as sort of the "Vanilla Ice" of the sport: big payday, national commercials (which few champions outside the heavyweight division could ever secure), heavy hype and flash, and zero substance to back it up.

McNeeley showed one trait that seemed to justify the continuation of his boxing career despite achieving everything he set out to accomplish. He showed courage and guts in rushing Tyson at the bell, exchanging punches with the hardest puncher in modern heavyweight history. Although he ended up on the losing end of those exchanges against Tyson, he showed more courage and grit than did Frank Bruno and Bruce Seldon did in fighting Tyson. (Both fighters were actually champions defending their belt in their fights with "Iron" Mike.) Most boxing insiders had little but scorn for McNeeley, but they grudgingly admitted that he could conceivably ride his newly found popularity into another big money fight. After all, losing in one round to Mike Tyson was certainly not career ending: Mike had blasted out many good heavyweights in the opening round.

Realizing that Peter was not completely out of the heavyweight picture despite the loss, Vecchione picked up where he left off before the Tyson fight. His first fight back was against the little known (and lightly regarded) Mike Sam for a minor championship (the USBF heavyweight title). It was an opportunity to give McNeeley a belt and pad his record against the usual soft opponent on whom he had spent most of his career feasting. McNeeley blasted out Sam in two rounds and proceeded to win his next three fights in dominant fashion.

There was little reason to suspect that his win streak over weak opposition would not continue against Lou Monaco. Although Monaco had one of the most impressive physiques in the heavyweight division, his record was unimpressive, winning only three of his eight fights and scoring only one knockout. In fact, most ringsiders wondered if Monaco was a step down for McNeeley (as hard as that was to comprehend considering his previous opposition). Although fighters like Juan Quintana and Mike Sam were lightly regarded, Monaco had already been starched in the opening round by Eric "Butterbean" Esch, a fighter who most experts felt was nothing more than a "carnival act." It seemed a safe bet that McNeeley would win and win big; he still was more highly regarded than "Butterbean" was at that time.

The "Butterbean" fight actually was an aberration for Monaco. He followed that loss with a draw (that most observers felt should have gone his way) against young prospect Rick Roufus, a fighter who possessed a fairly impressive record of 6–1 with five knockouts, and that draw with another impressive, albeit losing, effort to another prospect, undefeated Cody Koch, via a four-round decision. In fact, all three of his losses were to undefeated fighters. For the few boxing writers who actually were following his career, it actually appeared as if Monaco was improving each time he stepped in the ring. Still, the jump up from four rounders with inexperienced prospects seemed woefully inadequate to prepare Monaco for the experienced McNeeley, and considering how he folded in his only other high profile fight, it was assumed that he would do so again against the "Hurricane."

Buried on the undercard of a Michael Carbajal and Wayne McCullough doubleheader, McNeeley was clearly a man in hostile territory. Used to fighting in the safe confines of New England, he found himself roundly booed by the Denver fans, who rallied behind the local fighter Monaco. McNeeley seemed a bit angered by the slight, but it was likely that he would take it out on Lou, who appeared nervous during the referee's instructions. With twenty-three first-round knockouts, it was expected that McNeeley would come out swinging for the fences, and he fulfilled that expectation. At the bell McNeeley jumped all over Monaco, backing him up with hard combinations and solid left hooks. But as early as the first minute, two factors became abundantly clear: first McNeeley was loading up with every punch he threw, and second, the punches were having little serious effect on Monaco. By round's end it appeared that Monaco had taken control of the exchanges, with a handful of right hands sneaking through. McNeeley appeared winded after the opening session and ill-prepared to go past the first round, anticipating an easy knockout.

By the second round, McNeeley's offense began to settle into a fairly predictable patter. He would load up and throw hard combinations, but tended to fade out after only a few shots. When he wasn't throwing punches, he tended to pose rather than move. Most disturbing was the fact that he would pose with his left hand at his hip, making the opening for the right hand all the more inviting for Monaco. A straight right buckled McNeeley nearly a minute into the round, and despite trying to rally later in the round, it was becoming apparent that Peter was in serious trouble.

Ironically, manager Vinnie Vecchione tried to rally McNeeley after the second round, telling his fighter that "he's [Monaco] running out of gas fast." It seemed that Vecchione was talking about the wrong fighter. Monaco showed no signs of fatigue, whereas McNeeley was breathing heavily and dropping his hands lower and lower.

At the start of the third Monaco finally began to exploit Peter's weaknesses with urgency. After two rounds of success behind the overhand right hand, Monaco began to throw the punch with regularity and seldom failed to find McNeeley's chin with it. After timing a bobbing and weaving McNeeley perfectly, Monaco landed a picture perfect straight right that stunned McNeeley at the end of the round. McNeeley was a spent fighter in the fourth, but still managed to withstand the Monaco onslaught. But by the fifth round, it became apparent that he was ready to go. When referee Nomar Garcia separated McNeeley and Monaco from a clinch, McNeeley fell back into the ropes. Although Monaco failed to jump on McNeeley after what was a clear sign of McNeeley's fatigue, he did continue to pressure the retreating McNeeley. With seconds remaining in the round, Monaco's patience finally paid off when he landed another overhand right on Peter's chin. McNeeley buckled and fell back into the ropes (where Monaco landed one more shot for good measure). When referee Nomar Garcia jumped in to issue a standing eight count, a woozy McNeeley proceeded to literally run across the ring in falling face first in the opposite corner. Although he rose at the count of six, Garcia wisely waved the contest off, awarding the victory to Monaco.

For Monaco it seemed like he finally found lightning in a bottle with the win. However, the win would be only the first step in the rejuvenated career of Louis Monaco. When he proceeded to lose his next two fights to Michael Grant and Jeremy Williams, it seemed that the McNeeley win would be his only significant victory. But a shocking knockout over undefeated British power puncher Kevin McBride followed, as did a stunning upset over former WBA heavyweight champion Michael Dokes.

McNeeley, however, never recovered from the loss. With the possibility of another payday gone, McNeeley seemed to lose the desire and heart that marked his earlier career. Although he won his next five fights, he failed to score knockouts in any of those fights. When he finally stepped it up again to fight Brian Nielsen in Denmark, he found himself on the losing end again. McNeeley was stopped in the third round and appeared grossly overmatched again in that fight. However, there was one more payday for the "Hurricane," and it actually was a fight that most observers felt he had a great chance to win. The long anticipated fight with "Butterbean" finally materialized for McNeeley in 1999, and though few boxing experts considered it a quality match-up, most felt it was a toss up as to who would win. McNeeley, who struggled with drug addiction after the Tyson fight, would finally show the boxing world that he was, if not a great fighter, at least a legitimate fighter. A win over "Butterbean" might have even repair his battered reputation with boxing writers if he were successful in ending what many felt was the charade that was the boxing career of Eric Esch. But in what would be the single lowest moment in his career, McNeeley was stopped in the opening round against "Butterbean," a loss that effectively robbed him of what little legitimacy he had as a fighter.

September 12, 1996—Melville, New York
Bobby Joe Harris (18–0, 12 KOs) vs. Jesse Ferguson
   (20–16, 14 KOs)
Favorite: Harris
Result: Ferguson won a ten-round decision.

Perhaps no heavyweight in the 1990s was more familiar with the role of underdog than Jesse Ferguson, and perhaps no heavyweight pulled off quite as many upsets as Ferguson. But ironically when Ferguson was picked as undefeated Bobby Harris's nineteenth opponent in September 1996, it looked as if Jesse's upset over Ray Mercer in 1993 (page 84) would be his only highlight. After the win over Mercer, Ferguson's career went into a freefall, losing seven of his next eight fights. But perhaps more upsetting was that the determination and the toughness that made him such a popular fighter and tough opponent was beginning to wane. After weighing in at a career high 244 pounds, he was meekly stopped in the opening round by Frank Bruno in 1994. Most assumed that he would learn his lesson and return to the gym to train with some vigor, but he continued to weigh in the 240s, losing to Larry Holmes by decision and to Jeremy Williams by TKO in the seventh round. The Williams loss seemed to end any hope of a Ferguson revival: he appeared bloated and uninspired for much of the fight. Although he whipped himself back into reasonable shape against Alex Stewart in his next fight in

1995, he still ended up losing a decision, and when a TKO loss to Danell Nicholson followed, Ferguson faded from the scene for nearly a year.

Jesse returned to take on the undefeated Harris in 1996. With seven stoppage losses on his resume, and a six-fight losing streak that spanned three years, it looked like a safe pick for Team Harris. He needed exposure while taking on a slightly better grade of heavyweight opponent, and Ferguson fit the bill to a tee. At thirty-nine years old he was a full fifteen years older than Harris, and had shown that he could be easily outboxed or outpunched. It seemed the ideal coming out party for Harris, but Jesse was unwilling to just ride off into the sunset without one final run at a title. After whipping himself into great shape, Jesse stepped into the ring a fighter with all the tenacity and hunger of a man on a mission.

Ferguson came out in the opening round viciously attacking the body and stalking his younger foe. Harris, however, initially recognized Ferguson's strengths and weaknesses and worked behind a jab from the outside. But in the final minute of the round Jesse was able to bulldog his opponent into the ropes. Although Harris held his own in the exchanges, it was suddenly clear to Jesse that when push came to shove, Harris would be unable to handle the pressure. Jesse resumed his high-pressure attack in the second round, pumping hard right hands as he tried to pin down Harris. Although Harris continued to box from the outside, it was also becoming clear that he was somewhat tentative. His concern proved well warranted when Jesse finally found his mark at 0:45 of the round with a big right hand. Although Harris walked through it, a second right hand a minute later had the undefeated Harris holding on for dear life. By round's end, Harris was fighting inside with Ferguson, a troubling sign for his corner who recognized that an inside fight suited Ferguson considerably more than Harris.

Also recognizing the turning tide was Ferguson's trainer Eddie Mustapha Muhammad, who screamed "let your hands go!" at his fighter in between rounds. Jesse obliged, tagging Harris with a left hook thirty seconds in the third round. Although Harris appeared a bit less tentative and a bit more willing to open up against Ferguson, he paid for his foolishness. A right uppercut followed by a left hook shook up Harris and had him reeling towards the ropes. Ferguson followed up, but quickly emerged from the fray with a small cut over his left eye. Harris, sensing an opportunity, began to target the cut, but still dropped his left hand after firing the jab. With less than thirty seconds left in the round Ferguson made him pay for that mistake, dropping him with a right hand for an eight count. Harris struggled to rise and appeared without any legs at all, but was mercifully saved by the bell before Ferguson could finish him.

Harris did recover by the start of the fourth, but he again made another foolish mistake when he decided to slug it out with Ferguson to start the round. Jesse dropped Harris again with another left hook, this time only 0:35 into the round. Again Harris rose at the count of 8, and again Harris appeared badly wobbled. Ferguson swarmed all over Harris, who desperately tried to hold. Although Ferguson was unable to finish his wounded foe, Harris was also never able to recover, eating countless shots and getting stunned by two right hands at 2:30 of the round.

The fight began to slow in the fifth round, Ferguson's dominance continuing. Both fighters began to work the jab as the round started, with Jesse occasionally throwing a homerun shot. But Harris continued to make the same mistake he made in the first four rounds, backing into the ropes at 1:40 and allowing Jesse to attack his body. Ferguson again staggered Harris at 2:40 of the fifth, but failed to capitalize and allowed Harris to finish the round. It was the first major sign of fatigue that Jesse would show that night, and it would continue in the sixth as Jesse slowed his pace and allowed Harris to move and flick his jab. But Harris's inability to handle the power shots of Jesse Ferguson remained Jesse's great equalizer, and at 2:00 of the sixth Jesse again staggered Harris with a left hook. Thirty seconds later another right hand hurt Harris, and although Ferguson appeared totally winded at the bell, there was little question that he pulled out the round. The fight followed the Jesse Ferguson script for much of the remainder of the fight. Harris tried to box and move, but would get rattled every time Ferguson landed a big shot. In the seventh a straight right drove him into the ropes, and a minute later another right hand followed by a left hook hurt Harris while he covered up on the ropes. Ferguson's fatigue remained the only thing that kept Harris going, and although Jesse upped the pressure in the ninth round, he was unable to finish off Harris. Still, it appeared at the start of the tenth round that Harris's corner was stopping the contest. But they apparently decided to give Harris one more chance, realizing that a decision loss was considerably less damaging than a TKO loss. Harris fought bravely, but continued to eat leather from an onrushing Ferguson, cementing what became a very decisive unanimous decision win for Jesse Ferguson.

It was Ferguson's most meaningful win since his upset over Mercer, but few figured that anything would come of it. In fact, when *World Boxing* listed the Ferguson vs. Harris fight as one of the ten best heavyweight fights of the year, they also followed it up by claiming that it was "one old fighter's last frenzied stand against the forces of time."[2] But Ferguson would again prove the critics wrong when he went on a serious run for another title shot, and arguably most impressive run of his career. He followed up the win over Harris with two more impressive wins (over Everton Davis and Thomas Williams) before stepping up against Tongan heavyweight Samson Po'uha. Ferguson pulled out another upset, stopping Po'uha in eight. The win over Po'uha landed him a fight for the USBA heavyweight championship against Hasim Rahman. Although he would lose to Rahman by way of twelve-round decision in 1998, he still had one more impressive performance left, this time against Obed Sullivan, upsetting the younger man in his very next fight (page 290).

Initially most assumed that the loser, Bobby Harris, would still possibly have a bright future. He lost a lopsided decision to a seemingly washed up Jesse Ferguson, but he showed a lot of courage and grit in that fight. But many boxing insiders wondered if he took too much punishment from Ferguson, and if he could bounce back after taking such a beating. There questions seemed to be answered when Harris lost another fight that many expected him to win, this time against heavyweight Ray Anis—by way of tenth-round knockout in his next fight. It signaled the end of the line for Harris, and when he followed those two losses with an eight-round draw against clubfighter Will Hinton, even his most ardent fans admitted that a world title was not going to be in his future.

---

[2] William Dettloff, "The Top Ten Heavyweight Fights of 1996," *World Boxing*, Spring 1997, 65.

November 3, 1996—Tokyo, Japan
Alex Stewart (39–5, 38 KOs) vs. Craig Petersen (21–5-1, 8 KOs)
Favorite: Stewart
Result: Petersen won by way of eighth-round TKO due to
  swelling around Stewart's eyes.

For perennial heavyweight contender Alex Stewart, it looked as if he might just punch his way into one final big money fight. Although a lop-sided twelve-round decision loss, against Evander Holyfield in 1993, was the result of his last big fight Stewart had proved throughout the 1990s that he was a very resilient fighter. Besides, he finally had earned the right to be seen as a legitimate contender, something that eluded him for much of his early career. After winning twenty-four straight fights, all by knockout, Stewart was nonetheless seen as a grossly protected fighter when he stepped into the ring with Evander Holyfield the first time in 1989. Evander battered Stewart for the first four rounds, but in round five Stewart rattled Holyfield with several hard right hands. Although Holyfield rebounded to stop Stewart on cuts in the eighth round, Alex seemed to create at least some interest. He was stopped on cuts, never dropped, and had Holyfield in trouble at one point. It ap-peared as if Stewart could in fact become a legitimate contender, but the following year, Alex was dealt what appeared to be a career ending loss against Mike Tyson. Tyson destroyed Stewart in the opening round, but it was Alex's demeanor before the fight that sealed his fate in the eyes of many boxing fans. Stewart appeared terrified, almost to the point of tears, during the pre-fight introduction and fought accordingly. After getting dropped in the opening seconds of the fight Alex tried to hold on for dear life, but was quickly felled two more times, ending the fight. He never was able to test Mike Tyson's chin with his right hand and, more importantly, was never able to shake his pre-fight jitters.

Stewart seemed finished, and another knockout loss, this time to Mi-chael Moorer in 1991, seemed to confirm that. His reputation slipped so badly that George Foreman saw him as a soft touch and chose him as an opponent in 1992. But Alex finally put it all together against "Big" George. After getting decked twice in the second round Alex came back to batter Foreman over the next eight rounds. By the end of the fight Alex looked like the winner and Foreman looked like a man who swallowed a land mine. But by the slimmest of margins Foreman emerged victorious by decision. Still, it was enough to resurrect the career of Alex Stewart, and suddenly many boxing writers saw him as a legitimate challenger for Riddick Bowe's heavyweight championship. (In fact, several boxing writers felt that he was in fact more deserving than Foreman.) Stewart kept active, but stumbled against Jerry "Wimpy" Halstead in a fight in 1993. Although he stopped Halstead in seven, he was badly staggered by "Wimpy" and in fact was nearly dropped. It was enough to rob Stewart of just enough luster to remove his name from the list of potential Bowe opponents, but opportunity came in the form of an old nemesis: Evander Holyfield. Although Alex went on to lose a decision to Holyfield, he acquitted himself well, and many boxing insiders felt that he was still "in the hunt." So Alex cashed in on his newly found status as a contender, fighting frequently on *USA Tuesday Night Fights* against a steady collection of journeymen in an attempt to keep active. By the start of 1996 he found himself on the threshold of the top ten (he was ranked number fourteen by the WBC). But an eye injury (he had laser surgery on a detached retina) put him on the shelf for nine months and, by the time he was ready to return, his ranking had dropped eleven spots to number twenty-five. By October Alex was ready to fight, and when Michigan native Chris Byrd was forced to pull out of a fight on the undercard of George Foreman's WBU title defense against Crawford Grimsley, Alex jumped at the opportunity. Although it was on a mere two weeks notice, it was a very high profile fight, and one that could put him in position for a rematch with Foreman. Besides, there was little to indicate his opponent, Craig Petersen, would give him much trouble.

Although he had some success against regional fighters in Australia, New Zealand's Craig Petersen was a hardly an exciting international prospect. He was a fighter with little international experience and only moderate success at the local level. After losing a pair of fights early in his career to the forgettable Rod Carr in 1988, Craig bounced back to win his next six fights. But a fourth-round knockout loss to Apollo Sweet (for the British Commonwealth title) followed in 1989, and for many boxing fans in Australia, it appeared as if he would never become a serious contender in the world scene. But after another six-fight win streak Craig pulled off one of the biggest wins of his career, upsetting James Thunder for the Australian title in 1991. His reign was short lived however as he handed the title back to Thunder in 1992. In a fight with hard-punching prospect Herbie Hide later that year he found himself on the losing end again, this time by seventh-round stoppage. Although he did drop Hide in that fight, it was hardly enough to create much of a stir, and once again he appeared finished. But in 1993 he was given a most unusual opportunity.

After relocating to the United States to further develop as a fighter, The People's Choice Heavyweight Tournament (a one-night NCAA-style tournament with sixteen fighters) called. Despite his limitations, the People's Choice wanted an international flair, and Petersen would give them another fighter from an exotic location. Petersen went on to upset Bert Cooper in the first round by way of decision, and it looked like Petersen had the perfect tool to create a name for himself in the United States. Although he would go undefeated in the tournament, he would end up with a loss of sorts by the end of the night. He was expected to fold against Cooper, but there was little question that Cooper was in atrocious shape. That along with the nearly comical soap opera that nearly canceled the fight several times in the hours leading up to the fight seriously tainted his win. Also, Petersen was never able to completely recover from the first-round knockdown and dropped out of the tournament without moving on to the second round. Petersen completely disappeared after the Cooper fight and didn't step into the ring for nearly three years, and for his fans in Australia it appeared as if his career had come to an inglorious end. But in 1996 he returned and was quickly scouted by Chris Byrd as a potential opponent. Even at his best he was considered a long shot against Byrd, but he was also coming in with tons of ring rust and a full thirty pounds of added poundage over his ideal fighting weight. When Byrd pulled out, it looked as if things actually got worse for Petersen as Stewart was seen as a harder puncher and a more seasoned pro than Byrd.

But although both fighters came in after a long break with some added weight, it was in fact Petersen who was more prepared. He carried the extra weight surprisingly well (he weighed in at 250 pounds) and had much more time to prepare for the fight than Stewart. He also had an advantage in his southpaw stance, which gave most heavyweights trouble, including one as experienced as Stewart. Still, early on it seemed woefully inadequate to compensate for Stewart's advantage in natural talent. Although both fighters opened with the jab, it was not long before Alex began to take control with his, and by the end of the round he had neutralized Craig's offense and had him fighting defensively. Both fighters came out a little more aggressively in the second. Petersen, realizing that his normally solid jab and boxing skills were not enough against the skillful Stewart, mixed it up with the harder puncher. Surprisingly, Craig was not only holding his own, but in fact he was winning much of the inside action. The highlight for Craig came in the final thirty seconds of the round when Alex seemed to freeze after a hard inside combo from the Kiwi. Petersen fired a hard right hook that landed on Stewart's ear and robbed him of his equilibrium. Alex, clearly hurt, stumbled to the canvas. When he rose, there was little question that he was hurt. Saved by the bell, he returned to his corner with some serious swelling around his left eye, the seeds of his eventual defeat.

Alex, despite the swelling, gladly walked in and traded with Petersen at the start of the third (to which Craig gladly obliged). But the power and experience of Alex Stewart began to slowly turn the momentum back to his corner. After getting grazed with a right hand halfway through the round, Alex began to find a home for his own right hand and by round's end had Petersen on the ropes with hard combinations. The fourth saw the culmination of Alex's hard work and power. With Petersen again returning to the jab, Alex walked in throwing hard bombs. But Petersen was unable to keep Alex on the outside. Although Alex's left eye was nearly closed, he finally rocked Petersen with a hard right at 2:30. Petersen backed into the ropes and was quickly felled by a right hand to the body, and the early indications when he rose were that he was ready to call it a night. However, Alex was unable to finish his wounded foe as the bell sounded, ending the round.

However, if Craig Petersen needed some motivation to continue fighting, all he had to do was look at the face of Alex Stewart, which was becoming grotesquely swollen. Craig boxed and moved well in the early parts of the fifth, targeting his right jab on that swollen left eye of Stewart. Craig no longer was eager to mix it up on the inside either, holding whenever Alex got in close. In frustration, Alex pushed Craig back at one point and, with a little over a minute in the round, used a chopping right hand to find the chin of Craig Petersen and sent him back into the ropes. But a right hand of Craig Petersen's landed on the top of the head of Alex Stewart, causing him to stumble briefly, and Petersen was still in the fight.

Petersen began to target Stewart's eye even more in the sixth round, seeing it as his ticket to victory, and by the seventh round, he regained some of his courage. No longer moving around the ring as much, Craig held his ground firing one-two combinations from the outside with alarming regularity. Although Alex only needed to survive three more rounds (most ringsiders felt that he was still winning the fight on the scorecards), a disturbing sign greeted Stewart's cornerman, George Benton, as his fighter returned to the corner after the seventh. Now both of Alex's eyes were swollen; he could still see out of his right eye, but it was looking increasingly ugly. At the bell starting the round Benton wisely called the doctor to look at Alex Stewart. Stewart was allowed to continue, hardly coping with his damaged eyes. After Petersen lost a point early in the round for a headbutt, referee Frank Garza finally saw enough when the swelling in the right eye came close to blinding Stewart. He wisely waved the fight off in the final minute of the eighth round.

For Craig Petersen there was little question that it was the biggest win of his career, and one that opened the possibility of a big money fight in the United States. (A rubber match with old nemesis James Thunder was mentioned.) But in the end he chose to clear up some unfinished business with Chris Byrd. With his fight against Byrd now a serious, main event fight Craig knew that a win could finally put him into contention (he was still only twenty-seven years old). But underestimating the power of Byrd, as well as the effectiveness of Byrd's unorthodox style, Petersen was dominated for over five rounds before getting stopped in the sixth. It was a heartbreaking loss for Petersen, for coming back from such a loss to become a contender was next to impossible. But ultimately he would never get the chance. Less than three months later Craig died in New Mexico of a drug overdose.

For Alex Stewart, the loss to Petersen would end his run as a contender and introduce him to the world of opponent status. Although he fought well against Petersen, he was still dropped by a fighter with only eight knockouts (and five losses) in twenty-seven fights. The following year he lost by way of knockout to Oleg Maskaev, and over the next two years, losses to Phil Jackson and Lance Whitaker followed. The end came in June 1999 when Jorge Luis Gonzalez defeated him by way of an embarrassing second-round knockout, bringing his career to an end.

November 7, 1996—Vigo, Spain
Jukka Jarvinen (17–0, 9 KOs) vs. Peter Hrivnak (2–5, 1 KO)
Favorite: Jarvinen
Result: Hrivnak won by way of second-round TKO due to a
   cut.

By November 1996, it was becoming apparent that the long dormant heavyweight scene in Finland was coming alive. European boxing fans began to pay attention to some of the Finnish fighters, and although none of them had yet to fight for a world title (or even the European championship) there was growing evidence that a legitimate European heavyweight prospect was emerging in undefeated Jukka Jarvinen. Jarvinen won the Finnish heavyweight title in his previous fight against what was unquestionably the most recognizable boxer in Finland, a former WWF wrestler named Tony Halme (called Ludvig Borga in the WWF). Although Halme was not regarded as much of a fighter (he was a man with little experience despite better than average power) he was seen as the man any Finnish heavyweight needed to get by if he were to progress on to the European scene. Jarvinen's win, despite the fact that it came by way of controversial disqualification, did just that, and considering most Finnish boxing fans could not remember the last time Finland had an undefeated heavyweight with seventeen fights, he soon emerged as the top prospect in all of Finland. All that was left was to cause some excitement outside his native country, and possibly position himself for a shot at either the European heavyweight title or a minor world title.

Although Jukka had fought in the United States before (six of his wins actually came on U.S. soil), his first European fight outside his native country was to be an easy one against a little known Czech fighter named Peter Hrivnak in Spain. Hrivnak was a decent amateur fighter, representing Czechoslovakia in the 1992 Olympics (where he lost to Brian Nielsen by decision), but as a pro his career was hardly awe-inspiring. Against European fighters, Peter had lost five of his seven fights and managed only one knockout. More telling, in all five of his losses, he was stopped or knocked out. For most boxing fans in Europe, it appeared as if Jukka was taking no chances in his first fight outside of his country, and many did not question if Jukka would win, but rather, would he be able to stop Hrivnak early.

For those fans that had never seen the southpaw Jarvinen fight, it became clear that despite his record that he was a long way from becoming a European contender when his fight with Hrivnak began. Jarvinen fired his right jab with some effectiveness, but his technical shortcomings were glaring. Although he controlled the action in the opening round, many fans felt that he was not showing anything to justify a European title fight. When Hrivnak emerged from a competitive first round relatively unscathed, most fans concluded that Jarvinen was at best a few years from making a serious run for a title. But his title aspirations were dealt a most unfortunate blow early in the second round when an accidental clash of heads opened a small cut over his left eye. Due to the nature of the cut, most assumed that if it were to become a factor in the fight, it would either be declared a technical draw or go to the scorecards, and more likely the latter as the cut seemed way to small to threaten the fight yet. But several seconds later ringsiders were shocked to see the referee stop the action, examine the small cut, and declare Hrivnak the winner by way of TKO a little past the halfway point of the round. In controversial fashion, Peter Hrivnak emerged with the biggest win of his career.

For the young Czech, the win over Jarvinen did briefly buoy his career. He followed it with a disqualification win over undefeated Belgian heavyweight Geert Blieck. But in April 1997 he took the biggest step up in class, fighting German Mario Schiesser. Mario crushed Hrivnak in three rounds, exposing his soft chin once and for all and ending any possibility for the Czech becoming a contender in Europe.

For Jarvinen, it initially seemed that the win would not prove to be devastating. At his relatively advanced age of thirty-two a loss was always a major setback, but many of his fans felt (justifiably so) that he was robbed of a win, or at least a draw, by a referee who clearly dropped the ball. But Jarvinen's technical shortcomings, and a somewhat suspect chin of his own, would prove his undoing in his next fight. Against his old nemesis Tony Halme, Jarvinen was destroyed in the opening round. The loss robbed Jukka of his Finnish heavyweight title and effectively ended talk of Jukka as a possible prospect. Although an IBU world title fight did emerge in 2001 against Belgium's Dirk Wallyn (a fight in which he was stopped in the ninth round), it was clearly not the kind of title fight his fans envisioned back in 1996. Nor could anyone predict that the fighter who was regarded as the best Finnish heavyweight in the world in 1996 would, in the end, never make a successful defense of his Finnish championship.

November 9, 1996—Las Vegas, Nevada
"Iron" Mike Tyson (45–1, 39 KOs) vs. Evander Holyfield
    (32–3, 23 KOs)
Favorite: Tyson
Result: Holyfield won by way of eleventh-round TKO.

It took "Iron" Mike over six years (and eight fights), but by late 1996 he was once again the "baddest man on the planet." During his incarceration in an Indiana prison for rape, the heavyweight division descended into its worst state in over ten years, with three of the most forgettable heavyweight champions simultaneously holding the belts (Frans Botha, Bruce Seldon, and Frank Bruno). By the time he was released from prison in 1995 he was hailed as boxing's savior, the man who could bring back respect (and fans) to the sport. All this despite that in many ways he was the major reason that the heavyweight division was in such a sorry state. For the three fighters who were champions upon Mike Tyson's release were champions because of Don King, and more importantly remained champions because of King's desire to control Mike Tyson's return to championship boxing. While Riddick Bowe and Lennox Lewis (the two fighters widely regarded as the best heavyweights next to Tyson) saw themselves shut out of the heavyweight picture, Don King–controlled fighters Bruce Seldon and Tony Tucker saw their inflated ranking land them into a title fights. (Seldon and Tucker fought for the vacant WBA title as the number one and number two ranked contenders, this despite the fact that Seldon lost to Bowe and Tucker lost to Lewis.) After winning the title from Tucker, Seldon then avoided serious competition (fighting only Joe Hipp) in an attempt to keep the belt long enough to land the big money fight with Tyson. In fact, every fighter with a belt (even the more respected Michael Moorer) avoided Bowe and Lewis due to their fear of risking the potential huge payday that would await them if they were to fight Tyson.

By the time Mike Tyson returned, many boxing writers were simply glad that the charade of paper champions would be ending. Besides, it looked like Don King wanted Mike Tyson to unify the heavyweight title and like he would be able to do so (controlling two of the three champions). In fact, it didn't take Tyson long to win his first belt. With Don King pushing his weight around with the WBC, Mike found himself the number one contender before he even fought, and in a title fight against WBC champion Frank Bruno after only two fights. Tyson destroyed Bruno in three lopsided rounds, helping to reestablish himself as the biggest heavyweight in the world. King was determined to keep Mike's run as smooth as possible, and he realized that the way to do that was to avoid Riddick Bowe and Lennox Lewis. Bowe would be easier, as he was locked in a feud with Andrew Golota that would end his career. Besides, after dumping the WBC belt in the trash can shortly after winning it back in 1992, Bowe was permanently blacklisted by the WBC and virtually ignored in their ratings. Lewis, however, would be considerably tougher to avoid. He was the WBC number one-ranked contender and had won a WBC eliminator back in 1995 against Lionel Butler, forcing the WBC to grant him an immediate title fight. Lewis had allowed the Bruno vs. Tyson fight reluctantly, but he was not going to sit back and allow his title fight to slip away. As a result, King had Tyson vacate the WBC belt and fight the lightly regarded Bruce Seldon, who was the WBA champion. Tyson destroyed Seldon in one round and was now set to take on another lightly regarded heavyweight: former undisputed champion Evander Holyfield.

For Evander Holyfield, it looked like his best days were clearly behind him. He did not appeared to be the same fighter after his loss to Michael Moorer in 1994, and for many insiders, Don King was trying to cash in on the marketability of a Tyson-Holyfield fight before Holyfield slipped any further (making the fight unmarketable). After beating Ray Mercer by way of decision, Holyfield was stopped for the first time in his career against Riddick Bowe in November 1995. After dropping Bowe early, Holyfield inexplicably faded until he was stopped by the bigger man in the eighth round. Many called for his retirement after the Bowe fight, but he decided to make one more run at the gold. Struggling with Bobby Czyz in his next fight made it look like Evander was all but finished, and few could envision him landing a title fight, let alone winning it. Still, the cancelled Mike Tyson vs. Evander Holyfield fight from 1991 was widely seen as one of the biggest fights to never happen, and many boxing fans admitted that they felt Evander deserved a title fight much more than Bruce Seldon. Unlike Bruno and Seldon, Evander was respected as a fighter who feared no man; he would surely not freeze up and meekly fold like them. It was enough to motivate Don King to put together the fight five years too late under the heading "Finally."

Nonetheless, most saw it as another early knockout for Tyson. Vegas odds opened at 25–1 for Mike, and although they dropped to 6–1, much of that was seen as "sentimental" betting on the popular former champion. Although there were some reports that Mike Tyson was taking Holyfield lightly, his demeanor appeared angry during the press conferences, when he attacked Holyfield for an alleged comment made during Mike's trial for rape. When Mike weighed in at a fit 222 pounds, it appeared that the rumors of Mike's lack of readiness were unfounded. By fight night, only one of the reporters at ringside was picking Evander to win, and most felt that the thirty-four-year-old Holyfield would be hard pressed to get past the third round.

Although Evander entered the ring to cheers, it was in many ways an expression of appreciation for his many exciting years in the heavyweight division. Most of those fans expected a Mike Tyson victory. And as the bell rang to begin the fight, it appeared as if both fighters read the script. Tyson swarmed all over Holyfield, who seemed overwhelmed by the onslaught. Initially it appeared that Holyfield's response would be to hold, a strategy that tended to embolden Tyson in the past. But the onslaught slowed down in the second half of the round. Although Tyson was still aggressively attacking Holyfield with quick combinations upstairs, Evander appeared more composed as he responded with his own counterpunches. A Holyfield left hook upstairs briefly stunned Tyson, proving to both "Iron" Mike and the world that Evander was not about to go quietly. Mike quickly regained his composure, landing a straight right hand in the final thirty seconds of the round and another at the bell, but for "The Real Deal," he had survived the toughest round of any Mike Tyson opponent relatively unscathed.

Tyson started the second round again firing away with hard shots, but it was clear to most viewers that they had lost just a little bit of their snap. Also, his combinations were losing a punch or two with each flurry. Holyfield began to reveal what would become a very successful strategy. He would bounce and move a bit, and hold whenever Mike got inside. But rather than just wait for the referee to break his hold, Evander would grab Mike with his left arm while pounding away with his right. It was a strategy that nullified Mike's strongest weapons and wore out Tyson over the rounds, both physically and mentally. Holyfield briefly backed Mike into the ropes in the second round and, in the final ten seconds of the round, landed a hard left hand that caught Mike and cemented one of the most impressive rounds of his career. Holyfield continued his performance through the third and fourth rounds as well, "outspeeding" Tyson in the exchanges. Although Tyson tried to pump his much feared left hook in the fourth, Evander remained unfazed as he coolly dissected Mike Tyson.

Despite the fact that Evander had taken complete control of the fight, it appeared to many viewers and ringsiders that Tyson had in fact turned the tide in the fifth. After landing a right uppercut followed by a left hook to Holyfield's chin, Evander appeared hurt for the first time in the fight. Holyfield backed up as "Iron" Mike came forward in an attempt to finish off what he perceived as a wounded opponent. Tyson started taking control of the exchanges, although Evander seemed to have recovered (firing jabs and countering Mike Tyson). Showtime commentator Ferdie Pacheco observed that "Evander's punches no longer have the steam that they had . . . this power stuff [of Mike Tyson] that he's absorbing is wearing him out," a harsh, but seemingly legitimate observation. But the notion that Evander was wearing out would be quickly brought to an end in the sixth round. Still using his left hand clinch/right hand punch strategy, Holyfield backed Tyson into the ropes in the first minute of the round. Although Tyson landed a hard left hook inside, it became secondary to what followed seconds later. After an accidental clash of heads, Tyson emerged with a cut over his left eye. It was enough to revitalize Holyfield, who attacked with newly found vigor. As Evander fired hard shots upstairs, Tyson began to show signs of concern on his face. Coming alive in the final minute of the round

Evander stunned Mike with several hard shots upstairs. Tyson tried to answer with a hard right hand of his own, but a counter left hook dropped him for only the second time in his career. Although the knockdown did appear to be partially a result of poor balance on Mike's part and Mike was not seriously hurt (Tyson rose at the count of four), it was abundantly clear that the Evander was still in control and was not fading as had been predicted a round earlier. Evander was unable to completely capitalize on the knockdown as the bell ended the round, but from that point on "Iron" Mike was all but done. He would never again threaten Holyfield.

Tyson came out for the seventh looking confused and fighting tentatively. Holyfield even briefly taunted Mike halfway through the round, prompting a roar of approval from the crowd of over 17,000. No longer coming in with combinations, Mike became even easier to hit for Holyfield, who rattled Tyson with a straight left just past the halfway point of the round. Although Holyfield remained in complete control, the most damage done to Tyson in the seventh came from another accidental headbutt in the final seconds of the round, a jarring collision that buckled Tyson's knees and prompted referee Mitch Halpern to call time to allow Mike a few moments to recover (and to warn Holyfield for his reckless use of his head). Holyfield, however, would not be derailed. He began the eighth round boxing well behind a stingingly effective left jab and pounding Mike relentlessly every time he got inside. Still, many wondered if Holyfield's notoriously poor stamina (which failed him against Riddick Bowe, Michael Moorer, and, even to a lesser degree, Larry Holmes and George Foreman) would begin to falter as the fight headed into its final four rounds. But Holyfield was setting his own pace, holding when he wanted and punching when he wanted. Whenever Tyson tried to initiate a brawl Evander would either hold on (nullifying the assault) or respond in kind (winning the exchange).

Evander remained in complete control as the tenth round began, peppering Tyson with jabs on the outside that snapped his head back and firing left hook counters that robbed Tyson of what little resolve remained. The Tyson offense had slowed considerably as well, and although he briefly knocked Evander off balance with a right hand, Evander quickly responded with his own straight right on Mike's chin two minutes into the round. The beginning of the end would follow forty seconds later when a straight right badly wobbled Tyson. Holyfield jumped all over Mike, smothering him with devastating power shots upstairs that drove Mike Tyson back. Another right hand counter sent Tyson reeling into the ropes, on the verge of being knocked out, before being rescued by the bell. It was the most trouble Tyson had been in since Tokyo, and for the first time since 1990 it looked as if Mike would not only lose, but get stopped. To Tyson's credit however, he was determined to fight it out. He came out for the eleventh round swinging, hoping to catch a careless Holyfield coming in. It was, however, in vain. Holyfield retained his cool professionalism and quickly swarmed over Tyson again. A left hook to the chin jarred Tyson and opened up a assault to his head. Dazed, Tyson stumbled into the ropes and was snapped back with a hard straight right hand that prompted referee Mitch Halpern to stop the fight at thirty-seven seconds in the round.

With the impressive victory Evander Holyfield again revitalized a career that appeared all but finished and finally secured greatness in the ring. After his first loss to Bowe he was widely seen as a marginal champion, a caretaker who kept the belt warm in between two legendary championships. But he changed that perception after defeating Bowe in the rematch. However, after losing to Moorer and Bowe, it was widely assumed that despite his many accomplishments, the boxing hall of fame was probably not in his future. With the win over Tyson, Evander finally cemented his place in boxing history and, in fact, entered what is widely seen as his glory years. After winning *Ring Magazine's* "Fighter of the Year" award, he again stepped in the ring with Tyson, again as the underdog. Many assumed that Tyson simply underestimated Holyfield and would train with renewed vigor for the rematch. But Mike Tyson's psyche had been permanently scarred, and in one of the most infamous fights in the history of the sport, Evander again defeated Tyson, this time by way of disqualification when Mike bit off a small piece of Evander's ear in the third round. It was an ugly end to what many felt looked to be another dominant Evander Holyfield performance, and permanently turned Mike Tyson into a punch line for Jay Leno and David Letterman, erasing much of aura of Mike Tyson as a destroyer and replacing it with one of Mike as a complete basket case.

For Holyfield, a victory over old nemesis Michael Moorer in a rematch followed in his next fight (capturing the IBF belt). But age began

Evander Holyfield (right) defeated Mike Tyson not once but twice, reviving a seemingly finished career and cementing his place in boxing's pantheon of greats. *Pat Orr*

to catch up to him as he followed the win over Moorer with a fairly sloppy one over Vaughn Bean before being held to a draw with Lennox Lewis in a unification bout in 1999. Most observers felt that Holyfield was given a gift decision in a draw and that Holyfield was actually the loser. He fought Lewis again later that year (losing a close decision) before capturing his fourth world title, this time the vacant WBA title, against John Ruiz in 2000. Although he went on to lose a rematch with Ruiz the following year, Holyfield never slipped too far down the ranks. (A draw with Ruiz in their rubber match followed by a TKO over Hasim Rahman kept his career alive.) In fact, as late at 2003 he was again fighting for a world title (this time the vacant IBF title), losing a decision to Chris Byrd in what many felt was the most lopsided loss of his career. He followed that with a most embarrassing performance, getting stopped by blown-up former middleweight champion James Toney by way of ninth-round TKO.

For Tyson, he embraced his new persona as a fighter pushing the limits of sanity and decency from that point on, perhaps realizing that it was the only way he would ever be accepted again. His next two fights, against Frans Botha and Orlin Norris, saw Mike again flirting with disqualification. Although he regained some of his lost mystique after his knockouts over Julius Francis and, more notably, Lou Savarese (in which he blitzed Savarese in less than a minute), his comments after the fight played into the hands of the comedians when he indicated that he wanted to eat the unborn offspring of Lennox Lewis (this coming form a man with a prior history of using his teeth in such a manner). But his eagerness to call out Lewis was in many ways a mirage. Although he went on to knock out Andrew Golota and Brian Nielsen, Tyson made no serious attempt to fight Lewis immediately, citing a need for more tune-up fights. When he finally did fight Lennox in 2002 he was brutally battered for the better part of eight rounds before being knocked out. It was the first page of another personality change, as Mike congratulated Lennox after the fight, gently brushed some blood off his opponent's face, and in the post-fight interview gently caressed his infant child. Although few anticipated it would last more than a fight or two, it was one of the few times Mike acted with a humble degree of dignity in the ring, and one of the rare moments that he earned a degree of respect from boxing fans. Even his demeanor after his knockout victory over Cliff Etienne seemed uncharacteristically respectful, as when he appeared as a guest host on various television shows (including Fox's *Best Damn Sport Show* and ABC's *Jimmy Kimmel Live*). In fact, he became such a hit on *Jimmy Kimmel Live* (in once instance hamming it up with host Kimmel by sucking down helium balloons and singing to the crowd) that many boxing insiders were wondering if a Foreman-like personality change was possibly in the works. But when Mike Tyson was interviewed by Greta Van Susteren several months later on Fox, it appeared as if the old Tyson was back. (He said that he wished he had raped Desiree Washington.) The following year it was reported that he was bankrupt, with a little over $5,000 in his bank account, proving that predicting anything about Mike Tyson was never going to be easy.

December 14, 1996—Atlantic City, New Jersey
Courage Tshabalala (19–0, 16 KOs) vs. Brian Scott
**   (21–3, 12 KOs)**
Favorite: Tshabalala
Result: Scott won by way of second-round KO.

For young, undefeated heavyweight prospect Courage Tshabalala, it looked like his career was destined to take him all the way to a heavyweight championship fight. The young South African had personality in his power. He was a fighter with arguably the best one-punch power since a young Mike Tyson emerged on the heavyweight scene. Not only had he won his first eleven fights by way of knockout, but he also pulled together a most impressive amateur record of 70–1 with seventy first-round knockouts. Boxing fans were excited about the future of Tshabalala, and HBO commentator Larry Merchant proclaimed him one of the most exciting heavyweight prospects in years, saying shortly before the Scott fight that "he [Courage] is one of the best young natural punchers I've seen come along in the heavyweight division in a very long time."

Although many boxing fans were won over, a handful of critics began to emerge. After going the distance for the first time against little-known Carl McGrew in August 1995 many fans were stunned. Everyone agreed that sooner or later he would go the distance, it was a given, but with a record of 4–19 McGrew seemed the kind of opponent who would not challenge a knockout streak. Tshabalala then was extended the distance in his very next fight against Jesse Henry four months later, and fans began to openly question if his power was overrated. After winning an ugly eight-round split decision over Tim Nobel in May of 1996, even his most ardent supporters were left wondering what was going wrong. Courage began to win back some converts when he won his next three fights by way of knockout the following year, and by December he was ready for the big leagues, fighting journeyman Brian Scott on the undercard of Riddick Bowe's second fight with Andrew Golota on pay-per-view. It was a chance to showcase some of his power without seriously risking his undefeated record. Although his 6'5" opponent Brian Scott had a decent record of 21–3 with 12 KOs, almost all his wins were against second-tier heavyweights. The only times he stepped up in competition, he was defeated by way of early knockout (to Tommy Morrison and Jorge Luis Gonzalez). He seemed to be a perfect foil: a fighter with a better record than his skills could back up.

Those who were hoping that Brian Scott would at least look like a marketable opponent were left unhappy when Brian weighed in at a whopping 273 pounds, a full twenty-five pounds heavier than when he fought Morrison. With a soft midsection, it looked like Scott didn't give himself any chance at pulling off the upset and trained accordingly. And when Tshabalala entered the ring at a chiseled 225 pounds, there was little question as to which fighter was in better shape.

As the fight started, it appeared that Courage had an intelligent game plan considering his opponent. He wisely attacked the body while calmly stalking his taller foe. But although he impressed ringsiders with his body attack, he failed to do so with his left jab (which was almost non-existent) or his defense, which was porous at best. As Scott tried to out-box his shorter foe it became clear that Courage needed to work on ducking punches. If Brian Scott could land the jab with ease, than what would happen when he fought a ranked heavyweight? But as Courage began to attack upstairs at the bell ending the first, few anticipated that he would be called on it against Scott. Scott was a fighter with little "one-punch power," and Courage had yet to show that his chin was suspect. But in the second both perceptions would be blown apart. After continuing his body attack for much of the second round, Courage began to find his opponent getting braver and more adventurous. At 2:30 of the round Brian's courage paid off. A left hook behind a right hand caught Tshabalala and had him wobbling around the ring. Courage tried to hold on for dear life but Scott recognized that his opponent was seriously hurt and pumped a series of right hands. The last one landed flush on Tshabalala's chin and drove him to the canvas. Courage gamely tried to beat the count of referee Benji Esteves, but was out at 2:54 of the second round.

For Scott, the win was undoubtedly his biggest, and undoubtedly one that promised to open many doors. But his management team took a gamble and lost in his next fight when Brian signed to fight former champion James "Buster" Douglas three months later. It seemed a reasonable gamble; Douglas had one of the most recognizable names in the sport, and a win over him would propel Scott into the big leagues. Besides, there was ample evidence that he was not nearly the fighter he was when he fought Tyson. But James still had enough to take out a fighter like Brian Scott, and stopped the big man in six rounds. It was, for all intents and purposes, the end of any run at contention for Scott and his permanent induction into the journeyman's status. He would later go on to be knocked out by Ray Mercer in 2001 in his only other big fight.

For Tshabalala, the early effect of his first loss was stunned disbelief by many boxing fans. When the smoke cleared most boxing fans jumped off the bandwagon, assuming that there was little future for the young South African. Still, when it was announced that Courage would fight once-beaten Darroll Wilson in 1997, many assumed that Courage would prevail. Both fighters seemed to have soft chins, but the power and natural athletic ability appeared clearly in Tshabalala's corner. But in another upset (see page 255), Tshabalala was stopped in the fourth round after dropping Wilson in the first and third. It was the end of Courage's career as a prospect, and although he did land one more big fight (getting stopped by Oleg Maskaev in eight rounds) nobody ever looked at Courage as the second coming of Mike Tyson again. For Tshabalala, it was a disappointing end to a once promising career.

CHAPTER EIGHT

1997

"That was the best fight I've ever seen!"

Boxing historian Troy Harrington on the Tua-Ibeabuchi fight

January 14, 1997—Kansas City, Missouri
James Thunder (31–6, 25 KOs) vs. John Ruiz (29–3, 21 KOs)
Favorite: Thunder
Result: Ruiz won a twelve-round split decision.

Considering how James Thunder was being widely seen as the most likely next opponent for Lennox Lewis if he were successful in defeating Oliver McCall for the WBC heavyweight title, there was little question that Thunder had erased the stigma of his ugly loss to cruiserweight Franco Wanyama (page 187) in 1995 and had emerged as a legitimate heavyweight contender. He was on the threshold of fighting for a world title, and against a fighter that he had a "puncher's chance" against— Lewis (who had struggled against the likes of Ray Mercer and Frank Bruno as well get knocked out by Oliver McCall in two rounds). Thunder was increasingly looking like one of the more attractive heavyweights in the world with crushing performances against normally durable grade B opponents. In fact his five fights since the Wanyama loss were some of his best. Initially Thunder stepped in the ring with Ray Anis, a young prospect out of New York with only one loss in twenty fights. Many boxing fans saw it as a "pick 'em" fight, and some even gave the nod to Anis. But Thunder provided one of his most destructive performances ever in crushing the prospect in seven rounds. His next fight was against another prospect in Melvin Foster. Although Foster was coming off a decision loss to Michael Moorer, he was still seen as a

243

young fighter worth keeping an eye out for in the future. But again Thunder displayed brutal power in stopping Foster in eight rounds (showing considerably more firepower than the former champion had). With those two wins, the stigma of the Wanyama loss was effectively erased, and Thunder was again back on his way up the ladder to the top ten. He crushed the normally durable Will Hinton and followed it up with knockout victories over spoiler William Morris and former prospect Quinn Navarre in 1996. Thunder was a fighter who recognized the benefit of activity, and when he was presented with an opportunity to fight for the NABF title in early 1997, he jumped on it. The NABF belt would be just the cherry on top that he needed to add a final bit of legitimacy to his world title run, and would most likely boost his number twelve ranking up into the top ten—removing the only major potential roadblock to the fight. Even his opponent seemed to be the perfect foil; John Ruiz was a blown up cruiserweight with three losses (in fights where he tried to raise his game to the next level) and a reputation for folding against hard-punching Samoan fighters (Thunder was of Samoan decent). In his biggest fight to date Ruiz was destroyed in just nineteen seconds against David Tua less than one year prior, and few fans could forget such a brutal fight. Despite his glossy record, it was the loss to Tua that defined him, and the similarities between Tua and Thunder, though completely superficial, made the fight appear to be a setup for a Thunder blowout.

John Ruiz would prove to be one of the most intelligent and resilient fighters to emerge in the late 1990s, and as it would turn out, James Thunder would provide his coming-out party. Ruiz treated his loss differently than most fighters faced with the same situation: instead of losing confidence and losing heart, Ruiz gained determination. He wanted to prove that the Tua fight was a fluke and that he was a legitimate heavyweight, but he also intelligently looked at his situation and made some modifications on his style. Rather than try to box and move as he had in the past, he would emerge as one of the most effective in-fighters in the game. He would wrestle, he would hit in the clinch, and he would violate the unwritten law of machismo and actually milk the full five-minute break after a low blow. And he would win. Winning his next four fights by way of knockout, he was ready to take on the ghost of Tua as well as the hard-punching Thunder for the vacant NABF title. Even his previous run as a cruiserweight was something of a plus for Ruiz, as Thunder often had trouble (oddly enough) with blown-up cruiserweights (half of his losses were to those like Mike Hunter, Johnny Nelson, and Wanyama).

Before the fight began it looked as if all Ruiz's talk of rebuilding after the Tua debacle was just that, talk. He appeared apprehensive and scared, carrying an Alex Stewart look of terror during the pre-fight introductions. Many viewers on *USA Tuesday Night Fights* assumed that he was scared out of his wits and would fold the first time Thunder hit him. After all, he was a notoriously slow starter. But Ruiz would shock everyone, including Thunder, when he jumped all over the hard-punching Kiwi at the bell. Although Thunder calmly weathered the storm a quick combination upstairs to Thunder's head quickly rattled him enough to send shockwaves through the crowd. Ruiz then stepped back and boxed beautifully for the duration of the round, using a quick jab to pepper Thunder's face. When Thunder had second thoughts on a roundhouse right, leaving the punch in the "hanger" after starting the offensive motion, Ruiz quickly jumped on him for his caution and popped him with a right hand counter that cemented the round in his pocket.

But by the second round the "new" Ruiz began to emerge. He still landed hard right hands and mixed it up well with Thunder, but he also would clinch every time Thunder posed a threat and then punch relentlessly in the clinch. Although they were technically not point-scoring shots, it was impossible for the judges not to be impressed with the activity of Ruiz compared to Thunder. When Ruiz beat Thunder to the punch to start the third round, it became apparent that Ruiz would simply not be a pushover. It was a shockingly good start for a fighter with the reputation as a slow starter. Thunder continued to try and trap Ruiz for much of the fourth, but was unable to land anything significant against his unorthodox foe, who popped him with a hard left hook followed by a right hand at the bell. But the tide finally seemed to show signs of changing in the first thirty seconds of the fifth when Thunder finally caught Ruiz with a hard shot upstairs. But Ruiz easily clinched his way out of trouble and regained control seconds later. Thunder emerged from the round with swelling under his left eye and the early signs of fatigue, a bad sign considering Ruiz was known as a strong finisher. Still, Ruiz's corner was animated and upset over Ruiz's lack of movement and called on their fighter to show more of it in the sixth. He didn't, and though Thunder showed signs of getting his second wind, James smothered his own punches and failed to land any of them with much effectiveness. Thunder began to try and work his jab in the second half of the round, but Ruiz showed some of his slick boxing skills by out-jabbing Thunder.

The seventh showed the first signs of a change in repetition of the previous six rounds when a break was called early on due to some loose tape on Ruiz's glove. Although Ruiz still was beating Thunder to the punch, he ultimately paid a steep price in that round when he lost a point for an elbow to the head. Thunder tried to capitalize on the advantage by making it a 10–8 round with a solid flurry, but Ruiz again fought back well and refused to give any freebies to Thunder.

The loose tape became a regular occurrence as Ruiz again was forced to take a break in the eighth round to remove it, which proved to be a decisively dominant round for Ruiz thanks to his clever manipulation of a major James Thunder blunder. Thunder fired a low blow halfway through the round that actually landed nowhere near Ruiz's groin, but Ruiz knew that the referee saw it go south and dropped to the canvas grabbing his crotch and not his thigh (which had been hit). It was enough for the referee, who deducted a point from Thunder and handed the fight back to Ruiz. Moments after resuming, Ruiz emerged with an ugly cut over his right eye that again prompted a break in the action to allow the ringside doctor to examine the cut. Fans began to wonder if Ruiz's masterpiece would be snatched from him by way of a TKO due to the cut. But suddenly the ball was in Thunder's corner again. The cut, it was ruled, was due to an accidental headbutt, and if the fight had to be stopped it would go to the scorecards (which had to have favored Ruiz). Thunder was a man with a major liability. If he targeted the eye he could run the risk of losing the fight by way of technical decision.

As it would turn out, the cut would not play a factor in the fight. Ruiz continued to dominate while Thunder struggled to cope. Thunder lost another point in the ninth, making a knockout the only path to victory for him. But the knockout never came as Ruiz began to gain strength in the final three rounds while Thunder wilted. A solid combination buck-led Thunder in the opening minute of the eleventh round, and another right hand stunned him in the closing minute. There was little question in the eyes of ringsiders that Thunder needed to stop Ruiz to win, and his cornerman Eddie Mustafa Muhammad told him as much at the start of the final round. But any idea Thunder might have had about going out with guns blazing were quickly silenced when Ruiz landed a hard shot to the chin twenty seconds into the round. It was enough to keep Thunder honest for the rest of the round, and the rest of the fight.

However, although it appeared to be a lopsided decision in favor of Ruiz, fans were left in an uproar when it was announced that the decision was a split one. When the first judge's scorecard favored James Thunder by a score of 115–112 it looked as if Ruiz would be the victim of highway robbery. But the finally two scorecards favored John Ruiz (by scores of 115–112 and 116–111), giving him the well-earned victory as well as the NABF title.

For Ruiz there was little question of how important the win was for his career. John immediately jumped around the ring in a wild celebration, with tears nearly welling in his eyes. It was enough for USA commentator Al Albert to state that for John Ruiz "the nightmare of David Tua is over," unfortunately a premature assessment.

Although he immediately began to be touted as a heavyweight contender and proceeded to win his next six fights all by knockout, few boxing fans regarded him as a legitimate contender thanks to David Tua. Even after he lost a controversial split decision to Evander Holyfield for the vacant WBA heavyweight title in 2000, it was attributed more to how far Holyfield had slipped than how good Ruiz might have been. But by 2002 the perception was slowly changing. After winning a decision over Holyfield the following year, Ruiz racked up two successful defenses against quality opponents in Holyfield (by way of a twelve-round draw) and Kirk Johnson (by way of a disqualification victory). Although questions still lingered about the David Tua fight, Ruiz was emerging as not only a quality heavyweight, but also as a decent heavyweight champion. It did not take a victory to finally erase the stigma of the Tua loss: it took a defeat. In 2003 Ruiz made the highest profile defense of his WBA title against undisputed light-heavyweight champion Roy Jones. Although everyone agreed that Jones was by far the better fighter, many openly wondered if he would be able to overcome the size disadvantage. He did, battering Ruiz for the better part of twelve rounds and capturing a unanimous decision (as well as Ruiz's heavyweight championship). Suddenly nobody talked about how Ruiz was blown out in nineteen seconds by Tua anymore, all anyone was talking about was how he was completely dominated by a fighter who won his first world title at 160 pounds. Although he would bounce back with a decision over Hasim Rahman, he would still never recover from the stigma of his loss to Roy Jones.

For James Thunder it initially appeared as if he would quickly rebound from the loss just as he had done after the loss to Wanyama. He bounced back from the Ruiz fight with one of the most explosive fights ever seen on network TV, knocking out Crawford Grimsley in thirteen seconds (and, yes, that included the count). Considering how Grimsley was coming off a decision loss to George Foreman (a fight in which he was never dropped), it was a very impressive testament to the power of James Thunder. He followed the Grimsley win with the toughest loss of his career, a seventh-round upset loss to another blown-up fighter in Maurice Harris. The knockout proved to be as explosive as the one he racked up against Grimsley and, unfortunately for Thunder, just as devastating. He would follow the loss to Harris with a lopsided TKO loss to the light-punching Chris Byrd before pulling out his next big win against Tim Witherspoon. The win over Witherspoon proved to be his last significant victory as Thunder slid into journeyman status. By 2002 James Thunder was nowhere near the top ten, and it even became hard for boxing fans to envision the time when he was the prohibitive favorite against the reigning WBA champion, just five years prior.

January 29, 1997—New York City, New York
Richie Melito (16–0, 15 KOs) vs. Bert Cooper (33–17, 28 KOs)
Favorite: Melito
Result: Cooper won by way of first-round TKO.

Perhaps it was because Richie Melito looked just a little too marketable that boxing insiders were so skeptical, but in 1997 few were willing to "bet money" on the young, undefeated slugger from Flushing, New York. He just looked too media friendly, and boxing writers were becoming increasingly skeptical of white, marketable, heavyweights. (Initially it started out with Gerry Cooney in the early '80s, and Tommy Morrison in the early '90s.) Although those two fighters greatly benefited from their pigmentation, both were legitimately good heavyweights. They were given considerable more attention than most up-and-coming prospects and received much larger paydays than they probably warranted with their ring accomplishments. The mold was set, and by the mid-1990s, with the $800,000 payday given to Peter McNeeley for his destruction at the hands of Mike Tyson, it became all too common for club fighters with creative managers to try to package their product as the next great white hope (without ever explicitly saying so). White heavyweights with horrendously padded records were emerging all over the country, few with even a fraction of the skills of a Tommy Morrison or Gerry Cooney, and initially it seemed like Richie Melito was the New York City version of Peter McNeeley. Although he looked great against the "no-hopers" on which he had been feasting, it was widely assumed that he would fold as soon as he stepped up in competition, even a little bit. But in an unusual match-up of undefeated white heavyweights, Melito began to win some converts when, in 1996, he won the New York state heavyweight title over John Carlo. Although neither fighter was highly regarded going into the fight, the devastating fashion of Melito's second-round knockout attracted the attention of some boxing fans outside of the New York area. That, along with a first-round knockout over the usually more durable Nathaniel Fitch, convinced many boxing writers that, although the book was still out on exactly how good a fighter he might actually be, he was at least a better fighter than Peter McNeeley.

For some fans it looked like boxing was about to be introduced to a decent white heavyweight in Melito, a fighter who had never lost a fight in the ring in the professional ranks or the amateur ranks. The former baseball player was strong and handsome, and he was a college graduate (with a bachelor's degree from St. John's College), making him even more marketable. The "coming out" for Melito was going to be a nationally televised fight for the WBF heavyweight title against the rugged veteran "Smokin'" Bert Cooper. Despite the fact that Cooper was regarded as a very dangerous heavyweight, there was little to indicate that he would have what it took to pull off the upset. He was coming off six losses in his last eight fights (and two straight losses to punctuate a comeback after two years away from the ring). Although he had a reputation of a fighter who went through hot and cold streaks, it appeared that he was not in the middle of a slump, but a freefall. Melito was still not regarded as highly as Chris Byrd or even Samson Po'uha (the two fighters who beat Cooper earlier in the year), but he was still expected to extend Bert's losing streak.

Initially it appeared as if the twenty-seven-year-old Melito was in perfect condition to shine. He weighed in at a ready 221 pounds, and his training regimen (which included running 108 stories to the top of the World Trade Center three times a week) was impressive. Although Cooper appeared in decent shape, there seemed to be little improvement in conditioning from his previous fights (he weighed in at 233 pounds, two pounds more than what he weighed in against Po'uha). But mentally, it became abundantly clear that Melito was ill-prepared to fight the hard-punching former contender. Entering the ring, he had a worried look of anxiety, and when he refused to look at Bert Cooper at all during the referee's instructions, many began to wonder if Melito was actually scared of his older opponent.

Cooper, perhaps recognizing that Melito was in awe of the moment, jumped on him. Less than a minute into the round Cooper tagged the tentative Melito with a right hand that had Melito holding on. Although Melito fought back, a short right cross at 1:13 of the first round buckled his knees and nearly dropped him. Although he remained upright, he had to face a frightening onslaught from Cooper, who recognized a wounded opponent when he saw one. A crushing body attack robbed Melito of his wind and dropped him to the canvas (in a position that resembled an Islamic prayer). Melito rose on unsteady legs at seven, but with the damage done by both the hook to the chin and the body shots, it was clear that he was in big trouble. After resuming the fight, Melito tried to run for dear life. Cooper troubled Melito with the right hand, and the introduction of his renowned Joe Frazier–style left hook finally ended the night for Richie Melito: Cooper fired the shot from short range and found Melito's chin with ease. Melito dropped to the canvas, and although referee Wayne Kelly began to count, he quickly waved the fight off at five.

For Bert Cooper, the win gave him the WBF title, but more importantly, it gave him a final, devastating win on network TV for the fans to remember him by for, even with the belt and the win, he was unable to resurrect his career. He proceeded to lose his next fight to another New Yorker, Anthony "T-Bone" Green, by eight-round decision, and never again fought on network TV. For a fighter who possessed some of the most brutal knockouts of the decade, it was one final reminder of the potency of his vaunted left hook.

Initially it appeared as if Melito had been exposed, and the few boxing writers who had tentatively jumped on his bandwagon quickly jumped back off. After the loss to Bert Cooper it looked like his future was in Denmark as a Brian Nielsen opponent. Despite the fact that the loss was nothing short of devastating, Melito did not lose the dedication and determination that carried him through against the second tier heavyweights. The following year he rebounded with an impressive knockout over Melton Bowen, and by the decade's end had won six straight (all by knockout). Although he had yet to regain the respect of the boxing insiders, he had avoided the dangerous trap that many young prospects encounter after their first loss: he avoided cashing in on becoming an opponent. By 2000 it looked like he was on a solid comeback, that he had recovered about as well from the loss to Bert Cooper as was possible. When it was revealed that one of his opponents, Thomas Williams, allegedly took a "dive" against him later that year, Melito found himself in a world of trouble. Faced with potential legal actions (Williams in fact was indicted), Melito's career was suddenly tarnished even more than it had been after the Cooper loss. The allegations destroyed the small degree of credibility that he had garnered as a pro, and by the end of the year most boxing fans had little faith in the future of Richie Melito as a force in the heavyweight division.

April 3, 1997—Worley, Idaho
Terrence Lewis (20–1, 16 KOs) vs. Levi Billups
  (19–12–1, 11 KOs)
Favorite: Lewis
Result: Billups scored a sixth-round knockout.

By mid-1997 thirty-six-year-old journeyman Levi Billups looked like a fighter reborn. Although he never was regarded as a world-class heavyweight, most boxing insiders considered him to be about as good as you could get when looking for an opponent for much of the 1990s. He was tough, had a decent punch, and generally would give a respectable performance. Against Lennox Lewis and Buster Mathis Jr., he was able to last the distance, and against Nathaniel Fitch and former champion James "Bonecrusher" Smith, he was able to pull out the win. But by 1995, his reputation for resilience was quickly fading. It all started when undefeated South African Corrie Sanders knocked him out in the opening round. He followed that loss with a meek performance against contender Jeremy Williams, who knocked him out in the second round. At that point, it seemed safe to consider Billups a spent commodity and appeared that he was back on the journeyman road to oblivion (losing to prospects earlier in their career with each successive fight). After losing to Obed Sullivan and Clifton Mitchell, most observers assumed that Billups would disappear completely from the picture within a year or two. But then came his solid performance against undefeated Chris Byrd on *USA Tuesday Night Fights*, in which he broke the nose of the slick-boxing Byrd. The win seemed to temporarily halt the slide, and when Billups found himself on the questionable end of a ten-round draw with journeyman Everton Davis (who was younger and regarded as tougher journeyman than Billups) many in the sport realized that Billups had at least a few televised fights left in his tank.

It was that brief, two-fight resurrection that led to his selection on *Cedric Kushner's Heavyweight Explosion* as opponent for the rapidly rising puncher Terrence "K.O." Lewis. Lewis was already generating a great deal of excitement in the sport with his stunning knockouts. Although he lost a four-round decision to Levon Warner in his third pro fight, his career had been moving along quite nicely in the two years leading to his fight with Billups. Although he had yet to face any top-ranked opponents, his destruction of the normally durable William Morris (by way of second-round TKO) seemed to indicate that he would be able to compete with the top heavyweights in the power department. A fight with Billups would be the first major step on his rise to the top ten.

However, by the day of the fight it was abundantly clear that Lewis was ill-prepared for his first step up in class. Most observers agreed with commentator Bob Spagnola, who proclaimed Billups "the best ten-round fighter he's [Lewis] ever faced," but those professional assessments of Billups apparently had little impact on Lewis in the gym, as he weighed in a whopping 238 (Lewis's best weight was in the mid 220s). With the exception of his second pro fight, it was the most that Lewis had ever weighed. Billups, on the other hand, trained with a renewed dedication, shedding almost thirteen pounds from his fight with Dino Homsey the previous year (when he weighed in at a soft 240). For most ringsiders, it was clear that Billups was in the right shape (at least physically) to fight, and by fight time Lewis appeared nervous as the whispers of Lewis's conditioning floated around press row. That question of Lewis's weight was even mentioned by commentator Arnie "Tokyo" Rosenthal, who shortly before the start of the fight commented that "you have to question right off the bat, what is Lewis thinking about coming in as heavy as he is in what's probably the toughest fight of his career to date?"

By the start of the fight, many were wondering if Lewis would come out slugging, in an attempt to whack out Billups before his conditioning came into play. After all, Billups's past showed that a good puncher could take him out early, and many openly wondered if Lewis had the most power of any up-and-coming heavyweight. However, Lewis started the fight with the jab, apparently attempting to win the fight from the outside. Although a straight right hand pushed Billups back into the ropes at 1:20 of the first and a left hook caught Billups on the chin forty seconds later, Lewis's offense seemed curiously lacking power shots. Still, it seemed enough to win the round, until Billups bulldogged Lewis to the ropes at the end and tagged him with a solid right hand.

By the start of the second round Billups embraced the strategy that would carry him to victory. He began to pump right hands one after another. At the start a wide overhand right tagged Lewis, shaking up the twenty-four-year-old prospect. It became apparent that the conditioning of Lewis was indeed a serious liability, as he failed to generate hardly any offense for the next two minutes (and in fact spent a good amount of the round on the ropes). Although Lewis tried to steal the round at the end, it was ineffective against the determined Billups. Although implored to give Billups "angles" by his cornermen, Lewis entered the third almost identically to how he fought most of the second. He threw only one shot at a time (when he actually threw punches at all), hoping to land a "Hail Mary," prompting Arnie Rosenthal to comment, "Terrence Lewis just doesn't seem busy." When a pair of right hands seemed to shake up Lewis with thirty seconds left in the round it became apparent that Lewis was on a path to losing if he didn't turn things around quickly, and his mouth wide open indicated that he lacked the endurance to do so. He rallied in the last twenty seconds of the round, flaunting a sharp jab and beautiful footwork, enough to befuddle Billups for a short amount of time. Although Lewis showed that he could outbox Billups under ideal conditions, it was also clear that he was fatigued. Lewis returned to his "lethargic" style of fighting the following round, and when two Levi Billups jabs followed by a right hand pushed Lewis into the ropes early in the round, it was clear that Terrence Lewis's legs were rapidly weakening. Another wide overhand right tagged Lewis in the last minute, and many in attendance wondered if Lewis would be able to hold up against that sort of offense for six more rounds. About a minute and a half into the fifth round that question was answered in the negative when Billups staggered Lewis (whose back was to the ropes) with a (what else?) right hand. Billups exploded on his wounded opponent, throwing a collection of clubbing right hands that had Lewis slumped into the second rope. Although Idaho lacked a standing eight count, referee Jerry Armstrong correctly ruled that the ropes in fact were what kept Lewis from hitting the canvas, and issued a count. After the fight resumed, Lewis tried desperately to keep away from Billups and clear his head. Although Billups did indeed slow down later in the round, Lewis was unable to completely recover. As the round ended, Lewis's corner tried in vain to pump some life back into their damaged fighter, but Lewis came out for the sixth on unsteady legs. Billups appeared aware that Lewis was only one punch away from getting knocked out and stalked his opponent hoping to land the perfect shot. When a picture perfect overhand right landed on Lewis's chin and dropped him for a second time, it ended what was quite possibly the worst professional night of Terrence Lewis's career. He failed to beat the referee's count and was officially knocked out at 2:41 of the sixth.

With the win, it seemed that the Billups revival was complete. It was his biggest win since his upset over James "Bonecrusher" Smith six years prior. But the resurgence was short lived. In fact, it lasted only five days. Called upon to fill in as an opponent at the last minute, Levi traveled to Mississippi to take on another heavyweight prospect, Obed Sullivan, to whom he had already lost. Many boxing writers were aghast that Billups be allowed to take on such a tough fight five days after fighting another heavyweight prospect, and some wondered how the fight could have been allowed to take place at all. In the end though Billups lost his bid for the IBF Intercontinental belt when Sullivan stopped him in the twelfth and final round. Two months after that, Billups fought Terrence Lewis in a rematch. But this time Lewis used the boxing skills that he flaunted so briefly in the third round of their first fight to win a ten-round decision.

However, that win was quickly forgotten in his next fight when Lewis proceeded to lose to the fleshy James Gaines (whose physique hid his true boxing ability) by way of sixth-round knockout. It appeared that Gaines completely discredited Lewis as a heavyweight prospect until he was able to score an upset of his own against Darroll Wilson on *USA Tuesday Night Fights*. Although the revival was short-lived—he was disqualified in a fight against Mike Rush five months after the Wilson victory—his power ensured that he would still be a familiar face in the division for years to come.

June 3, 1997—Philadelphia, Pennsylvania
Courage Tshabalala (20–1, 17 KOs) vs. Darroll Wilson
   (18–1–2, 12 KOs)
Favorite: Tshabalala
Result: Wilson won via fourth-round KO.

By mid-1997, it appeared as if Darroll Wilson had gone full circle. Going into his fight with Shannon Briggs in 1996, Wilson saw himself a prohibitive underdog against a fighter widely regarded as the best heavyweight prospect in the sport despite the fact that he, like Briggs, was also undefeated. That lack of respect was all the more questionable considering the fact that his opposition was slightly better than his heavily favored opponent. For Wilson, he had something to prove that night, and when he scored the upset knockout over Briggs (see page 208) it seemed that he finally earned the respect as not only a top prospect in the division, but more importantly as a legitimate contender. But the brief flirtation with legitimacy was short-lived. In his first fight after his win over Briggs, Wilson looked very ordinary in out-pointing journeyman Rick Sullivan (who brought in a less than impressive record of 6–11 with 4 KOs). When he was knocked out in the opening round in his next fight by another undefeated prospect (David Tua), it appeared as if Wilson was done as a top-rated heavyweight. The immediate assumption was that Wilson was never that good, and Briggs was just that bad.

For Courage Tshabalala, there was a determination to get his career back on track after his upset loss to Brian Scott. Although many boxing writers jumped off the Tshabalala bandwagon after the loss, he was still considered a better fighter than Wilson. After all, Tshabalala was at one time one of the most feared prospects in the division. Even though his record was nearly identical to Wilson's, and his opposition was nowhere near as good, he was expected to win based on the merit of his punching power alone. Yes, for Darroll Wilson, things had come full circle for him.

Despite the fact that many boxing insiders ignored Tshabalala's glaring deficiencies in the ring and overplayed Wilson's drawbacks—neither fighter had a great chin, but Wilson's knockout loss to Tua was considerably more acceptable than Tshabalala's loss to the lightly regarded Brian Scott— Wilson realized that this was very much a winnable fight. More than that, it was a "must win" fight for him. If he were to lose, it would bring to an end his dreams of becoming a champion and almost surely end any legitimacy to his bid to become a contender again. Wilson entered the ring as a man who knew that he simply could not afford to lose.

Regardless of his determination, Wilson quickly discovered that the left jab of Courage Tshabalala was a major obstacle in his quest for redemption. Less than thirty seconds into the fight Wilson was felled by a Tshabalala jab, and though he quickly got up (and appeared clear headed) the power of Tshabalala was indeed going to be a major problem for Wilson. Hoping to test his opponent's chin with an actual power punch, Tshabalala exploded on Wilson immediately after referee Rudy Battle waved him in. However, Wilson fought defensively (although several jabs did push him back into the ropes). Wilson was able to avoid getting tagged with any serious shots for most of the round, however, as soon as he tried to establish his own offense towards the round's end he found himself the recipient of a solid Tshabalala left hook at the bell that seemed to rattle him.

Going into the second, Wilson tried to establish his jab to take Tshabalala out of his game. But it proved ineffective as Courage tagged Darroll with a solid right cross nearly halfway through the round that had the fans in attendance on their feet. By the round's end, Courage had

Wilson hurt on the ropes, and many wondered if Wilson would survive another round of punishment. When Courage picked up where he left off at the start of the third (backing up Wilson with solid power shots to the head and stunning Wilson with a left hook less than a minute in the round) it appeared as if Courage would score his eighteenth knockout inside of three rounds. A picture-perfect right hand with less than five seconds left in the round seemingly did the trick. Wilson dropped to the canvas, and though he tried to rise at the referee's count of five, he was clearly too hurt to continue, and he fell flat on his back. At referee Rudy Battle's count of seven Wilson was still down, and it appeared that Tshabalala would score the knockout. But inexplicably Rudy Battle stopped counting at "eight" and allowed Wilson to rise to his feet despite clearly being given the benefit of a long (and unusually slow) count. Realizing that the round was over, Battle then proceeded to tell the timekeeper to ring the bell rather than to see if Wilson was fit to continue (despite the fact that Pennsylvania did not allow a fighter to be saved by the bell at the end of a round). A clearly groggy Wilson stumbled back to his corner, with a full minute to recover. Courage Tshabalala's trainer Lou Duva became infuriated, rushing the center of the ring to confront Battle, but realizing that the fight was still on, he quickly regained his composure and attended to his fighter.

Although Tshabalala was clearly tired and never scored a knockout past the third round, it was hard to imagine Wilson being able to recover from such a damaging knockdown. Most fans expected to see Tshabalala quickly end the show with a dominant knockout in the fourth. Early on, it appeared as if he would. Tshabalala exploded on a glassy-eyed Darroll Wilson, who was still out on his feet. But in one of the most memorable comebacks in the heavyweight division in recent memory, Wilson began to up his punch output as Tshabalala slowed down. Within a minute the fight was an out and out Philly slugfest, and when Darroll landed a right hand that had Tshabalala holding on seconds later, it was clear that Courage was quickly losing the momentum in the fight. Although Tshabalala was clearly fatigued (and somewhat stunned by the Wilson right), it seemed as if he survived Wilson's brief comeback when Wilson also slowed down. With less than thirty seconds left in the round, Tshabalala tried to regain control of the fight with a brief flurry, and though his heart was in the right place, his conditioning was not. With his back to the ropes, Wilson then proceeded to "rope-a-dope" Courage, tagging him repeatedly with shots. When a short right hand stunned Tshabalala it became apparent that Courage was in serious trouble, something that proved correct when another right (followed by a short left hook) dropped Tshabalala to his hands and knees. Although Courage didn't appear seriously hurt, it was clear that the gas tank was empty for the South African. Apparently not wanting to slug it out further with Wilson (or perhaps assuming that Battle would give him a long count as well) Tshabalala rose at the count of $10\frac{1}{2}$, and dropped out of the heavyweight picture completely.

With the victory over Tshabalala, Wilson saw his career as a heavyweight contender back on track. For some fans he was considered a sort of Matthew Saad Muhammad, a fighter who could come back from the brink of defeat and still win. But once again, his career went in full circle. The resurrection was short-lived as he lost eight months later in an upset to Terrance Lewis.

For Tshabalala, it effectively marked the end of his career as a heavyweight prospect. Although he continued his career, winning several fights after the Wilson loss, he never regained the respect he garnered early in his career. When he was stopped by Russian heavyweight prospect Oleg Maskaev the following year, it effectively marked the end to Tshabalala's career.

June 7, 1997—Sacramento, California
David Tua (27–0, 23 KOs) vs. Ike Ibeabuchi (16–0, 12 KOs)
Favorite: Tua
Result: Ibeabuchi won a twelve-round unanimous decision.

For boxing fans, there was little question as to which fighter was the hottest prospect in the heavyweight division in 1997. With explosive power in both fists, David Tua had established himself as the most talked about heavyweight prospect since Riddick Bowe. Although there were many other undefeated, talented heavyweights, none could excite fans like Tua. It started with Tua's first ever fight on HBO on March 15, 1996, a nineteen-second knockout over John Ruiz. The speed and brutality of the knockout, along with Shannon Briggs's upset loss to Darroll Wilson, jumpstarted Tua to the front of the pack of heavyweight prospects. Tua cemented his position with another brutal first-round KO, this time over Briggs's conqueror Darroll Wilson, a win that had boxing fans talking world title by the end of 1997. Although some critics began to emerge when Tua struggled with the likes of David Izonritei and Oleg Maskaev (scoring late-round knockouts in close fights in his next two fights), most boxing insiders felt that it was a testament to Tua's power, and a shining example of his ability to remain dangerous throughout a fight. Besides, Tua's opposition was clearly a level above that of any other heavyweight with the arguable exception of Chris Byrd, and Tua had a big advantage over Byrd in regards to public appeal.

With such public appeal as well as the strong support of HBO, Tua decided to remain active with another defense of his rather meaningless WBC International Heavyweight Championship, this time against little known Ike Ibeabuchi. It seemed a typical Tua fight, against a fellow prospect with just as much grit and determination as he had, but not nearly as much power. In fact, for many fans Ibeabuchi appeared a small step down for Tua. Although undefeated, his record was littered with unknown fighters and limited journeymen, and in the eyes of many boxing insiders, he was only the second best Nigerian heavyweight in the world (David Izonritei being the best). Even HBO commentator Larry Merchant admitted during the telecast that he had "never heard of him [Ibeabuchi] until this fight was made." Besides, he was a product of *Cedric Kushner's Heavyweight Explosion*, which produced some interesting fights but had yet to produce a championship-caliber heavyweight contender.

As it would turn out, being unknown was Ibeabuchi's only drawback, and he would soon remedy that situation with one of the most exciting performances in heavyweight history. For Ike Ibeabuchi would redefine what activity in the ring would be for a heavyweight. From the moment the bell rang to start the fight, Ibeabuchi was punching. Working behind a quick, hard jab, Ibeabuchi outhussled David Tua early on, landing combinations upstairs that had the hard punching Samoan unable to keep up. The normally fast starting Tua was relegated to slowly stalking his opponent, waiting for the moment that he would stop punching so that he could launch his own offense. Although Ibeabuchi was starting strong, many assumed that once he tasted the power of David Tua he would become a little more safety conscious and more conservative with his punch output. But after Ibeabuchi walked through a Tua overhand right just inside of a minute into the opening round, it became clear that Ike had the chin to match up to Tua's power. The domination continued for Ike, prompting HBO commentator Jim Lampley to say "it's Tua who looks a little bit overwhelmed." Although Tua came on strong in the final twenty seconds of the round, it was not enough to compensate for the amazing ninety-one punches thrown by Ike.

But Ike had yet to win over the critics. For many ringsiders and viewers, it appeared as if Ibeabuchi would simply be unable to maintain that kind of activity for long. Although he came on equally strong in the second round (throwing another ninety-one punches) most assumed he would slow down in the third. But after briefly backing up David Tua in the first forty seconds of the round, Ibeabuchi incorporated an effective uppercut to his arsenal and actually increased his punch output to ninety-five punches.

However, the pressure of David Tua finally began to take its toll in the fourth round, when Ibeabuchi began to slow down just a bit. Although both fighters began to incorporate the body attack in the fourth, it appeared as if Ibeabuchi was the more winded fighter at the bell. Ike worked behind his jab early in the fifth round before abandoning it and letting David Tua get inside and initiate a phone booth war for much of the round. In the final thirty seconds of the round, however, both fighters tried to steel what was a razor-thin round with a brawl in the center of the ring. When David Tua briefly buckled Ibeabuchi over at the bell with a hook to the body it looked as if the tide was in fact, finally turning.

The jab of Ibeabuchi appeared to have lost its zip early in the sixth round, and the thudding blows of David Tua began to finally start moving Ike back as the round progressed. In fact, Ike spent much of the round on his bicycle, leading to a solid round for David Tua. Although Ike tried to regain the momentum early in the seventh, the pressure of David Tua still moved the Nigerian back. Tua also began to land more right hands, something that signaled the end of both David Izonritei and Oleg Maskaev after their fast starts, and many ringsiders were anticipating a similar turn for Ibeabuchi. Ibeabuchi allowed the fight to return to the phone booth in the eighth round, and even tried to slug it out with the hard punching Samoan early, something that few felt was in his best interest. But those fans underestimated the chin and resolve of Ibeabuchi as he held his own against Tua. When the pace began to slow in the final minute, Ibeabuchi stepped up the pressure, landing a left hook that surprised Tua and stole the round for him.

It looked as if Ibeabuchi was getting his second wind early in the ninth as his jab began to find some of its missing snap. But Tua was unwilling to hand the fight to Ike just yet, and after landing a crushing uppercut at 1:40 of the round, a shot that briefly stunned the Nigerian, Tua had Ike fighting a bit more cautiously again. Tua attacked the body in the final minute and came on strong himself in the closing ten seconds of the round, conscious of how he allowed a close round slip away just three minutes earlier.

Although Ike was able to keep the tenth round close, it was the eleventh that appeared to seal his fate. After coming out strong in the first two minutes, Ike was stunned with a hard combination upstairs that hurt him and had him holding on for dear life for the first time in the fight. Tua, a fighter whose skills at finishing a wounded foe were legendary, jumped all over Ike and at the bell had his opponent hurt and just a punch or two from hitting the deck. For fans, it appeared as if Tua would duplicate his final-round knockout over Izonritei. But Ike Ibeabuchi was a fighter with skills of his own, and his skills of recovery came through in the twelfth round. Ike came out slugging, clearly unafraid of David Tua's power and more than held his own. As Tua marched in Ibeabuchi threw a hard uppercut that snapped his head back, and actually fought his best round since the fourth. As the bell ended the slugfest both fighters continued to wail away at each other, and in the process set an all-time record for punches thrown in a heavyweight fight with an astounding 1,730!

Although Ibeabuchi fought admirably, throwing a stunning 975 punches, it seemed to most ringsiders that Tua was still the winner. They felt that Ike won the first three and the final rounds clearly while Tua won most of the other rounds. But in a somewhat surprising decision Ibeabuchi captured the unanimous decision by scores of 117–111, 116–113, and a more realistic 115–114. For the winner, it was a rewarding victory. Suddenly he was the most talked about heavyweight thanks to his chin, his grit, and his endurance. Immediately talk began to cen-

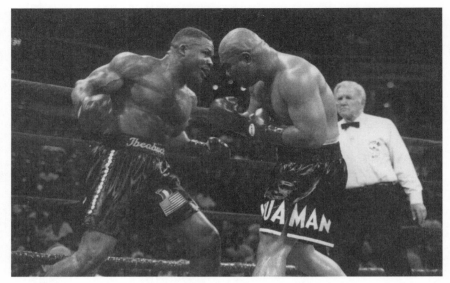

Ike Ibeabuchi (left) set a frenetic early pace in his win versus David Tua, and the two set a heavyweight record with 1,730 punches thrown. *Tom Hogan*

ter on another fight with an undefeated heavyweight in Kirk Johnson, a fight that would most likely propel the winner into a title fight. But trouble began to emerge outside the ring for Ibeabuchi. Two months after his career defining win, Ibeabuchi was arrested and charged with kidnapping and attempted murder. After his girlfriend left him Ibeabuchi allegedly grabbed her young son, took off with the child in a speeding car, and rammed into a freeway overpass at sixty-five miles per hour. After being diagnosed with a possible chemical disorder, it appeared as if the promising career of Ibeabuchi was over before it even got off the ground. But Ike did have friends in high places and was able to return to the ring nearly a year after patching up his legal problems. Still, the book was out on Ibeabuchi and his reported instability. After signing to fight Chris Byrd, Ike again added fire to that claim when he attacked a sparring partner, Ezra Sellers, after being cut during sparring (an incident that reportedly led Sellers to file, and later drop, a criminal complaint on Ibeabuchi). But when Ibeabuchi shocked Chris Byrd with a stunning fifth-round knockout in March 1999, he again found himself back on top of the boxing world. With a number-two rank-ing with the IBF, it looked as if Ibeabuchi was going to get his title fight by the end of the year.

But in July trouble again arose outside the ring. While staying at the Mirage hotel-casino in Las Vegas, Ibeabuchi called a Las Vegas stripper to his hotel room. At that point he allegedly detained the woman against her will and then sexually assaulted her. When the police arrived at 5:30 in the morning after a hotel guest reported a commotion coming from the room they found Ibeabuchi barricaded inside the bathroom, unwill-ing to allow the police to arrest him. Police on the scene had to use pep-per spray under the bathroom door to get Ibeabuchi to come out. For boxing fans, it was another bizarre and frightening step taken by a fighter with so much talent. With such serious charges like kidnapping and sexual assault facing him, Ibeabuchi was faced with the very real possibility that he would spend the rest of his life in prison. Although Bob Arum tried to help Ibeabuchi legally, hiring Richard Wright to rep-resent him, Arum soon changed his mind after Ibeabuchi continued his erratic behavior during the trial. At one point Ibeabuchi was removed from the courtroom after an outburst, and he was later medicated with mood-stabilizers and anti-psychotic drugs against his will by the judge. By October 2001 Ibeabuchi was represented by a public defender, Bob Arum unwilling to invest any legal fees into what was looking like a lost cause. Arum wasn't the only one to have given up on Ibeabuchi; most boxing fans admitted that the prospects of him ever stepping into the ring again were slim at best.

For David Tua however, the loss to Ibeabuchi proved to be nothing more than a brief bump in the road on his way up he heavyweight lad-der. The nature of the loss made it considerably more excusable to box-ing fans, and many were eager to see David Tua in the ring again. Initially Tua took on the lightly regarded southpaw Jeff Wooden in March 1998. Although he struggled against Wooden, winning a close de-cision, he was able to erase much of the stigma of that performance with three straight knockout wins to follow it. But Tua's return to the big leagues came in December 1998 when he met with undefeated Hasim Rahman. Against Rahman, Tua proceeded to get outboxed for the better part of nine rounds before rallying to stop Rahman in the tenth round in controversial fashion. (Rahman was hurt after getting hit after the bell in the ninth round, which led to the unusually quick stoppage the following round.) It was a win that put David Tua back on the map, and after stopping his next four opponents in impressive fashion, Tua finally landed his title shot against Lennox Lewis in November 2000. Although Tua went on to lose a lopsided decision to Lewis and followed the meek loss to Lewis with another decision loss to Chris Byrd in 2001, he rebounded the following year with stunning knockouts over Fres Oquendo and Michael Moorer. He did stumble in a rematch with Hasim Rahman, but it still looked like a world title was in his near future when Roy Jones appeared ready to vacate the WBA heavyweight title in late 2003. But managerial problems sidelined him, and an old nemesis, John Ruiz, ended up with the opportunity, defeating Hasim Rahman over twelve rounds for the interim WBA heavyweight championship.

September 15, 1997—Edmonton, Alberta, Canada
Trevor Berbick (45–9–1, 32 KOs) vs. Lyle McDowell
    (19–5–1, 11 KOs)
Favorite: Berbick
Result: McDowell won a twelve-round split decision.

For the forty-three-year-old Berbick, the possibility of making a serious run at a world title was brought to a rather decisive end when undefeated Hasim Rahman won a lopsided decision over him the previous year. It seemed, in fact, that he had only two options. He could become a name opponent, getting pounded on by the young up-and-comers in the heavyweight division (like Rahman) or he could retire. Most boxing experts hoped that he would choose the latter, but few believed he would, for on the other side of the Atlantic a new force was giving life to the sagging careers of many a former heavyweight champion. Already James "Bonecrusher" Smith, Tony Tubbs, and even Larry Holmes saw a fairly impressive payday accompany a free trip to Europe. Although all three ended up on the losing end in their fights, they found themselves given considerably more respect as opponents than they were receiving from the American fight fans. Holmes, in fact, saw his fight (for the IBO title) given all the accolades and legitimacy from local fans that would accompany a legitimate title shot. The rejuvenating force was Denmark's Brian Nielsen, a chunky brawler with an undefeated record who was already the biggest sports celebrity in that tiny country. Nielsen was making a decent living knocking out former champs and contenders on his home turf and was in fact establishing himself as one of the better prospects in Europe by many American boxing writers (who did not share in the opinions of their Danish compatriots that Nielsen was already a world champion). As IBO champion Nielsen wanted to take advantage of the relative naivety of European fight fans in regards to the sanctioning bandits and their former champions, calling on any washed-up fighter who once held a world title belt. Suddenly Berbick was back in demand.

But unfortunately for Trevor, the IBO was attempting to act like a legitimate sanctioning organization and balked at allowing Nielsen to defend his title against a fighter who lost his last fight and had been inactive for nearly a full year. Berbick, however, was given a golden opportunity to eliminate that problem with an easy win, a minor title belt, and a follow up title shot. All he had to do was beat the lightly regarded Lyle McDowell. The IBO sanctioned Berbick-McDowell for the vacant IBO Intercontinental heavyweight championship, a belt that would put Berbick in the IBO rankings and make him more marketable to Danish fans. Although nobody felt Berbick was still a world-class fighter, the view was that the twenty-seven-year-old McDowell simply did not have the chin to handle the hard punching former champion. McDowell had already been knocked out by Lou Savarese and Jerry Ballard, and even was stopped by the feather-fisted Buster Mathis Jr. in a bid for the USBA title. (Mathis had only three knockouts in seventeen fights at that time.) If those setbacks weren't enough to ensure a Berbick victory McDowell had also been knocked out in the second round by club fighter Exum Speight (who brought in a terrible record of 8–31–2 going into that fight) earlier in the year. Although McDowell was a southpaw, it seemed that Berbick had found the perfect foil in him, a fighter with a flashy record and no chin. When the fight landed in Canada (Berbick's home country) it seemed to further stack the deck against McDowell.

By fight time however, it became apparent that Trevor made a mistake in undertraining for the fight. He weighed in at a fleshy 254 pounds (to McDowell's 230), underlining the fact that Berbick didn't think highly of McDowell as an opponent. It was likely a twenty-eight-year-old Berbick could have gotten away with it, but not one who was in his forties.

When the fight started, the notoriously slow-starting Berbick failed to mount any offense. He simply kept his hands up high and followed the quicker McDowell around the ring, allowing the "Iceman" to pepper him with right jabs. Hardly enthralling, it seemed to have a purpose in wearing down the younger man (who also looked a bit soft around the middle). In fact, commentator Ken Lakusta likened it to Ali's famous rope-a-dope, calling it a "robot rope-a-dope." By round's end, Berbick began showboating, putting both his hands on his head and letting McDowell unload to his body. Although it seemed that Berbick gave away the round, the question of Lyle's chin still lingered, and the assumption was that when Trevor hit his younger opponent, he would knock him out. Even after Lyle won the next two rounds against a lethargic Berbick, most assumed Berbick would win as soon as he chose to pick up the pace. When he slowly upped the pressure in the fourth, it appeared that the tide was changing, but soon conditioning played a role, as his offense quickly fizzled. After five rounds most ringsiders felt McDowell had swept them all, and many were now wondering if Berbick could pull the trigger.

But in the sixth round, both Berbick and McDowell were able to answer the lingering questions about each other. When McDowell began brawling with Berbick on the inside, a move that clearly played into the hands of the older man, he found himself the recipient of a Berbick left hook that dropped him into the ropes for what appeared to be a knock down at the halfway point of the round. Although the referee erroneously ruled the knockdown a slip, it seemed that McDowell was indeed in trouble. He was clearly rattled and had to survive nearly half the round against a forward-moving Berbick. But luck intervened in the form of a timekeeper's error when the round ended about twenty seconds later, with well over a minute remaining.

Berbick pressed his advantage over the next three rounds, and although they seemed tied, the assumption was that Berbick would be more likely to be given the benefit of the doubt than McDowell. But once again, poor conditioning combined with age did the former champion in. When McDowell found his second wind in the tenth round and proceeded to sweep the last three rounds (even having a badly fatigued Berbick staggered and holding on in the final round), there was no question about who won. The only question was whether the hometown fighter would be given a gift decision or not. Although judge David Nars gave Berbick the nod by a unrealistic score of 115–110, he was overruled by judges Billy Warwick Jr. and Gary Hart, who both voted for McDowell by sizeable margins, giving the career journeyman his biggest win and the IBO Intercontinental belt.

For McDowell, it initially appeared that he finally laid to rest the questions about his chin. He was tagged repeatedly by the hard-punching Berbick and withstood the blows. He even seemed to be a viable opponent for Nielsen when, five months later, he defended his title with a seventh-round knockout over former Olympic silver medallist and light heavyweight contender Egerton Marcus. It appeared to some that 1998 was going to be a breakthrough year for the "Iceman." Unfortunately for McDowell, his chin was still suspect. In what was supposed to be a time-killing fight for Lyle four months later, McDowell was upset by journeyman Linwood Jones (who knocked out McDowell in the fifth round). With a record of 10–25 with 6 KOs, Jones was considered a soft touch and the kind of fighter that a contender (even one for the IBO) should have easily beaten. It was the first setback in what quickly deteriorated into a disastrous year for the "Iceman." McDowell proceeded to lose to Zebielee Kimbrough (fighting in only his second pro fight) and Lovi Page before the year ended, ending his run at a title fight with Brian Nielsen and the talk that had been emerging about McDowell as an up-and-comer.

For Berbick, it appeared to be a devastating loss. Although he could be heard shortly after the decision was announced trying to line up a rematch with McDowell (who quietly let the older man blow his steam) it seemed clear that he was no longer a contender, even for a lightly regarded title like the IBO. There was one title which he was still highly qualified to fight for—the Canadian heavyweight title. He took on the popular Canadian champion Shane Sutcliffe in 1999, scored an upset of sorts over him, and became the Canadian heavyweight champion, a move that gave new life regionally to his dead end comeback.

November 17, 1997—Tunica, Mississippi
Gary Bell (15–0, 10 KOs) vs. Robert Hawkins (14–2, 4 KOs)
Favorite: Bell
Result: Hawkins won via tenth-round TKO.

For a little over a year, Gary Bell had been at the top of the list of top prospects in the heavyweight division. Although he had yet to produce a breakthrough performance like Michael Grant, David Tua, or even Chris Byrd had, he was given one of the biggest endorsements of the 1990s from a man whose opinion carried a good deal of sway with the boxing public. Shortly after knocking out "Iron" Mike Tyson for the heavyweight championship, Evander Holyfield admitted that he was having some doubts in training camp. It seemed that one of his sparring partners, Gary Bell, had been manhandling him in sparring, something that discouraged Holyfield as he prepared for Mike Tyson. In fact, Evander went so far as to say "Gary Bell, he was just whuppin' me up."

The next day that story became an insert in almost every sports page in the country, and suddenly casual boxing fans wanted to see the man who "whupped" the man who beat the man. It was free publicity that was worth a million dollars to the career of an undefeated fighter. For casual boxing fans and sports fans across the country, Gary Bell jumped to the front of the class of young heavyweights in the division. The natural assumption was if he could give Holyfield trouble, he must be pretty good.

But for the serious boxing fans, Bell still had a lot to prove. It had already been a widely accepted assumption by boxing insiders that sparring didn't necessarily reveal how good a fighter was or how he would do against top-ranked fighters. One prime example that had already become a legend of sorts was Carl "The Truth" Williams and Mike Tyson. Allegedly Williams destroyed Tyson in sparring early in their careers, but the result of a fight was quite different (with Tyson scoring a first-round TKO). Oliver McCall and even Greg Page also held their own against Tyson quite well in sparring—Page even knocked Tyson down—but few thought they would have stood much of a chance if Tyson actually fought either in a real match. Even lightly-regarded journeyman Garing Lane allegedly held his own against Lennox Lewis when he worked as Lewis's sparring partner. For boxing experts, Bell would need to prove his merit in front of the crowds.

Despite the more critical position held by most boxing insiders, the general assumption was that he had in fact passed his first test. Against Lou Monaco (a fighter coming off big wins over Peter McNeeley, Michael Dokes, and undefeated Kevin McBride), Bell scored a lopsided decision.

Although Monaco had lost his last major fight against James "Buster" Douglas, most felt he was robbed of the win (when Douglas refused to continue after getting dropped a split second after the bell to end the first). The Bell fight was his first fight since the Douglas debacle, and he carried all the accolades of his "knockout" over Douglas into the ring that night. It seemed Bell was ready to step it up another notch, and Robert Hawkins seemed the perfect opponent—after all, he had beaten him once before.

Robert Hawkins was a fighter who had rebounded from two back-to-back losses early in his career to win eleven straight. His competition seemed a bit more solid than Bell's, with a recent win over one time prospect Melvin Foster, and in fact he seemed to discover some power that had been missing early in his career in knocking out Foster. Hawkins, in fact, had scored three of his four professional knockouts in the four fights leading up to his matchup with Bell. On paper he seemed a dangerous opponent, perhaps too dangerous, but at the time Bell appeared not to be taking too big a chance in picking Robert. Since Bell had already beaten him (the last time Hawkins tasted defeat as a pro), the assumption was that he had Hawkins's "number." Also, with Hawkins weighing in at 240 pounds, a full ten to fifteen pounds over his admitted ideal weight, there was a question about conditioning.

But though Gary Bell might have seen Robert Hawkins as a safe opponent, Hawkins was obsessed with extracting revenge for his loss to Bell. The first Bell-Hawkins fight was filled with controversy, Robert Hawkins saw victory (or more accurately a draw) robbed from him when the referee erroneously called a slip and a low blow knockdown, and he was determined to rectify what he perceived as a great injustice done to him.

It took less than ten seconds for boxing fans to realize that this was not the same Robert Hawkins who fought Gary Bell three years prior. A Hawkins right cross dropped Bell, who appeared more embarrassed than hurt. The controversy from the first fight seemed to carry into the second, as referee Paul Sita ruled the knockdown a slip. It was a questionable call, and the assumption was it might go on to play a role in the scoring of the fight (after all, the first fight was close). But Hawkins would not be denied. He was determined to rob the judges of any doubt as to who was the aggressor, and who was more effective. He proceeded to bulldog his way into Bell with solid left hooks and overhand rights. Bell was unable, or unwilling, to attempt to control the fight from the outside, abandoning his jab and allowing his shorter opponent to march inside. Bell briefly rallied at the end of the second, but by the start of the third, it seemed Bell needed to turn things around to pull out the victory.

Although the third round began like the previous two, Bell did finally land an effective shot. Unfortunately, it was to the crotch. Hawkins dropped from the low blow, and referee Paul Sita made another questionable call in deducting a point from Bell. The low blow actually did little to deter Hawkins. In fact, it seemed actually to anger him. He swarmed all over Bell, and had him in trouble at round's end. Bell tried to use his body shots more effectively in the fourth, but Hawkins continued his forward moving pressure. When Hawkins landed a looping right hand to drop Gary Bell, it seemed clear that it was not to be Bell's night. Bell struggled to rise, and was the recipient of another boneheaded call by the referee, who ruled the knockdown a slip.

Although Bell was saved from further punishment by the bell (ending the round) he was clearly still groggy when he came out to start the fifth. By the sixth Hawkins had taken control from the outside as well, landing more jabs than his taller opponent, and when both fighters came out of their corners after the seventh, it seemed that Hawkins was pitching a shutout.

Less than twenty seconds into the eighth Bell landed another low blow that dropped Hawkins. Initially assuming that he knocked down his opponent, Bell raised his arms into the air. But they quickly came back down when he saw Hawkins grab his groin. Bell proceeded to turn to referee Paul Sita to argue that it was a legitimate shot that dropped Hawkins. Sita sent Bell to a neutral corner (from which Bell proceeded to walk over to his own corner to get some water) and allowed Hawkins several minutes to recover. Bell's trainer, Lou Duva, unimpressed, screamed at Sita, questioning why Hawkins was allowed time to recover. Sita took another point from Bell, who maintained his innocence. Duva felt that it was a legitimate body shot that dropped Hawkins and went so far as to tell commentator Sean O'Grady "he's pulling a Riddick Bowe out there!" (a reference to Bowe's alleged overacting in his response's to low blows from Andrew Golota in his win over the Duva-trained Pole). Although Bell fared somewhat better in the eighth, he sealed his fate when another low blow dropped Hawkins with less than twenty seconds left in the round. Sita, who at that point had dropped the ball more than a Detroit Lions quarterback, ruled it a knockdown.

After a slow ninth round that saw more clinching than fighting, it appeared as if the fight would indeed go to the scorecards (where Hawkins was most likely ahead). Bell, it seemed, needed a big tenth round if he were to win the fight; anything less than a knockout would have fallen short. However, it was Hawkins who came out on fire, throwing bombs and backing up Bell. Remembering the close decision in their first fight, Hawkins set out to eliminate any possibility of the judges giving it to Bell. A left hook a minute into the round seemed to stun Bell, and a straight right also snuck through Bell's defense a minute later. It proved to be the end for Bell, as Hawkins followed up the shot with a left hook that had Bell holding on. With Bell on the ropes, Robert walked in throwing bombs. Although Bell was covering up quite well, a right uppercut snapped his head back and set him up for the wide overhand right. When another overhand right behind it landed, it effectively sent Gary Bell to Queer Street. Recognizing how hurt Bell was, referee Paul Sita jumped in to administer a standing eight count (as soon as Hawkins was pulled off, Bell fell back into the ropes and would have hit the canvas had the ropes not held him up). After reaching eight, Sita decided that Bell was in no condition to continue and waved it off with thirty-five seconds remaining in the fight.

With the win, Robert Hawkins effectively washed away the stain of his loss to Bell that had followed his career for over three years. The win was his most impressive, and boxing experts regarded him as a legitimate contender. Although he struggled with Boris Powell four months later in his next fight, he still emerged victorious (winning a decision), and it seemed to many that Hawkins was on the verge of a big fight (perhaps even an HBO televised fight). Although many felt he would be the underdog against the top-ranked heavyweights, he already proved himself to be capable of pulling off the upset, if he were to win again on HBO a title fight could be his. But Hawkins never got his big money fight. The win over Powell was his last fight.

Gary Bell never recovered from the loss. In his first fight after the loss to Hawkins, Bell struggled with limited Ron McCarthy, winning a six-round decision. A loss later that year to journeyman Artis Pender-grass destroyed his comeback, and when Bell landed an HBO televised fight in 1999 against David Tua, he was so lightly regarded that the fight was seen as a total mismatch. It proved to be a correct assessment as Bell was stopped in the first round.

October 11, 1997—Erlanger, Kentucky
Michael Dokes (53–5–2, 34 KOs) vs. Paul "Rocky" Ray Phillips
    (19–3, 17 KOs)
Favorite: Dokes
Result: Phillips won by way of second-round knockout.

By 1997 boxing fans had yet to recover from the disgraceful perform-ance of Michael Dokes in his challenge of WBA-IBF heavyweight cham-pion Riddick Bowe over four years earlier. His poor conditioning along with his shameless demands for a rematch after the fight left many fans and writers in a near uproar. After all, here was a man who hardly quali-fied for a title shot at all. Most hoped that Dokes would simply "take the money and run." If nothing else, the payday he received against Bowe seemed sufficient enough to ensure that fans would not be forced to sit through another Dokes comeback. Initially it appeared that that was the case; Dokes disappeared from the scene immediately after the fight. But after a two-year layoff, the now grossly obese former WBA cham-pion was back in the ring to see if he could land at least one more pay-day. It wasn't bad enough seeing a nearly three-hundred-pound Michael Dokes; for fans it was also a sad reminder of how good he could have been.

Winning the title in controversial fashion against Mike Weaver in 1982 (he stopped Weaver in the first round in a fight that was widely regarded as the most premature stoppage ever in a championship fight), Dokes was initially groomed as a potential "legend." The comparisons to Ali and Joe Louis began to come in, and though fans still regarded Larry Holmes as the true champion, many were drooling over the poten-tial unification bout. But rumors began to surface of problems with drugs, and after struggling with Mike Weaver in a rematch (he was held to a fifteen-round draw) his self-destructive lifestyle began to over-whelm him. When he signed to fight Gerrie Coetzee in Cleveland (only twenty minutes from his hometown of Akron), he was unable to avoid the negative influences that began to destroy his life, and by fight time rumors of rampant cocaine use (even in the days leading up to the fight itself) were floating around the boxing world. A tenth-round knockout loss to Coetzee ended his title reign and seemed to end his career. After remaining inactive for much of the following three years (he had only three fights in the three years after the Coetzee fight) Dokes cleaned up his life and made a serious run for another title in 1988. His comeback initially failed to impress many people—Dokes struggled with the likes of K.P. Porter, Ken Lakusta, and Eddie Richardson—but in 1989 an impressive (albeit losing) performance against Evander Holyfield revitalized his career. Suddenly Dokes found himself regarded as one of the top heavyweights in the world, a position he held until a knockout loss to Donovan "Razor" Ruddock interrupted his career again in 1990.

It was hard to envision Dokes coming back from the knockout loss to Ruddock. "Razor" was highly regarded, and the knockout was so brutal that many wondered if Dokes could possibly recover from such a devastating defeat. But after a one-year hiatus Dokes returned in winning an ugly decision over John Morton for a measly $500 payday. Although the second comeback of Michael Dokes failed to impress anyone, he was still able to land the Bowe fight after winning nine in a row. Bowe confirmed what many already suspected: that drugs, age, and punishment had robbed Dokes of his once impressive skills in the ring. When he returned to the ring in 1995, he was unable to convince anyone that he should be taken seriously as a contender again (his weight didn't help the situation), and most boxing writers felt that he would lose, and lose badly, when he stepped up in competition.

It initially appeared as if he was going to undertake the same comeback that landed him the Bowe fight earlier in the decade: remain active until a giant payday fell in his lap. After winning three in a row against weak opposition Dokes stepped in the ring against his first "live" opponent: Louis Monaco. Monaco was hardly world class, but he had a pair of impressive wins over Peter McNeeley and Kevin McBride. Dokes was dropped in the opening round and battered for much of the fight in losing a ten-round decision, and it appeared as if the ill-advised comeback had come to an end. But a mere six months later Dokes was back, this time fighting Paul "Rocky" Ray Phillips in Kentucky.

Considering Phillips had a somewhat glossy record of 19–3 and Dokes had just lost to a fighter with a 5–6–2 record, on paper it seemed a fairly solid match. But most boxing insiders felt that Phillips was a step down from Monaco. Fighting primarily in the Kentucky and Ohio circuits, Phillips seemed to be one of the countless midwestern fighters with limited skills and a padded record. In his only fights against quality opposition Phillips found himself on the losing end, getting stopped by Trevor Berbick and losing in three to Shane Sutcliffe. But "Rocky" was a deceptively solid puncher and obsessively motivated with beating Dokes for a most unlikely reason. As it turned out, Phillips was involved in a legal entanglement (he worked as a bodyguard for a man who was later arrested as a drug dealer) that threatened to not only to end his career, but also rob him of his freedom. Facing prison time, Phillips was determined to prove to the sentencing judge that he had put his mistakes behind him and that he was a legitimate heavyweight boxer who dedicated himself to the sport. If he could prove that he was a world-class heavyweight (and not just some hired thug) he felt that he could ensure a more lenient sentence, and a win over Dokes was just the thing to put him in that position. Phillips trained with a newly found vigor, and by the fight time, there was little question which fighter was in better condition. Whereas Phillips weighed in at a solid 218 pounds, the thirty-nine-year-old Dokes weighed in at an obscene 280 pounds.

Still, a Dokes win seemed a surefire bet, as Phillips had yet to show the durability against world-class opposition in the past to suggest that he could hang with Dokes. As soon as the bell rang, it was clear that Phillips was no pushover. Using a stiff jab and a solid body attack Phillips pressured the former champion mercilessly. Dokes was unable to keep his younger foe at bay, and nearly halfway through the round a hook to the body dropped Dokes. Although the punch was ruled a "low blow" by the referee, and Dokes was given time to recover, there was little question that Phillips had the power to hurt his bigger opponent. For much of the second round he further proved that point, landing hard shots to the body throughout the round. But it was a shot to the chin that cemented that fact. In the final seconds of the second round, Phillips fired a right hand followed by a left hook to the chin that dropped Dokes in a heap. The punch not only knocked Dokes out, but also broke his jaw. With one shot the thirty-three-year-old Paul

"Rocky" Ray Phillips was suddenly a real heavyweight, and one of only five men to knock out the former WBA champion.

For Phillips the win did help to ensure that he ended up with a reasonable three-year sentence, and after serving one year, he was back in the ring to continue his career. However, he struggled in his return. Traveling to Denmark in his first fight back Phillips was stopped by Brian Nielsen in two rounds, and followed that loss with another knockout loss to Alex Zolkin.

For Dokes, it was the end to his career. Although initially some wondered if another deadend comeback was down the line, that question was put to rest when Michael ended up in legal trouble of his own the following year. After a domestic dispute with his live-in fiancée, Dokes allegedly beat and then sexually assaulted her. His subsequent conviction ensured that Dokes would not resume his career, which ended with a most disturbing quote from the arresting officer (Lt. Tom Monahan) who said of the victim: "I've never seen anybody walk out of the ring after fighting Michael Dokes that looked this bad."

CHAPTER NINE

1998

"I think I might have rubbed him the wrong way."

Obed Sullivan on Jesse Ferguson shortly before they fought

April 11, 1998—Southwark, England
Kevin McBride (22–2–1, 19 KOs) vs. Michael Murray
(15–16, 8 KOs)
Favorite: McBride
Result: Murray won by way of third-round TKO.

When 6'6" Irishman Kevin McBride first exploded on the British heavy-weight scene there was no shortage of those proclaiming him a poten-tially solid European heavyweight prospect. He seemed to have everything needed to be a legitimate heavyweight contender as well as the intangibles to make him an attractive prospect. He was a devastat-ing puncher with a solid amateur career (he went on to fight in the 1992 Olympics), he had solid management in the form of Frank Maloney and Panos Eilades (the men who guided Lennox Lewis to a world title), and he was white. But the critical American boxing press was wary of a six-round draw in his pro debut against club fighter Gary Charlton (who had a less than stellar record of 1–6–1 with 1 KO). But as the wins con-tinued in impressive fashion, he began to raise eyebrows in the United States as well. When he was featured as an upcoming prospect in the December 1995 issue of *Boxing Illustrated* it looked like he was indeed on the right track towards a world ranking. But his defeat in Nevada at the hands of Louis Monaco in February 1997 sent his American fans (and quite frankly many of his Irish and British fans) jumping off the bandwagon in rapid fashion. Maloney, recognizing that his prospect was

277

at least temporarily taken out of the world scene with the loss, continued to try and maintain the career of the "Clones Colossus" in the European scene. He brought McBride back to Europe, where he scored a pair of meaningless wins before taking on his first world-class foe, German Axel Schultz. Although many boxing insiders thought that Schultz would probably win, the manner of the victory seemed to end any notion of McBride becoming even a player in the European theater. Stopped in the ninth round against a fighter widely regarded as a light puncher, it appeared to many that McBride simply lacked the chin or the stamina to ever compete with a world class opponent. Perhaps sensing that, and perhaps unwilling to abandon a fighter who had already cost him over half a million pounds, Maloney again tried to sell McBride, this time back to the British boxing public. Although McBride would never be able to fight for the British heavyweight title due to his nationality, a streak of wins in Britain could land him a WBO title fight against a Herbie Hide or Henry Akinwande. After knocking out Yuri Yelistratov in the opening round in England, there was talk of matching McBride up with former heavyweight champion Greg Page or former contender Phil Jackson. But first McBride was put in with one of Britain's most recognizable opponents to further pad his record: Michael Murray.

Murray was after all a very safe pick. After scoring a ten-round decision victory over Julius Francis in 1996, Murray went on a seven-fight losing streak, with four of the losses coming inside the distance. Although he was at one time regarded as a decent, if not exceptional, British heavyweight (he fought Herbie Hide for the British title in 1993, getting stopped in five), at thirty-three-years-old most regarded his best days as behind him. Most British boxing fans felt that if would be a surprise if he were able to last the distance. But Murray recognized the weaknesses in McBride's armor and saw the fight as very winnable for him, something that carried through in his training.

At the bell Murray rushed into his bigger foe. McBride responded by trying to establish the jab and keep Murray on the outside of his long reach. Unable to out-jab his bigger foe, Murray began to find the strategy that would carry him to victory, jumping in with wild, but hard, overhand rights. It was enough to raise the possibility of the unthinkable for the SKY Television commentator, who recognized that "it would be a catastrophic setback for the plans of McBride and promoter

Frank Maloney if Murray was to derail him here." By the end of the first, McBride seemed to silence the fears when he hurt Murray with a left hook to the body.

Perhaps sensing blood, McBride came out in the second, stalking and looking for the knockout. But Murray still had his most effective weapon, and seconds into the round it finally found its mark. Firing a solid right hand thirteen seconds into the round, Murray dropped the forward-moving McBride. McBride quickly rose at the count of four, but there was little question that he was hurt. Murray jumped on McBride, unloading shots on his wounded foe, mostly right hands. When a right uppercut snapped back his head at the halfway point of the round, it looked like the Irishman was close to hitting the canvas again. McBride seemed more than just hurt, he seemed tired. Fighting in slow motion and breathing heavily, he elected to slug it out with Murray, trying desperately to land something that could turn the tide of the fight quickly. But after missing a left hook near the end of the round, McBride stumbled into the ropes. No longer was the question on the minds of fans in attendance how long would Murray survive, but rather could McBride survive. Twenty-three seconds into the third round the question was answered. A chopping right hand badly hurt him, and after another right, McBride was again on the canvas. Although the referee allowed McBride to continue, a right uppercut followed by two more overhand rights prompted the referee to rescue McBride from further punishment, awarding the TKO victory to Murray at 1:20 of the round.

The shocked TV commentator admitted that the Murray win was "definitely not in the pre-fight script for the McBride camp." It all but ended any hope of McBride ever becoming a serious contender (although he would go on to win three more fights before losing to DaVarryl Williamson in 2002). He would never go on to fight for the world title or even the European title. Still, his pigmentation and power kept him in line for a major payday, and in 2004 he was seen as a strong candidate to fight Mike Tyson in what would be the biggest fight of his career.

Murray also saw his career fizzle after the win over McBride. Although the victory brought his record to .500, he would go on to lose his next six fights (all by decision) in the European scene to fighters like Timo Hoffman, Scott Welch, and Matthew Ellis.

July 4, 1998—Gold Coast, Australia
**James "Bonecrusher" Smith (43–15–1, 31 KOs) vs. Joe Bugner
(67–13–1, 40 KOs)**
Favorite: Smith
**Result: Bugner won by way of second-round TKO when Smith
dislocated his shoulder.**

For many boxing fans, the Bugner-Smith fight was about as ugly a
match-up as possible. Two fighters, both of them decades removed from
their primes, battling for a "world title" despite having a combined age
of ninety-three. Most American boxing fans were indifferent, and the
few who noticed the fight at all were less than supportive. For a commission to sanction the fight seemed to many a travesty of decency, and the
fact that a sanctioning organization had the audacity to call the winner
the heavyweight champion of the world was insulting. Although the
WBF was hardly a highly regarded organization (even among the third-
tier championships) it seemed to have sunk to a new low.

When push came to shove and asked whom the winner would be, almost every reputable boxing writer in the United States felt Smith
would emerge victorious.

It wasn't because Smith was still regarded as a viable heavyweight
that made him the favorite. For all intents and purposes, he was considered finished after his loss to Levi Billups in 1991 (see page 29) and had
become a "name" opponent since then (losing six of his next fifteen
fights). It was because most boxing writers felt that Smith was a little
less "washed-up" than Bugner. He had pulled off a handful of decent
wins in the 1990s (though few and far between), and more importantly,
he was closer to his prime. While Bugner was remembered for fighting
Joe Frazier and Muhammad Ali (both in 1973), Smith was remembered
for his fights in the mid-eighties with Larry Holmes and Mike Tyson.
Though he had become an opponent for fighters like Brian Nielsen and
Lionel Butler, he was also coming into the fight on the heels of a four-
fight winning streak.

In many ways the statistics were misleading. Despite the fact that
both fighters fought in distinctively different eras they were separated
by only three years in age. Also, Bugner himself had also put together a
decent run in the 1990s, winning the Australian title as well as the

PABA heavyweight championship. These accomplishments were easily overlooked by the American boxing public, which still retained an ethnocentric view of the heavyweight division. But Joe's accomplishments were not lost on his native home of Australia.

Even his most diehard Australian supporters regarded his comeback as only moderately successful (he was destroyed by Scott Welch in his only fight against a decent opponent), but Bugner was able to finally capture the appreciation and admiration from fans in his comeback that was missing in his previous career. Based initially in Great Britain, Bugner beat the popular Henry Cooper in 1971 for the European heavyweight championship. Rather than win the support of British fans, the win permanently tainted his career as a professional boxer in Britain. The controversial decision that gave him the belt caused a great deal of resentment in British boxing fans (a factor that was further complicated by the fact that Cooper never fought again after the loss to Bugner) and for the duration of his career, Bugner faced a cool reception from his hometown crowd. When Bugner launched his ill-advised comeback in 1995 he based it out of the country of his birth (Australia), and the reception was overwhelming. Bugner found the Australian boxing public to be the complete opposite of the British boxing fans. They cheered him with gusto and warmed to him personally. Suddenly, Joe Bugner became an Australian version of George Foreman—a dour, bitter young man who was transformed into a likeable, popular senior citizen. When his fight with Smith was announced, many fans of Australian boxing were excited. It seemed to many Aussies that it was a very winnable fight for Joe (even if their American counterparts did not agree). He had momentum going his way, and the fight would be in Australia, with all his fans firmly behind him. A world title, even the lightly regarded WBF, seemed to be the perfect way to cap off an emotional (albeit meaningless) comeback, and both Joe Bugner and his fans realized that.

By fight time it was clear that Joe had one other thing working in his favor: conditioning. Bugner weighed in at a reasonable 261 pounds, a full twelve pounds less than when he fought Waisiki Ligaloa in 1997. Although it was hardly awe inspiring, it was a far cry from Smith's conditioning. Smith walked into the ring weighing in at a career high 282 pounds. Although he had never been regarded as one of the "fat" heavyweights from the 1980s, his physique that night was not dissimilar to that of Tony Tubbs and Tim Witherspoon. He appeared as flabby and soft as he ever appeared for a fight, and it was clear that if the fight did extend into the championship rounds, that the edge would be in Bugner's corner.

Perhaps realizing at the bell that he could ill-afford to let the fight go more than a few rounds, Smith opened with an impressive offensive flurry. He fired a hard overhand right in the first few seconds that backed Joe into the ropes. A second right hand clipped Joe's chin and had him briefly stunned, and it initially appeared as if Joe was in for a tough round. Although Smith maintained solid pressure for the next 30 seconds, he inexplicably slowed down to a near crawl afterward. Bugner tried to take control with his jab, but it hardly appeared as if he was bothering Smith much with it. In fact, it seemed to many that the only decent shot that Bugner landed was a left hook to the body. Despite Bugner's inability to get his jab working well, Smith continued to slow down, and many were wondered just how bad his conditioning was when the bell ended the round. As the second round started, however it became clear to everyone in attendance that there was another reason for the "Bonecrusher" meltdown. Complaining of an injured right shoulder, ringsiders and television viewer's immediately recognized from the ugly lump protruding from Smith upper right arm that he had in fact dislocated his shoulder. It was clear to everyone that the fight needed to be stopped immediately, but unfortunately fans and viewers were forced to watch the disturbing actions of the ringside physician who tried to crudely reinsert Smith's shoulder back into the socket right there in the ring. However, the attempts of the ringside physician were to no avail, and a few seconds later the match-up was appropriately stopped by the referee.

With the win, the poor man's fairy tale that had been Joe Bugner's comeback was given a happy ending. Although Joe did fight once more after that, winning over Levi Billups, he never stepped up to fight one of the top-ranked fighters of the world (although he probably would have jumped at the opportunity to fight George Foreman). Australian fans were never forced to witness the potential massacre that a fight with David Tua might have been, and Joe was able to take a world title belt with him into the greener pastures of retirement, something he never won in his first career. (Of course, the WBF was not around in the

1970s, and defeating Muhammad Ali proved an impossible task, even for a Joe Bugner in his prime.)

October 22, 1998—Reseda, California
Alonzo Highsmith (27–0–1, 23 KOs) vs. Terry Verners
(7–20–2, 4 KOs)
Favorite: Highsmith
Result: Verners won by way of third-round TKO.

When Alonzo Highsmith announced his intentions to begin a career as a professional boxer in 1995 after a successful career as a running back in the NFL, the response from boxing writers was overwhelmingly negative. Going into 1995 it seemed as if boxing had finally overcome the negative stigma that followed Mark Gastineau's brief foray into the sport, and few were eager to witness another circus show. Gastineau's career involved all the elements that made boxing such a pariah among professional sports: crooked promoters, fixed fights, undeserving paydays (in his proposed matchup with George Foreman), allegedly drugged opponents, and a fighter who couldn't fight. It became abundantly clear early on that, regardless of what Highsmith would accomplish as a fighter, he was no Mark Gastineau. Turning pro in February 1995 (after eighteen months of intense training) Highsmith took on the seasoned, hard punching Marcos Gonzalez (a fighter with a 14–2–1 record). It was a shocking move for the untested Highsmith, as few "legitimate" prospects took on such tough opposition in their first fight. Highsmith struggled at times against Gonzalez, but emerged victorious, winning a four-round decision. From that point on Highsmith worked hard at his new profession, and though he struggled often, his heart and determination won over many of his critics. Though nobody envisioned a potential title in his future, he clearly was a man trying to become a world champion and do so legitimately. Even after padding his record early on, he never jumped at the big money fights on the horizon that would have relegated him to the role of sacrificial lamb. He fought to improve his game and to become a better boxer. Early on Highsmith became a common fixture on the undercards of high profile fighters such as Julio Cesar Chavez, Oscar De La Hoya, Tommy Morrison, Hector Camacho, and Donovan "Razor" Ruddock, and in 1996 he even performed a great service to the sport when he brutally knocked out Gastineau in the second round. It was a win of which almost everyone in boxing was appreciative (and many crossover fans from the NFL also relished in the image of the cocky and arrogant Gastineau getting pounded by the likeable Highsmith). By 1998 things were beginning to unravel for Highsmith. Unable to improve his "game" enough to take the next step up in competition, Highsmith was relegated to fighting weak opposition in an attempt to find the missing piece of the puzzle (in fact, after twenty-eight fights, his toughest opponent was still Gonzales). It was becoming clear to some that his dedication was beginning to show early signs of faltering, and some boxing insiders wondered how much longer the boxing career would continue before he returned to his "first" love in football.

Still, it seemed as if he picked a safe opponent in Terry Verners. The thirty-four-year-old Verners turned pro in less than impressive fashion when he was held to a four-round draw against Glendon Vernon in 1984, and by the end of the 1980s he had been relegated to "journeyman" status in the light heavyweight division (losing to fighters like future cruiserweight champion Arthur Williams as well as the oft-beaten Exum Speight). His jump to the heavyweight division in 1991 failed to revitalize his career (he was knocked out in one round by Lionel Butler) and after getting starched the following year by Gerard Jones, Verners decided to hang up the gloves. But after a nearly six-year hiatus Verners returned, losing a six-round decision to Ahmed Elsayed before being picked as Highsmith's opponent. It was hard to envision Verners pulling out the victory, even against the seemingly vulnerable Highsmith. In his so called "prime" he was defeated by fighters like Exum Speight, and with six years of ring rust added to his soft chin, it appeared that he would fold as soon as Highsmith found his chin.

When the fight started it was clear that Highsmith was using his weight advantage well (he weighed in at a solid 234 pounds to Verners's 210). He successfully pressured the veteran (who was eight years removed from his last victory) and by the round's end had him badly rattled. It appeared as if the fight was close to completion, and by the second round Highsmith picked up where he left off, battering the smaller man with thudding shots. But Verners was proving that, if nothing else, he was not folding after one punch. Rather, he intended to make Highsmith work for his knockout. But at the start of the third round Verners was rewarded for his resiliency, coming out of nowhere to stagger the bigger man with a shot to the chin. Although Highsmith had come back from adversity before in his career, he was unable to keep Verners off long enough to clear his head and quickly found himself on the canvas. Highsmith rose on wobbly legs, and it was clear to everyone in attendance that Highsmith was in serious trouble. Unfortunately for Alonzo, it was also clear to Verners who jumped on his wounded foe. A hard combination to the head ended matters when the referee rescued the badly dazed Highsmith at 1:19 of the third round, awarding Verners his first heavyweight victory.

Unfortunately for Verners, it also was his last. Given new life by his recent performance Verners landed a fairly tough opponent in Charles Shufford in his very next fight. He wasn't expected to win (he still had an 8–20–2 record) but based on his come-from-behind victory over Highsmith, a decent performance was not out of the question. But Shufford destroyed the veteran inside of one round, a loss that sparked a five-fight losing streak. By the end of the decade Verners had again retired. But he was able to take with him a rewarding and satisfying upset win over an undefeated heavyweight prospect with a most recognizable name.

The loss effectively ended Highsmith's career. Although he did fight Reggie Miller in his next fight, an ugly draw with the journeyman convinced him to hang up the gloves for good. For a competitor like Highsmith, the possibility of becoming anything less than the best was unacceptable, and he was clearly not going to become one of the best heavyweights in the world. He quickly returned to football as a scout for the Green Bay Packers, a position he not only relished, but at which he also excelled. And his boxing career was hardly a complete failure. He was arguably the most successful former NFL football player to turn boxer, and when he left the ring many boxing insiders were impressed with his career as a whole. Although he never accomplished what he set out to by winning a world title, he never discredited himself nor the sport, and that was something that few envisioned when he first laced up the gloves.

December 5, 1998—Kiev, Ukraine
Wladimir Klitschko (24–0, 22 KOS) vs. Ross Puritty
 (23–13–1, 21 KOs)
Favorite: Klitschko
Result: Puritty won by way of eleventh-round TKO.

By the late 1990s it was becoming increasingly clear that Europe was becoming a major powerhouse in the heavyweight division, and many boxing writers admitted that not since the 1930s (when Primo Carnera and Max Schmeling were two European fighters who won the title) had the division seen such activity from the continent. Not only had Lennox Lewis broken the infamous British heavyweight curse, but fighters like Henry Akinwande, Herbie Hide, Brian Nielsen, and Zeljko Mavrovic were establishing themselves as top contenders. In 1997 the most exciting European prospects were two Ukrainians fighting out of Germany: Wladimir and Vitali Klitschko. The two towering bombers had racked up an impressive combined record of 46–0 with forty-four KOs, and although their opposition was not impressive, there was little question that they appeared to be two of the best young prospects in the game. Although both brothers were held in high regard by boxing fans, many experts thought that Wladimir was the better prospect. With an Olympic pedigree, as well as his youth (he was nearly five years younger than Vitali), Wladimir was the fighter who tended to get bigger headlines after each fight. His destruction of Marcus McIntyre for the WBC Intercontinental title in 1998 came of the heels of older brother Vitali's KO over Dick Ryan for the WBO version of that title, and many experts assumed that Vitali was being groomed for a WBO title, whereas Wladimir was being groomed for bigger things. Even with Vitali's capture of the European title, many still gave the slight edge to younger brother Wladimir. Nothing in the matchmaking seemed to indicate differently when both brothers fought in front of their hometown crowd for the first time in December 1998. While Vitali took on unknown European Francesco Spinelli in defense of his European title, Wladimir took his first major step up in class, fighting rugged Ross Puritty, a fighter widely regarded as the toughest journeyman in the heavyweight division.

After starting his career in dismal fashion, going 8–8 (5 KOs) in his first sixteen fights, Ross was called upon as a last minute replacement for William Morris in a fight against Tommy "The Duke" Morrison on ESPN. Puritty shocked the world when he dropped the hard-punching Morrison twice en route to a ten-round draw. The fight helped to resurrect a career that was all but dead, and Ross went on to win his next nine fights, all by knockout. But after losing back-to-back decisions against Hasim Rahman and Michael Grant in 1996 it appeared that his brief flirtation with contention had come to an end. However Ross proved considerably more resilient than anticipated when he strung together another win streak, knocking out his next five opponents. With knockouts over former contenders Jorge Luis Gonzalez and Joe Hipp, Ross found himself again on the threshold of the top ten. But again Ross was knocked back when he lost a decision to Corrie Sanders for the WBU heavyweight championship. That loss was followed by two more (by decision) to Larry Donald and Chris Byrd. Few anticipated another rebound for the gritty Puritty, and although he was able to secure a fight with Klitschko when he knocked out undefeated Mark Hulstrom in the second round, most assumed it was more a reflection of Hulstrom's protected record than Ross's skills as a fighter. When Ross was given only one week's notice for the fight, it seemed to seal his fate. The question became would Ross's granite chin fail to hold up against the hard punching Ukrainian or would he once again lose a decision.

However, as soon as the bell rang it soon became clear that Wladimir was not going to try to seriously test the chin of Puritty. He came out with superior footwork and pumped a surprisingly effective jab that kept the forward-moving Puritty at bay. Whenever Ross tried to bull-rush his taller opponent, Wladimir easily sidestepped him and peppered him with counterpunches, and by round's end it was becoming increasingly clear that if it were to remain a "chess match" the edge was Klitschko's. Ross proceeded to cover up while stalking his bigger opponent in the second, but the results remained the same. Wladimir boxed, jabbed, countered, and hit Ross while taking very little punishment in return. By the third round the pro-Wladimir crowd began chanting "Klitschko! Klitschko!" in appreciation of the dominant performance put forth by their countryman. It wasn't until the fifth round that Ross landed anything of significance, when a few of his own jabs snuck in and caught Wladimir enough to set up a decent right hand two minutes into the round. Although Ross jumped on Wladimir and fired a combination to the body shortly thereafter, it failed to capture the round for him when Wladimir erased his effective offensive attack with a quick combo to Ross's head in the final seconds of the round.

It was enough to upset the corner of Ross Puritty, who implored their fighter between rounds to jab more and follow it with the right (the only combination that worked against Klitschko) and not to "sit" and let Wladimir tee off on him so much. Entering the sixth, it appeared as if Ross in fact took that advice to heart when he followed that strategy to rough up Wladimir in the first thirty seconds. But it was short-lived, as his bad habit of "sitting" and waiting for Wladimir took over. When an overhand right stunned Puritty briefly in the round it appeared as if Wladimir might in fact score the rare knockout. Wladimir threw a quick follow up combo that drove Ross into the ropes and then snapped his head back with a solid straight right that had the crowd on their feet. But by round's end Ross had recovered enough to resume his ineffective stalking.

By the eighth round there was little question that Ross needed a knockout to win, and there was little to indicate that it would come. Although Wladimir was showing some signs of fatigue, it hardly seemed out of the ordinary considering the pace of the fight as well as Wladimir's lack of experience in the later rounds. The assumption was as long as Wladimir didn't do anything stupid, he could lose every remaining round and coast to a decision. But Wladimir actually upped the pressure in an attempt to rob Ross Puritty of his heart and possibly score the knockout. Firing quick jabs and hard overhand rights, Wladimir again snapped Ross's head back early in the round and then fired a beautiful eight-punch combination to the head at 2:45 seconds of the round. Although the combination was indeed quite impressive, it became clear that Wladimir had expended too much energy in the eighth round, as he emerged looking for all the world like a tired fighter. When Puritty fired a left hook that failed to land cleanly, fans were shocked to see Wladimir stumble around the ring like a staggered fighter. Ross tried to jump on his seemingly wounded foe, pumping right hands, but was reprimanded for holding and hitting. It seemed that his golden opportunity was gone when Wladimir bounced back with a quick combination to the head at the bell to steal the round.

When Wladimir returned to his footwork in the ninth there was little question that he was tired. He threw considerably less than he had in the previous eight rounds. But there was also little to indicate that Ross could capitalize on Wladimir's condition, as he was still unable to get inside to land any serious punches. When Ross landed a left hook–right hand combo in the final thirty seconds Wladimir was able to fire a left jab counter of his own that snapped the head of Ross back, and it looked as if he would in fact survive the fight.

With only three rounds to go, fatigue finally caught up with Wladimir. Although Wladimir continued his successful strategy of jabbing and moving to start the tenth, a Ross Puritty right sent the giant Ukrainian reeling and trying desperately to hold. Wladimir's jab lost all its snap, and the combinations became mere movements of his arms. Sensing the advantage, the corner of Ross Puritty screamed, "He's tired Ross! Now push him!" which prompted Ross to oblige. Throwing hooks and uppercuts, Puritty dropped the big Ukrainian with thirty seconds remaining in the round, Referee Daniel Vande Wiele incorrectly waved the knockdown off, claiming Klitschko slipped. As soon as he rose he was again felled as he tried to back away from the onrushing American. As he crumbled into a neutral corner, the referee this time ruled it a knockdown and began counting. With only seconds remaining in the round Wladimir was able to rise and was saved by the bell, but few doubted that he was in for the longest two rounds of his career.

As it turned out, the two rounds lasted a mere sixteen seconds. Ross continued to pound away at his opponent, prompting Wladimir's corner to enter the ring to rescue their fighter from serious injury. Gone was the undefeated record of the giant Ukrainian.

For Wladimir, it initially appeared as if he was a pretender, and when brother Vitali won the WBO heavyweight championship with a decisive second-round knockout over Briton Herbie Hide, it appeared to many fans that he was going to be the Leon Spinks to Vitali's Michael. Although he regained some respect with a brutal knockout over German Axel Schultz for the European championship, it wasn't until he avenged his brother's loss to Chris Byrd (winning a decision over Byrd for the WBO title) that he was able to effectively erase the stigma of his loss to Puritty. In fact, by 2003 he was widely seen as the second best heavyweight in the world behind Lennox Lewis, and many boxing writers were predicting that if he were ever to fight Lewis, he would elevate himself to number one. But a shocking upset loss to Corrie Sanders that year (by way of second-round knockout) sent him back to the drawing board.

For Ross, the win should have been the shining moment of his career and the first step to making a third run for contention. But the victory was squandered by inactivity, as he fought a mere three times over the next two years. It wasn't until he met up with older brother Vitali in 2002 that he capitalized on his win, and by then a draw with journeyman Frankie Swindell had already tarnished his run. Older brother Vitali was able to accomplish what few thought was possible when he stopped Puritty in the eleventh.

December 8, 1998—New York City, New York
Obed Sullivan (29–3–1, 20 KOs) vs. Jesse Ferguson
(25–17, 16 KOs)
Favorite: Sullivan
Result: Ferguson won a ten-round split decision.

For career journeyman Jesse Ferguson, it looked as if his unlikely run at contention at the ripe age of forty-one was finally coming to an end. After losing seven of eight after his unlikely upset victory over Ray Mercer (see page 84), Ferguson dropped off the boxing map. It appeared an appropriate end to his career, towards the end he was coming into fights grossly out of shape and mentally unready (which was most clearly exemplified by his first-round knockout loss to Frank Bruno) and after losing by way of stoppage to Danell Nicholson in 1995, there appeared to be no future for Jesse Ferguson except one as a punching bag for a steadily declining class of heavyweight. With the memory of a world title fight and the knowledge that the skills were there to upset many top ranked heavyweights, Ferguson rededicated himself to the sport and reemerged against undefeated Bobby Harris in 1996 (see page 221), winning a ten-round decision. Ferguson then wisely tried to resurrect his career with solid wins over tough, but limited opposition to follow up the Harris fight. After winning his next two against journeymen Everton Davis and Thomas Williams, Ferguson took on his second name heavyweight in the comeback, this time Samson Po'uha. Although Po'uha was no longer seen as much of a prospect after knockout losses to Craig Payne and Andrew Golota, the conventional wisdom was that he lost those fights due to poor conditioning. However, against Ferguson he weighed in at a reasonable 258 pounds, and many were assuming that Po'uha would emerge victorious. But again Ferguson exposed another limited heavyweight with a brutal upset, this time by way of an eight-round knockout. It was enough to earn Jesse the respect of many boxing insiders and also enough to put him within a fight of his dream of another big payday. He initially was being considered as a potential opponent for George Foreman, but when that fell through he stepped in against undefeated Hasim Rahman in January 1998 for the IBF Intercontinental heavyweight championship and the USBA heavyweight title. A win would put him in line for a title fight, or at the very least a big money, pay-per-view fight, but after twelve lopsided rounds, Hasim Rahman emerged victorious, brutally taking advantage of Ferguson's inability to deal with quickness or movement to control the fight. For Ferguson it seemed to expose once and for all his limitations, and most assumed that he would not be able to recapture the dedication that marked his recent revival. But for Jesse, there was one fighter in which he had something to prove, there was one fighter that he had to beat: Obed Sullivan.

By late 1998 Sullivan appeared on his way out of the heavyweight picture. After starting his career with an impressive 28–1–1 record (with his only loss coming in his third pro fight) Obed found himself in the top ten and a fan favorite due to his personality and aggressive style. However in 1997 Sullivan dropped a close, majority decision to undefeated Hasim Rahman, a loss that derailed his run at a title. Although he rebounded with an impressive knockout over Keith McKnight, he went on to lose a heartbreaker to Michael Grant in May of 1998. Unlike the loss to Rahman, the loss to Grant was lopsided and decisive (Grant stopped Sullivan in the ninth round). That seemed to show that Sullivan would clearly never be a top-notched heavyweight, but there was little to indicate that it would end his status as a contender. After all, Grant was widely seen as the best heavyweight prospect in the world, the man who would go on to beat Lennox Lewis. Sullivan may never be a world champion with Grant and Rahman around, but he would still have too much for a forty-one-year-old fighter like Jesse Ferguson.

But in a chance meeting after Jesse Ferguson's knockout over Samson Po'uha, Obed unwittingly gave Ferguson all the motivation he would need. After congratulating Ferguson for his impressive win, Obed took a light-hearted jab at his fellow heavyweight by arrogantly promising that if they ever fought that he would win. Ferguson was taken aback by the slight, and although Sullivan later admitted that it was done somewhat tongue-in-cheek, he also admitted shortly before the fight "I think I might have rubbed him the wrong way." It was a very correct assessment, as Ferguson trained with renewed fire and entered the ring at a fit 235 pounds.

Even without the added weight, it was not enough to compensate his lack of speed and his inability to deal with it. Sullivan was fed a very effective fight plan, one that involved the jab and lots of foot movement,

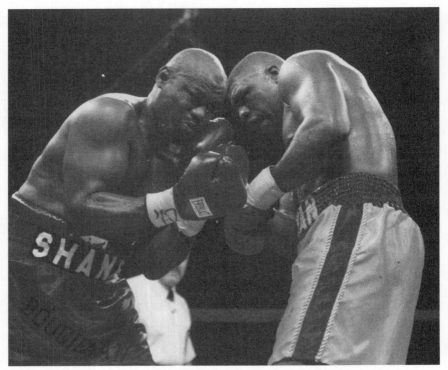

After a perceived slight from Obed Sullivan, Jesse Ferguson (left) came out determined to win, and took a split decision victory. *Pat Orr*

and for much of the first he executed it quite well. Ferguson tried to wade in and attack the body, one of his assets, but he was unable to pin down Sullivan, who dominated from the outside. But in the last thirty seconds of the round, Jesse finally was able to catch Sullivan as he moved in. Two hard right hands rattled Sullivan as the round closed, turning a Sullivan round into one very difficult to score.

However, Obed returned to the jab in the second, and again continued to dominate from the outside. A minute into the round a jab followed by an overhand right actually forced the ever forward moving Ferguson to take a step back. But the halfway point of the round saw Sullivan make a critical error in altering his game plan. Standing in front of Ferguson, Sullivan began to bang away at him, who gladly obliged. Initially it appeared as if Obed would hold his own against Ferguson, but a right hand cut Sullivan over his left eye, prompting him to take a backward step. There was little question that if the fight would be waged inside, Ferguson would do considerably well, and by round's end he was landing the overhand right with alarming regularity.

Sullivan's corner recognized Obed's mistake and instructed their fighter to return to the jab. Initially Sullivan followed instructions, but the fighter known as "stubborn" throughout his career picked the worst possible moment to ignore his corner. Within a minute he was again standing on the inside with Jesse, and although he tagged Ferguson with a hard combination upstairs in the final ten seconds, there was little question that he was fighting exactly the type of fight Jesse wanted. For much of the remainder of the fight the rounds followed a similar pattern, with Obed boxing and moving in the opening minute before abandoning his game plan to fight inside with Sullivan in a classic phone booth war. The effect of Jesse's punches began to show in the fifth when, a minute into the round, Ferguson drove Sullivan into the ropes briefly with a hard combination. Although Ferguson showed early signs of fatigue after the round, his conditioning along with Sullivan's foolish strategy allowed him to continue his solid performance. Near the halfway point of the sixth Ferguson landed a hard right hand to the chin, and followed it with a hard combination upstairs which landed cleanly. Although Obed showed more grit than fighters like Bobby Harris and Samson Po'uha in taking the punches and holding his ground, they were proving decisive on the scorecards.

By the seventh round it appeared as if Obed was finally listening to his corner, boxing well early on and even throwing Ferguson to the canvas a minute in, when Jesse did close the gap and get inside. But in the final minute of the round, Obed again returned to what was not working. He stood still and actually started to stalk Ferguson, and then paid for his mistake by eating a right hand (a shot that again robbed him of a clear cut round on the judges scorecards).

When the ninth round saw Obed open by eating a right hand, it looked like another big Ferguson round. However, Jesse eased up in the round, clearly saving some gas for the final round. It was perhaps the first good round for Obed since the second, and he even had Jesse backing up in the final thirty seconds, although he never had the veteran seriously hurt. Still, going into the final, most ringsiders felt that Obed needed a big round to turn around what was clearly a Jesse Ferguson fight. Although Sullivan did well in the tenth, it was hardly the dominant round that would turn things around on the scorecard. Steve Weisfeld scored the fight for Sullivan (96–94) but was overruled by Harold Letterman and Melvina Lathan, both who gave the fight to Ferguson by identical scores of 96–94.

For Jesse, it was one of the biggest wins of his career, and initially it appeared as if his dream for another big money fight might still be alive. But his win over Sullivan was only able to land one more big fight, against Andrew Golota. It looked like a smart fight: although Golota was a heavy favorite, he was the kind of fighter Jesse tended to do well against. But in the middle of a rebirth as a boxer of sorts, he easily outboxed Ferguson from the outside. It was another dominant loss for Ferguson, but few felt that it would hurt Jesse's attempt to land another fight against a name opponent (after all, there seemed to be a market for a potential rematch with Sullivan). However, Ferguson decided to call it a career, never fighting again.

For Sullivan, the loss was nothing short of devastating. No longer considered a contender, Obed's career began to become defined as a "name opponent" for the younger, fresher, prospects. Sullivan's career continued its free fall, when he lost his next big fight in 1999 to undefeated Derrick Jefferson by way of close decision. A shot at the WBO title later that year followed, but again he fell short against a top heavyweight, losing by way of ninth-round knockout to the undefeated Vitali Klitschko. It would be his only world title fight.

CHAPTER TEN

1999

"He may have been hurt, Francis, by being made the underdog in this fight."

TV commentator on Julius Francis during
his fight with Pele Reid

January 30, 1999—London, England
Pele Reid (13–0, 13 KOs) vs. Julius Francis (18–7, 10 KOs)
Favorite: Reid
Result: Francis scored a third-round TKO.

Although Great Britain was never known for its production of great heavyweights, it never seemed to have a shortage of easily marketable fighters with personalities that rivaled Muhammad Ali's, and by the late 1990s that phenomenon had hit an all-time high. It began with WBO middleweight and super middleweight champion Chris Eubank, whose brash personality and cocky attitude complimented his skills as a fighter to make him one of the most talked about British fighters of the decade. After he faded from the scene following a defeat at the hands of Steve Collins, a new Brit quickly picked up his position, and in fact raised the bar even higher. Featherweight "Prince" Naseem Hamed became one of the most recognizable fighters in the world, in part due to his one punch power, his unorthodox style, and his unique personality (that often resulted in some of the most memorable ring entrances in the history of the sport). Although he had no shortage of critics, most boxing experts admitted that he was in fact one of the better fighters in the world. But it was almost an aberration that Hamed would emerge as such a dominant fighter because of it. He was often unbalanced, threw punches from bizarre angles, and tended to violate such fundamental rules of the ring such as keeping his hands low and his chin high. Still, his success was undeniable, and when a heavyweight version of Hamed seemed to emerge from the United Kingdom in the form of Pele Reid (a stablemate of Hamed), the boxing world took notice.

Reid was a prospect with power in both fist and an undeniably outgoing personality that made him a favorite of many of the boxing press. Unfortunately, he also possessed many of the bad habits that Hamed also possessed, something that would prove to be a major stumbling block in his career if he lacked Hamed's natural talent. He tended to keep his hands low and his chin high and often relied on his quick reflexes and his power to keep him out of trouble. It seemed to catch up with him when, in the fight prior to the one with Francis, he found himself on the canvas courtesy of a forty-one-year-old African journeyman named Ikomoniya Botowamung (a fighter with a 10–8–1 record). Although Reid would come back to knock out Botowamung in the fourth round, the boxing world began to show signs of skepticism. Nonetheless, few anticipated anything short of an early knockout for Pele when he was called upon to fill in for fellow undefeated Briton Danny Williams in challenging Julius Francis for the British and Commonwealth heavyweight title.

Francis, who would emerge in the following years as a sort of British version of Jesse Ferguson, was still seen as something of a ordinary and limited fighter in the British scene (and nobody regarded him as a fighter of note on the world scene). He won his first six fights as a pro, but against John Ruiz he was stopped in the fourth round, and followed the loss with a collection of losses against such forgettable fighters like Michael Murray and Nikolaj Kulpin. Although he was able to put up a respectable performance in getting stopped in the eighth round against European champion Zeljko Mavrovic in 1997, a second-round knockout loss to Vitali Klitschko the following year seemed to bring to an end his status as a contender in Europe. By the start of 1999 it appeared with the emergence of such attractive British prospects like Danny Williams and Pele Reid that it was only a matter of time before he would lose his British and his Commonwealth titles, thus ending his status as a British contender as well.

But the world had yet to see the last of Julius Francis, and he recognized the flaws in Pele Reid's style in the ring. Reid, however, had different ideas, and as the first round began it looked like he was going to have his way with Francis. He came out jabbing but it wasn't long before he was firing bombs in an attempt to test the chin of the thirty-four-year-old veteran. Within a minute he had Francis covering up on the ropes, and it soon appeared as if Francis lacked anything that really could discourage Reid. Even when Francis landed a solid right with less than 30 seconds left in the round, it seemed to do little serious damage to Reid.

The assumption that Francis was unable to hurt his younger foe was shattered less than fifteen seconds into the second round. After coming out swinging, Pele Reid found himself the recipient of a powerful right hand that nearly decapitated the flashy slugger. Recognizing his opportunity Francis jumped on his injured opponent, unloading power shots that trapped Reid against the ropes. Reid no longer looked like a "world beater," but rather a very vulnerable young fighter in serious trouble, but he seemed to do well in surviving the onslaught. He held and clinched his way out of trouble and seemed to have weathered the storm by the halfway point of the round. However, the flaws in Reid's style were still intact, and Francis did not forget where he found his success against Pele. When a looping left hook caught Reid on the chin at the 2:00 mark Reid was again on Queer Street, trying desperately to survive. Francis again unloaded against a hurt Reid, and even knocked his mouthpiece out at 2:35, but Reid was able to survive the round. Still, there was no doubt that Pele needed something big to turn things around.

However, it again looked as if Pele had recovered as the third round began. He tried to fight his way back into the fight, but his porous defense and exposed chin were still prevalent, and it only became a matter of time. A minute later a left jab followed by a devastating overhand right again staggered Reid. When Reid was again hurt at the 2:00 mark by another right, he again found himself in a dire situation, trying to survive the Francis onslaught. Trapped on the ropes it appeared as if Francis was finally able to rob Reid of his heart, as the battered fighter seemed to be slowly turning his back to Francis in a sign of surrender. But Reid resisted the temptation and was given a break when the referee separated the fighters, allowing Pele a chance to get off the ropes. The reprise was short lived; Francis again pounded Reid into the ropes, tagging him with hard shots that landed with a dangerous degree of accuracy. It was enough for referee Richie Davis, who stopped the fight at 2:28, giving Francis the victory.

There was little question that it was a shocking result. Even the boxing fans that picked Francis did not envision such a display of power. It was enough to cause ringside commentator to proclaim "Julius Francis confounded those who made him an underdog in this fight."

However Francis, who would admit to commentator Adam Smith in the post-fight interview that the win was his "best night ever," was not done. In his next fight he met up with another undefeated British heavyweight: Danny Williams. Williams, who was the originally planned opponent for Francis before being replaced by Reid, was favored. However, he also saw his undefeated record brought to an end by Julius Francis.

Reid, however, was all but finished. He was thrown in with the rugged Orlin Norris in his next fight, a fight he was not expected to win. But when Norris, who was not regarded as a particularly devastating puncher, destroyed Reid in the opening round it was clear that Pele lacked the durability to match up with any quality heavyweight. A third knockout loss, to unknown Jacklord Jacobs, brought his career to an inglorious and disappointing end, and although he made a comeback several years later, he continued to struggle against British journeymen like Luke Simpkin (a draw in six rounds) and Michael Sprott (who knocked him out).

April 1, 1999—Worley, Idaho
Greg Page (55–13–1, 45 KOs) vs. Artis Pendergrass
    (14–13, 14 KOs)
Favorite: Page
Result: Pendergrass won a ten-round split decision.

By 1999 the frequent and unrelenting barrage of Foreman-like comebacks had worn out their welcome with even the cable networks. Although initially embraced by *USA Tuesday Night Fights* and ESPN boxing (former champions often would draw more viewers than young up-and-coming fighters) the lack of success of these comebacks eventually led to their demise. With the exception of George Foreman (who actually had graduated to HBO fights after his war with Evander Holyfield in 1991) and Larry Holmes (who used his Foreman-like comeback to land two title shots) there was little interest in any of the countless former champions and contenders, and few were able to land televised fights against unknown opponents. When *USA Tuesday Night Fights* was canceled in 1998, it was a fatal blow for the comebacks of many of these fighters, as *Tuesday Night Fights* was the one show that regularly showcased older fighters. ESPN, never a big fan of the forty-year-old fighter, tended to ignore all but the biggest named veterans. But there was one final avenue for the elder heavyweight, *Cedric Kushner's Heavyweight Explosion*. With nearly a card a month, Kushner promoted cards on occasion suffered from lack of quality (although many cards were in fact quite strong) and *Heavyweight Explosion* was no exception. Although they offered younger fighters rare opportunities to showcase their skills, and occasionally offered great matches, the quantity of cards led to main events with such fighters as Rick Sullivan (a fighter with a dismal 6–11, 4 KOs record).

It appeared that the Page-Pendergrass match was going to be one of those cards when it was put together at the last minute. Few anticipated a big payday for the former WBA champion Greg Page even if he were to win, but he badly needed a televised fight to rekindle interest in his career. After losing by way of knockout to Bruce Seldon in 1993, Page initially retired to embrace a career as a trainer. It was a natural step for the articulate former champion, and he showed a genuine knack for it. In fact, his success as a trainer was so impressive (and surprising) that he was quickly becoming one of the more respected young trainers in the sport. Working primarily with Don King–associated fighters, Page also had no shortage of clients. His crowning moment came when one of his fighters, Oliver McCall, went on to win the heavyweight championship with a second-round knockout over Lennox Lewis (although Emanuel Steward took over as head trainer shortly before the fight, Page still remained a co-trainer and received a great deal of credit for his work with McCall). Despite his success at his new profession (or perhaps because of it), Page decided to make another run as a fighter, and in 1996 launched an ill-advised comeback. He began it in impressive fashion, knocking out his first nine opponents in the first round, but without the television exposure it proved to be futile. After winning fourteen straight (thirteen by knockout) he took on the up-and-coming Jerry Ballard and held the younger fighter to a ten-round draw. The draw did prove that he still was a fighter to reckon with, and it helped him land another big fight, this time against prospect Monte Barrett. Although Page ended up on the losing end of a ten-round decision he hardly embarrassed himself. However, most fans wanted to see the former champion retire. He held his own with Barrett and Ballard, but it was hard to see how he could go on to win a title or land a big payday based of those performances. Although both Ballard and Barrett were prospects, they tended to be regarded as second-tier prospects, and the assumption was that if he were to jump up to fight a contender, he would lose and lose badly. But Page continued his career, and following the winning recipe that he hoped would lead to a title fight, he remained very active. In fact, Page agreed to take the fight with Pendergrass despite fighting only five days prior; the opportunity to fight a journeyman on television was simply too good to turn down (and Page didn't really think too highly of Pendergrass as a fighter anyway). His record was close to .500, he was a small heavyweight (starting his career as a middleweight), and there were questions about his chin.

Pendergrass was actually a very underrated fighter. Even at heavyweight his power was very good, and he had pulled off several heavyweight upsets, including his knockouts over Gary Bell and Josh Dempsey. Although he had been stopped three times in his career, it was in fact more the norm for him to go the distance before losing. But Page made the same mistake that Josh Dempsey did nearly two months prior in assuming that his power would overwhelm the smaller man, and ultimately he paid the same price that Dempsey did.

As soon as the bell rang starting the fight, the forty-year-old Page jumped all over Pendergrass, forcing his smaller opponent to cover up. It appeared as if the flabby-looking Page, who weighed in at a somewhat fleshy 252 pounds, wanted to make quick work of things before his stamina (or potential lack of) came into play. But the offensive blitz was short lived, and by the end of the round the punch output of Page had slowed considerably. Still, he was able to win the round convincingly and continued his dominance into the second. By the third round it appeared as if Page would cruise to a victory, but unfortunately for Greg Page, Pendergass was a determined man, who had just discovered a weapon that proved to be effective against the former champion: the overhand right.

After winning the third round Artis took control of the fight in the fourth when, less than a minute into the round, a three-punch combination to the face followed by a big right hand had Page in trouble. Pendergrass, seizing the opportunity, trapped the staggered Page on the ropes, and although he was unable to drop the cagey veteran, there was little question which fighter won the round. Throwing solid hooks to the body throughout the fifth with effective overhand rights thrown in for good measure, Pendergrass went on to take the next two rounds as well (even getting a two-point round in the sixth when Greg Page had a point deducted for a low blow). Ironically, Pendergrass also employed a veteran trick with big flurries in the last ten seconds to cement his lead in both rounds. With a solid body attack robbing Page of his energy, it appeared as if Pendergrass had everything going his way going into the seventh, but Page began to find his second wind and won the round with solid right hands. In fact, Page appeared the fresher man in the eighth as both fighters exchanged right hands. For Page, the target was now clear, the left eye of Artis Pendergrass was quickly swelling shut, and Pendergrass was increasingly having trouble seeing out of that eye. Sensing his opportunity, Greg Page came out in the ninth round looking to end the show. He started the round strong, and for the first time in the fight began to dance and jab like the Greg page of old. It was proving to be highly effective as well, as Pendergrass seemed unable to avoid the solid lefts of the former champion. Although he could no longer get in with the overhand right, he was still able to exchange jabs with Page, and a hard left jab caught Page flush on the chin with less than a minute left in the round. It was a good shot, but it seemed unlikely that a mere jab could seriously hurt a good fighter like Page, but in fact that was what the shot did. Page briefly doubled over and a Pendergrass assault had Greg Page on the ropes and nearly out on his feet. Although Greg survived the onslaught without going down, Pendergrass was able to effectively steal the round when a body attack had Greg Page in trouble at the bell. Going into the tenth round, it appeared that the underdog had again stolen the momentum of the fight, and determined to punctuate his performance with a solid finish, Artis came out bombing at the bell to start the tenth. Page was clearly winded, the second wind that had carried him through the middle rounds was now depleted and he spent most of the round clinching. It was enough to ensure that Pendergrass won the round, and ultimately the fight. Although one judge had Page winning by a point, the other two judges appropriately voted for Pendergrass, giving him the first decision victory of his career.

Although it was his biggest win, Artis failed to become a contender after the victory over Page. Despite his thirteen losses, his small size and hard punch meant that a run as a cruiserweight contender was hardly out of the question (in fact British cruiserweight Johnny Nelson, a fighter with twelve losses, had just won the WBO cruiserweight title four days earlier). Artis initially seemed willing to take the necessary steps to maximize his newly found status as potential contender when he promised to take a few months off to rest (he had in fact fought seven times in the one year period leading up to his Page fight). However, the journeyman mentality took over when a potential payday reared its career ending head. Within three weeks Pendergrass was fighting again, this time against Boris Powell. With his swollen eye still damaged, and serious signs of burnout, Pendergrass was meekly stopped in the sixth round.

For Greg Page however, the loss in actuality set up a big fight against an old nemesis Tim Witherspoon. He seemed the perfect foil for the rapidly declining Witherspoon, he was unable to beat him in his prime, and the ease upon which Pendergrass was able to tag him with the overhand right (a punch that was Witherspoon's bread and butter shot) indicated that he would most likely be unable to compete with the fighter who seemed closer to his prime than Page was. But in another upset, Greg Page emerged victorious, briefly salvaging a career that appeared over with the loss to Pendergrass. The revival was short-lived however, and within two years, the career of Greg Page would take a tragic turn. Initially it appeared as if Page could emerge as an opponent for Larry Holmes, but the fight never materialized, and Holmes eventually picked Mike Weaver as an opponent the following year. Page followed his win over "Terrible" Tim with a fight against Witherspoon KO victim Jorge Luis Gonzalez. Although he lost that fight by decision, the fight was competitive, and Page saw his stock as an opponent for young up-and-comers rise with the loss. A follow-up win over Terrence Lewis followed by a loss to Robert Davis seemed to confirm the reputation he had gained as one of the better "test" for young fighters. However, many insiders were hoping that he would retire. It was, after all, depressing to see a former champion like Page relegated to getting beat up by guys like Jorge Gonzalez. Besides, the possibility was there that he could get hurt; after all, he was over forty years old and had been fighting professionally for over twenty years. But Page ignored those who were calling for his retirement, continuing his career against the advice of almost every neutral observer in the sport. Tragically, the worries proved prophetic when a loss to Dale Crowe nearly ended his life. Hospitalized, Page nearly became the first former heavyweight champion killed in the ring. Although he survived, and is currently recovering, he never stepped in the ring again.

June 17, 1999—Worley, Idaho
David Bostice (17–0–1, 10 KOs) vs. Israel Cole (14–8–4, 9 KOs)
Favorite: Bostice
Result: Cole won a ten-round decision.

There was little question leading up to his fight with Israel Cole that David Bostice was confident of victory, and few felt that his confidence was unwarranted. Proclaiming before the fight that "it'll take me a couple of rounds for me to figure him out. And then that'll be it,"[1] Bostice was clearly a man who didn't think too highly of his opponent's chances of victory. After all, there was little on paper that indicated Cole could pull off the upset. After making it to the quarterfinals in the 1984 Los Angeles Olympics for his native country of Sierra Leone (he was one the most successful Olympic boxers in the history of the tiny west African nation) Cole turned pro in 1985 in the middleweight division, knocking out a fighter named Ondre Williams in the first round. But his success was short-lived when in his second pro fight he was knocked out by the unknown Henry Johnson. Things seemed to fall apart from that point on, as he went on to lose two more fights at middleweight the following year (to Steve Darnell and Tim Williams) all before his tenth fight.

---

[1] Hilary Kraus,"Confident Bostice in Fightin' Mood," *The Spokane-Review*, June 17, 1999.

Although he was able to land a fight with Reggie Johnson for a regional version of the WBA title, by the mid 1990s he was firmly established as an opponent for various up-and-comers in the light heavyweight division. But after an eight-round loss to Ernie Magdaleno in 1992, Cole retired from the ring and became a regular fixture in various Las Vegas gyms as a sparring partner. When Cole decided to lace up the gloves one more time, many felt that he could conceivably still have a career as an "opponent." But when he stepped into the ring at heavyweight against journeyman Ken Bentley, many boxing insiders worried about what could happen if he were to fight a hard-punching big heavyweight. And hard punching and big were two phrases that seemed to define David Bostice.

The undefeated Bostice had just begun to excite boxing fans with his quick fist and his above average power. But critics began to notice his inconsistency. Bostice followed an impressive win with an ugly performance, and many were wondering what to make of him as a fighter. After being held to a draw against unknown Maurice May in his third pro fight, Bostice followed it with a devastating knockout over Craig Brinson, but inconsistency continued to plague his career. Still, he had a good punch, a solid chin (he had yet to be dropped as a pro), and the size to overwhelm his smaller opponent (he outweighed Cole by thirty-five pounds). It was enough to convince many insiders that even if he were due for a bad performance, it was highly unlikely that he would lose the fight.

Cole had some tricks up his sleeve as well. Despite his early knockout loss to Johnson, he had developed into a fairly resilient fighter, losing only one other fight inside the distance. He also had developed his power with the added weight, a factor that was evident when he knocked out Bentley in his first heavyweight fight. (Although Bentley was a journeyman, he did have the ability to go the distance at times, taking Shannon Briggs to the scorecards.)

When the fight began, Cole wisely tried to avoid Bostice's power in the early rounds. In fact, for much of the first three rounds it was looking like Bostice was en route to a victory. But nearly halfway through the fourth round Cole turned the tide when he landed a big overhand right to drop his undefeated opponent. Bostice was clearly on Queer Street as he rose at the count of eight, and suddenly it appeared as if the smaller man was about to score the biggest win of his career. Cole jumped on his injured foe, badly staggering him throughout the round but was unable to put him away, and by the fifth round it seemed clear that his opportunity had slipped away. In fact, Bostice was able to pull out the fifth and sixth rounds, and it looked increasingly like the Cole right hand was just a "lucky punch." But Cole's luck had yet to run out when, in the seventh round, he found his mark with the right hand again. Bostice was again felled, and though he survived the ensuing onslaught, he was unable to effectively rally from it. Cole went on to dominate the eight and ninth rounds, and although Bostice did try to force the knockout in the tenth, he failed to find his suddenly elusive foe (although it was enough to steal the round for him in the eyes of many ringsiders). By the time the final bell rang, there was little question which fighter won the fight. When the scorecards were tallied Israel Cole, the former Olympian turned sparring partner, had finally put it together as a pro and captured the unanimous decision (by scores of 96–91 twice and 95–94).

Nonetheless the swan song was short-lived when Cole went on to lose his next fight to another journeyman-turned-prospective contender, Maurice Harris, three months later. It ended what could have been a successful run as a heavyweight for Cole, but he did prove his worth in that fight as well. Against a fighter coming off a win over Jeremy Williams, he was able to last the distance (something fighters like Lou Monaco and James Thunder were unable to do against Harris), thus ensuring that his brief career as a heavyweight was by no means a failure.

For Bostice, the fight epitomized his inconsistency, and although he would go on to become a borderline contender, he would never completely put it together to emerge as a legitimate, top-notched heavyweight. After winning his next five fights, he was destroyed by the giant Ukrainian Wladimir Klitschko in two rounds in 2000. However, he was able to bounce back, winning decisions over Ed Mahone and Al Cole later that year. The roller coaster career had another drop when aging former champion Tim Witherspoon knocked him out in the first round in 2001. By 2002, the ride was still continuing, as Bostice was able to extend Francois Botha the distance in losing a highly questionable decision before getting blitzed early by Jeremy Williams.

June 18, 1999—Vejle, Denmark
Brian Nielsen (49–0, 33 KOs) vs. Dick Ryan (47–4, 40 KOs)
Favorite: Nielsen
Result: Ryan won by way of tenth-round TKO.

For boxing fans in Europe, the 1990s saw a complete reversal of their fortunes in the heavyweight division. Not only had Lennox Lewis established himself as the one true champion by decade's end, but also fighters like Frank Bruno, Herbie Hide, and Henry Akinwande (all Brits) would go on to hold world titles (Bruno captured the WBC title while Hide and Akinwande won the WBO crown). But Britain was not the only country to produce world-class heavyweights. Great fighters emerged from Germany (in the form of Vitali and Wladimir Klitschko) and even Croatia (in the form of Zeljko Mavrovic), giving the heavyweight division its most international feel since the 1930s. But one of the most unlikely fighters to emerge as a top contender was Denmark's Brian Nielsen.

Nielsen was a fighter with an impressive amateur background, winning the bronze medal in the 1992 Barcelona Olympics while compiling an amateur record of 104–7. But that alone was not enough to convince critical American fans that he was a fighter worth watching. Many fine amateurs from Europe proved inept as pros, and the common assumption was that Nielsen was no different. Physically Nielsen appeared ridiculously out of shape and early on he appeared to lack power (scoring only one knockout in his first nine fights). But Brian began to win over the converts in 1994 when he stopped former heavyweight champion James "Bonecrusher" Smith in his thirteenth fight. Slowly, boxing insiders outside of Denmark began to pay attention to the chunky Dane. When Brian stopped another former champion, Tony Tubbs, in 1995 he jumped to the front of the pack of heavyweight prospects in Europe, and the following year he captured the lightly-regarded IBO heavyweight title. Although the IBO wasn't an organization held in high regard and most Americans ignored the significance of his belt, it did prove beneficial in strengthening his fan base in Denmark, where boxing fans tended to hold the IBO in higher regard (although arguably that was more due to the title holder than the title itself).

After stopping Phil Jackson and Mike "The Bounty" Hunter in 1996 (as well as racking up five other less meaningful wins), Brian was ready to take on a fighter that would make or break him, a fighter who would either expose him as a fraud or establish him as one of, if not the, best European heavyweight contender in the world: Larry Holmes. Although Larry was still a good fifteen years removed from his prime, he still was a widely respected heavyweight, not only because of his accomplishments as a champion, but also due to his performances in his comeback. In the only two losses of his comeback Larry dropped close decisions to reigning champions (Evander Holyfield and Oliver McCall), and many boxing insiders felt that Larry still had more than enough in his tank to take Nielsen to school. But Nielsen fought surprisingly well, winning a twelve-round split decision in his home country. Although most neutral observers felt that the decision was somewhat suspect, and that Larry was the victim of a hometown decision, few could argue with the fact that the win propelled Brian into the big leagues. Suddenly Brian was in line for a big money fight against the likes of an Evander Holyfield, and although few felt that he could beat Holyfield, even his harshest critics grudgingly admitted that he earned the shot.

But Team Nielsen realized something right away, that there was in fact a lot of money to be made in cashing in on the most recognizable athlete in Denmark, as recognizable to the average Dane as Michael Jordan was to the average American. Nielsen fought eight more times in 1997, against a collection of fighters who all had something in common: almost all were fighters with little skill and grossly inflated records, many coming from the Midwest. None better exemplified this than South Carolina's Don Steele, who Brian stopped in November 1997. Steele came to Denmark with an impressive record of 42–0 with forty-two knockouts, only to be crushed in two rounds. It appeared that Team Nielsen was interested in cashing in (and to a lesser degree conning) the Danish public, and by the start of 1999 much of the momentum Brian built up in beating Larry Holmes was gone. Suddenly, Brian found himself scorned by many boxing writers for what they saw as his attempt to tarnish a sacred record in boxing: Rocky Marciano's 49–0 record as a heavyweight champion. Few questioned that Rocky's record was somewhat inflated, most of his wins coming before he won the heavyweight title in his forty-third fight. But over the years it became a record that rivaled Joe DiMaggio's fifty-six-game hitting streak, or Wilt Chamberlain's 100 points in a game. For Marciano retired undefeated and stayed retired, something that proved impossible for any other heavyweight champion to do since. As a result, the record remained unchallenged until Larry Holmes racked up a record of 48–0 as a champion, putting him within one win of tying the record. But fate intervened when he lost a decision to Michael Spinks in fight number forty-nine. But unlike Holmes, who won the title in his twenty-eighth fight and defended the title successfully twenty times, Nielsen had yet to make the argument that he was even a champion. He won an illegitimate belt against Tony LaRosa (a fighter who hardly deserved to be in a title fight) in his twenty-fourth fight and defended it only five times over the next three years while fighting countless non-threatening, non-title affairs. Although he tied the record with an impressive win over Tim Witherspoon in April 1999, it was not enough to silence the boxing historians. One boxing historian even used the analogy that if Eric Lindros scored 250 empty net goals, while playing for a European minor league team, that Wayne Gretzsky's record for points in a hockey season would still stand. But although nobody questioned that logic in the United States, it looked like Denmark would treat Nielsen's accomplishment as legitimate, something that infuriated boxing insiders.

Nielsen's promoter Mogens Palle decided to take no chances, calling on Nebraska heavyweight Dick Ryan to pad his record for fight number fifty. Ryan was the classic Nielsen opponent: he was white, from the Midwest, generally seen as a clubfighter in the United States, and came to Denmark with a glossy record of 47–4. But despite the glossy record Ryan was a fighter couldn't overcome the top of the line heavyweights. After winning thirty of his first thirty-one fights Ryan was given his first taste of the big leagues when he was matched up with Mike "The Giant" White in the main event of an ESPN fight card. But Ryan failed miserably against White, dropping a decision. The loss seemed to close the book on Ryan as a prospect, and although he won ten fights over the next six years he never was able to earn much respect in the eyes of boxing insiders. After dropping a decision to James "Buster" Douglas, Ryan appeared to accept his future as an opponent and traveled to Germany to get pounded on by Vitali Klitschko the following year, losing by way of knockout in five. The Nielsen fight appeared to be another example of Dick cashing in on a free trip to Europe, and even the naive Danish boxing public did not see Ryan as much of a threat.

But there was more than one myth regarding Rocky Marciano's record, one that would gain even more merit after Nielsen's inexplicable loss to Ryan. No heavyweight was ever able to overcome that mythical barrier of 49–0, it was a sports curse that rivaled the one that "The Bambino" had over the city of Boston, and one that would hold up against Brian Nielsen's early dominance.

Early on Nielsen controlled the fight, driving Dick Ryan into the ropes with hard, winging shots upstairs in the opening minute of the fight. Ryan tried to slug back, but the defense of Brian Nielsen was surprisingly competent and few of Ryan's shots landed. With a minute left in the round, both fighters began to wage a phone booth war, but revealing his solid schooling, Nielsen attacked the body relentlessly, something that he would do throughout the fight.

Although Ryan came out strong in the second, hitting inside the clinch and trying to remain more active than Nielsen, he was unable to hold his own against the active Nielsen. Nielsen quickly took control of the slugfest and had Ryan on the ropes inside of a minute. Although Nielsen showed early signs of fatigue in the third round, he continued his impressive punch output in the third. Responding to Ryan's inside hooks and uppercuts, Nielsen again had Ryan on the ropes covering up, and although he was failing to utilize the jab, there was little to criticize in his performance.

In the fourth it appeared as if Nielsen had taken complete control of the fight. Unlike the previous three rounds, in which Ryan would come out swinging at the bell and briefly control the action, round four saw Nielsen take complete control. He also began to attack the body with greater intensity. Nielsen pushed Ryan down with a looping right hand midway through the round, and at 2:30 Nielsen gave the local fans something to get excited about when he unloaded on Ryan in the corner. Seconds later Ryan appeared to be dropped, by a left hook to the body, but the punch was ruled a slip by referee Jess Andreasen (who saw Ryan block the punch). As the bell sounded to start the fifth round Nielsen jumped on Ryan before he even got out of his corner and attacked with vicious intensity. By round's end Brain even began to showboat with the increasingly fatigued looking Dick Ryan. The showboating continued in

round six, as Brian appeared to invite Ryan in with playful taps to his
own belly. Ryan also began showing troubling signs of his fatigue and
frustration as he began to walk away from Nielsen in what looked like
the early signs of a "no mas." Ryan appeared as if he simply didn't want
to fight anymore, prompting Nielsen to stick his arms out in mocking
anger towards Ryan. Seconds before the bell Ryan turned his back away
from Nielsen and walked away, prompting Nielsen's cornerman Pepe
Correa to scream in between rounds "He's trying to quit! He wants to
quit but you won't let him go!"

Initially it appeared as if Ryan had in fact quit, in between the sixth
and seventh round, as Nielsen's corner saw the Nebraskan sitting on
his stool at the bell. However, it proved premature as Ryan wearily rose
to keep fighting for one more round. It appeared as if the seventh would
prove to be a test of wills, if Brian could force the American to quit or
at least give him an opportunity to. But in what proved to be a major
mistake on Nielsen's part, he let his wounded foe off the hook. Ryan
spent much of the seventh round holding and clinching. Although Nielsen began to tee off on Ryan in the final minute, signs of frustration
would begin to emerge on Nielsen's face, whose expression revealed
what many ringsiders were thinking: "Why is he still standing?"

Although Nielsen was pitching a virtual shutout for the first seven
rounds, the eighth would prove to be the turning point in the fight. Initially the round followed the same patter of the previous seven, with
Nielsen attacking the body and outpunching his overmatched foe on the
inside. Although both fighters were clinching and holding quite a bit, it
still was Nielsen who was the more active fighter on the inside. Nielsen
actually had Ryan on the canvas again in the eighth round, although
once again it was not the result of a punch but rather his leaning on the
back of Dick Ryan. But a peculiar thing began to emerge halfway
through the round. Nielsen's offense became completely nonexistent as
he began to dance around in front of Ryan like a man badly hurt. Being
that nobody saw Ryan land a punch, most assumed Nielsen was merely
showboating again. But it continued in the ninth, and even got worse.
Brian stumbled around the ring like a drunkard at the start of the
ninth, and in fact did not leave his corner when the round started, too
weak to walk across the ring. Initially Ryan assumed that Brian was
trying to set a trap and he refused to walk in, but seconds later Ryan

realized that it was no play-acting, Brian Nielsen was seriously hurt. He jumped all over Brian Nielsen, winging punches from all angles in an attempt to put away his curiously wounded foe. Nielsen, to his credit, continued to try and survive by holding on for dear life, but he lacked the energy and the mental faculties to do even that. At one point Brian was so weakened that he actually put his arms around Dick Ryan while grabbing the ropes behind the Nebraskan while Ryan fired short hooks to his chin. It was clear that Brian was in dire straits, and at the bell many wondered why the fight was not being stopped. But for referee Jess Andreasen and Nielsen cornerman Pepe Correa, the simple fact was that Brian Nielsen was only one round away from winning the fight, and it seemed hard to rob him of the win when he was so close.

Initially Nielsen appeared to be making the choice for them, indicating in between rounds that he wanted to quit. But Correa screamed at him, "you can't give up! Three minutes to win!" prompting Nielsen to reluctantly come out for the tenth. But things did not improve for him, as Ryan again swarmed all over Nielsen. Brian lacked the energy to even clinch with Ryan, who easily pushed Nielsen off and into the referee. When Brian then fell back from the referee and into the ropes, Andreasen finally saw enough, waving the fight with a little over two minutes to go.

Initially it appeared as if Brian lacked the toughness to be a legitimate heavyweight contender, and for many boxing insiders watching the fight live it appeared as if Brian could never regain that image of toughness that he lost. But it proved short-lived when seconds later Brian collapsed in the ring. Brian was rushed to an ambulance, and for many Danish boxing fans it looked like the courage of Nielsen might rob him of his life. Brian slipped into a coma and remained unconscious for sixteen hours, but after waking he made a full recovery and actually walked out of the hospital two days later. In the end it was dehydration and lack of fluids that did Brian in, something that appeared to be confirmed by the claim that Brian lost twenty-two pounds before and during the fight.

Still, many boxing insiders were confused. Dehydration usually occurred when a fighter struggled to make weight in the lower weight classes, something that Brian clearly did not have to worry about. But the answer soon became apparent when it was revealed by Nielsen that his trainer Pepe Correa did not let him drink water in between rounds.[2]

Brian returned to the ring less than three months later against rugged Canadian Shane Sutcliffe (stopping him in the fifth round) and by year's end he had racked up three more wins. Critics began to notice a pattern as Nielsen's fights were predominantly eight-rounders rather than ten- or twelve-rounders. In 2000 Nielsen captured another lightly regarded title (this time the IBC) against another unworthy contender (this time Troy Weida) and three months later he scored the biggest win of his career, stopping Jeremy Williams in five rounds. The win over Williams, however, was not without controversy. Shortly after the win Williams claimed that he threw the fight and later changed his story to claim that he was poisoned. Although most insiders felt that both claims were unlikely, it was enough to taint the victory. Besides, for many boxing fans in Denmark and out, there was still the strong opinion that Brian needed to avenge his lone defeat if he wanted to truly revitalize his career. Recognizing the blemish on his career Nielsen signed to fight Ryan in a rematch in October 2000. Although most felt that he should have fought Ryan in defense of his IBC title (which would have made the fight twelve rounds) or at the very least fought a ten-rounder like the first fight, Nielsen stacked the deck in his favor just a little bit more, fighting Ryan in an eight-round fight so that his endurance would not be tested again. Nielsen easily outpointed Ryan, but few boxing insiders were impressed. Still, Nielsen continued to win and by the end of 2001 he was ready to fight in front of his first major American audience when he fought Mike Tyson on Showtime. Although Tyson battered Nielsen for the better part of six rounds before scoring the stoppage, Nielsen earned some credit for his toughness and durability, and it was only then that fans began to notice that, despite what appeared to be his technical limitations, after sixty-four fights he had yet to be knocked down.

For the unlikely winner Ryan, the victory revived his career and put him in the top ten (he was ranked number ten by the WBA shortly after the fight), but success would be short-lived. Unable to capitalize on his

---

[2] Roy Freddy Andersen, http://www.kronkgym.com. (Accessed in February 2002.)

win in the United States, Ryan returned to Denmark to fight Nielsen again. After dropping the decision he quickly faded from the scene, fighting only once in 2001 (although the fight was for the vacant IBC super heavyweight title). Nonetheless he still had a big name in Denmark, and in 2002 he was called upon to face undefeated Dane Steffen Nielsen in Denmark, dropping an eight-round decision.

June 19, 1999—New York City, New York
Jeremy Williams (34–2, 31 KOs) vs. Maurice Harris
 (14–9–2, 9 KOs)
Favorite: Williams
Result: Harris won a ten-round unanimous decision.

After he was starched by Henry Akinwande in three rounds in a bid for the WBO heavyweight title back in 1996, most boxing insiders closed the book on Jeremy Williams. He simply lacked the size or the chin to mix it up with the top-line heavyweights. But when he followed the loss to Akinwande with a first-round knockout over "Wimpy" Halstead and another first-round knockout over former contender Phil Jackson, there was little question that he still had dangerous power. Jeremy Williams was a puncher and could "whack out" just about any heavyweight whose chin he found. And if he could overcome that final obstacle, if he could beat a top-ranked heavyweight at the right time, he knew that he could end up right back in the title fight picture. Realizing after eight straight knockout victories that he was no closer to the top ten, Jeremy agreed to an HBO-televised fight with top ranked prospect Ike Ibeabuchi. It was a critical fight for Jeremy, but the potential rewards were huge. Ike was coming off two big wins over David Tua and Chris Byrd, and a victory over Ike might lead to a title fight and the payday that came with it. But, unhappy with a mere $575,000, Ibeabuchi refused. Enter Hasim Rahman, who despite a knockout loss to David Tua, was still widely regarded as one of the better heavyweight prospects in the game. Many felt that Rahman was unjustly robbed of a victory when his fight with David Tua was halted in the tenth round, and he was eager to land another high-profile fight to prove that was, in fact, the case. But Rahman also dropped out of the fight with less than a week's notice, leaving both HBO and Jeremy Williams hanging. Maurice Harris, who was coming off a first-round knockout over Lou Monaco only four weeks earlier, came into the picture. Harris had revitalized his career after a dreadful start, beating David Izon and James Thunder before losing a controversial decision to Larry Holmes in 1997. With only five days to prepare, it appeared to most insiders that Harris was getting caught up in the classic "opponent" trap. He lacked the patience to develop his career, instead chasing the high profile and big money fights (if $13,000 could be considered big money). Besides, with Jeremy's reputation as a puncher, it appeared to many that the real winner of the whole musical chairs of opponents was Jeremy. He had an HBO-televised fight against an ill-prepared journeyman, a recipe for an impressive knockout victory.

For much of the first round, things seemed to follow the script. Jeremy Williams came out pressuring while Harris tried to jab and hold. "Harris seems a little taken aback by the early aggression," commented Jim Lampley during the round, a sentiment many ringsiders shared. But oddly enough, Jeremy began to abandon the forward-moving pressure for the jab, something that was considerably less effective. From the outside Jeremy was a sitting duck for the one big weapon in Maurice Harris's arsenal: his right hand. Although Jeremy dominated the early part of the first round, perhaps the most telling sign of the round was when Maurice Harris landed a big right hand in the last thirty seconds that opened up a cut over the left eye of Jeremy Williams.

With that the tide began to turn, as Maurice began to outbox his shorter foe from the outside. Jeremy continued to play into the game plan of Harris, jabbing from the outside as well. At 1:20 of the second round a big right hand staggered the hard punching Williams, backing him into the ropes. It was clear that Harris's effective boxing was frustrating Williams when, seconds later, Williams fired a shot from behind his back, prompting Harris to laugh at Williams.

But things began to turn back in Williams's favor in the third. Starting the round with a badly bloodied nose, Harris showed signs of fatigue as he failed to fire his jab, instead choosing to lean back on the ropes. He began to pump the right hand a bit in the final minute, but it was still not enough to win the round. It looked to be a last hurrah as he came out for the fourth round badly fatigued. Williams began to up the pressure again, backing Harris into the ropes as he gasped for air. But in a little less then a minute the tide would again turn, for the last time.

Maurice Harris (right) keeps Jeremy Williams at bay during his ten-round unanimous-decision victory. *Ray Bailey*

Harris fired a hard straight right that found the chin of Williams and nearly dropped him. Suddenly it was Williams holding on for dear life as Harris unloaded on him as he covered up on the ropes. For ringsiders it appeared as if Williams was not going to make it out of the round as Harris pounded him from pillar to post. An uppercut snapped Jeremy's head back at 1:50, sending him reeling back into the corner. In a complete role reversal, it was Williams who looked fatigued as the round ended.

Gun-shy and timid, Jeremy fought cautiously in the fifth. Unfortunately for Williams, he decided caution was best fought on the outside, which left him susceptible to the Harris jab and, more importantly, the Harris right hand (another one would rattle him a minute into the round). Harris returned to his corner all smiles after the fifth and continued his dominance well into the sixth. It was clear to everyone that

Maurice gained his second wind just as Jeremy's tank ran out, and with that the fight became a complete mismatch. Jeremy's offense became virtually nonexistent in the sixth and would not return for the duration of the fight. Williams either laid on the ropes or moved back and away from Harris, not a strategy for victory for a compact puncher. Rocked again in the final twenty seconds of the round (this time courtesy of the left hook), Jeremy was unable to cope with the versatile arsenal of Harris. After a slow and tactical seventh round, Harris dominated the eighth, despite badly hurting his right hand. Using only the left jab and the left hook, Harris continued his domination sans his most potent weapon (even stunning Jeremy with a quick triple left hook to the face). Jeremy looked all the part of a defeated fighter in the ninth, moving away from Harris despite the fact that he needed to knock him out to win. A left hook inside of a minute into the round helped confirm why, when it sent Jeremy back into the ropes. Jeremy seemed a fighter without his legs, as jabs snapped his head back and sent him reeling.

Going into the tenth round, there was little question that Jeremy needed to knockout Harris to win, but Jeremy was a defeated fighter already. He continued his ineffective strategy of self-preservation. Never in the round did he seriously pressure Harris at all, and several ringsiders were left to question his heart and desire during the round. Jeremy simply was not fighting with the desperation that the situation required. So few found fault when the decision went to Maurice Harris by a lopsided margin. (No judge gave Williams more than two rounds. Melvina Lathan scored it 99–89, while Fred Ucci and Steve Weisfeld scored it 98–91 and 98–90 respectively.) The hard-luck Maurice Harris had finally put it all together, prompting Jim Lampley to call him "the best 15–9 fighter in the division." But the glory was short-lived. Maurice was knocked out in his next fight against undefeated Derrick Jefferson in a Fight-of-the-Year candidate. It hurt Maurice's career, but he still was able to land a fight with Chris Byrd in an IBF title eliminator. It was as close as he would come to a title fight (a win over Byrd would have put him only one more win away from a mandatory title fight with Lennox Lewis). But in one of the most dismal performances of his later career, Harris was virtually shut out by the slick boxing southpaw. He followed that loss with one of the worst of his career, a first-round knockout loss to Henry Akinwande. Although Harris did briefly bounce back in 2002 (winning a one-night NCAA-style tournament as well as knocking out undefeated Serguei Lyakhovich), he again stumbled with only one step to a world title fight, losing to Fres Oquendo in a IBF heavyweight eliminator the following year.

For Jeremy, the loss initially seemed introduce him to the journey-man class. He immediately took a fight in Denmark with Brian Nielsen, getting stopped in the fifth. Although Jeremy claimed that he threw the fight (and, later, claimed he was poisoned), few gave the excuse much credence. To most neutral observers, it was sour grapes from a fighter who was simply beaten. He disappeared after the Nielsen loss, initially dabbling in acting and hinting at a return to boxing as a cruiserweight. But in 2002 Jeremy resurfaced as a heavyweight and did what he did best: he blew out journeyman Louis Monaco in the opening round.

December 9, 1999—Mt. Pleasant, Michigan
Joe Hipp (41–5, 28 KOs) vs. Jeff Pegues (16–6, 13 KOs)
Favorite: Hipp
Result: Pegues won by way of fifth-round TKO when Hipp
  injured his knee.

When former heavyweight contender Joe Hipp entered the ring for his showdown with little-known Jeff Pegues, it was clear that he was ripe for the taking. It just didn't seem plausible that Jeff Pegues would be the man to take him. Most observers anticipated a quick Hipp victory, but few felt it would do anything for his career other than help market him as an opponent for a young up-and-comer. Although Hipp had never been regarded as a top-of-the-line heavyweight, even when he was ranked, he was still a fighter who fought for the world heavyweight championship. Unfortunately for Joe he lost, and lost in most dominat-ing fashion, to a fighter who was widely regarded as one the worst heavyweight champion in boxing history, namely Bruce Seldon. Al-though he was able to take some comfort in being the first Native Amer-ican to fight for a world title, it was hardly the performance that his supporters envisioned. After all, this was the man who broke Tommy Morrison's jaw before the blonde bomber rallied back to score a dra-matic knockout in the ninth round. This was the man to dominate the once feared Alex Garcia in capturing the NABF heavyweight champion-ship. Those performances may not have helped to sell him against a

Mike Tyson or Michael Moorer, but it seemed plausible that against the soft-chinned Seldon, he could shine. But after losing by way of tenth-round TKO, Hipp quickly faded from the heavyweight picture. Few felt that he deserved another shot after getting beat by Seldon (who later would be discredited against Tyson) and when Joe was stopped in ten rounds by Ross Puritty in 1997, it seemed that his career was over or would continue as a "name opponent" for the young guns in the division. But Hipp decided to carefully reconstruct his career, winning his next two fights against limited opponents before fighting Everett "Bigfoot" Martin in June 1999 in a bout for the lightly-regarded WBF heavyweight title. Hipp struggled but was still able to win a twelve-round decision. Still, the title hardly guaranteed respect. Its previous holders included Joe Bugner and Bert Cooper, two fighters who were clearly past their prime when they won it, and few felt that Hipp was the exception to the norm in regards to WBF champions—after all, at thirty-seven years old, Hipp appeared well past his prime. Also, although Hipp never resembled a bodybuilder in regards to his physique; he weighed in at an embarrassing 282 pounds, a full forty-nine pounds heavier than when he fought Bruce Seldon for the WBA heavyweight title four years earlier.

Still, Hipp was the prohibitive favorite. For despite his limitations, he was a man who did carry some pop behind his punches, and Jeff Pegues's history in the ring indicated that he lacked anything resembling a chin. Pegues had already been stopped in five of his six losses, and had been starched in the opening round by the likes of Orlin Norris, Monte Barrett, and Shazzon Bradley. He had yet to go past the sixth round and to show any durability against quality fighters.

By the start of the fight Pegues was showing a newly found durability in the ring, trading punches with Hipp without folding as envisioned. At the end of the first round Hipp began to show signs of swelling around his eyes, although that was not uncommon for the big Native American (who had trouble with swelling in his eyes for almost his entire career). Nonetheless, despite Pegues's surprising resiliency, it was clear that Hipp was winning. The only question appeared what would happen in the later rounds. Would the out-of-shape Hipp fade due to fatigue in the later rounds? Or would the untested Pegues fall apart when he entered the seventh round for the first time? It was a question that began to have the fans in attendance intrigued when the unexpected happened. Falling to the canvas in the fifth round, Hipp twisted his right knee badly (the same knee he injured early in his career). Although he initially indicated his desire to continue, it was clear that the fight was over, and that Jeff Pegues would be awarded the victory by way of TKO.

It was a career ending fight for Hipp, who initially indicated that he would return again after shedding some weight. But when he was stripped of his WBF title (not on the line against Pegues) it became clear that he was without a foundation on which to base his comeback, and he faded from the heavyweight picture without ever stepping in the ring again.

For the unlikely victor Jeff Pegues, the win propelled him into the status of "opponent" for the more named contenders in the division (rather than the undefeated, untested prospects). But his soft chin was still a factor in his performances, and when he fought Ray Mercer in 2001, Pegues was stopped in the second round in one of the most brutal knockouts of the year. The following year he was brutally dominated by Chris Byrd before succumbing to a knockout in the third round.

EPILOGUE

It is hard to say where the sport will go as we look forward into the twenty-first century. Some will point to the heavyweight division and predict the demise of the sport, whereas others will simply smile and remember the Gatti-Ward trilogy. But one thing is for sure: the upset will be with us in boxing and in the heavyweight division. Already we've seen a former American Olympian, groomed as a future contender at the least, defeated before he even fought in his first eight-rounder. We've seen one of the most intimidating fighters to emerge from Europe get derailed by a hard luck South African who put it together when it counted. We've seen his brother, only minutes away from victory, succumb to the pain of a rotor cuff injury and meekly hand victory to one of the most elusive fighters in the sport. And we've seen a seemingly dominant heavyweight champion derailed in Africa against a little known challenger who had already been knocked out twice before.

But maybe, just maybe, the 1990s will stand out. As boxing fans grew more cynical over the decade, the "white-hope" money-making scam no longer became the guaranteed moneymaker that it once was. Richie Melito, Jim Strohl, Don Steele, and even Butterbean were unable to garner a payday like the one McNeeley earned. And by the decade's end, we were finally seeing the never-ending comebacks decline in number. Although, the tragedy of former champion Greg Page's near death in the ring certainly was a wake up call for many older fighters, most began to slowly realize that the payday would just not be there for them. Most simply faded away, many with losses that defied reason on their record. And perhaps most importantly, the obsession with the undefeated fighter finally began to abate in the new century. Suddenly a loss was not a sign that the fighter was not championship caliber, and with it an important dynamic that defined the 1990s lessened in importance: where a "zero" under losses meant more than the caliber of opposition.

Perhaps we will look back on the 1990s as the era of the heavyweight upset. Though it is likely that some of the smaller upsets have already lost their impact, and we may not remember that at one time we actually thought James Thunder would beat John Ruiz, there are some fights that we will never forget were upsets. To any boxing fan that watched Mike Tyson fumble with his mouthpiece in Tokyo, or George Foreman pray in the corner after the count of ten, it will be a memory that he or she will carry forever. To the day he or she forgets what a great sport boxing is and will always be, so long as there are underdogs who believe when others don't.

The expert's pick of the biggest upsets in the 1990s:

1. James "Buster" Douglas KO10 Mike Tyson
2. George Foreman KO10 Michael Moorer
3. Oliver McCall TKO2 Lennox Lewis
4. Michael Bentt TKO1 Tommy Morrison
5. Evander Holyfield TKO11 Mike Tyson

BIBLIOGRAPHY

Periodicals

Boxing 94

Boxing 95

Boxing Illustrated

Boxing Record Book, Fight Fax, Inc. (yearly publication)

Boxrec.com (www.Boxrec.com)

Cyber Boxing Zone (www.cyberboxingzone.com)

Fightnews.com (www.fightnews.com)

Flash

International Boxing Digest

Jerry Quarry Foundation (www.jerryquarry.com)

KO Magazine

Kronk Gym (www.kronkgym.com)

People Magazine

Ring Magazine

Spokane Review, Spokane, Washington

State Paper, Columbus, South Carolina

World Boxing

INDEX

325

About the Author

David E. Finger was born in Honolulu, Hawaii. His earliest boxing memories were of watching Larry Holmes defend his title on ABC with his father. By 1990 he had become a "diehard" boxing fan and began researching what would eventually become *Rocky Lives!* as early as 1996. In 1999 he began writing for various Internet boxing sites and by 2001 he was a regular contributor to Fightnews.com. Finger graduated with a BA in history and anthropology from the University of Michigan–Flint in 2000 and is currently a second year law student at the University of Denver–College of Law.